Creation and Chaos

Creation and Chaos

A Reconsideration of Hermann Gunkel's Chaoskampf *Hypothesis*

edited by

JoAnn Scurlock

and

Richard H. Beal

Winona Lake, Indiana
Eisenbrauns
2013

Printed in the United States of America

www.eisenbrauns.com

Library of Congress Cataloging-in-Publication Data

Creation and chaos : a reconsideration of Hermann Gunkel's chaoskampf hypothesis / edited by JoAnn Scurlock and Richard H. Beal.
pages cm
Includes bibliographical references and index.
ISBN 978-1-57506-279-2 (cloth : alk. paper)
1. Mythology, Middle Eastern. 2. Creation—Mythology—Middle East. 3. Monsters—Middle East. 4. Religion and politics—Middle East—History—To 1500. 5. Gunkel, Hermann, 1862–1932. I. Scurlock, Jo Ann, 1953– II. Beal, Richard Henry, 1953–
BL1060.C74 2013
202′.4—dc23

2013035853

The paper used in this publication meets the minimum requirements of the American National Standard for Information Sciences—Permanence of Paper for Printed Library Materials, ANSI Z39.48–1984.⊗™

Contents

Part 1

Creation and Chaos

Part 2

Monster-Bashing Myths

Part 3
Gunkel and His Times

Part 4
Power and Politics

Part 5
Kampf and *Chaos*

Part 6
Chaos and (Re)Creation

Preface

The 17 papers in this volume were, with 2 exceptions, originally delivered as part of the annual meeting of the Midwest branch of the American Oriental Society, held in conjunction with the Midwest branches of the Society of Biblical Literature and the American Schools of Oriental Research in February 2011. We would like to thank Olivet Nazarene University in Bourbonnais, Illinois, for hosting us. We would especially like to thank Richard Choi of Andrews University and Kevin Mellish of Olivet Nazarene for their organizational skills and irrepressible good humor, without which this conference would have been impossible. One of the participants, Wilfred G. Lambert, was eager to come, but his doctors would not allow him to attend. Consequently, the paper that he wrote to be delivered as a plenary speech was instead ably delivered by Karen Sonik. Prof. Lambert's illness unfortunately proved fatal. We hope that he would not have minded that we are dedicating this volume to his memory.

Introduction

JoAnn Scurlock

Hermann Gunkel was of the generation of the origins of Assyriology, the spectacular discovery by George Smith of the Babylonian version of the flood story, and the *Babel-Bibel* debate. He was also contemporary with the development of higher criticism and liberal theology. His contributions to the field included smoothing ruffled feathers, acquiring respectability for the field, and being one of the founding fathers of form criticism. Gunkel's thesis, inspired by materials that were supplied by the Assyriologist Heinrich Zimmern, was that the *Chaoskampf* motif of Revelation was an event that would not only occur at the end of the world but also had already happened once, in the beginning, before creation. In other words, by this theory, God in Genesis 1 first battled Rahab, Leviathan, and Yam (the forces of Chaos) in a grand battle, and only then did he begin to create.

Monster bashing is a feature common to all the mythologies of the ancient world and, not only that, but there is *Kampf* between the good guys and the bad guys in which the good guys (eventually) win. Chaos is, moreover, often involved in these battles, so we may speak with a straight face of *Chaoskampf*. Finally, it is hard not to notice that something very important—whether humankind (by Prometheus), Baʿal's palace in the *Baʿal Epic*, or Babylon in the *Enūma eliš*—is created after the battle that would probably never have been created if the *Chaoskampf* had not taken place. Thus, there was a relationship among creation, Chaos, and *Kampf* in quite a wide range of cultures across the ancient Near East.

The problem with Gunkel's theory is that it did not simply identify these elements; it also imposed on them a structure dictating the relationships among the elements—a structure that was based on inadequate knowledge and the forced interpretation of his sources. In other words, Gunkel wrote a myth, his own myth, that I would argue is essentially false. False in two ways: It fits the *Zeitgeist* of his own time rather than the time frame of his study and, indeed, was intended to do so because Gunkel was avowedly looking for the primordial tradition from which his historical present had evolved. Moreover, in its fullest formulation, Gunkel's myth corresponds to no real myth of either his own time or the ancient world writ large, including Greece and Rome and extending into the Christian era. I do not need to add that Gunkel also required all myths of the ancient Near East to be telling essentially the same story—the sort of analysis I believe we have long outgrown.

On the other hand, there is far too much fire under the Gunkel smoke for there to be nothing in common among the mythical complexes of various cultures in the ancient Near East. Nor are we entitled to insist that there was no cultural conversation between peoples who spent the better part of several millennia trading with, fighting, and conquering one another.

So, the question that I posed to all of the participants in this program was this: what is all the fuss about, anyway? I have divided the participants' answers into several categories, each of which forms a section.

Part 1, entitled Creation and Chaos, contains reflections on creation narratives in various cultures of the ancient Near East and beyond. We begin with Karen Sonik's paper, entitled: "From Hesiod's Abyss to Ovid's *rudis indigestaque moles*: Chaos and Cosmos in the Babylonian 'Epic of Creation,'" which provides a fine introduction to the problem of precreation Chaos in the *Enūma eliš*. Of special interest is a detailed discussion of current scholarship on Hesiod and Ovid's accounts of creation, which continue to inform modern Western scholarship on creation and Chaos. We are also introduced to a modified form of Jan Assman's distinction between cosmogonic and kratogenic chaos. As Sonik argues, the chaos that is represented by Tiʾāmat is kratogenic rather than cosmogonic chaos, with significant implications for our understanding of the *Enūma eliš*.

The next essay in part 1, Dennis R. M. Campbell's "On the Theogonies of Hesiod and the Hurrians: An Exploration of the Dual Natures of Teššub and Kumarbi," continues the Greek theme but with a twist. Early Sumerian accounts of creation quite frequently involve androgenous beings who, while being on some level specifically male in gender, are essentially both male and female.[1] Also curiously ambiguous in Mesopotamian religion of all periods is the relationship between astral and chthonic divinities, to the point that it is often not helpful to make the distinction. In his essay, Campbell explores the ways in which ambiguities of this sort color the myths of Greeks and Hurrians, with specific reference to Hesiod's *Theogony* and the Song of Kumarbi. Another analogy in Indo-European mythology is represented by the Indian god Shiva, who is both male and female, Creator and Destroyer.

W. G. Lambert's "Creation in the Bible and the Ancient Near East" is his paper as read at the original conference. He unfortunately did not have time

1. For a discussion of this issue, see Joan Goodnick Westenholz, "Heaven and Earth: Asexual Monad and Bisexual Dyad," in *Gazing on the Deep: Ancient Near Eastern and Other Studies in Honor of Tzvi Abusch* (ed. Jeffrey Stackert, Barbara Nevling Porter, and David P. Wright; Bethesda, MD: CDL, 2010) 293.

to revise it, and we decided to publish it as it is, without any artificially added footnotes. Of special interest is the fact that Lambert calls to our attention the Sumerian creation accounts and the god lists that the author of *Enūma eliš* used as his starting point. These are seldom-used sources that help us to decode the true nature of figures such as Tiʾāmat, who is not, as he points out, actually the sea as we know it but female cosmic water.

Part 1 is rounded out by my "Searching for Meaning in Genesis 1:2: Purposeful Creation out of *Chaos* without *Kampf*," in which I address the issue of the relationship between Genesis 1 and *Enūma eliš*, with specific reference to the nature of the creative act and the presence or absence of imagined *Chaoskampf* as a prelude to creation.

In part 2, entitled Monster-Bashing Myths, we explore in regional perspective the phenomena of monsters and divine combat, the strongest fire beneath Gunkel's smoke. The first essay, Douglas Frayne's "Fifth Day of Creation in Ancient Syrian and Neo-Hittite Art," serves as an introduction to this fascinating topic. Frayne surveys textual references to Leviathan and Behemoth in rabbinic sources and seeks similar monsters in textual and visual evidence from Mesopotamia and Syria. Of particular interest is his analysis of the little-known Ebla stele, and parallels between the Sumerian myth of Inanna and Šukaletuda and the Greek myth of Apollo and the Raven.

The next two papers, Amir Gilan's "Once upon a Time in Kiškiluša: The Dragon-Slayer Myth in Central Anatolia" and Joanna Töyräänvuori's "Northwest Semitic Conflict Myth and Egyptian Sources from the Middle and New Kingdoms," explore dragon myths among the Hittites and Egyptians, respectively. Gilan surveys the Hittite material and analyzes the two versions of the Illuyanka myth from the perspective of comparative mythology and possible performance in ritual contexts. In the process, he takes the opportunity to reassess now-classic studies of the relationship between myth and ritual that have largely fallen out of favor in other disciplines of ancient Near Eastern studies but are still "alive and kicking" in Hittitology. Töyräänvuori explores the relationship between Egyptian monster-bashing tales such as the battle between the sun-god Re and the Apep snake and the Astarte papyrus on the one hand and the Ugaritic *Baʿal Epic* on the other. Although the direction of influence is usually understood as flowing from Egypt to Ugarit, Töyräänvuori persuasively argues that the tales are just as likely to have come to Egypt from a West Semitic context. She also warns against too-quick an assumption that Egyptian realities (such as, for example, the pharaoh's political role as symbolic combater of chaos) can be projected beyond Egypt's borders.

We return to the theme of Leviathan with Brendon C. Benz's paper: "Yamm as the Personification of Chaos? A Linguistic and Literary Argument for a Case of Mistaken Identity." Benz uses a careful philological analysis to demonstrate that Yamm is not, in fact, a monstrous force of primordial Chaos but instead a legitimate political rival of Baʿal for divine kingship.

Part 3, Gunkel and His Times, examines the political maelstrom in which Gunkel himself operated and reminds us that neither his theories nor the form criticism that he helped to initiate were free of political or religious agendas. Steven Lundström's "Chaos and Creation: Hermann Gunkel between Establishing the 'History of Religions School,' Acknowledging Assyriology, and Defending the Faith" outlines contemporary developments in Assyriology and higher criticism and explains the prominence of Assyriology in the European culture wars of the late-nineteenth and early-twentieth century. As a relative newcomer on the world scene, Germany was especially eager to "pitch her tent on the palm-crowned banks of the streams of Paradise!"[2] Lundström also demonstrates the ways in which, despite the ostensible divorce between Assyriology and biblical studies, theology-driven approaches continue to haunt the field.

Peter Feinman's "Where Is Eden? An Analysis of Some of the Mesopotamian Motifs in Primeval J" continues this theme, engaging some of the debates within liberal theology and tracing religiously and politically motivated arguments into the next generation of scholarship. In the process, Feinman argues persuasively that current higher criticism is far too inclined to assume that accretions to the narrative represent "free-floating, immature, hazy, primitive, oral tradition that somehow of its own accord attached itself to an existing narrative tradition or was grabbed from thin air by an author." Feinman also makes the interesting suggestion that the motivations of redactors were as much embedded in then-current religious and political debates as those of the scholars who now study them. "An alternative approach to understanding the biblical texts is that the Mesopotamian motifs are the products of writers who were in dialogue with each other, just as Langdon, Jastrow, Albright, and Kramer were in dialogue when they reinterpreted the same texts. The difference is that the biblical writers operated in the political arena and not the ivory tower. Inconsistencies within J, therefore, may reflect the different viewpoints of different contemporary authors."

Aaron Tugendhaft completes part 3 with his offering "Babel-Bible-Baal" on the subject of the modern scholarly version of culture wars, in which the claims of Assyriology, Ugaritology (and, occasionally, Egyptology) to relevance for the interpretation of the biblical narrative and to representing the

2. Friedrich Delitzsch, *Babel und Bibel. Ein Vortrag: Neue durchgesehene Ausgabe mit Anmerkungen* (Leipzig: Hinrichs, 1903) 51–52; translation from Bill T. Arnold and David B. Weisberg, "A Centennial Review of Friedrich Delitzsch's 'Babel und Bibel' Lectures," *JBL* 121 (2002) 445.

"original" form of the *Chaoskampf* myth are pitted against one another. Tugendhaft criticizes this scholarly one-upmanship in favor of an approach that seeks to understand the differing uses that each ancient Near Eastern culture made of common motifs in "understanding the relationship among politics, history, and the divine." His suggestion for a new typology includes making a distinction between "diachronic" and "synchronic" applications of the divine combat to this problem.

The essays in part 4, Power and Politics, explore the religiopolitical issues that would have been the concern of the original myth-makers. Wayne T. Pitard's article "The Combat Myth as a Succession Story at Ugarit" outlines the power politics of divine (and human) succession at Ugarit. As he points out, all of Baʿal's mighty efforts to the contrary notwithstanding, the god was forever trapped in the position of heir apparent to El. Moreover, not even he could defeat death. Pitard also seconds Tugendhaft's call for understanding the Combat Myth in local rather than regional terms. Indeed, Baʿal's position was not unlike that of the ruler of the small state of Ugarit, which was wedged between empires.

Robert D. Miller II's "What Are the Nations Doing in the *Chaoskampf?*" makes a similar argument for *Chaoskampf* imagery in the book of Psalms as having to do with "Judean royal propaganda in the context of Neo-Assyrian expansion." Specifically, he argues that the *Völkerwallfahrt*, which has no clear antecedent in Ugaritic mythology, is not a postexilic addition but represents the imperial aspirations of Judean kings whose "systemically distorted communications"[3] were intended to "legitimate [their] domination and power."[4]

Of course, it is important not to go too far in disenchanting ancient texts with clear mythological content. But how far is too far? And how far is not far enough? And which mythological elements from various ancient Near Eastern cultures actually match, and in which passages? The two papers in part 5, *Kampf* and Chaos, constitute a sort of debate within a debate.

We begin with Bernard F. Batto's essay "The Combat Myth in Israelite Tradition Revisited," which is a thoroughgoing review of Rebecca S. Watson's 2005 monograph *Chaos Uncreated: A Reassessment of the Theme of "Chaos" in the Hebrew Bible*. In the process, Batto provides a full definition of his current thinking on the subject of the "Combat Myth." Batto argues, quite persuasively, that Watson has gone too far in arguing that "Israel proper was unacquainted with a 'chaos' motif"—unacquainted, that is, until they learned of it in Babylonian Exile. Given the full-volume blast of the Wrathful-Marduk-as-

3. Ian Hodder, *Reading the Past: Current Approaches to Interpretation in Archaeology* (Cambridge: Cambridge University Press, 1986) 165.

4. Louis Althusser, *Essays on Ideology* (London: Verso, 1984) 17, 20.

Raging-Flood motif being leveled at Judah by the expanding Neo-Babylonian state, it is hard to imagine tone deafness in Jerusalem on this point. It does not, of course, necessarily follow that divine combat is present in Genesis 1.

Richard E. Averbeck's paper "The Three 'Daughters' of Baʿal and Transformations of *Chaoskampf* in the Early Chapters of Genesis" is in agreement with Batto that mythemes are an important part of the biblical text and that among the motifs readily traceable in the narrative are those of divine combat. Nonetheless, Averbeck argues for a combat-free creation narrative in Genesis 1. Where Averbeck sees a use of the divine-combat motif in the biblical text is in the Garden of Eden story, between the snake and God, with human beings as the battleground—a cosmic struggle that will ultimately (in Revelation 12) involve the destruction and re-creation of the world.

Part 6, Chaos and (Re)Creation, brings us back full circle to our starting point. It begins with my article "*Chaoskampf* Lost—*Chaoskampf* Regained: The Gunkel Hypothesis Revisited," in which I agree with Averbeck that there is no mention of *Chaoskampf* in Genesis 1 but give as the reason the fact that Marduk is not actually a Creator but a (Re)Creator who is reassembling what he has first destroyed. I further argue that the divine combat was artificially introduced into the narrative of *Enūma eliš* to facilitate Marduk's rise to the head of the pantheon and that, by removing it from the narrative, Genesis 1 made it literally impossible for Marduk to have created the universe. Finally, I argue that the combat mytheme in the biblical text has to do, not with original creation, but with the un-creation and re-creation of the divine community.

We end with David Melvin's "Making All Things New (Again): Zephaniah's Eschatological Vision of a Return to Primeval Time." His interest is in the origins of apocalyptic literature, a trajectory in which Zephaniah would represent a transitional stage between prophecy and apocalyptic. Melvin argues in favor of de Roche's suggestion that Zephaniah involves a literal and figurative reversal of creation and return to primordial Chaos, in which God "sweeps away" his creation in inverse order to his creating of it and further connects Zephaniah's Oracles against the Nations with the Table of Nations in Genesis. I personally would argue this particular connection in reverse, with oddities in the Table of Nations in Genesis to be explained with reference to a preexisting text of Zephaniah. This would also allow us to understand Cush as 26th-Dynasty Egypt, which was, we tend to forget, a "loyal vassal state" of Assyria to the bitter end. Finally, Melvin connects the scattering of the nations in the Tower of Babel story with the ingathering of nations in Zephaniah, a link recognized in the three-year cycle of Torah reading. "The book of Zephaniah begins with the 'un-creation' of the world and ends with the re-creation of the unity of primeval humanity."

Abbreviations

General

A.	siglum for Mari texts in the Louvre
Akk.	Akkadian
ANE	ancient Near East
Arab.	Arabic
Aram.	Aramaic
b.	tractate in the Babylonian Talmud
BM	tablets in the collections of the British Museum
chap(s).	chapter(s)
col(s).	column(s)
EA	El-Amarna
EB	Early Bronze Age
ed.	edited by; editor(s); edition
ED	Early Dynastic
Ee	*Enūma eliš*
ET	English translation
Gk.	Greek
Heb.	Hebrew
Hh	ḪAR.RA = ḫubullu lexical list
Hitt.	Hittite
KJV	King James Version of the Bible
km	kilometer(s)
m	meter(s)
MB	Middle Bronze Age
Metam.	Ovid, *Metamorphoses*
ms	masculine singular
NAB	New American Bible
ND	field numbers of tablets excavated at Nimrud (Kalḫu)
NEB	New English Bible
NJPS	New Jewish Publication Society version of the Bible
n(n).	note(s)
no(s).	number(s)
NRSV	New Revised Standard Version of the Bible
OB	Old Babylonian
obv.	obverse
Opif.	Philo of Alexandria, *De opificio mundi*
OT	Old Testament
P	Priestly Writer/source
PAmherst	Papyrus of Aquila's LXX Gen 1:1–5 (first half of fourth century C.E.)

PBremner	British Museum papyrus no. 10188, also known as the Bremner-Rhind Papyrus
PE	Eusebius of Caesarea, *Praeparatio Evangelica*
PHearst	Hearst Medical Papyrus, one of the medical papyri of ancient Egypt, from first half of second millennium B.C.
pl.	plural
PT	Pyramid Texts (see R. Faulkner, *The Ancient Egyptian Pyramid Texts* [Oxford: Clarendon, 1969])
RS	Ras Shamra
RSV	Revised Standard Version of the Bible
SBV	Standard Babylonian version of a text
sing.	singular
s.o.	someone
s.t.	something
Theog.	Hesiod, *Theogony*
trans.	translated by
Ug.	Ugaritic

Reference Works

AB	Anchor Bible
ABD	Freedman, D. N., editor. *The Anchor Bible Dictionary*. 6 vols. Garden City, NY: Doubleday, 1992
ABL	Harper, R. F., editor. *Assyrian and Babylonian Letters Belonging to the Kouyunjik Collections of the British Museum*. 14 vols. Chicago: University of Chicago Press, 1892–1914
AfO	*Archiv für Orientforschung*
AJA	*American Journal of Archaeology*
AJSL	*American Journal of Semitic Languages and Literature*
AKA	Budge, E. A. W., and King, L. W. *The Annals of the Kings of Assyria*. London: British Museum, 1902
ANEP	Pritchard, J. B., editor. *The Ancient Near East in Pictures Relating to the Old Testament*. 2nd ed. Princeton: Princeton University Press, 1969
ANET	Pritchard, J. B., editor. *Ancient Near Eastern Texts Relating to the Old Testament*. 3rd ed. Princeton: Princeton University Press, 1969
AnOr	Analecta Orientalia
AOAT	Alter Orient und Altes Testament
AoF	*Altorientalische Forschungen*
ARET	Archivi Reali di Ebla: Testi vol. 5: Edzard, D. O. *Hymnen, Beschwörungen und Verwandtes aus dem Archiv L. 2769*. ARET 5. Rome: Missione archeologica italiana in Siria, 1984
ARM	Archives royales de Mari
AS	Assyriological Studies
AuOr	*Aula Orientalis*
BA	*Biblical Archaeologist*
BAI	*Bulletin of the Asia Institute*

BAR	*Biblical Archaeology Review*
BASOR	*Bulletin of the American Schools of Oriental Research*
BBB	Bonner Biblische Beiträge
BDB	Brown, F.; Driver, S. R.; and Briggs, C. A. *Hebrew and English Lexicon of the Old Testament*. Oxford: Clarendon, 1907
Bib	*Biblica*
BibOr	Biblica et Orientalia
BN	*Biblische Notizen*
BO	*Bibliotheca Orientalis*
Borger, *Ash.*	Borger, Rykle. *Beiträge zum Inschriftenwerk Assurbanipals: Die Prismenklassen A, B, C = K, D, E, F, G, H, J und T sowie andere Inschriften*. Wiesbaden: Harrassowitz, 1996
BSOAS	*Bulletin of the School of Oriental and African Studies*
BZ	*Biblische Zeitschrift*
BZAW	Beihefte zur Zeitschrift für die Alttestmentliche Wissenschaft
CAD	Oppenheim, A. L., et al., editors. *The Assyrian Dictionary of the Oriental Institute of the University of Chicago*. 21 vols. (A–Z). Chicago: Oriental Institute, 1956–2011
CahRB	Cahiers de Revue Biblique
CANE	Sasson, Jack, editor. *Civilizations of the Ancient Near East*. 4 vols. New York: Scribner, 1995
CAT	Dietrich, M.; Loretz, O.; and Sanmartín, J. *The Cuneiform Alphabetic Texts from Ugarit, Ras Ibn Hani and Other Places*. Abhandlungen zur Literatur Alt-Syriens-Palästinas 8. Münster: Ugarit-Verlag, 1997
CBQ	*Catholic Biblical Quarterly*
CBQMS	Catholic Biblical Quarterly Monograph Series
CC	Continental Commentaries
CHANE	Culture and History of the Ancient Near East
CHD	Güterbock, Hans G., and Hoffner, Harry A., editors. *The Hittite Dictionary of the Oriental Institute of the University of Chicago*. Chicago: Oriental Institute, 1980–
ChS	Haas, V., et al., editors. *Corpus der hurritischen Sprachdenkmäler*. Rome: Multigrafica, 1984–
COS	Hallo, W. W., and K. L. Younger Jr., editors. *The Context of Scripture*. 3 vols. Leiden: Brill, 1997–2003
CP	*Classical Philology*
CRAIBL	*Comptes-rendus des séances de l'Académie des Inscriptions et Belles-Lettres*
CT	Cuneiform Texts from Babylonian Tablets in the British Museum
CTA	Herdner, A., editor. *Corpus des tablettes en cunéiformes alphabétiques*. Paris: Imprimerie Nationale, 1963
CTH	Laroche, E. *Catalogue des textes hittites*. 2nd ed. Paris: Klincksieck, 1971
DDD	Van der Toorn, K.; Becking, B.; and van der Horst, P. W., editors. *Dictionary of Deities and Demons in the Bible*. Leiden: Brill, 1995
FAT	Forschungen zum Alten Testament
FRLANT	Forschungen zur Religion und Literatur des Alten und Neuen Testaments

HALOT	Koehler, L.; Baumgartner, W.; and Stamm, J. J. *The Hebrew and Aramaic Lexicon of the Old Testament*. Translated and edited under supervision of M. E. J. Richardson. 5 vols. Leiden: Brill, 1994–2000
HO	Handbuch der Orientalistik
HR	*History of Religions*
HS	*Hebrew Studies*
HSM	Harvard Semitic Monographs
HUCA	*Hebrew Union College Annual*
IB	Buttrick, G. A., et al., editors. *Interpreter's Bible*. 12 vols. New York: Abingdon-Cokesbury, 1951–57
ICC	International Critical Commentary
IDB	Buttrick, G. A., editor. *Interpreter's Dictionary of the Bible*. 4 vols. Nashville: Abingdon, 1962
Int	*Interpretation*
JAAR	*Journal of the American Academy of Religion*
JANER	*Journal of Ancient Near Eastern Religions*
JANES(CU)	*Journal of the Ancient Near Eastern Society (of Columbia University)*
JAOS	*Journal of the American Oriental Society*
JBL	*Journal of Biblical Literature*
JCS	*Journal of Cuneiform Studies*
JEA	*Journal of Egyptian Archaeology*
JESHO	*Journal of the Economic and Social History of the Orient*
JHS	*Journal of Hebrew Scriptures*. http://www.jhsonline.org
JHS	*Journal of Hellenic Studies*
JNES	*Journal of Near Eastern Studies*
JNSL	*Journal of Northwest Semitic Languages*
JSOT	*Journal for the Study of the Old Testament*
JSOTSup	Journal for the Study of the Old Testament Supplement Series
JSPSup	Journal for the Study of the Pseudepigrapha Supplement Series
JSS	*Journal of Semitic Studies*
JTS	*Journal of Theological Studies*
KAR	Ebeling, E., editor. *Keilschrifttexte aus Assur religiösen Inhalts*. 2 vols. Leipzig: Hinrich, 1919–23
KB^3	Koehler, L.; Hartmann, B.; and Kutscher, E. Y. *Lexicon in Veteris Testamenti libros*. 6 vols. 3rd ed. Leiden: Brill, 1967–96
KBo	Keilschrifttexte aus Boghazköi
KTU	Dietrich, M.; Loretz, O.; and Sanmartín, J., editors. *Die Keilalphabetischen Texte aus Ugarit*. Alter Orient und Altes Testament 24. Kevelaer: Butzon & Bercker / Neukirchen-Vluyn: Neukirchener Verlag, 1976. 2nd ed.: Dietrich, M.; Loretz, O.; and Sanmartín, J., editors. *The Cuneiform Alphabetic Texts from Ugarit, Ras Ibn Hani, and Other Places*. Münster: Ugarit-Verlag, 1995
KUB	Keilschrifturkunden aus Boghazköi
LCL	Loeb Classical Library
MAD	Materials for the Assyrian Dictionary
MARI	*Mari: Annales de Recherches Interdisciplinaires*
MDOG	*Mitteilungen der Deutschen Orient-Gesellschaft*

MSL	Materialien zum sumerischen Lexikon
MVAG	Mitteilungen der Vorderasiatisch-ägyptischen Gesellschaft
NICOT	New International Commentary on the Old Testament
OBO	Orbis Biblicus et Orientalis
OEANE	Meyers, E. M., editor. *The Oxford Encyclopedia of Archaeology in the Near East*. 5 vols. New York: Oxford University Press, 1997
OLZ	*Orientalische Literaturzeitung*
Or	*Orientalia*
OrAnt	*Oriens Antiquus*
OTL	Old Testament Library
PBS	Publications of the Babylonian Section, University Museum, the University of Pennsylvania
PRU	Le palais royal d'Ugarit
PSBA	*Proceedings of the Society of Biblical Archaeology*
3R	Rawlinson, H. C. *The Cuneiform Inscriptions of Western Asia*. Vol. 3 of 5 vols. London: British Museum, 1861–1909
RA	*Revue d'Assyriologie et d'Archéologie Orientale*
RHA	*Revue Hittite et Asianique*
RHR	*Revue de l'histoire des religions*
RIH	Rougé, J. de. *Inscriptions hiéroglyphiques copiées en Égypte*. Études égyptologiques 9–11. Paris: Vieweg, 1877–79
RINAP	The Royal Inscriptions of the Neo-Assyrian Period
Rit. Acc.	Thureau-Dangin, F. *Rituels accadiens*. Paris: Leroux, 1921
RlA	Ebeling, E., et al., editors. *Reallexikon der Assyriologie*. Berlin: de Gruyter, 1928–
SAA	State Archives of Assyria
SAACT	State Archives of Assyria Cuneiform Texts
SAAS	State Archives of Assyria Studies
SBLWAW	Society of Biblical Literature Writings from the Ancient World
SBT	Studies in Biblical Theology
SCCNH	Studies on the Civilization and Culture of Nuzi and the Hurrians
SEÅ	*Svensk Exegetisk Årsbok*
SJOT	*Scandinavian Journal of the Old Testament*
TAPA	*Transactions of the American Philology Association*
TS	*Theological Studies*
TUAT	Texte aus der Umwelt des Alten Testaments
UBL	Ugaritisch-biblische Literatur
UF	*Ugarit-Forschungen*
USQR	*Union Seminary Quarterly Review*
VAB	Vorderasiatische Bibliothek
VC	*Vigiliae Christianae*
VT	*Vetus Testamentum*
VTSup	Vetus Testamentum Supplements
WBC	Word Biblical Commentary
WZKM	*Wiener Zeitschrift für die Kunde des Morgenlandes*
ZA	*Zeitschrift für Assyriologie*
ZÄS	*Zeitschrift für Ägyptische Sprache und Altertumskunde*

ZAW	*Zeitschrift für die Alttestamentliche Wissenschaft*
ZDMG	*Zeitschrift der Deutschen Morgenländischen Gesellschaft*
ZTK	*Zeitschrift für Theologie und Kirche*

Part 1

Creation and Chaos

From Hesiod's Abyss to Ovid's rudis indigestaque moles

Chaos and Cosmos in the Babylonian "Epic of Creation"

Karen Sonik

Brown University

In 1895, Hermann Gunkel published what has since become an extremely influential study in the interpretation of biblical and Mesopotamian literature, *Schöpfung und Chaos in Urzeit und Endzeit*. Taking as his central concern the mythological motif of *Chaoskampf*[1] (the battle against chaotic agents by divine representatives of order) and its association with subsequent accounts of cosmogony or creation, Gunkel suggested that multiple references to this motif were to be found within the Hebrew Bible, discerning traces of it even within the seemingly peaceful and orderly creation account in Genesis 1.[2]

Author's note: Thanks are due to the Institute for the Study of the Ancient World, where I conducted much of this research, and to a New Faculty Fellows award from the American Council of Learned Societies, funded by the Andrew W. Mellon Foundation, which facilitated the completion of this work. Thanks are due also to JoAnn Scurlock and Richard Beal for the invitation to contribute to this volume with an investigation of the impact of Gunkel's work on the interpretation of *Enūma eliš*.

1. Although the concept of *Chaoskampf* was investigated in detail by Gunkel, the term itself does not appear in his study; see Hermann Gunkel, *Creation and Chaos in the Primeval Era and the Eschaton: Religio-Historical Study of Genesis* 1 and Revelation 12 (trans. K. William Whitney Jr.; Grand Rapids, MI: Eerdmans, 2006) 287 n. 26.

2. "In the beginning God created the heavens and the earth. / The earth was still a desert waste, and darkness lay upon the primeval deep and God's wind was moving to and

More striking even than this hypothesis, however, was that Gunkel located the origins of this tradition, violent *Chaoskampf* followed by methodical creation, not in the ancient environs of Israel but in Mesopotamia—specifically, in the then-recently-discovered and translated text of *Enūma eliš*, the so-called Babylonian Epic of Creation.[3]

Likely dating to the late second millennium B.C.E.,[4] *Enūma eliš* seemed to offer a single unified account of the tradition with which Gunkel was concerned, recording not only the battle between the Babylonian chief god Marduk and the feminine and threatening personified sea Tiʾāmat but also Marduk's subsequent structuring of the cosmos from Tiʾāmat's corpse.[5] While no similar such savage confrontation was explicit in Genesis 1, Gunkel constructed a detailed case for its relationship to *Enūma eliš* on the basis of two main points. The first was his association of the *tĕhôm* of Gen 1:2 with the Tiʾāmat of *Enūma eliš*; the second was his collection and elucidation of passages from elsewhere in the Hebrew Bible that apparently referenced divine conflict with chaos, the chaos therein taking an array of forms, including that of the primeval sea.[6]

fro over the surface of the waters. / And God said: Let there be light! And there was light (Gen 1:1–1:3)," translated in Claus Westermann, *Genesis 1–11* (CC; Minneapolis: Augsburg, 1984) 1, 76.

3. The first fragments of the composition were recovered in 1848–49 during the excavations of Austen Henry Layard at the Library of Ashurbanipal at Nineveh, but a translation of the text did not appear until its 1876 publication in George Smith, *The Chaldean Account of Genesis, Containing the Description of the Creation, the Fall of Man, the Deluge, the Tower of Babel, the Times of the Patriarchs, and Nimrod: Babylonian Fables, and Legends of the Gods; from the Cuneiform Inscriptions* (New York: Scribner, Armstrong, 1876). While *Enūma eliš* may still be popularly known as the Babylonian Epic of Creation, the text is less concerned with providing an account of creation than with justifying the ascension of the Babylonian god Marduk to the kingship of the gods (many of whom are older and have a clearer claim to rule); see, for example, Piotr Michalowski, "Presence at the Creation," in *Lingering over Words: Studies in Ancient Near Eastern Literature in Honor of William L. Moran* (ed. Tzvi Abusch, John Huehnergard, and Piotr Steinkeller; Atlanta: Scholars Press, 1990) 384. Gunkel's suggestion that "the Babylonian *Tiʾâmat-Marduk* myth was taken up by Israel and there became a myth of YHWH" was a bold and striking one for his time; much of the evidence on which he built his theory, however, has been significantly reevaluated based on new discoveries over the last 100+ years.

4. Its composition is generally but not universally dated to ca. 1100 B.C.E.; for a brief summary of the debate on the subject spanning the past 70 years, see Tzvi Abusch, "Marduk," *DDD* 543–49, esp. pp. 547–48.

5. The term *cosmos* is used throughout, unless otherwise noted, in the specific sense of an organized universe. The dictionary definition of "*orderly harmonious systematic* universe" (italics mine; see *Merriam-Webster's Collegiate Dictionary* [11th ed.; Springfield, MA: Merriam-Webster, 2003] 282) also serves, but it suggests, incorrectly in the context of the Mesopotamian cosmos, an absence of chaotic or disruptive elements within the system.

6. Gunkel, *Creation and Chaos*, 22, 35; K. William Whitney, *Two Strange Beasts: Leviathan and Behemoth in Second Temple and Early Rabbinic Judaism* (HSM 63; Winona Lake, IN: Eisenbrauns, 2006), esp. chap. 1.

In the 100+ years that have passed since Gunkel's initial publication, the sheer number of scholarly responses written in support of or opposition to various aspects of his original hypothesis testify to its ongoing influence. The discovery of much new material, the Ugaritic *Baʿal Cycle* especially,[7] and significant refinements in the understanding of the ancient Semitic languages have significantly complicated the question of whence exactly the *Chaoskampf* tradition might have been introduced into the biblical materials.[8] Nevertheless, the impact of Gunkel's broader vision continues to resound in contemporary scholarship in points both subtle and explicit. It is one unique legacy of his work—the embedding of chaos into the discourse on *Enūma eliš* in particular (and the cosmogonic and theogonic accounts of Mesopotamia in general)—that is the subject of this essay.[9]

7. Dating to perhaps the thirteenth century B.C.E., the first fragments of the *Baʿal Cycle* were discovered in 1929 in the "House of the High Priest" at Ugarit. The cycle was published with detailed commentary in Mark S. Smith, *The Ugaritic Baal Cycle: Introduction with Text, Translation and Commentary of KTU 1.1–1.2* (vol. 1; VTSup 55; Leiden: Brill, 1994); and Mark S Smith and Wayne Thomas Pitard, *The Ugaritic Baal Cycle: Introduction with Text, Translation and Commentary of KTU/CAT 1.3–1.4* (vol. 2; VTSup 144; Leiden: Brill, 2009). For the privileging of the Canaanite material in relation to the Genesis account, see, for example, John Day, *God's Conflict with the Dragon and the Sea: Echoes of a Canaanite Myth in the Old Testament* (University of Cambridge Oriental Publications; Cambridge: Cambridge University Press, 1985) esp. p. 4; and for a consideration of creation in the *Baʿal Cycle*, see Loren Fisher, "Creation at Ugarit and in the Old Testament," *VT* 15 (1965) 313–24; idem, "The Temple Quarter," *JSS* 8 (1963) 34–41. Arguing for a close relationship between *Enūma eliš* and Genesis 1, see Bernard Frank Batto, *Slaying the Dragon: Mythmaking in the Biblical Tradition* (Louisville: Westminster/John Knox, 1992) esp. pp. 77–82; and, for an overview of scholarly work on the subject, see David Toshio Tsumura, "Genesis and Ancient Near Eastern Stories of Creation and Flood: An Introduction," in *I Studied Inscriptions from before the Flood: Ancient Near Eastern, Literary, and Linguistic Approaches to Genesis 1–11* (ed. Richard S. Hess and David Toshio Tsumura; Sources for Biblical and Theological Study 4; Winona Lake, IN: Eisenbrauns, 1994) 31–34.

8. For the relationship between *tĕhôm* and Tiʾāmat, see David Toshio Tsumura, *The Earth and the Waters in Genesis 1 and 2: A Linguistic Investigation* (JSOTSup 83; Sheffield: JSOT Press, 1989) chap. 3, esp. pp. 45–47; and, more recently, David Toshio Tsumura, *Creation and Destruction: A Reappraisal of the Chaoskampf Theory in the Old Testament* (Winona Lake, IN: Eisenbrauns, 2005) esp. pp. 42–53. His position is briefly summarized (Tsumura, "Genesis and Ancient Near Eastern Stories of Creation and Flood," 31): "[I]t is phonologically impossible to conclude that *tĕhôm* 'ocean' was borrowed from *Tiamat*. The Hebrew *tĕhôm* 'ocean' together with the Ugaritic *thm*, the Akkadian *tiāmtu*, the Arabic *tihāmat*, and the Eblaite *ti-ʾà-ma-tum /tihām(a)tum/* is simply a reflection of a common Semitic term **tihām-*."

9. The difficulties inherent in mapping chaos onto the biblical materials have been recently and thoroughly explored in Rebecca Sally Watson, *Chaos Uncreated: A Reassessment of the Theme of "Chaos" in the Hebrew Bible* (BZAW 341; Berlin: de Gruyter, 2005) esp. pp. 13–19; and Tsumura, *Creation and Destruction*. Watson in particular traces the application (and the arguments against the application) of chaos to the account in Gen 1:2 from as far back as the Fathers through to Delitzsch and Wellhausen. Watson notes here

While Gunkel's mapping of chaos—which is properly at home in the cosmogonies and philosophies of Classical antiquity—onto the alien Babylonian creation account of *Enūma eliš* was not original even at the early date of his writing, his specific linking of chaos with the themes of both combat and creation introduced certain lingering ambiguities into the interpretation of that text.[10] Notable among these is the conflation of what should be understood as two distinct concepts: cosmogonic chaos, in the manner of the neutral (neither "good" nor "evil") chasm or jumbled primordial matter that appears at the origins of cosmic differentiation in Hesiod's *Theogony* or Ovid's *Metamorphoses*, respectively; and kratogenic chaos, referring to the specifically harmful forces of disorder or confusion that exist *within* the organized universe and that actively threaten the establishment and maintenance of divine order and civilization.[11] While these two concepts may in some contexts overlap or even

also the reference by George Smith, in his initial publication of *Enūma eliš*, to Ti'āmat as sea-chaos (Watson, *Chaos Uncreated*, 15–16).

10. See, for example, Gunkel, *Creation and Chaos*, 18: "The Babylonians asserted with pride that their god *Marduk* was the ruler of the world, since he had defeated chaos and created the world."

11. Jan Assmann (*The Mind of Egypt: History and Meaning in the Time of the Pharaohs* [Cambridge: Harvard University Press, 2003] 189) offered an elegant distinction between cosmogonic chaos and what he termed "cratogonic" chaos (Gk. *kratos* "strength"), the latter standing in opposition to the order represented by the state, in a discussion of Middle Kingdom Egypt:

> The purpose of the state is the aversion of "chaos," and this chaos is represented as the quintessence of all evil. But this idea of chaos should not be confused with cosmogonic chaos, the primal state of the fore-world from which sprang the order of creation. Cosmogonic chaos is amorphous primal matter devoid of any connotations of evil or imperfection. . . . The chaos that the Middle Kingdom pits itself against is not cosmogonic, but "cratogonic"; the opposite of chaos is not the birth of a world but the establishment of rule.

He further defines *cratogony* specifically as "the emergence and evolution of power," in Jan Assmann and David Frankfurter, "Egypt," in *Religions of the Ancient World: A Guide* (ed. Sarah Iles Johnston; Harvard University Press Reference Library; Cambridge: Belknap, 2004) 158. The concept is adapted here for application in a specifically Mesopotamian context to encompass the establishment (and active maintenance) of civilization as it is housed and contained (and protected by the gods) within the cities: the term is consequently altered to *kratogeny*, still derived from the Gk. *kratos* ("strength, stronghold"), but drawing on the role of kratogen (more recently, craton or cratonic) as incorporating the concept of stability and carrying also the connotation of stronghold. The term *kratogen* is well known from geological scholarship, in which Kratogen (the consolidated and stable parts of the earth's crust) is defined in opposition to Orogen (the unconsolidated and mobile zones); see J. Aubouin, *Geosynclines* (Amsterdam: Elsevier, 1965) 24. A distinction may alternately be drawn between precosmic (cosmogonic) and cosmic chaos, the latter contained within the cosmos or ordered universe (Gk. *kosmos* "order" or "world") rather than existing at its point of origin. A caveat is that the current scholarship does not always reflect such a distinction.

be jointly personified in a single entity,[12] a productive analysis of *Enūma eliš* depends on their distinction. In seeking to define where, exactly, chaos is to be located within *Enūma eliš*, then, this paper comprises three distinct sections: (1) an exploration of the definition and function of chaos within its original contexts, the Greek and Roman mythological texts in which cosmogonic or precosmic chaos is explicitly referenced; (2) a consideration of the extent to which cosmogonic chaos may be legitimately mapped onto the Mesopotamian cosmogonies, specifically the cosmogony contained in *Enūma eliš*; and (3) a treatment of kratogenic chaos, its role in the Mesopotamian world view, and its specific manifestation in the text of *Enūma eliš*.

Defining Cosmogonic Chaos: From Hesiod's Theogony *to Ovid's* Metamorphoses

Deriving originally from the Greek (χάος), chaos appeared prominently in various ancient Greek and Roman cosmogonic and philosophical accounts in which it served a striking variety of functions,[13] appearing variously as the abyss or chasm from which arose all things, a gap that initiated the process of

12. It is tempting to see the Chaos of Ovid's *Metamorphoses* in this manner, given that the "instability of form and confusion of boundaries" that distinguishes primordial Chaos poses a persistent threat to the organized world; see Richard Tarrant, "Chaos in Ovid's Metamorphoses and Its Neronian Influence," *Arethusa* 35 (2002) 349–60 esp. pp. 349–51. It is important to note, however, that Chaos in this context is not an active or specifically hostile force working against the ordered world but, rather, an initial state to which it is possible to return: "Now if the sea, the lands, the heaven perish, / all will be plunged in chaos once again! / Save from the flames whatever still is left, / take measures to preserve the universe!" *Metamorphoses* 2.394–97, translated in Charles Martin, *Metamorphoses: A New Translation, Contexts, Criticism* (New York: Norton, 2010) 36; see also Tarrant, "Chaos in Ovid's Metamorphoses," 351.

13. West (Martin Litchfield West, *The East Face of Helicon: West Asiatic Elements in Greek Poetry and Myth* [Oxford: Oxford University Press, 1997] 288) notes that "the word *khaos* is related to the verbs *khainō* and *khaskō*, 'gape, yawn', and the idea is perhaps related to the concept of the earth itself gaping open to swallow someone up so that he is never seen again." For a broad overview of ancient Greek philosophical and poetic treatments of Chaos, see Robert Mondi, "ΚΑΟΣ and the Hesiodic Cosmogony," *Harvard Studies in Classical Philology* 92 (1989) 1–41; Elaine Fantham, *Ovid's Metamorphoses* (Oxford Approaches to Classical Literature; New York: Oxford University Press, 2004) 21–26; also G. S. Kirk, J. E. Raven, and M. Schofield, *The Presocratic Philosophers* (2nd ed.; Cambridge: Cambridge University Press, 1983) 17–41. See also Norman Wentworth De Witt, *Epicurus and His Philosophy* ([Minneapolis: University of Minnesota Press, 1954] 42) for the impact of Hesiod and his mysterious Chaos on Epicurus; see David Bolotin, *An Approach to Aristotle's Physics: With Particular Attention to the Role of His Manner of Writing* ([Albany: State University of New York Press, 1998] 23, 79), for Aristotle's discussion of Hesiod's Chaos; and, for Aristophanes' location of Chaos, see J. Henderson, *Aristophanes Birds, Lysistrata, Women at Thesmophoria* (LCL; Cambridge: Harvard University Press, 2000) 114–17; and Leo Strauss, *Socrates and Aristophanes* (Chicago: University of Chicago Press, 1966) 171.

differentiation, a primordial personified or divine entity, and a mass of jumbled and conflicting elements of every type in a state of constant disarray. This section focuses on those texts, Hesiod's *Theogony* and Ovid's *Metamorphoses*, which have significantly shaped or contributed to modern Western thought on the subject of chaos.

In Hesiod's ca. eighth-century B.C.E. *Theogony*, which recounts the origins and genealogies of the gods, Chaos serves as the starting point for cosmic differentiation, originating without antecedent and functioning as an apparent abyss or chasm.[14] Key to its understanding and to the understanding of Hesiod's cosmos overall is the fact that, while Chaos appears at the beginning of all things, and while it superficially represents a void, empty space, it too is described with the language of "coming to be."[15] If it is nothing, it is yet an "articulated nothing."[16] Already in 1983, Bussanich argued persuasively for this more nuanced treatment of Chaos within the context of the *Theogony*, identifying it as a mythological symbol that was properly interpreted qualitatively rather than quantitatively and that was not to be confused with an empirical void: "Since its function is cosmogonic, Chaos must be defined as unidimensional or principial space . . . it is the barest indication that there is a qualitative something, from and in which cosmic differentiation occurs. . . . As the least differentiated divinity in the *Theogony*, Chaos denotes the limits of the cosmic process, beyond which mythical representation cannot go."[17]

Following Chaos onto the scene of Hesiod's developing cosmos are Gaia, the earth and essential matrix of creation; misty Tartara (pl.), which at this point may represent *either* the independent netherworld Tartarus (sing.) as it is

14. John Bussanich, "A Theoretical Interpretation of Hesiod's Chaos," *CP* 78 (1983) 214. *Chaos* is conventionally capitalized where it refers specifically to Hesiod's primal principle, a convention that is followed here. This convention is extended to the Chaos of Ovid's *Metamorphoses* only in order to distinguish the term in its classical context from its mapping onto alien contexts. All other appearances of the term, as in the discussion on *Enūma eliš*, appear in lower case.

15. See Jenny Strauss Clay, *Hesiod's Cosmos* (Cambridge: Cambridge University Press, 2003) 15–16. See also Bussanich ("A Theoretical Interpretation of Hesiod's Chaos," 212–13) for the argument that, while Chaos, Gaia, and Eros "come to be," their existence is not dependent, as in the case of all of the other deities, on procreation; thus, in his treatment of them, Hesiod "isolates a timeless moment, an *Urzeit*, that is qualitatively distinct from subsequent stages of the cosmogony"; and the discussion in Drew A. Hyland, "First of All Came Chaos," in *Heidegger and the Greeks: Interpretive Essays* (ed. Drew A. Hyland and John Panteleimon Manoussakis; Studies in Continental Thought; Bloomington: Indiana University Press, 2006) esp. pp. 9–10.

16. Bussanich, "A Theoretical Interpretation of Hesiod's Chaos," 216.

17. Ibid., 214.

later described in the *Theogony* (lines 729–819) *or* the initial interior space or inner dimensions of the earth that will only later become "sufficiently differentiated and separated from the Earth to emerge in a final manifestation as the personified Tartarus";[18] and Eros, the procreative force and actual mechanism of creation that accompanies Gaia, the matrix or matter. The relationship of these three entities to Chaos, as their relationship to each other, is not clearly explicated in the text, so that they have been variously characterized as "self-generated, autonomous agents in [this] cosmology, primary entities, beyond which it is not possible to penetrate,"[19] or (at least, in the case of Earth and Tartarus) as the *by-products* of the appearance of Chaos. In this reconstruction, then, Chaos would function as the "underworldly gap" that separated and defined Earth and Tartarus (see figs. 1–3 for several proposed reconstructions of the place and functioning of Chaos within Hesiod's cosmos).[20] It is only after these two elemental loci have come into being that Chaos is implicated in a deliberate act of creation or generation. Erebos, the primordial darkness, and Nyx or Night are subsequently described as emerging from it (through scissiparity or parthenogenesis)[21] before sexual procreation is initiated through the union of Erebos and Nyx:

18. Clay, *Hesiod's Cosmos*, 15–16. For the argument against the role of Tartara as a primal principle and the assertion that it appears in the opening lines not in the nominative but in the accusative, see E. F. Beall, "Once More on Hesiod's Supposed Tartarus Principle," *Classical World* 102 (2009) 159–61; and his proffered alternate translation: "Well first of all arose Chasm; and then (came) broad-breasted Earth, ever the firm seat of all the immortals who hold the peak of snowy Olympus and the murky underworlds [Tartara] in the recess of the ground with its wide courses, and Love, who as the most beautiful among the deathless gods, and as the limb-relaxer, subdues the mind and sensible will in the breast of all gods and all humans," *Theogony* 116–22, translation on p. 159. Such a reading, of course, would preclude any interpretation of Chaos as "gap."

19. Norman Austin, *Meaning and Being in Myth* (University Park: Pennsylvania State University Press, 1990) 55.

20. The most compelling argument for interpreting Hesiod's Chaos as "gap" appears in Mitchell Miller, "'First of All': On the Semantics and Ethics of Hesiod's Cosmogony," *Ancient Philosophy* 21 (2001) 251–76, esp. p. 254; see also the useful summaries of the issues in Hyland, "First of All Came Chaos"; and Edward S. Casey, *The Fate of Place: A Philosophical History* (Berkeley: University of California Press, 1997) 9–10. For a thorough account of the various interpretations of Chaos and its function at the origins of Hesiod's cosmos, see also Gerard Naddaf, *The Greek Concept of Nature* (SUNY Series in Ancient Greek Philosophy; Albany: State University of New York Press, 2005) 48–50; H. Podbielski, "Le chaos et les confins de l'univers dans la théogonie d'Hésiode," *Les études classiques* 54 (1986) 253–63. If Chaos in the context of the opening lines of Hesiod's *Theogony* is indeed correctly interpreted as a gap rather than an abyss, it is a gap not between earth and heaven (as it was once interpreted) but between Earth and Tartarus; see Miller, "'First of All': On the Semantics and Ethics of Hesiod's Cosmogony," 253–60, esp. p. 257.

21. Clay, *Hesiod's Cosmos*, 16.

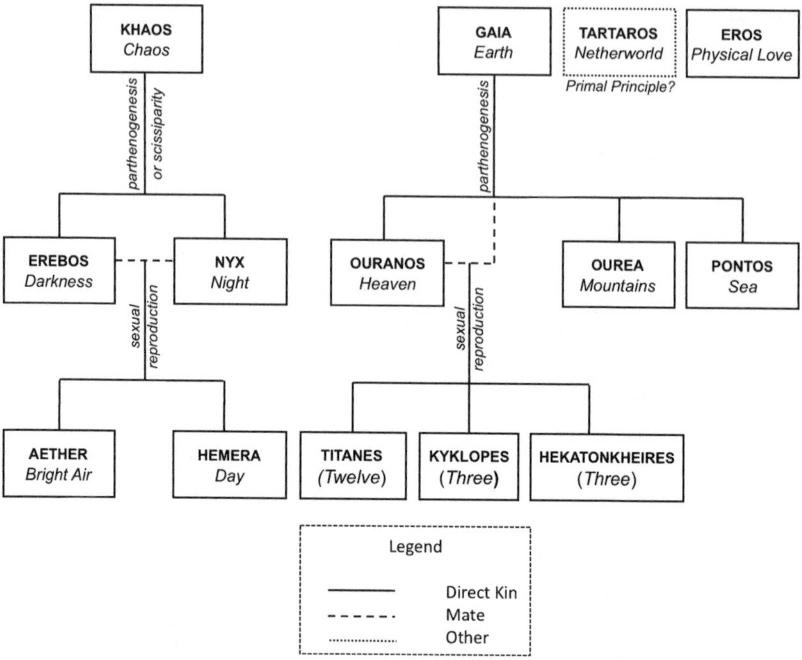

Fig 1. Reconstruction 1: Chaos and cosmogony in Hesiod's *Theogony*.

> First came [Chaos] the Chasm; and then broad-breasted [Gaia] Earth, secure seat for ever of all the immortals who occupy the peak of snowy Olympus; the misty Tartara in a remote recess of the broad-pathed earth; and Eros, the most handsome of the gods, dissolver of flesh, who overcomes the reason and purpose in the breasts of all gods and men.
>
> Out of the Chasm came Erebos [Darkness] and [Nyx] dark Night, and from Night in turn came [Aether] Bright Air and [Hemera] Day, whom she bore in shared intimacy with Erebos. Earth bore first of all one equal to herself, starry [Ouranos] Heaven, so that he should cover her all about, to be a secure seat for ever for the blessed gods.[22]

The driving impetus of the *Theogony*, then, is one toward increasing differentiation as Gaia gives birth to Ouranos, who further defines as he encloses her, and as Erebos and Nyx emerge out of Chaos, subsequently coupling to

22. Translated in Martin Litchfield West, *Theogony; and, Works and Days* (Oxford World's Classics; Oxford: Oxford University Press, 1999) 6.

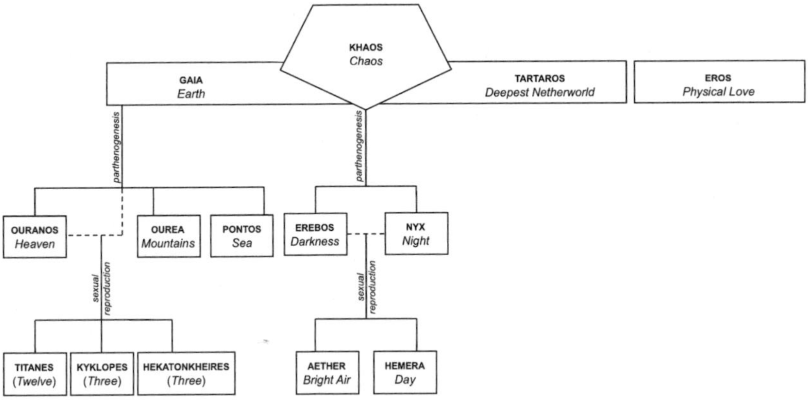

Fig 2. Reconstruction 2: Chaos and cosmogony in Hesiod's *Theogony*.

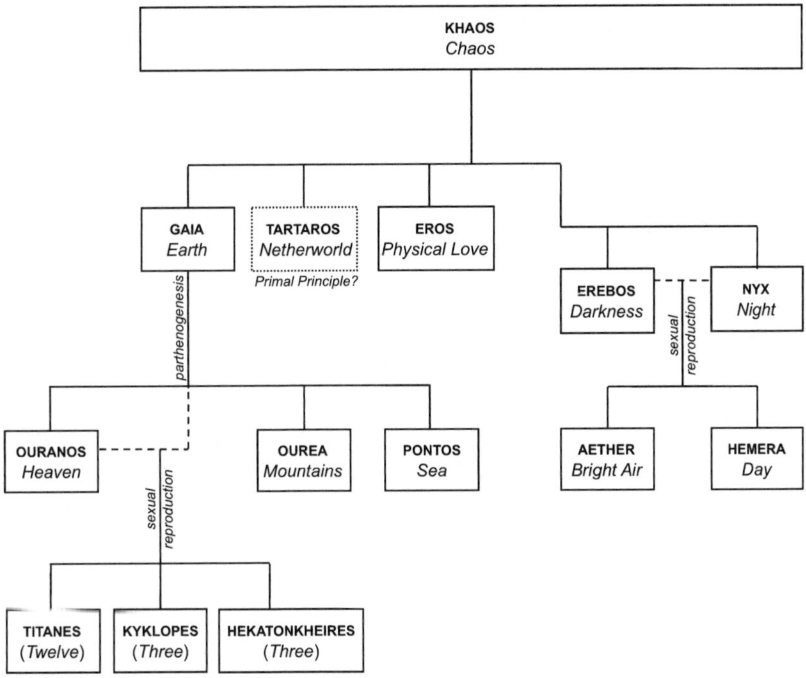

Fig 3. Reconstruction 3: Chaos and cosmogony in Hesiod's *Theogony*.

produce their opposite numbers Aether and Hemera. In so doing, they signal the beginning of measurable time through an eternal cycle of nights and days.[23]

If Chaos, in Hesiod's account, is a yawning abyss, a barely articulated nothing that has little in common with the contemporary use of the term as meaning "complete disorder and confusion,"[24] it takes on quite a different guise in other poetic and philosophical accounts, even those dating from Classical antiquity.[25] The depiction of chaos perhaps most diametrically opposed to that appearing in Hesiod's *Theogony* is found some eight centuries later, in the early first-century C.E. *Metamorphoses* of the Roman poet Ovid:

> Before the seas and lands had been created,
> before the sky that covers everything,
> Nature displayed a single aspect only
> throughout the cosmos;[26] Chaos was its name,
> a shapeless, unwrought mass of inert bulk
> and nothing more, with the discordant seeds
> of disconnected elements all heaped
> together in anarchic disarray.
> The sun as yet did not light up the earth,
> nor did the crescent moon renew her horns,
> nor was the earth suspended in midair,
> balanced by her own weight, nor did the ocean
> extend her arms to the margins of the land.
> Although the land and sea and air were present,
> land was unstable, the sea unfit for swimming,
> and air lacked light; shapes shifted constantly,
> and all things were at odds with one another,
> for in a single mass cold strove with warm,
> wet was opposed to dry and soft to hard,
> and weightlessness to matter having weight.[27]

Described rather graphically as a *rudis indigestaque moles*, Ovid's Chaos is a rude and disordered mass "marked above all by instability of form and confusion of boundaries."[28] Far from Hesiod's featureless chasm, this dark primordial bulk contains already within it, albeit in a state of perpetual conflict, the seeds of

23. Clay, *Hesiod's Cosmos*, 15.

24. Elizabeth Knowles, *The Oxford Dictionary of Phrase and Fable* (Oxford: Oxford University Press, 2005) s.v. "chaos."

25. See n. 5.

26. *Cosmos* is here used in its generic sense as the totality of all existing matter and space.

27. *Metamorphoses* 1.6–25, translated in Martin, *Metamorphoses*, 5.

28. Tarrant, "Chaos in Ovid's Metamorphoses," 350.

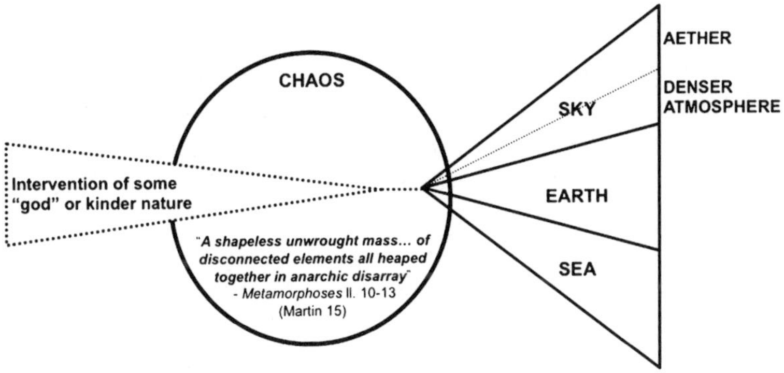

Fig 4. Chaos and cosmogony in Ovid's *Metamorphoses*.

as-yet unstable and disconnected elements. Further, the transition from this "anarchic disarray" to the structured cosmos known to Ovid and his contemporaries is attributed by the poet to the intervention of some unknown god or "kinder nature" who gave Chaos form, separating and redefining it, "dividing it into parts which he [the god] arranged" (fig. 4).[29] How and when this creator god arose is not clear, and the exact relationship between Chaos and the line of gods culminating in those worshiped in Ovid's day is but briefly suggested as the narrative moves swiftly forward to the creation of the humans, who take pride of place in this account of creation. Following the separation of elements and the structuring of the cosmos by the creator, every part of the world took on "its own distinctive forms of life,"[30] the gods and the beasts among them. "The constellations and the shapes of gods occupied the lower part of heaven; the seas gave shelter to the shining fishes, earth received beasts, and flighty air, the birds,"[31] and humans—akin to the gods in form and perhaps in substance as well—appear at last on the scene.[32]

29. *Metamorphoses* 1.41–43, translated in Martin, *Metamorphoses*, 6.

30. *Metamorphoses* 1.100, translated in ibid., 7.

31. *Metamorphoses* 1.101–4, translated in ibid., 7.

32. Humans are created out of either the divine substance of the "framer of all things," the creator god, or through Prometheus's deliberate shaping of them from a clod of ether; see *Metamorphoses* 1.105–17, translated in ibid., 7. The typically anthropocentric universe of the Greeks and Romans contrasts sharply with the theocentric universe of Mesopotamia; see, for example, Jean Bottéro, Clarisse Herrenschmidt, and Jean-Pierre Vernant, *Ancestor of the West: Writing, Reasoning, and Religion in Mesopotamia, Elam, and Greece* (Chicago: University of Chicago Press, 2000) 42–43; also the Sumerian composition *Enki and Ninmah* and the Akkadian composition *Atraḫasīs*, which recount the creation of humans to labor on behalf and in place of the gods.

The distinction between Hesiod's abyss and Ovid's rude and disordered mass is not limited, then, to a question of form or even substance. In the *Theogony*, Chaos stands at the beginning of not only the process of differentiation, but also of a line of ever more-complex gods that emerge organically into and out of the abyss, the earliest of which themselves serve as the foundations of the familiar cosmos. In the *Metamorphoses*, in contrast, while Chaos contains the raw matter from which the cosmos might be shaped, the process of differentiation must be deliberately initiated through the agency of some unknown divinity or kinder nature who succeeds—at least temporarily—in imposing order upon it.[33]

While Hesiod's and Ovid's competing visions of precosmic Chaos (and the philosophers' meditations on and adaptations of these) have been predominant in the shaping of Western thought on the subject,[34] to what extent can the concept of cosmogonic chaos be productively mapped onto the creation account contained in *Enūma eliš*?[35]

Cosmogony: Chaos and Creation in Enūma eliš

The Mesopotamian cosmogonic accounts, including that contained in *Enūma eliš*, are distinguished from those of both Hesiod's *Theogony* and Ovid's *Metamorphoses* in that they originated neither in an articulated nothing nor in an anarchic mass of heterogeneous matter. Instead, typically, they "went back to a single element in the beginning," with Lambert identifying four such original elements: Earth, Time, Heaven, and Water.[36] As a consequence,

33. The precariousness of this imposed order is underlined in the mutability of physical forms and instability of the boundaries between different classes of being in the *Metamorphoses*.

34. Anthony Grafton, Glenn W. Most, and Salvatore Settis, *The Classical Tradition* (Harvard University Press Library; Cambridge: Belknap, 2010), s.v. "chaos."

35. Tiʾāmat's explicit identification with cosmogonic Chaos is more prominent in now outdated works of Mesopotamian scholarship or in works by scholars taking up the threads of Gunkel's work and retaining his terminology; however, it persists in casual reference in other works as well. See, for example, L. W. King, *The Seven Tablets of Creation, or the Babylonian and Assyrian Legends concerning the Creation of the World and of Mankind* (London: Luzac, 1902) xxv, xxxiii, xxxviii n. 1, lxxxi, 3; Batto, *Slaying the Dragon*, 76; Sjoerd Lieuwe Bonting, *Creation and Double Chaos: Science and Theology in Discussion* (Minneapolis: Fortress, 2005) 51–54, esp. p. 52; J. W. Rogerson and Philip R. Davies, *The Old Testament World* (London: T. & T. Clark, 2005) 112. Tiʾāmat is also occasionally identified as a "chaos monster" (see, for example, Day, *God's Conflict with the Dragon and the Sea*, 7, 11): in these cases, the concepts of cosmogonic and kratogenic chaos may be conflated.

36. W. G. Lambert, "Kosmogonie," *Reallexikon der Assyriologie und Vorderasiatischen Archäologie* 6 (1980–83) 219. In her article on Sumerian cosmogonic strands, Westenholz begins with the statement, "None of the various Mesopotamian cosmogonies envisages a *creatio ex nihilo*; rather, they posit a primeval material" (Joan Goodnick Westenholz, "Heaven

the scholarly discourse on the Mesopotamian cosmogonies is typically framed with terms referencing primary elements or primary matter, recalling less the mythological accounts of cosmogonic Chaos from Classical antiquity and more (if still only superficially) the doctrines of the Greek philosophers—as, for example, the seventh-century B.C.E. Thales of Miletus. Thales, according to Aristotle, posited that the first or primary principle (ἀρχή or *arkhē*) was not chaos in the Hesiodic or Ovidian sense but, rather, a specific element, water, the unity of all things:

> Following an explanation involving elements and the preservation of the permanent substance through the processes of change, Aristotle returns, in 983 b19, to the number and nature of the ἀρχή (first cause) on which they (the first philosophers) had made their declarations. In the next line, 983 b20, Aristotle then made his imperative statement that Thales, the first of the natural philosophers, had, however, decided on the number and nature of ἀρχή, declaring it to be a single material, water.[37]

The language of chaos is, however, retained in reference to *Enūma eliš*, a partial legacy certainly of Gunkel's work and the ongoing scholarly responses to it. Westenholz's discussion of Sumerian cosmogonies originating with An and Ki (Heaven and Earth), for example, is cast in terms of primary matter or primary elements. Her single reference to the cosmogonies that originate in water (*Enūma eliš* prominent among them) is particularly telling in this context. "In Mesopotamian thought there were three types of primary matter: earth, sky, and water . . . the theology concerning a watery chaos at the beginning of time held sway in the city of Eridu and later Babylon."[38] The application of chaos to *Enūma eliš* in such contexts should generally be read as more conventional than deliberately descriptive, the term used in the most generic and neutral possible sense as a synonym for primordial matter (in whatever form this might take) or, more simply, for the original state of the universe. The question is, however, whether the persistence of the term in reference to the cosmogony in *Enūma eliš* is wholly due to convention or whether it has any real basis in the unfolding of events in that text. In order to answer this question, the cosmogonic account in *Enūma eliš* is divided into two parts, the

and Earth: Asexual Monad and Bisexual Dyad," in *Gazing on the Deep: Ancient Near Eastern and Other Studies in Honor of Tzvi Abusch* [ed. Jeffrey Stackert, Barbara Nevling Porter, and David P. Wright; Bethesda, MD: CDL, 2010] 293).

37. Patricia F. O'Grady, *Thales of Miletus: The Beginnings of Western Science and Philosophy* (Aldershot: Ashgate, 2002) 31, 76–77; see Aristotle, *Metaphysics* 983 b20–b33. For a discussion of and argument against the suggestion that Thales was influenced by Near Eastern cosmogonic accounts such as, for example, *Enūma eliš*, see O'Grady, *Thales of Miletus*, 76–81.

38. Westenholz, "Heaven and Earth," 293.

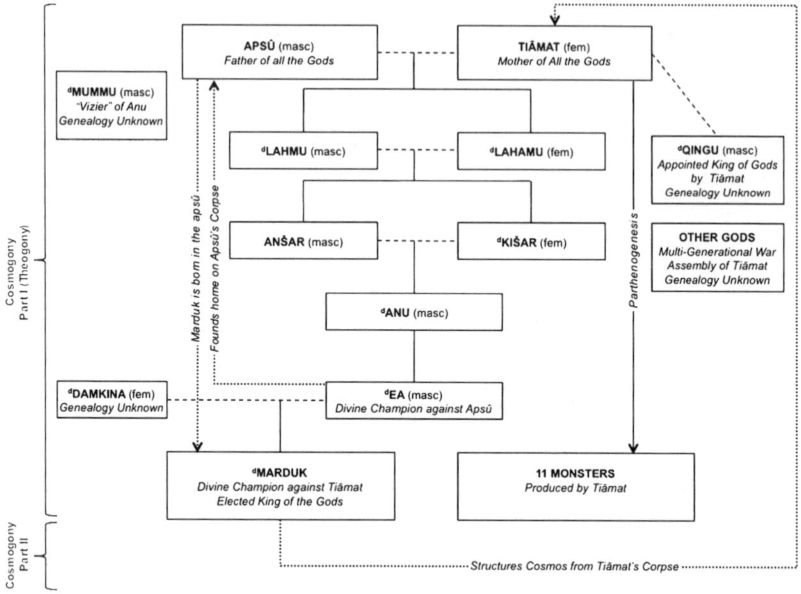

Fig 5. Modeling cosmogony in *Enūma eliš.*

first essentially comprising a theogony and the second comprising a deliberate cosmic organization undertaken by a creator god (see fig. 5).

Enūma eliš opens on a scene devoid of those features that defined the familiar Mesopotamian landscape, lacking not merely marsh or meadow-lands but even the fundamental frame of heaven and earth, and containing as yet no trace of the gods themselves. What it does, contain, however, is water and, more, water already separated into the masculine Apsû and the feminine Tiʾāmat.[39] The mingling of these two elemental entities is sufficiently potent to initiate an organic process of differentiation:

When the heavens above did not exist,
And earth beneath had not come into being—
There was Apsû, the first in order, their begetter,
And demiurge Tiāmat, who gave birth to them all;
They had mingled their waters together

39. The common distinction between these as representing the sweet (Apsû) and salt (Tiʾāmat) waters, respectively, was challenged in W. G. Lambert, "The Apsû," in *Landscapes: Territories, Frontiers, and Horizons in the Ancient Near East. Papers Presented to the XLIV Rencontre Assyriologique Internationale, Venezia, 7–11 July 1997* (ed. L. Milano et al.; Padua: Sargon, 1999) 75; thus, it is not included here.

Before meadow-land had coalesced and reed-bed was to be found—
When not one of the gods had been formed
Or had come into being, when no destinies had been decreed,
The gods were created within them:
Laḫmu and Laḫamu were formed and came into being.[40]

The first gods generated from this mingling of the waters, Laḫmu and Laḫamu (their names, unlike those of the elemental Apsû and Tiʾāmat, marked with the divine determinative),[41] are followed onto the scene by Anšar and Kišar, representing perhaps heaven and earth, who "excel" beyond the original pair.[42] These, in turn, produce the sky-god Anu, the traditional head of the Mesopotamian pantheon and equal of his father, Anšar; and Anu in turn produces Ea (Nudimmud), lord of the *apsû* or subterranean fresh waters. Rivaling his father Anu, exceeding his grandfather Anšar, and peerless among his brothers,[43] it is Ea who becomes the first champion of the gods in a developing conflict with Apsû, who has been plotting to destroy his divine heirs on account of their unceasing clamor: "I will destroy and break up their way of life / That silence may reign and we may sleep."[44] While Ea is successful in his task, binding and slaying Apsû and founding his own home upon the corpse of his progenitor,[45] it is with Ea's son Marduk[46]—a god who is awe-inspiring and remarkable from birth and who soon grows to surpass all his forebears—that this process reaches

40. *Enūma eliš* (henceforth *Ee*) I 1–10, translated in W. G. Lambert, "Mesopotamian Creation Stories," in *Imagining Creation* (ed. Markham Geller and Mineke Schipper; IJS Studies in Judaica: Conference Proceedings of the Institute of Jewish Studies, University College London; Leiden: Brill, 2008) 37.

41. The absence of the divine determinative for the names of Apsû and Tiʾāmat distinguishes them from their children, the gods proper. Though they later take on the role of active and powerful beings, the mother and father of all the gods, the opening of *Enūma eliš* depicts Apsû and Tiʾāmat as passive at best.

42. Thorkild Jacobsen (*The Treasures of Darkness: A History of Mesopotamian Religion* [New Haven, CT: Yale University Press, 1976] 256 n. 332) linked Laḫmu and Laḫamu to mud or silt through a connection to /*lhm*/; this reading was challenged by W. G. Lambert ("The Pair Lahmu-Lahamu in Cosmology," *Or* n.s. 54 [1985] 199); see also Wiggermann, *Mesopotamian Protective Spirits*, 165–66. Anšar and Kišar were identified by Jacobsen (*The Treasures of Darkness*, 168) as together representing "the horizon, the circular rim of heaven and the corresponding rim of earth." Anšar and Kišar are presumably the children of Laḫmu and Laḫamu, though this is not absolutely clear in the text. It is possible, though I think not plausible, that they derive also from Apsû and Tiʾāmat; see my "Gender Matters in Enuma Eliš," in *In the Wake of Tikva Frymer-Kensky* (ed. S. W. Holloway, J. Scurlock, and R. H. Beal; Piscataway, NJ: Gorgias, 2009) n. 13.

43. *Ee* I 16–20, translated in Lambert, "Mesopotamian Creation Stories," 37.

44. *Ee* I 39–40, translated in ibid., 38.

45. "He bound Apsû and killed him. . . . He set his dwelling upon Apsû," *Ee* I 69–71, translated in ibid., 37.

46. For a discussion of Marduk's genealogy and birth, see my "Bad King, False King, True King: Apsû and His Heirs," *JAOS* 128 (2008) 737–43.

its culmination: "Anu rendered him perfect: his divinity was remarkable, / And he became very lofty, excelling them [the gods] in his attributes. / His members were incomprehensibly wonderful, / Incapable of being grasped with the mind, hard even to look on."[47] When a second, greater threat to the gods arises in the form of a furious Tiʾāmat, stirred to action against her own children by Ea's slaying of her mate, Apsû, it is Marduk who steps forward as the new divine champion and who demands—and is awarded—the kingship of the gods as his prize.

There is as yet no trace of cosmogonic or precosmic chaos here except in its most generic sense as primeval matter, no hint of disorder or disarray in the placidly mingling waters, and no attempt to penetrate beyond the existence of the elemental entities Apsû and Tiʾāmat. If there is a resemblance to the mythological cosmogonies from Classical antiquity considered in the previous section, this is to be found primarily in the trend in *Enūma eliš* (somewhat comparable to that found in Hesiod's *Theogony*) toward not only increasing differentiation but also the production of ever more powerful and sophisticated gods, with each new generation rivaling or surpassing the previous one until they culminate in Marduk, the clearly predestined king of the gods.

There is a second phase to the cosmogonic account, however, which assumes quite a different aspect from the first. Rooted in the developing conflict between Tiʾāmat and her children,[48] it sees the watery Tiʾāmat, one half of the elemental pair that stands at the beginning of all things in *Enūma eliš*, bring forth 11 monsters to aid in the destruction of her own divine children: "She created the Hydra, the Dragon, the Hairy Hero / The Great Demon, the Savage Dog, and the Scorpion-man, / Fierce demons, the Fish-man, and the Bull-man."[49] More, Tiʾāmat's own form, variously suggested in earlier portions of the narrative to be that of a body of water or a woman, itself takes on a distinctly monstrous aspect following her death,[50] being attributed with a tail and described as a *kūbu*, a word otherwise referring to an abortion or monstrous form.[51] Dismembered by Marduk and the elements of her corpse used

47. *Ee* I 91–94, translated in Lambert, "Mesopotamian Creation Stories," 39.

48. This conflict is precipitated both by Ea's killing of Tiʾāmat's mate, Apsû, and by the terrible disturbances created by the young and enormously precocious god Marduk, *Ee* I 105–9.

49. *Ee* I 141–43, translated in ibid., 39.

50. *Ee* II 144; V 57, 59.

51. *Ee* IV 136: UZU.*ku-bu ú-za-a-zu i-ban-na-a nik-la-a-ti*; see Philippe Talon, *The Standard Babylonian Creation Myth: Enuma Elish* (SAACT; Helsinki: The Neo-Assyrian Text Corpus Project, 2005) 17, 56. *CAD* K 487, s.v. *kūbu* A1; more recently, see the detailed discussion by Stol (in Marten Stol and F. A. M. Wiggermann, *Birth in Babylonia and the Bible: Its Mediterranean Setting* [Cuneiform Monographs 14; Groningen: Styx, 2000] 28–32), who clarifies that a *kūbu* "is not a still-born child but must be a foetus that already has clear

to form the features of the familiar cosmos, Tiʾāmat at last comes to resemble something of chaos as it appears—that anarchic mass divided and reassembled by an unnamed creator god (or nature)—in the *Metamorphoses*.

> Bel rested, surveying the [Tiāmat's] corpse,
> In order to divide the lump by a clever scheme.
> He split her into two like a dried fish:
> One half of her he set up and stretched out as the heavens.
> Gates he opened on both sides,
> And put strong bolts at the left and the right.
> He placed the heights (of heaven) in her (Tiāmat's) belly,
> The foam which Tiāmat [. . .
> Marduk fashioned [. . .
> He gathered it together and made it into clouds.
> The raging of the winds, violent rainstorms,
> The billowing of mist—the accumulation of her spittle—
> He appointed for himself and took them in his hand.
> He put her head in position and poured out . [. .] .
> He opened the abyss and it was sated with water.
> From her two eyes he let the Euphrates and Tigris flow;
> He blocked her nostrils, but left . .
> He heaped up the distant [mountains] on her breasts,
> He bored wells to channel the springs.
> He twisted her tail and wove it into the Durmahu,
> [. . .] . . the Apsû beneath his feet.
> [He set up] her crotch—it wedged up the heavens—
> [(Thus) the half of her] he stretched out and made it firm as the earth.[52]

It is this portion of the text, certainly, that facilitated the mapping of cosmogonic chaos (in the manner of Ovid's rude and disordered mass) onto *Enūma eliš*, as in Heidel's identification within the text of "a watery chaos . . . chaos as living matter and as being an integral part of the first two principles, Apsû and Tiʾâmat, in whom all the elements of the future universe were commingled,"[53] and that continues to cast a shadow, albeit lightly, over even more recent

human features"; and the brief note in Francesca Rochberg, *The Heavenly Writing: Divination, Horoscopy, and Astronomy in Mesopotamian Culture* (Cambridge: Cambridge University Press, 2004) 89, discussing *kūbu* as a synonym for *izbu*, "malformed newborn human or animal." For the *kūbu* as demon, see also JoAnn Scurlock and Burton R. Andersen, *Diagnoses in Assyrian and Babylonian Medicine: Ancient Sources, Translations, and Modern Medical Analyses* (Urbana: University of Illinois Press, 2005) esp. pp. 387, 476.

52. *Ee* IV 135–38; V 9–11, 56–62, translated in Lambert, "Mesopotamian Creation Stories," 48–49.

53. Alexander Heidel, *The Babylonian Genesis: The Story of Creation* (2nd ed.; Chicago: University of Chicago Press, 1963) 97.

scholarly analyses. The resemblance, however, is at best a superficial one: there is no evidence that Ti'āmat—despite her monstrous corpse, her capacity to independently generate creatures hybrid in form, and her de- and reconstruction at the hands of Marduk—ever herself *physically* comprises the type of dark primordial array of disparate and conflicting elements that characterizes Ovid's *rudis indigestaque moles.*[54] She may be dismembered, as Ovid's mass was divided, but she possesses a coherent body that serves, after her death, as a conveniently coherent corpse.[55]

Chaoskampf? *Chaos and Cosmos in* Enūma eliš

If cosmogonic or precosmic chaos may be mapped only uneasily onto the extant Mesopotamian accounts of cosmogony and theogony, it is to be sharply distinguished from "kratogenic" chaos, specifically defined here as chaos that stands in opposition to the establishment *and maintenance* of civilization and its apparatuses.[56] Vitally, kratogenic chaos is to be understood not as external or alien to the cosmos: the organized Mesopotamian cosmos has chaotic elements embedded deeply within it and, if these are constantly in conflict with the representatives of order and civilization, they nevertheless preclude a de-

54. Ti'āmat, of course, is certainly capable of roiling or raging in response to provocation (*Ee* I 116; IV 60, 76), but there is nothing of cosmogonic Chaos in the Ovidian sense, or of chaos in its modern sense as "a state of complete disorder and confusion" (Knowles, *The Oxford Dictionary of Phrase and Fable*, s.v. "chaos") in the placid mingling of waters at the opening of the composition. Ti'āmat's creation of the monsters is, however, quite interesting in light of the later accounts of hybrid creations by Berossus and Empedocles, discussed briefly by Stephanie Dalley, "Evolution of Gender in Mesopotamian Mythology and Iconography with a Possible Explanation of *ša rešen*, 'the Man with Two Heads,'" in *Sex and Gender in the Ancient Near East: Proceedings of the 47th Rencontre Assyriologique Internationale, Helsinki, July 2–6, 2001* (ed. Simo Parpola and Robert M. Whiting; Helsinki: Neo-Assyrian Text Corpus Project, 2002) 117–22, esp. p. 119; see also Stanley M. Burstein, *The Babyloniaca of Berossus* (Sources from the Ancient Near East 1/3; Malibu: Undena, 1978) 13–15.

55. Her various parts are conveniently attributed to account for the features of the known cosmos (*Ee* IV and V): her breasts are heaped up to form the mountains, her eyes give forth the twin rivers, and her "tail" is shaped into the Durmahu, the great or cosmic bond; see Wayne Horowitz, *Mesopotamian Cosmic Geography* (Mesopotamian Civilizations 8; Winona Lake, IN: Eisenbrauns, 1998) 120. The several different guises in which she appears over the course of *Enūma eliš* are not random shifts in form but seem linked, rather, to her developing place in the cosmos; see my "Gender Matters in Enūma eliš."

56. Distinguishing between the two types of chaos in reference to Ti'āmat in *Enūma eliš* is especially difficult because Ti'āmat is both a primordial elemental being and mother of the gods, and she is referred to as a "watery chaos" (cosmogonic chaos) on this account; later, she is the mother of monsters and would-be destroyer of her divine children, on which account she may be referred to as "watery chaos," again, or "chaos monster" (kratogenic chaos).

scent into stagnation or moribundity. This section explores the role played by kratogenic chaos in Mesopotamian literary and visual contexts in general and in *Enūma eliš* specifically.

While it is not possible to speak of a single Mesopotamian cosmography or cosmogony, any more than it is possible to speak monolithically of Mesopotamian religion, the inhabitants of the land between the rivers yet seem to have had something of a common world view, a shared perception of the overarching principles that shaped and defined their cosmos. Though not explicitly articulated, these principles, in place of the opposing and monumental forces of good and evil that might be regarded as characterizing our own world view, may best be characterized as those of order and chaos. Order was associated with the gods and their cities, the bastions of divinely organized and guarded civilization; chaos, in this context, was affiliated with all that threatened from the wild and untamed zones beyond the city walls, from the mountains, the steppes, the deserts, and the seas. These latter regions were the birthplaces and proper homes of not only the mundane but also the supernatural threats to the cities—among these the monsters that sought to usurp or overthrow the gods and their order, the malevolent *daimons* that wished to inflict harm or practice their destructive mischief on hapless or innocent mortals, and the terrible human enemies that arose at periodic intervals to sweep violently over the cities of the land between the rivers. If chaos was the antithesis of order—its representatives seeking perpetually to undermine the civilized world and its ties, conventions, and customs—it must nevertheless be understood as fundamental to the overarching Mesopotamian cosmos, inserting a vital dynamic element into the established order and its hierarchy and ensuring continuing growth and development.[57]

The struggle between order and chaos, between the civilized world and the wilderness, was one eternally played out, the theme discernible already in the earliest visual and literary compositions of the region. On cylinder seals, it was strikingly manifested in the form of the contest scene, a popular and recurring composition originating in Uruk period images of natural animals engaged in acts of predation but removed to a mythical plane by the Early Dynastic period—a shift signaled by the new vertical orientation of all the participants and by the frequent intervention on behalf of vulnerable animals or domesticates by the bull-man or hero-with-curls.[58] In the perpetual and

57. Among other things, agents of chaos such as monsters offered young hero-gods the chance to make their names or to advance significantly within the ranks of the divine hierarchy through successful battle (*Chaoskampf*).

58. See the brief but illuminating discussion on contest scenes and the hero and bull-man in Eva A. Braun-Holzinger, "Apotropaic Figures at Mesopotamian Temples," in

ongoing engagement between the forces of order and those of chaos, neither proved capable of gaining a permanent upper hand. On steles and later on orthostat reliefs, kings played their own part in the cosmic struggle, defeating human enemies from the mountains or ritually battling ferocious lions on foot or from chariots.[59] And, in both mythological texts and pictorial representations, hero-gods were depicted in the act of making their names and reputations by slaying the terrifying monsters (creatures of the wilderness, born in or of the mountains, the steppes, or the tumultuous seas) that had arisen to overturn or to usurp the divine order or kingship.[60] On a more mundane level, humans waged their own personal battles against the malevolent and harmful *daimons*, seeking the assistance of the gods to cast these out of the civilized world, where they were not properly at home and which they sought constantly to undermine or destroy:

> They whose clamour is unpleasant were born on the western slopes,
> and those whose features changed were raised on the eastern mountains . . .
> They are the waves in the sea,
> they are the terrors of the marsh.
> In the proper time of cultivation, (the demons) cry out malevolently and suppress the 'life of the land.'
> They are the ones who sweep away the inhabitants in the steppe, and devastate the land,
> who malevolently flatten the city, the settlements, the sprawling villages.[61]

Whether rendered in image or in text, all of these types of combats may arguably, in a specifically Mesopotamian context, be filed under the rubric of *Chaoskampf*, the battle by agents of order against agents of chaos. But, if this is how (kratogenic) chaos ought properly to be defined and understood—as encompassing the hostile and actively threatening forces of disorder and confusion contained within the cosmos; as chaos in its modern sense of disarray, turmoil, and disruption; as that which stands outside rather than prior to the

---

Mesopotamian Magic: Textual, Historical, and Interpretative Perspectives (Ancient Magic and Divination 1; ed. Tzvi Abusch and Karel van der Toorn; Groningen: Styx, 1999) 160–63.

59. Images of the king engaged in the lion hunt date back to the Uruk period Warka stele, although they are, perhaps, best known from the orthostat reliefs that lined the walls of the Neo-Assyrian palaces.

60. In addition to the narratives recording battles between gods and monsters, such as the Sumerian *Ninurta and Azag* or the Akkadian *Anzû*, there are texts recording the interactions between heroes (such as Gilgameš and Lugalbanda) and monsters (such as Ḫuwawa and Anzû); and various images of gods battling hybrid monsters, such as the ninth-century B.C.E. relief from Nimrud depicting Ninurta routing a lion-eagle hybrid (BM 124572).

61. Markham J. Geller, *Evil Demons: Canonical Utukkū Lemnūtu Incantations* (SAACT 5; Helsinki: The Neo-Assyrian Text Corpus Project, 2007) 242: tablet 13–15 (lines 3–4, 10–11, 16–18).

divinely instituted and guarded order[62]—then where is chaos properly located in the text of *Enūma eliš*? And what role does it play in the unfolding of that narrative?

Wilfred Lambert in 1986 compellingly situated *Enūma eliš* within the tradition of the myths (the Mesopotamian *Chaoskampf* texts proper) of the divine monster slayers and their adversaries, though most of these (except perhaps *Lugal-e*, in which Ninurta wars against Azag) do not include a subsequent creation from the enemy corpse.[63] While noting the similarity in basic plot outline between *Enūma eliš* and *Labbu*, in which the god Tišpak defeats a 60-league-long "fantastic *bašmu* that was created in the sea,"[64] Lambert focused on the apparently deliberate adoption and adaptation of details of the god Ninurta's mythology and deeds in *Enūma eliš*, especially as they were presented in the Akkadian *Anzû Epic*: "[I]t can be argued that not only was *Enūma eliš* consciously based on Anzû, but other items of Ninurta mythology were deliberately worked in so as to present Marduk as Ninurta redivivus."[65]

62. The forces of chaos, of course, are not wholly destructive: they are, indeed, vital to divine mobility and the evolution of the pantheon. Similarly, not all that existed beyond the city-walls was definitively harmful or threatening: the inhabitants of Mesopotamia were adept at developing long-distance trading networks and exploiting far distant resources from very early periods (Guillermo Algaze, *The Uruk World System: The Dynamics of Expansion of Early Mesopotamian Civilization* [2nd ed.; Chicago: University of Chicago Press, 2005]; idem, *Ancient Mesopotamia at the Dawn of Civilization: The Evolution of an Urban Landscape* [Chicago: University of Chicago Press, 2008]; Gil Stein, *Rethinking World-Systems: Diasporas, Colonies, and Interaction in Uruk Mesopotamia* [Tucson: University of Arizona Press, 1999]; Klaas R Veenhof, "'Modern' Features in Old Assyrian Trade," *JESHO* 40 [1997] 336–66) and continued these activities throughout the thousands of years of their history.

63. Wolfgang Heimpel ("The Natural History of the Tigris according to the Sumerian Literary Composition Lugal," *JNES* 46 [1987] 316) suggests that

> the story about making the Tigris what it was for the Babylonians was built on speculation about the origin of the yearly flood. The flood was recognized as deriving from snow-melt and spring waters in the mountains facing the Babylonian plains. The mountains provided the slope that allowed the water to run off, in the process carving channels by which the far-off plains were reached. . . . The consequence was scarceness of water in the plains. Enter Ninurta, the protagonist and champion of the valiant farmer of the plains, to provide with the Tigris the desired abundance of water by creating that which made it possible to tap the abundant sources of the Kur, namely, the mountains and valleys.

For a quite different reading of the antagonist of the text, at least, see Karen P. Foster, "Volcanic Landscapes in *Lugal-e*," in *Landscapes: Territories, Frontiers, and Horizons in the Ancient Near East. Papers Presented to the XLIV Rencontre Assyriologique Internationale, Venezia, 7–11 July 1997* (ed. L. Milano et al.; Padua: Sargon, 1999) 23–39.

64. Horowitz, *Mesopotamian Cosmic Geography*, 35; Theodore J. Lewis, "CT 13:33–34 and Ezekiel 32: Lion-Dragon Myths," *JAOS* 116 (1996) 32.

65. W. G. Lambert, "Ninurta Mythology in the Babylonian Epic of Creation," in *Keilschriftliche Literaturen: Ausgewählte Vortäge der XXXII. Rencontre Assyriologique Internationale, Münster, 8.–12.7.1985* (ed. Karl Hecker and Walter Sommerfeld; Berlin:

Among the striking and persuasive points offered in support of this view are: Anšar's initial and failed attempts to dispatch the gods Ea and Anu against Ti'āmat prior to Marduk's challenging of her in *Enūma eliš*, akin to Anu's attempt in the *Anzû Epic* to dispatch the gods Adad, Girra, and Šara against Anzû prior to Ninurta's taking up of the challenge; the deliberate attempt to make the monsters in *Enūma eliš* number 11, corresponding to the 11 monsters defeated by Ninurta; Marduk's use of a net against Ti'āmat, a weapon better suited to a bird monster such as Anzû than to a water entity; and the bearing up of the slain Ti'āmat's blood in the same manner as the feathers of the dead and defeated Anzû.[66] If Marduk is cast as Ninurta redivivus, however, the unspoken implication is that Ti'āmat should be read as Anzû redivivus, a chaos monster on a par with Azag or Labbu. I argue, however, that Ti'āmat is not cast easily among such company.

While Lambert's case for *Enūma eliš* as "highly composite [in] nature . . . combin[ing] numerous mythological threads into a single narrative"[67] is persuasively argued, any attempt at the text's interpretation must still contend with the fact that it *is* a single narrative and not a series of disconnected scenes and motifs. The primary combat scene in *Enūma eliš*, specifically the confrontation between Marduk and Ti'āmat (there is, of course, a preceding encounter between Ea and Apsû), does not exist—and should not be read—independently of the rest of the composition. Inextricable from the scene of Marduk's structuring of the cosmos, the brutal and methodical violence of Ti'āmat's defeat and dismemberment at Marduk's hands is not only a necessary precursor to the subsequent creation account, providing as it does the vital matter, but also the culmination of a quite intricately contrived preceding narrative. This preceding narrative traces Ti'āmat's slow progression from primary matter, an elemental liquid entity mingling her waters with those of

Reimer, 1986) 56. Lambert notes also the unexpected use of *mu-tir gi-mil-li-ku-un* in *Ee* II 123, which deliberately references *mutīr gimilli abīšu*, a stock epithet of Ninurta (pp. 58–59).

66. For Anšar's sending of Anu and Ea against Ti'āmat and the two gods' failure to placate her, see *Ee* III 71–126; for the comparable episode in *Anzû* I 88–158, see Marianna E. Vogelzang, *Bin šar dadmē: Edition and Analysis of the Akkadian Anzu Poem* (Groningen: Styx, 1988) 34–37, 43–45. For the 11 monsters of Ti'āmat, see *Ee* I 133–46; these are comparable to the 11 monsters defeated by Ninurta and hung by him as trophies on his chariot, see *Angim, lines* 52–62 (Jerrold S. Cooper, *The Return of Ninurta to Nippur: An-gim dím-ma* [AnOr 52; Rome: Pontifical Biblical Institute, 1978]). For the bearing up of Ti'āmat's blood, see *Ee* IV 131–32 (Marduk "severed her arteries / And let the North Wind bear up [her blood] to give the news," translated in Lambert, "Mesopotamian Creation Stories," 48), comparable to *Anzû* II 135 ("Let the winds carry his wings as [good] tidings," translated in Vogelzang, *Bin šar dadmē*, 66); see, more recently, Amar Annus, *The Standard Babylonian Epic of Anzu* [SAACT 3; Helsinki: The Neo-Assyrian Text Corpus Project, 2001] 11, 25).

67. Lambert, "Ninurta Mythology in the Babylonian Epic of Creation," 56–57.

Apsû to generate the first gods, to a developing proto-goddess, a wife to Apsû and indulgent mother to her divine children. Her transformation into a raging mother of monsters comes only as the third and final stage in her development, when she yields at last to the plea of a particularly torpid faction of her divine children to destroy her own and Apsû's rightful heirs—the line of the enormously potent, dynamic, and disruptive great gods that has culminated in the remarkably precocious and troublesome Marduk.[68] Setting up a new dynasty in challenge to them, Tiʾāmat replaces the dead Apsû with Qingu as her new spouse and bestows upon him the Tablet of Destinies, which in the right hands functions as both an emblem of power and a receptacle of divine power and rulership.[69] While Qingu is later explicitly derided as unworthy to bear the tablet or to exercise such rulership,[70] Tiʾāmat's right to bestow it is never challenged, suggesting that she is its proper guardian and emphasizing her role as a significant—and legitimate—power in her own right. It is this legitimacy that most acutely divides Tiʾāmat from the ranks of the monstrous would-be usurpers in *Lugal-e* or the *Anzû Epic* and that casts the conflict between Tiʾāmat and Marduk as much in the light of a theomachy as a *Chaoskampf*, a battle between two divine champions, each with some claim to legitimacy but with mutually exclusive visions of the future of the cosmos.

On the one side, Marduk and his forefathers are the legitimate heirs and most powerful descendents of Apsû and Tiʾāmat, the original ancestral pair, and Marduk himself is cunningly located as not only the ultimate but also

68. It is worth noting that the forces of disorder and disarray seem most explicitly showcased in *Enūma eliš* by the god Marduk, the ostensible hero of the composition: "He [Marduk] formed dust and set a hurricane to it, / He made a wave to bring consternation on Tiāmat. / Tiāmat was confounded; day and night she was frantic," *Ee* I 107–9, translated in Lambert, "Mesopotamian Creation Stories," 39. This disruption, however, is either a necessary by-product of creation (which in other texts such as *Atrahasīs* is undertaken by lesser gods) or signifies Marduk's extraordinary potency and creative potential; see *Ee* IV 22–26 for Marduk's destruction and re-creation of a constellation. For the discussion of Tiʾāmat's changing depiction depending on the needs of the text, see my "Gender Matters in Enuma eliš." All of the gods in *Enūma eliš*, with the possible exception of Marduk (see my "Bad King, False King, True King"), are the "children" or descendents of Tiʾāmat, mother of all. Only the great gods, however, which reach their zenith with Marduk, are named and their genealogies defined: the other gods, in particular those who convince Tiʾāmat to turn against her heirs, are neither named nor endowed with individual personalities.

69. For the definition of the Tablet of Destinies, its significance in the context of *Enūma eliš*, and its implications for where legitimate power is located in *Enūma eliš*, see my article "The Tablet of Destinies and the Transmission of Power in *Enūma Eliš*," in *Organization, Representation, and Symbols of Power in the Ancient Near East: Proceedings of the 54th Rencontre Assyriologique Internationale at Würzburg, 20–25 July 2008* (ed. G. Wilhelm; Winona Lake, IN: Eisenbrauns, 2012) 387–95.

70. *Ee* IV 81–82, 121–22.

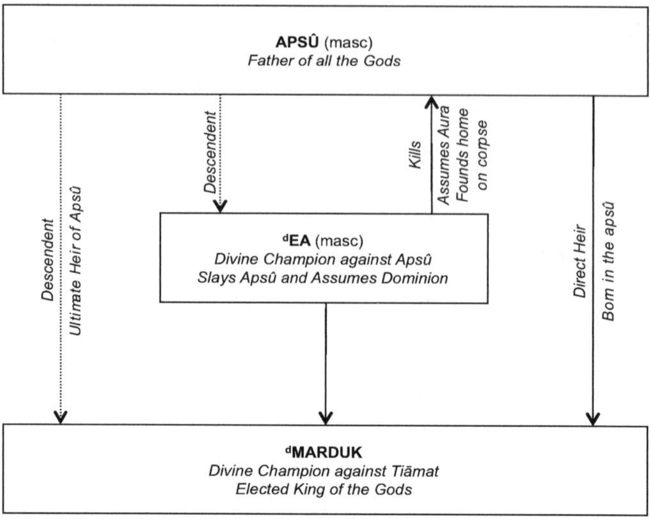

Fig 6. Marduk's lineage in *Enūma eliš*.

the direct heir of Apsû (see fig. 6).[71] Enormously noisy and disruptive, these gods still offer the potential for action and further creation.[72] On the other side, Ti'āmat and her new spouse, Qingu, stand at the head of a mass of other gods, perhaps lesser in stature but characterized here as neither the lower class worker gods nor the rebellious mountain gods that appear in conflict with the established pantheon in other literary and visual contexts.[73] While these have a legitimate grievance against their noisy and disruptive siblings, their vision

71. Though he is the child of Ea and Damkina, Marduk is born within the *apsû*, the corpse of the father of all the gods; see my "Good King, Bad King, False King."

72. This, of course, is ultimately achieved by Marduk through his structuring of the cosmos and, subsequently, his ordering of the creation of Babylon (*Ee* VI 57–66).

73. In the Sumerian *Enki and Ninmaḫ*, for example, it is the minor gods, condemned to unceasing labor, who are on the verge of rebellion against the senior or great gods when Namma intervenes on their behalf with Enki. In the Akkadian *Atraḫasīs*, similarly, it is the minor divine laborers who revolt against the heavy labor imposed on them and come to threaten Enlil himself. On cylinder seals, such as BM 89119, 136776, 116586, 89802, images of mountain gods chastened in defeat are well known from the Akkadian period; see Dominique Collon, *Catalogue of the Western Asiatic Seals in the British Museum*, vol. 2: *Cylinder Seals II: Akkadian, Post-Akkadian, Ur III Periods* (London: British Museum, 1982) 68, s.v. "Battle of the Gods," pls. 19:135, 136; 28:198; 30:210. The lesser stature of the gods championed by Ti'āmat is suggested but not conclusively indicated by the fact that these gods are not attributed distinct names or genealogies.

of the cosmos—a tranquil place where they may rest passive and inert—is one of ultimate stagnation. The state of permanent quiescence that they seek not only entails the violent destruction of the current developing order but also precludes any further creation.[74] The implications of Tiʾāmat's choice in casting her lot with this latter group are made immediately and graphically clear as the mother of the gods is transformed into a mother of monsters, bearing these new and terrible children parthenogenetically to bolster the ranks of the quiet-seeking gods she has agreed to champion. Her monsters are weapons directed against the established pantheon of gods and the order and creative potential they represent, and are intended to be eternally on the attack: "She clothed the fearful monsters with dread, / She loaded them with an aura and made them godlike. / (She said,) 'Let their onlooker feebly perish, / May they constantly leap forward and never retire.'"[75] Kratogenic chaos, such as will thenceforth seek constantly to undermine or overthrow the gods and the order they uphold, here gains form and gathers flesh, endowed with a line of descent distinct (but not wholly independent) from that of the gods (see fig. 5 above).[76] With regard to Tiʾāmat herself, the complexity of her position—standing as she does at the point of origin of developing divine order, even as she ultimately comes to be located external to it, and the true magnitude and nature of the threat she poses to her legitimate line of divine heirs—is not easily encapsulated. She does not begin as a primeval chaos monster, and it is not clear, despite her ultimately monstrous form or progeny, that she ends as one. What is clear is that, in turning against her own heirs, she completes the dissolution of the social and kinship ties that had integrated her within the developing divine order, until she stands at last outside and pitted against it,[77] and that it is through her agency that kratogenic chaos comes to gain a permanent foothold in the developing cosmos of *Enūma eliš*.

74. Michalowski ("Presence at the Creation," 385) noted that "throughout the text [*Enūma eliš*], and in other Mesopotamian literary compositions, noise and silence are symbols of action and inaction." The quiet sought by the gods championed by Tiʾāmat would be incompatible with any significant further creation.

75. *Ee* I 137–40, translated in Lambert, "Mesopotamian Creation Stories," 40.

76. The gods, of course, are born of the mingling of Tiʾāmat and Apsû, while the monsters are born only of Tiʾāmat; see the discussion in my "Gender Matters in *Enūma eliš*." The resilience of monsters is notorious: no matter how many times one slays or binds them, they have a disquieting tendency to reappear. Tiʾāmat may be slain at Marduk's hands, but the danger she poses remains: the threat of her return or resurrection is indicated both by the annual recitation of her defeat (*Enūma eliš*) during the *akītu*-festival and by several lines in the text itself (*Ee* VII 129–34).

77. As a feminine entity, Tiʾāmat is expected to fulfill her responsibilities dutifully as both wife (to Apsû) and mother (to the gods): these are the ties that bind her to the developing civilized world and that she is ultimately unable to maintain; see my "Gender Matters in *Enūma eliš*."

On the Theogonies of Hesiod and the Hurrians

An Exploration of the Dual Natures of Teššub and Kumarbi

Dennis R. M. Campbell
San Francisco State University

Zeus's swallowing of his wife Metis (*Theog.* 886–900) is a pivotal moment in Hesiod's *Theogony*. This act of divine consumption is ostensibly prophylactic for Zeus, eliminating the possibility of any future rivals for his position as foremost of the gods. It has, however, a deeper function in the myth—the unification of male *bie* "violence" and female *metis* "cunning."[1] Kronos and Prometheus before him *almost* manage this union through their status as *ankulometis*, "crooked of counsel," but it is only through the ingestion of his spouse that Zeus achieves this fusion of the masculine and the feminine. This is the ultimate act of control whereby the procreative force of the feminine, which itself brings about a regular influx of rivals, is appropriated by the supreme male deity.[2] The binding of binary forces (male : female, *bie* : *metis*, *eros* : *eris*) is

1. Jenny Strauss Clay, *Hesiod's Cosmos* (Cambridge: Cambridge University Press, 2003) 18. See also Raymond Prier Jr., "Archaic Structuralism and Dynamics in Hesiod's 'Theogony,'" *Apeiron: A Journal for Ancient Philosophy of Science* 8/2 (1974) 8; Friedrich Solmsen, "The Earliest Stages in the History of Hesiod's Text," *Harvard Studies in Classical Philology* 86 (1982) 18; E. E. Pender, "Chaos Corrected: Hesiod in Plato's Creation Myth," in *Plato and Hesiod* (ed. G. R. Boys-Stones and J. H. Haubold; Oxford: Oxford University Press, 2010) 231; Carolina López-Ruiz, *When the Gods Were Born: Greek Cosomogonies and the Near East* (Cambridge: Harvard University Press, 2010) 142–43. On Metis's role in the *Theogony*, see Jean-Pierre Vernant, "Mètis et les mythes de souveraineté," *RHR* 180 (1971) 29–76. The swallowing of Metis has been analyzed in a number of different ways: as a way of eliminating her dangerous "cunning" (Marcel Detienne and Jean-Pierre Vernant, *Cunning Intelligence in Greek Culture and Society* [trans. Janet Lloyd; Chicago: University of Chicago Press, 1991] 107–30) or as a way of integrating her wisdom, knowledge, and justice with Zeus (Christopher A. Faraone and Emily Teeter, "Egyptian Maat and Hesiodic Metis," *Mnemosyne* 4th series 57 [2004] 205–6; Carl Joachim Classen, *Aretai und Virtutes: Untersuchungen zu den Wertvorstellungen der Griechen und Römer* [Beiträge zur Altertumskunde 283; Berlin: de Gruyter, 2010] 19). According to the latter, after her ingestion, Metis still acts as his counselor or *sumboulos* (Carl Curry, "The Theogony of Theophilus," VC 42 [1988] 323).
2. Clay, *Hesiod's Cosmos*, 28.

combined with the negation of the female procreative force (e.g., Hecate's virginity and her concurrent status of *kourotrophos* "rearing children" and Zeus's assimilation of Styx's children)[3] to ensure that Zeus as supreme god does not face any challenges to his position.

The merging of opposing forces within a deity is a theme in Hesiod's *Theogony* and in Greek religion. This joining together of aspects can result from the actions taken by a god, such as the swallowing of Metis mentioned above, or it can be inherent in the very nature of the deity. An example of this latter sense is the integration of the celestial with the chthonic in a god. The issue of the distinction between Olympian (celestial) and chthonian (earthly) has been problematic for Classicists. Many have sought to create a strict divide between the two, but it is most likely that the way in which mortals approached a god (through either Olympian or chthonian ritual) was dependent on the internal nature or temperament of that god.[4] As Scullion notes: "There are powers, in no sense chthonian, that are yet of such similar temper . . . that the chthonian mode of worship seems best suited to them."[5] Even these binary modes of worship are not to be strictly separated but should be seen as fluid. The sacrifices made to Zeus Meilichios, "the protector of those who invoked him with propitiatory offerings,"[6] have both chthonian (a holocaust or burnt offering) and "normal" Olympian (consumption of the burnt offering) aspects, and the same can be seen with the offerings to Zeus Polieus, "Guardian of the city," on Kos (chthonian—holocaust of piglet; Olympian—participatory sacrifice of an

3. I follow here the argument in Clay, *Hesiod's Cosmos*, 132–33. On Hecate, see Deborah Boedeker, "Hecate: A Transfunctional Goddess in the Theogony?" *TAPA* 113 (1983) 79–93, esp. p. 82.

4. See Scott Scullion, "Olympian and Chthonian," *Classical Antiquity* 13 (1994) 75–119 on this issue. The tradition of a more strict differentiation between celestial (Olympian or *ouranic*) and netherworld (or chthonic) still holds today; see, for example, D. Felton, "The Dead," in *A Companion to Greek Religion* (ed. Daniel Ogden; Oxford: Wiley-Blackwell, 2007) 90. For the difficulty of this strict division between celestial and chthonic, especially concerning heroes and hero-worship, see Gunnel Ekroth, "Heroes and Hero-Cults," in ibid., 114; see also Gunnel Ekroth, *The Sacrificial Rituals of Greek Hero-Cults in the Archaic to the Early Hellenistic Periods* (Kernos supplement 12; Liège: Centre international d'étude de la religion grecque antique, 2002); and Robin Hägg and Brita Alroth, eds., *Greek Sacrificial Ritual, Olympian and Chthonian: Proceedings of the Sixth International Seminar on Ancient Greek Cult, Organized by the Department of Classical Archaeology and Ancient History, Göteborg University, 25–27 April 1997* (Skrifter utgivna av Svenska institutet i Athen 8° 18; Sävedalen, Sweden: Svenska institutet i Athen, 2005).

5. Scullion, "Olympian and Chthonian," 118.

6. On this deity, see, for example, Martin P. Nilsson, *Greek Folk Religion* (Philadelphia: University of Pennsylvania Press, 1998) 69–71. Nilsson discusses the character of Zeus in part as a consideration of the deity as a god of the "house."

ox).[7] It is notable that this duality of aspect is seen with hypostases of Zeus and therefore with Zeus himself, the highest of gods.[8]

The connections between the Hurrian (via the Hittites) *Kumarbi Cycle* (including the Song of Kumarbi,[9] i.e., the Hurrian Theogony)[10] and Hesiod's *Theogony* have long been noted by scholars of both the ancient Near East and Classics.[11] The focus of these works has been on two particular incidents in

7. See Georges Dauch, "La grande démarchie: Un nouveau calendrier sacrificial d'Attique (Erchia)," *Bulletin de corréspondance hellénique* 87 (1963) 603–34; Michael Jameson, "Notes on the Sacrificial Calendar from Erchia," *Bulletin de corréspondance hellénique* 89 (1965) 154–72; and the study of Scott Scullion, "Olympian and Chthonian," 79–89.

8. This can also be seen with other deities such as the chthonic Hermes, who attained his chthonic attributes through his role of accompanying the souls of the dead to Hades (Felton, "The Dead," 90).

9. CTH 344.A: KUB 33.120 + KUB 33.119 + KUB 36.31 + KUB 48.97 + KBo 52.10. For earlier translations, see Harry A. Hoffner Jr., *Hittite Myths* (2nd ed.; SBLWAW; Atlanta: Society of Biblical Literature, 1998) 95; and Ahmet Ünal, "Der Mythos vom Königtum der Götter und Kumarbi, CTH 344," in *Weisheitstexte, Mythen und Epen* (ed. Karl Hecker et al.; TUAT 3/4; Gütersloh: Gütersloher Verlag, 1994) 828. For a more recent translation/transliteration, see the online publication of Elisabeth Rieken et al., "CTH 344: 'Das Lied von Ursprung': Das Königtum im Himmel oder die Theogonie," last modified August 12, 2009, http://www.hethport.uniwuerzburg.de/txhet_myth/intro.php?xst=CTH%20344&prgr=&lg=DE&ed=E.%20Rieken%20et%20al, with bibliography.

10. On the issues with the naming of this group of myths, see Carlo Corti ("The So-Called 'Theogony' or 'Kingship in Heaven': The Name of the Song," *Studi Micenei ed Egeo-Anatolici* 49 [2007] 109–21), who proposes a reading of "Song of Genesis/Beginning" based on the restoration of the colophon with the join of KBo 52.10 (= 1194/u) to KUB 33.120+. This new reading of the colophon seems to put the emphasis not on Kumarbi but on Teššub (i.e., the mythic cycle would concern the rise of Teššub and his challenges and triumphs). I argue that, regardless of its title, this mythic cycle is not simply focused on one or the other character but on the interplay of both Teššub and Kumarbi, as the latter, after having himself been dethroned, attempts to regain the throne for his direct line of chthonic offspring.

11. The following are just samples of the work done on this topic: R. D. Barnett, "The Epic of Kumarbi and the Theogony of Hesiod," *JHS* 65 (1945) 100–101; Hans-Gustav Güterbock, *Kumarbi: Mythen vom churritischen Kronos aus den hethitischen Fragmenten zusammengestellt, übersetzt und erklärt* (Istanbuler Schriften 16 [Zurich: Europa, 1946]); idem, "The Hittite Version of the Hurrian Kumarbi Myths: Oriental Forerunners of Hesiod," *AJA* 52 (1948) 123–34; Heinrich Otten, *Mythen vom Gotte Kumarbi: Neue Fragmente* (Deutsche Akademie der Wissenschaften zu Berlin: Institut für Orientforschung Veröffentlichung 3; Berlin: Akademie, 1950); O. R. Gurney, *The Hittites* (2nd rev. of 2nd ed.; London: Penguin, 1990) 157–62; Norman Brown, *Introduction to Hesiod: Theogony* (New York: Liberal Arts, 1953); Uvo Hölscher, "Anaximander und die Anfänge der Philosphie II," *Hermes* 81 (1953) 391–94; Ugo Bianchi, *Dios Aisa: Destino, uomini e divinità nelljepos, nelle teogonie e nel bulto dei Greci* (Rome: Signorelli, 1953); D. Thompson, "The Possible Hittite Sources for Hesiod's Theogony," *Parola del Passato* 22 (1967) 241–51; Gerd Steiner, *Der Sukzessionmythos in Hesiods "Theogony" und ihren orientalischen Paralleln* (Ph.D. diss., University of Hamburg, 1958); Edmund S. Meltzer, "Egyptian Parallels for an Incident in Hesiod's Theogony and an Episode in the Kumarbi Myth," *JNES* 33 (1974) 154–57; Friedrich Solmsen, "The Two Near Eastern Sources of Hesiod," *Hermes* 117 (1989) 413–22; Walter Burkert, "Oriental and Greek Mythology: The Meetings of Parallels," in *Interpretations of Greek Mythology* (ed. Jan

the cycle: the castration of Anu by Kumarbi[12] and the Ullikummi episode.[13] These represent the most visible parallels between the older Hurrian mythic cycle and Hesiod's *Theogony*.[14] The following analogies have been derived—Kumarbi : castration of Anu :: Kronos : castration of Uranus and Teššub : Ullikummi :: Zeus : Typhoeus.[15] These analogies are not exact thematic matches, however, because they are used in different ways by these two sets of myths. It is better to term them imperfect reflections of one another. We are rightly cautioned that we should not be too hasty in jumping to the conclusion that Hesiod's *Theogony* is derived from the *Kumarbi Cycle* based on the presence of these reflections.[16] It is not my intent here to revisit these arguments.[17] In what follows, I explore the possibility of new thematic parallels between the *Kumarbi Cycle* and Hesiod, in particular with regard to the union of binary parts. The fusion of masculine and feminine is found in both myths to

---

Bremmer; London: Routledge, 1988) 10–40; Giovanni Casadio, "A proposito di un recente volume su problem di storia della religione greca," *Quaderni Urbinati di Cultura Classica* n.s. 36 (1990) 163–74; Reinhard Hillmann, "Otto Eissfeldt und die orientalische Religionsgeschichte," *Oriens* 32 (1990) 260–92; Roger D. Woodard, ed., *The Cambridge Companion to Greek Mythology* (Cambridge: Cambridge University Press, 2007).

12. Martin L. West gives a series of correlations/parallels between the Song of Kumarbi and Hesiod's *Theogony* in his *East Face of Helicon: West Asiatic Elements in Greek Poetry and Myth* (Oxford: Oxford University Press, 1997) 279–80.

13. Edited by Hans-Gustav Güterbock, "The Song of Ullikummi: Revised Text of the Hittite Version of a Hurrian Myth," *JCS* 5 (1951) 135–61; 6 (1952) 8–42; E. Rieken et al., eds., "CTH 345.I.1: Das Lied von Ullikummi—Hethitische Version, Erste Tafel," last updated August 31, 2009, http://www.hethport.uniwuerzburg.de/txhet_myth/intro.php?xst=CTH%20345.I.1&prgr=&lg=DE&ed=E.%20Rieken%20et%20al. The Song of Ullikummi (CTH 345) is treated by the Hittites as its own individual text (note the colophon, KUB 33.96+ left edge 1: [. . .] DUB.1.KAM SÌR [d]*ul-li-kum-m*[*i* . . .]), "First tablet, Song of Ullikummi [. . .]," but its placement in the larger cycle is likely, because it concerns Teššub's position as king of the gods and Kumarbi's latest attempt to dethrone him through the creation (engendering) of a giant deaf-and-blind stone monster.

14. It is important to note here that the Hurrians were a distinct linguistic group from either the Indo-European Hittites and Luwians or the Semitic peoples of Syria and Mesopotamia. For a history of the Hurrians, see Gernot Wilhelm, *The Hurrians* (trans. Jennifer Barnes; Warminster: Aris & Phillips, 1989).

15. Woodard calls these parallels "'[c]ognate' figures and events" and goes on to list several of them in *The Cambridge Companion to Greek Mythology*, 95–96.

16. See especially G. S. Kirk, *Myth: Its Meaning and Functions in Ancient and Other Cultures* (London: Cambridge University Press / Berkeley: University of California Press, 1970) 219, where he suggests that Hesiod's *Theogony* "derived from a pre-Hurrian *koine* account." For a recent study on the transmission of Near Eastern theogonic material to Greece, see López-Ruiz, *When the Gods Were Born*. For a different take, see Robert Mondi, "The Ascension of Zeus and the Composition of Hesiod's *Theogony*," *Greek, Roman and Byzantine Studies* 25 (1984) 325–44, esp. p. 343 (citation provided by Mary Bachvarova).

17. Of additional interest is the theogony of "Sanchouniathon" transmitted by Philo of Byblos, which displays certain affinities to both the Hurro-Hittite theogony and Hesiod. This connection has long been noted (see already Güterbock, *Kumarbi*, 110–15).

drastically different effects. Also to be explored is the blending of the celestial and the chthonic in the *Kumarbi Cycle*, already noted above in connection with our discussion of ritual offerings to the hypostases of Zeus.

The Fusion of the Masculine and the Feminine

In the *Theogony*, goddesses (in particular Gaia and then Rhea) perform a vital role in the succession of gods. As female, these goddesses embody flux, while the gods, as males, represent stasis. It is the female's role to give birth, and the creative act of birth results in change, because the new gods eventually attempt to replace the old.[18] It is Gaia who convinces Kronos to castrate and thereby depose his father, her mate, Uranus (*Theog*. 164–66, 179–82). It was she who engendered the titan Typhoeus, the final challenger to Zeus's position of primacy (*Theog*. 820–22). It was Rhea, daughter of Gaia and Uranus, sister to her husband, Kronos, who gave birth to Zeus (*Theog*. 478–79), who would then usurp the throne of his father. Not coincidentally, Zeus is, in part, raised by his grandmother Gaia (*Theog*. 479–80). As Clay puts it: "Gaia will always be on the side of birth and of the younger against the older generation."[19] This cycle of a goddess giving birth to her husband's eventual replacement is only halted when, as mentioned above, Zeus swallows his wife Metis, who also happens to be a daughter of Gaia.

One of the most striking and immediate differences between Hesiod and the succession myth in the Song of Kumarbi is the latter's lack of a birthing goddess.[20] The characters involved in the succession are the gods Alalu, Anu, Kumarbi, and Teššub. There are no goddesses included to fill the roles of mothers and wives analogous to Gaia, Rhea, Metis, and others.[21] What makes this lack of goddesses all the more remarkable is that the feminine plays a pivotal role in the creation of Teššub, the ultimate king of the gods. This position, which is held by Rhea in Hesiod, is fulfilled in the *Kumarbi Cycle* by the eponymous god. Through the castration and subsequent consumption of

18. Clay, *Hesiod's Cosmos*, 17.

19. Ibid.

20. While this is specifically in reference to the lack of mother goddesses such as Gaia and Rhea who have an active role in the succession of divine kings, it can also be extended to the lack of any Muse-like characters in the Hurrian Theogony (on these, see López-Ruiz, *When the Gods were Born*, pp. 51–54).

21. This is not to say that there are no goddesses in the *Kumarbi Cycle*. The goddess Šauška (Ištar) plays a major role in both the Hedammu and Ullikummi episodes. In the Song of Silver, Kumarbi sires Silver with a human woman (see Harry A. Hoffner Jr., "The Song of Silver: A Member of the Kumarbi Cycle of 'Songs,'" in *Documentum Asiae Minoris Antiquae: Festschrift für Heinrich Otten* [ed. Erich Neu and Christel Rüster; Wiesbaden: Harrassowitz, 1988] 143–66).

Anu's penis and sperm, Kumarbi has not only usurped the throne of the gods from him, but he has also assumed the role of the feminine creator.[22]

Before going further it is necessary to step back and briefly explore the nature of succession in the *Kumarbi Cycle*. After an initial invocation to the "primeval gods" (Hitt. *karūil*]*is* DINGIR.MEŠ), the text states that "Alalu was king in heaven. Alalu sits upon the throne."[23] His cupbearer Anu, served him for nine years, after which time Anu rose up and defeated Alalu in battle.[24] Alalu is then demonstrated to be chthonic in nature as "he went down into the dark earth."[25] Anu was then king of the gods with Alalu's son Kumarbi serving as his cupbearer.[26] It is clear from external evidence that Kumarbi, like his father, is to be considered a chthonic deity. In fact, he is likely to have been a grain god,[27] a position similar to that of Kronos.[28]

After ruling for nine years, Anu is attacked by Kumarbi. Anu, a celestial deity, flees into heaven, but is chased by Kumarbi. According to the text: "Kumarbi rushed after him, seized Anu by the feet/legs, and dragged him downward from the sky. He (Kumarbi) bit his (Anu's) loins (i.e., his genitals), and his (Anu's) manhood united with Kumarbi's inside like bronze."[29]

---

22. Harry A. Hoffner Jr. ("Hurrian Civilization from a Hittite Perspective," in *Urkesh and The Hurrians: Studies in Honor of Lloyd Cotsen* [ed. Giorgio Buccellati and Marilyn Kelly-Buccellati; Urkesh/Mozan Studies 3; Malibu, CA: Undena, 1998] 191) is correct in noting that, through the swallowing of Anu's penis and semen, he "has become . . . the womb which will bear Anu's children."

23. ^{d}*a-la-lu-uš* AN-*ši* LUGAL-*uš e-eš-ta* ^{d}*a-la-lu-uš-ša*$^{!}$*-an* $^{9\text{GIŠ}}$ŠÚ.A-*ki e-eš-zi* (KUB 33.120+ i 8–9).

24. KUB 33.120+ i 12–15.

25. *pa-i-ta-aš-kán kat-ta-an-da da-an-ku-wa-i ták-ni-i* (KUB 33.120+ i 15).

26. ^{d}*ku-mar-bi-iš* ^{d}*a-la-lu-wa-aš* NUMUN$^{!}$-*ŠU* "Kumarbi, the seed of Alalu" (KUB 33.120+ i 19).

27. Volkert Haas (*Die hethitische Literatur* [Berlin: de Gruyter, 2006] 131) considers Kumarbi to be "ein Gerstengott." Since at least the sixteenth century B.C., western Syrians had made a connection between Kumarbi and Enlil and between Kumarbi and the grain-deity Dagan (Güterbock, "The Hittite Version of the Hurrian Kumarbi Myths," 132–33; Emmanuel Laroche, "Les dieux des Yazılıkaya," *RHA* 27/84–85 (1969) 70, with additional references in n. 15; Alfonso Archi, "Translation of Gods: Kumarpi, Enlil, Dagan/NISABA, Ḫalki," *Or* n.s. 73 [2004] 322; Haas, *Die hethitische Literatur*, 131). The syncretism between Kumarbi and Enlil was not complete, however, and there are texts, including parts of the *Kumarbi Cycle*, in which both Kumarbi and Enlil appear as separate actors (Archi, "Translation of Gods," 321). On Kumarbi, see the seminal study in Hans Gustav Güterbock, "Kumarbi," *RlA* 6:324–30.

28. H. A. Hoffner Jr., "Hittite Mythological Texts: A Survey," in *Unity and Diversity: Essays in the History, Literature, and Religion of the Ancient Near East* (ed. Hans Goedicke and J. J. M. Roberts; Baltimore: Johns Hopkins University Press, 1975) 139; López-Ruiz, *When the Gods Were Born*, 108. The nature of Kronos is more difficult to ascertain, but he has been seen by many as a god associated with the harvest, a position that would be very similar to Kumarbi (see West, *East Face*, 280).

29. EGIR-*an-da-aš-ši ša-li-ga-aš* ^{d}*ku-mar-bi-iš na-an* GÌR.MEŠ *e-ep-ta* ^{d}*a-nu-un* ^{24}*na-an-kán ne-pí-ša-az kat-ta ḫu-it-ti-et* § ^{25}*pár-ši-nu-uš-šu-uš wa-ak-ki-iš* LÚ-*na-tar-še-et-kán*

Upon castrating Anu, Kumarbi begins to celebrate his great triumph. Not only has he defeated Anu, but he has taken away the essence of the god's masculinity.[30] Kumarbi's triumph soon turns bitter as Anu reveals to him the consequences of his action. Through the biting off and subsequent swallowing of Anu's genitals and semen, Kumarbi has become pregnant with the Storm-god Teššub and other deities.[31] This impregnation of Kumarbi by Anu through Anu's castration ultimately results in the Kumarbi's downfall.[32]

The act of castration began as an act of emasculation but ended with unexpected consequences for the aggressor. Kumarbi, a masculine god, assumes the female sexual role when he consumes the penis and semen of Anu. Although he is assaulted and violated by Kumarbi, Anu still plays the masculine role of the penetrator, while Kumarbi, despite his being a male god and by virtue of his being penetrated, assumes the role of the female. The ultimate result of this atypical sexual union of Anu and Kumarbi, a union of the celestial with the chthonic, is the Storm-god Teššub. Although not preserved in the Song of Kumarbi, it is likely that by the end of this myth, Teššub has usurped the throne from Kumarbi and become the king of the gods. Anu's mutilation becomes his ultimate victory.

Kumarbi: Masculine Mother

Kumarbi's role in the creation of Teššub should not be downplayed. Kumarbi is not to be seen as a mere vessel holding the gods that Anu has placed

A-NA ^{d}*ku-mar-bi* ŠÀ-*ŠU an-da* ZABAR ^{26}*ma-a-an ú-li-iš-ta* (KUB 33.120+ i 23–26). The phrase "his manhood united with Kumarbi's inside like bronze" is quite interesting. Just as bronze is made by the fusion of copper and tin, Teššub was "cast" and was literally the fusion of Anu and Kumarbi. In other words, Teššub is not simply Anu's son (pace López-Ruiz, *When the Gods Were Born*, 141) but the union of both Anu and Kumarbi.

30. *ma-a-an* ^{d}*ku-mar-bi-iš* ŠA ^{d}*a-nu* LÚ-*na-tar kat-ta pa-aš-ta* ^{27}*na-aš-za du-uš-kit*$_9$*-ta na-aš-za ḫa-aḫ-ḫar-aš-ta* "When Kumarbi swallowed the genitals (lit., manliness) of Anu, he rejoiced and laughed out loud" (KUB 33.120+ i 26–27).

31. *I-NA* ŠÀ-⸢KA-*ták*⸣-*kán an-da a-im-*⸢*pa*⸣*-an* ^{1} *te-eḫ-ḫu-un a-aš-ma-at-ta ar-ma-aḫ-ḫu-un* ⸢d!IM⸣-*ni-it na-*⸢*ak*⸣*-ki-*⸢*it*⸣ "I have placed inside you a burden. First, I have impregnated you with the noble Storm God" (KUB 33.120+ i 30–31; translation Hoffner, *Hittite Myths*^{2}, 43).

32. López-Ruiz (*When the Gods Were Born*, 142), in contradiction with her other statements alluding to Kumarbi as only a vessel for the seed of Anu (= Teššub), writes that "the swallowing of Sky's genitals highlights the creative force of the aggressor (Kumarbi, Zeus [in the Derveni Theogony]), who gains from the cosmos the power of generating the universe anew." In the Hurrian Theogony, Kumarbi's initial gloating indicates that he intended his castration of Anu to be the emasculation of his predecessor. The (feminine) creative power that Kumarbi gains from this act is completely unexpected by the god and is an undesired outcome. On the Derveni papyrus, see, for example, André Laks and Glenn W. Most, eds., *Studies on the Derveni Papyrus* (Oxford: Clarendon, 1997).

within him.[33] He is an active, albeit unwilling, partner in the creation of the gods through his castration of Anu. The penetration of Kumarbi parallels and subverts the sexual union of man and woman, but it is this very subversion that causes Kumarbi to transcend gender bounds and assume the creative role of the feminine.[34] That this particular event is to be seen not just as a figurative but as a literal transformation of Kumarbi is indicated by the Hurrian "Prayer to Teššub of Aleppo" (KUB 47.78 i 9′–14′ = ChS 1/8 no. 8):[35]

adall(i)≈ā≈mma tal≈av≈ā≈šš(e)≈a	You (are) the strong one which I *tal-*,
fūtki pedāri ^{d}Ani*≈ve*	the bull calf[36] of Anu!

33. This is distinct from Hesiod's *Theogony*, where the gods can be vessels for other gods. It seems that López-Ruiz (*When the Gods Were Born*, 93) is taking a similar approach when she writes: "Teshub is *not* Kumarbi's son but Anu's, though born *through* Kumarbi" (italics hers).

34. This is in part the view of Alberto Bernabé, "Generaciones de dioses y sucesión interrumpida: El mito hitita de Kumarbi, la 'Teogonía' de Hesíodo y la del 'Papiro de Derveni,'" *AuOr* 7 (1989) 176 (see a slightly more conservative approach taken by West, *East Face*, 283: "[H]e [Teššub] can also be considered the son of Kumarbi inasmuch as he is born from his body"). Based on the available information, we cannot accept Kumarbi as Teššub's father (pace E. van Dongen, "The 'Kingship in Heaven'-Theme of the Hesiodic *Theogony*: Origin, Function, Composition," *Greek, Roman, and Byzantine Studies* 51 (2011) 195.

35. Edited by Hans-Jochen Thiel and Ilse Wegner, "Eine Anrufung an den Gott Teššup von Ḫalab in hurritischer Sprache," *Studi micenei ed egeo-anatolici* 24 (1984) 187–213; see also Daniel Schwemer, *Die Wettergottgestalten Mesopotamiens und Nordsyriens im Zeitalter der Keilschriftkulturen: Materialien und Studien nach den schriftlichen Quellen* (Wiesbaden: Harrassowitz, 2001) 454–55 with analysis in nn. 3752–56; Haas, *Hethitische Literatur*, 251–52.

36. Schwemer (*Wettergottgestalten*, 454) translates literally as "Sohn (und) Stier." A word for calf, *hobidi*, is known, but I believe that we have here a compound that is synonymous to it. We find such compounds in the ritual texts. Note, for example, ChS 1/2 no. 1 i 24, where we find the *ši(e)≈āi aġr(i)≈āi* "(Ḫebat, may you wash your hand) by means of aromatic water (lit., through water [and] through incense)" (Dennis R. M. Campbell, *Mood and Modality in Hurrian* [Ph.D. diss., University of Chicago, 2007] 134 n. 134). Gernot Wilhelm ("Der hurritische Ablativ-Instrumentalis /*ne*/," ZA 73 [1983] 109) translates literally as "um Wasser und Weihrauch," but since this is an act of washing (*až-*; see Volkert Haas and Ilse Wegner, "Beiträge zum hurritischen Lexikon: Die hurritischen Verben *ušš-* 'gehen' und *ašš-* 'abwaschen, abwischen,'" in *Investigationes Anatolicae: Gedenkschrift für Erich Neu* [ed. Jörg Klinger, Elisabeth Rieken, and Christel Rüster; Studien zu den Boğazköy Texten 52; Wiesbaden: Harrassowitz, 2010] 102–9), it must be assumed that the water has been infused with the incense. Note the following Hittite example from KUB 45.3(+) i 10–11 (= ChS 1/2 no. 40): ZAG*-it-ma-az ki-iš-ši-it* $^{\text{11}}$GAL A *da-a-i* ^{GIŠ}ERIN*-ia-aš-ša-an an-da-ma* "but he takes a cup of water with his right hand, and cedar is within (it)," which is resumed by the Hurrian *šīae aḫarrai*$^{!}$ in i 13; Haas and Wegner, "Beiträge," 108. The two nouns are separate, despite representing a physical substance that is actually a combination of the two. See ibid., where Haas and Wegner translate *ši(e)≈āi aġar(i)≈r(e < ne)≈ā[i* in ChS 1/2 no. 1 ii 30–31 as "mit der Wasser-Weihrauch(-Ingredienz)." Note also the use of *ši(e)≈ai aġri≈v(e)≈ai* "through the water *of* the incense" (ChS 1/1 no. 3 rev. 11; Volkert Haas, *Materia Magica et Medica Hethitica: Ein Beitrag zur Heilkunde im Alten Orient* (2 vols.; Berlin: de Gruyter, 2003) 151–52.

adall(i)≈ā≈mma tal≈av≈a≈šš(e)≈a	You (are) the strong one which I *tal-*.
atta≈i≈v≈u(ǯ)≈mma ^d^*Ani≈ǯ fūt(≈)t≈oǯ≈a*	Your father Anu begot you.
. . . *≈mma*[37] *nera≈v≈ū(ǯ)≈mma*	. . . , your mother
^d^*Kumarbi≈ne≈ǯ un≈ō≈v/b*	Kumarbi brought you (into the world?).

Kumarbi is explicitly called Teššub's mother (Hurrian *nera*), while Anu is his father (*atta*). The gender roles of woman and man are fulfilled, respectively, by these two gods in the act of creating Teššub and his siblings.[38]

The switch in gender roles that Kumarbi undergoes was apparently not without conceptual difficulties for the ancient Hurrians and Hittites. In the "Prayer to Teššub of Aleppo" cited above, both parents of Teššub are mentioned together, and Kumarbi is specified as "mother." Anu clearly fills the masculine role of sire in that it is his penis and semen that penetrate Kumarbi. It is only logical then that Kumarbi is placed in the role of mother. There is abundant evidence, however, that when mentioned alone Kumarbi is given the masculine role of father.[39] This is not to be taken literally—Kumarbi is the functional equivalent of a mother—but as a concession to the masculine nature of the god, and is to be taken as metaphorical.

The text KUB 45.21 (ChS 1/5 no. 1) contains Hurrian recitations belonging to the Allaituraḫḫi ritual (CTH 780). In line 24′, we find the following passage:

---

37. The form(s) preceding the second person enclitic *≈mma* is/are difficult to determine: *wu*$_{u}$*-u-ri(-)*[(x)] (*-*)*ur-tu-pa-ta-a-am-ma*. It is possible that the first three signs are to be taken as one form (*fōr*[≈]*i*) from *fōr-* "to see" (either antipassive verb ["he sees (x)"] or absolutive singular noun "eye") as per Schwemer, *Wettergottgestalten*, 455 n. 3755, but its function here is uncertain. Immediately preceding the *≈mma*, we have either *≈ubadā* (as in ibid.), which can be analyzed as either either *≈ubad(i)≈a* in the essive or *≈ubada(<i)* with vowel harmony with *≈mma* or, less likely, a nominal form ending in the directive *≈da* (this would then require the noun to have a root vowel of *-a*, but given the length of the form, the *-a* preceding the *-da* is unlikely to be part of the root).

38. Although Kumarbi expectorates spittle and semen together (the word for semen is actually lost in a break), thereby creating Mount Kanzura (KUB 33.120+ 39–41), he still has other deities within him. Anu reveals to Kumarbi that not only has he been impregnated with the Storm god, but also with the Aranzah River, the god Tasmisu, and "two terrible gods." What is preserved of the birthing concerns Teššub, the main protagonist in the *Kumarbi Cycle*, but we can safely assume that other gods are birthed as well. Gary Beckman ("Hittite and Hurrian Epic," in *A Companion to Ancient Epic* [ed. John Miles Foley; Oxford: Oxford University Press, 2005] 260) is correct in writing that "Kumarbi is in a sense his [Teššub's] mother!" but incorrectly identifies Alalu as the father.

39. Note the introduction to the Song of Ullikummi (composite following Rieken et. al., eds., www.hethiter.net/: CTH 345.I.1 (INTR 2009–08–31): *ḫūmantas* DINGIR.MEŠ *addan* ^d^*Kumarbin isḫamiḫḫi* "I sing Kumarbi, father of all of the gods" (KUB 33.102+ i 3–4; dupl. KUB 33.96+ i 3–4); see also Volkert Haas, *Geschichte der hethitischen Religion* (HO 1/15; Leiden: Brill, 1994), 300; and Archi, "Translation of Gods," 319.

> *[fud]≈uš≈t≈a avaḫḫ(i)≈a* ^{d}*Kuma<r>bi attā≈n(i)≈o≈nn(i)≈ia≈ž en(i)≈n(a)≈až≈a*
>
> Kumarbi, their fatherhead, *gave birth* to the gods *as*? an *avaḫḫi*. (ChS 1/5 no. 1:24′)

The verb is the intransitive *[fud]≈ušt≈a*, either in the preterite *≈ož≈* plus *≈t≈* morpheme[40] or with the derivational morpheme ≈V*št≈* with vowel harmony with the root vowel.[41] The restoration of *[pu-d]u-*, taken here as the root *fud-* "to give birth" is certain based on the high number of occurrences of this root in this section of the text.[42] It is possible that the verb should be analyzed as *pud-* "to transfer, transport; to report (s.t./s.o. to authorities)," which would make this passage an evocation of gods.[43] It is my opinion that *fud-* fits the context of the passage better than *pud-*, although the choice of verb does not affect the present argument.

In this passage, Kumarbi is called *at-ta-a-nu-un-ni-ia-aš*, an absolutive case noun derived from the root *atta* "father," which stands in apposition to Kumarbi. The final element of the form is the third-person plural possessive *≈ia≈ž* "their,"[44] which can only refer here to the gods. The root is adjectivized by the morpheme *≈ni*[45] (*atta* "father"; *atta≈ni* "fatherly?") and then made into

40. On the combination of *≈ož≈* and *≈t≈*, see Christian Girbal, "Der Pluralisator /*t*/ in ḫurritischen Verbformen," *AoF* 16 (1989) 78–83; Mauro Giorgieri, "Schizzo grammaticale della lingua hurrica," *Parola del Passato* 55/310–315 (2000) 226; Gernot Wilhelm, "Hurrian," in *The Cambridge Encyclopedia of the World's Ancient Languages* (ed. Roger D. Woodard; Cambridge: Cambridge University Press, 2004) 111; Ilse Wegner, *Hurritisch: Eine Einführung* (2nd ed.; Wiesbaden: Harrassowitz, 2007) 92.

41. The derivational morpheme ≈V*št≈* (where V typically shows vowel harmony with the preceding vowel) is of uncertain function despite being highly productive. See Wegner, *Hurritisch*, 88–89.

42. *pu-du-na-a-en* (23′); *[pu-d]u-uš-ta* (24′); *[pu-d]u-uš-du* (25′); *pu-du-uš-du-uš* (30′); *pu-du-uš-du* (32′); *pu-du-uš-du-uš* (33′)

43. The root is originally taken by Volkert Haas and Hans-Jochen Thiel (*Die Beschwörungsrituale der Allaituraḫ(ḫ)i und verwandte Texte: Hurritologische Studien II* [AOAT 31; Kevelaer: Butzon & Bercker / Neukirchen-Vluyn: Neukirchener Verlag, 1978] 261) as /*fu*ⁿ*d*/ "(wirk-)kräftig [machen oder sein]," based on the earlier works of A. Gustavs ("Abd-ḫiba ≈ Put-i-Ḫepa," *OLZ* 14 [1911] 341–43) and Ferdinand Bork (*Die Mitannisprache* [MVAG 14.1–2; Berlin: Peiser, 1909] 106), who equate the Hurrian name Pudi-Ḫeba with Semitic *Abd-ḫiba*. This reading is no longer possible (an issue that I cover in an article in progress). There are currently two accepted (near) homophonous roots, *pud-* in *pud≈ang-* "to transfer, report, etc." (see Gernot Wilhelm, "Hurritische Lexikographie und Grammatik: Die hurritisch-hethitische Bilingue aus Boğazköy," *Or* n.s. 61 [1992] 133) and *fud-* "to give birth, sire" (Wegner, *Hurritisch*, 274).

44. Erich Neu, "Die hurritischen Pronomina der hurritisch-hethitischen Bilingue aus Ḫattuša," in *Hittite Studies in Honor of Harry A. Hoffner Jr. on the Occasion of His 65th Birthday* (ed. Gary Beckman, Richard Beal, and Gregory McMahon; Winona Lake, IN: Eisenbrauns, 2003) 303; Wegner, *Hurritisch*, 63

45. Giorgieri, "Schizzo grammaticale," 210–11; Wegner, *Hurritisch*, 55.

an abstract through the morpheme *≈o≈nni* (*atta≈n[i]≈o≈nni* "fatherhead" or "patriarch").[46] Rather than simply calling Kumarbi "their father" (**atta≈ia≈ž*), he is called their "fatherhead." I believe that the use of this derived form is the direct consequence of the difficulties of Kumarbi's dual nature—a masculine god who is at the same time a mother.[47]

Divine Genealogy

The passage of kingship from Alalu to Anu to Kumarbi is a succession that is accomplished through violence. It is through conflict and combat that a new king claims the throne. Furthermore, we find that this conflict occurs between two different lines of gods–one chthonic, Alalu and Kumarbi, and one celestial, Anu.[48] The throne of Alalu is usurped by Anu but eventually regained by his son Kumarbi. This creates the following schema (solid arrows represent passage of throne; dashed arrows represent filiation):

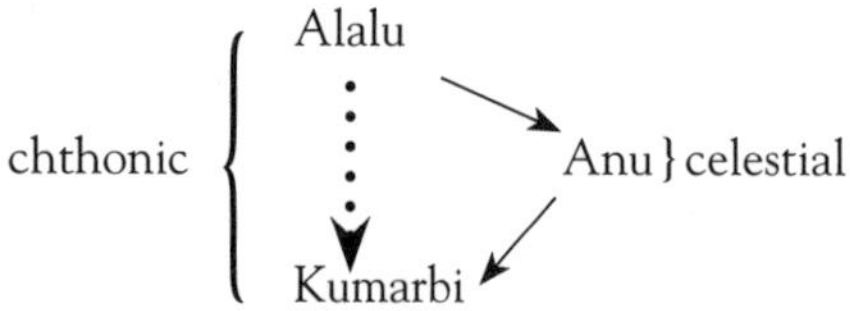

The throne of the gods is in heaven (Hitt. ^{d}*a-la-lu-uš* AN-*ši* LUGAL-*uš e-eš-ta* "Alalu was king in heaven"), regardless of the aspect, chthonic or celestial,

46. Giorgieri, "Schizzo grammatical," 211; Wegner, *Hurritisch*, 55–56. I use the term "fatherhead" for *attanonni* as analogous to "godhead" (the quality of being divine), because this term best fits the Hurrian.

47. This does not preclude identifying Kumarbi as "father" of the gods, as mentioned above.

48. This was put forward by Hoffner, "Hittite Mythological Texts," 139, and generally followed since then (see Trevor Bryce, *Life and Society in the Hittite World* [Oxford: Oxford University Press, 2002] 225). Woodard (*The Cambridge Companion to Greek Mythology*, 96–97) notes that the chthonian—celestial lines in the *Kumarbi Cycle* are paralleled in Hesiod by the conflict between the Olympian (= celestial) gods and the Titans (= chthonian). In a different approach, Haas (*Geschichte der hethitischen Religion*, 85; and idem, *Hethitische Literatur*, 136) treats the myth as related to the calendar: Kumarbi (March–July), Teššub (July–September), Alalu (September–January), Anu (January–March). This conception of the myth is unlikely, as pointed out by Manfred Hutter, "Religion in Hittite Anatolia. Some Comments on 'Volkert Haas: Geschichte der hethitischen Religion,'" *Numen* 44 (1997) 75. Whatever the cultic function of this mythic cycle was, it is unlikely that it was as simple as a myth in which "the sequence is explicitly a dynastic one: the focus is on who is king" (West, *East Face*, 283). The focus is instead on the position of Teššub as the ultimate king of the gods through his multiple natures and the challenges that Kumarbi poses. It is highly unlikely, however, that the primeval gods are gods "as a result of their defeat in a confrontation with the storm-god"; *pace* van Dongen, "The 'Kingship in Heaven,'" 187. The primeval underworld deities achieve their status as gods for other reasons (see below).

of the ruling deity.[49] This has been seen by some as a reflection of an original earthly conflict between two lines for control of kingship, but it is not necessary to look for historical origins for this conflict.[50] As I hope to demonstrate, the conflict exists in the divine realm for a particular reason.

The birth of Teššub as son of Anu can be seen as the restoration of the celestial to the throne of the gods.[51] This would be represented by the following diagram:

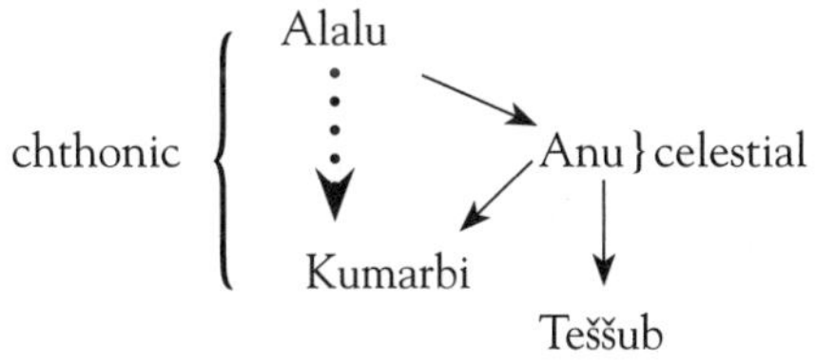

If we accept the "Prayer to Teššub of Aleppo" as representing the actual parentage of the Storm god, however, this picture becomes more complex. Kumarbi was no mere surrogate for Anu's progeny but played the active role of the pregnant female. Teššub is not just the son of Anu but the son of Anu and Kumarbi. He is not only a celestial god, although through his father, Anu, this is his prominent aspect, but has a chthonic aspect as well—his inheritance from his "mother," the god Kumarbi. As such, when Teššub usurps the throne from Kumarbi, he is not simply restoring it to the celestial line but completing the circuit by joining the two lines:

49. Note that, despite Alalu's chthonic attributes, as king of the gods he ruled not from his earthly (or netherworld) realm but, rather, in heaven. An interesting parallel may be found in the Ugaritic text KTU 1.2 (= RS 3.367) iv 22–23, which reads: *yprsḥ ym wyql larṣ*, "May Yam crumple and fall to earth" (following Wilfred Watson, "Ugaritic Poetry," in *Handbook of Ugaritic Studies* [ed. Wilfred Watson and Nicolas Wyatt; HO 1/39; Leiden: Brill, 1999] 181). Yam, the sea god, is the designated heir to El in the *Baʿal Cycle*, who is then defeated by the Storm-god Baʿal. It is possible, if not likely, that Yam's throne was not in the waters (i.e., of the earthly realm) but, rather, up on high, as it was for Alalu and Kumarbi in the Hurrian myths. René Lebrun ("From Hittite Mythology: The Kumarbi Cycle," *CANE*, 1973) takes a different approach and sees "gods dethroned from heaven and then relegated to the netherworld," a trope that is "Mesopotamian in origin." There is no sense that Alalu is forced to go to the underworld, especially considering that, after Anu's dethronement, he himself did not go down to the earth but rather (further?) up into the heavens.

50. See Emmanuel Laroche, "Les dieux des Yazılıkaya," *RHA* 27/84–85 (1969) 134. This is not to say that an earthly parallel could not have existed, but it is my opinion that the succession myth in the Song of Kumarbi may not be teleological in nature but, rather, an element of the mythology concerning the divine rule of Teššub.

51. Bryce, *Life and Culture*, 225.

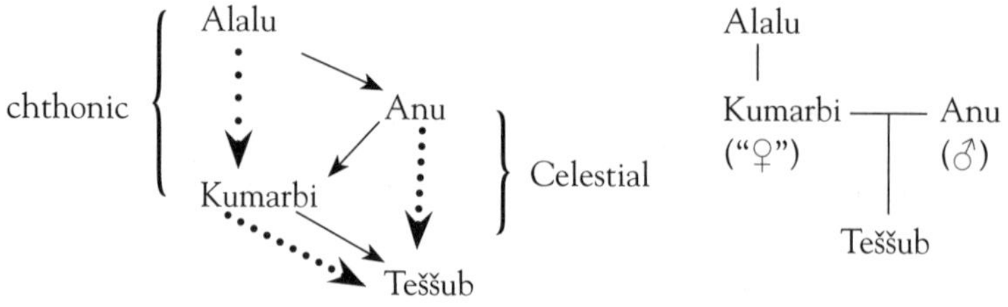

This revised lineage is of key importance to the *Kumarbi Cycle*. The abbreviated reigns of the first three kings indicate that there are two lines between which the throne passes in the pattern: chthonic → celestial → chthonic. Teššub, as the son of Anu, seemingly brings the throne back to the celestial line. As such, Teššub should not only be at risk from the chthonic side (presumably through his cupbearer, who would be a son of Kumarbi, according to the pattern) but eventually should fall to that other line, continuing the pattern. Although this nearly happens several times as LAMMA, Silver, (presumably Ḫedammu), and Ullikummi all initially defeat Teššub, the Storm god always regains the throne at the end of each conflict.[52] Kumarbi's right to sire an offspring who would eventually become the newest king of the gods, however, has been eliminated by the unusual circumstances of Teššub's birth.[53]

Kumarbi does not concede his right as a masculine god to sire a future king, despite the fact that he is the birth mother of Teššub and that in this guise he has already fulfilled his destiny. Kumarbi repeatedly attempts to regain this right by creating offspring to challenge Teššub.[54] The goal is not for Kumarbi

52. Bryce (*Life and Society*, 185) notes that a common theme of *theomachias* is that "the loser can re-emerge to fight the victor another day."

53. This is presaged by Hoffner (*Hittite Myths*², 192), who writes that with each successive cycle of the *Kumarbi Cycle*, "Kumarbi is described as creating still another plot whereby he can thwart the dire prediction by Anu of his eventual demise at the hands of Teššub." This is also the position taken by Alberto Bernabé ("Generaciones de dioses," 176) when he writes, "De ahí que Tesub no tenga que intervenir para detener el proceso; él mismo es la detención del proceso." See also Haas, *Hethitische Literatur*, 136. It is not so clear that "Kumarbi . . . refuses to accept Teshub's victory, and thus attempts to defeat him by creating 'a rebel against the Weather God'" (López-Ruiz, *When the Gods Were Born*, 93–94). Even if we simply accept Teššub as the son of Anu (and not of Kumarbi), then Teššub's rightful place is as king of the gods. His rule would not be eternal, however, but would be brought to an end by Kumarbi's progeny following the pattern established for succession in this myth. This point is similar to López-Ruiz's statement that one of the functions of male impregnation is "to provide a solution to the problem of how to end the succession, so that Zeus [and Teššub] may be the last unchallenged god" (*When the Gods Were Born*, 143).

54. Woodard (*The Cambridge Companion to Greek Mythology*, 154) is not correct in stating that these offspring were "all denizens of the Netherworld." Silver, according to the myth, is not a netherworld deity but the earthborn offspring of Kumarbi and a human woman (see Hoffner, "Song of Silver"). A different approach is taken by Bernabé, who

himself to regain the throne but for his progeny to do so, usurping it from Teššub and returning it to the chthonic line.[55] Despite their initial successes, Kumarbi's monstrous and semihuman offspring cannot hold onto the throne of the gods.[56] Teššub wins it back from his usurpers every time. The explanation for the fact that Teššub manages always to regain his position as king of the gods derives from his parentage. From the very moment of his conception, Teššub is destined to bring the rivalry between the chthonic and the celestial to an end.[57]

On the Celestial and Chthonian: The Dual Nature of Teššub

The Hittites recognized celestial and chthonic deities in their pantheon, although the latter group takes a variety of forms. In its early stages, Hittite religion was heavily influenced by Hattic beliefs. A number of chthonic deities from the Hattic strata played important roles in the Hittite pantheon,

writes that, "[p]or el contrario, todos los intentos de destronar a los 'nuevos dioses' [here Teššub] procede siempre de las fuerzas del pasado, de las fuerzas oscuras, telúricas, aherrojadas por el Nuevo orden, y está por tanto condenado al fracas" ("Generaciones de dioses," 172). I argue here that later offspring of Kumarbi who pose as challengers to Teššub's rule are part of the "new" gods. Teššub, as the offspring of both Anu *and* Kumarbi, is the culmination of the divine cycle of kings. These challengers are not doomed to failure by virtue of their being "from the past" or from "darker forces." They are, in fact, viable challengers to Teššub in that they are Kumarbi's offspring and therefore represent the possible return of the throne to the chthonic line. Their ultimate failure lies in the fact the Teššub is of both celestial and chthonic lines. Franca Pecchioli Daddi and Anna Maria Polvani (*La mitologica ittita* [Testi del Vicino Oriente antico 4-I; Brescia: Paideia, 1990] 126) see the battles between Teššub and Kumarbi's monstrous offspring as the true indication of his right to rule as king of the gods, not any conflict between Teššub and his "mother." The connection between Zeus's challengers and Kronos are not as immediate as the connection between Kumarbi and his offspring, such as Ḫedammu and Ullikummi. But note that the scholion on the *Iliad* in which "Typhon originated from an egg impregnated by Kronos in Cilicia" (López-Ruiz, *When the Gods Were Born*, 111; citing Güterbock, *Kumarbi*, 131).

55. I do not believe that Bernabé is completely correct when he writes, "[P]ero las fuerzas ctónicas del pasado, representadas por Kumarbi y por sus sucesivos hijos engendrados para rivalizar con Tesub . . . , están siempre al acecho, dispuestas a combatir en todo momento contra el poder de los dioses nuevos" (A. Bernabé, "El extraordinario embarazo de Kumarbi," in *Reconstructing a Distant Past: Ancient Near Eastern Essays in Tribute to Jorge R. Silva Castillo* (ed. Diego A. Barreyra Fracaroli and Gregorio del Olmo Lete; AuOr Supplement 25; Barcelona: AUSA, 2009) 29. It is not that the chthonic offspring of Kumarbi are *always* lurking and ready to fight the "new" gods, the offspring of Kumarbi and Anu, but that Kumarbi is trying to restore the cycle of rule back to the (completely) chthonic line.

56. This is distinct from the Hesiodic tradition in which Zeus "appears particularly strong and powerful, and superior to his predecessors beyond doubt" (van Dongen, "The 'Kingship in Heaven,'" 191).

57. I completely agree with Bernabé ("Generaciones de dioses," 176; idem, "El extraordinario embarazo de Kumarbi," 29) in this matter.

most notably deities such as Lelwani[58] and the Sun goddess of the Earth (also known as the Sun goddess of Arinna), who was the wife of the weather god (Tarḫunt) and queen of the gods.[59] By the fourteenth century, Hurrian religion began to exert a strong influence over the Hittites (or at least those of the ruling class). With the influx of this southeastern religious system, we find a new set of underworld deities who were closely associated with Mesopotamian (Akkadian and Sumerian) gods. These *karuiles siunes*, "former gods" (Hurrian: *ammadi≈na en[i]≈na*) are also called *katteres siunes*, "gods of the earth" (Hurrian: *en[i]≈na turi≈na*, "lower gods") in Hittite rituals and political treaties.[60] These new underworld deities are equated with the Akkadian *Anunnaki*.[61]

Along with this influx of "new" underworld deities through Hurrian intermediaries, we find a new type of offering that appears to be directed at them.

58. See Ben H. L. van Gessel, *Onomasticon of the Hittite Pantheon* (HO 1/33; 3 vols.; Leiden: Brill, 1998–2001) 1:280–83 with additional bibliographical references.

59. See Hutter, "Religion in Hittite Anatolia," 79.

60. See, for example: Heinrich Otten, "Eine Beschwörung der Unterirdischen aus Boğazköy," ZA 54 (1961) 115, 145–48, 157; Alfonso Archi, "The Names of the Primeval Gods," *Or* n.s. 59 (1990) 114–29. It is to these new underworld deities that Mesopotamian imports such as Alalu, and even Anu belong. It is interesting to note the passage in KBo 10.45+ (CTH 446) iii 45–47: ^{d}U*-aš-ša-ma-aš-kán* ⸢*ku*⸣*-wa-pí* GAM*-an-ta* GE$_{6}$*-i ták-ni-i* ^{46}*pé-en-ni-eš-ta nu-[u]š-ma-aš-kán ki ši-ip-pa-an-du-wa-ar* ^{47}*da-a-iš*, "When the Stormgod drove you (pl.) down to the dark earth, he set for you this offering" (transliteration: Otten, "Eine Beschwörung," 130–32; translated by Billy Jean Collins, "Purifying a House: A Ritual for the Infernal Deities (1.68)," in COS 1:168–71; Jared Miller, "4. Ein Ritual zur Reinigung eines Hauswesens durch eine Beschwörung an die Unterirdischen (CTH 446)," in *Omina, Orakel, Rituale und Beschwörungen* (ed. T. Abusch et al.; TUAT 4; Gütersloh: Gütersloher Verlag, 2008) 206–17; for additional bibliography, see the online *Konkordanz der hethitischen Keilschrifttafeln*, http://www.hethport.uni-wuerzburg.de/hetkonk/, sub CTH 446). Here, the Storm god is said actually to have forced (driven) the primordial deities underground (see Volkert Haas and Gernot Wilhelm, *Hurritische und luwische Riten aus Kizzuwatna: Hurritologische Studien I* (AOAT 3; Kevelaer: Butzon & Bercker / Neukirchen-Vluyn: Neurkirchener Verlag, 1974) 51–53; Archi, "The Names of the Primeval Gods," 119. These primordial deities do not include the offspring of Kumarbi, and although the ritual appears to draw on aspects of the *Kumarbi Cycle*, it does so only in a general way. Perhaps this is simply a general exposition explaining how the primordial deities in general ended up in the earth, or it may even represent an alternative version in which an event of this sort is detailed (Mary Bachvarova, personal communication).

61. See Otten, "Unterirdischen," 114–15; Erica Reiner and Hans Gustav Güterbock, "The Great Prayer to Ishtar and Its Two Versions from Boğazköy," *JCS* 21 (1967) 265–66. We should perhaps also question the strict division between celestial and chthonic as being considered absolute characteristics for the Hittite gods (Mary Bachvarova, personal communication). In the Hurro-Hittite pantheon, the above-mentioned primordial or former gods are assigned the status of chthonic in as much as they are of an older generation that has been relegated to the back/underground. In the following discussion, I will be exploring, albeit briefly, the earthly or chthonic associations of the Hurrian Storm god in order to demonstrate that he was able to transcend the boundary between celestial and chthonic, whatever implications these states may have held for the Hurrians.

In the ritual texts, we begin to find mention of $^{(d)}$*ābi* ($^{(d)}$*a-a-bi*) pits.[62] Based on evidence from Hittite, Akkadian, and Greek sources, Hoffner, following Vieyra, demonstrates that "[the *ābi*] was primarily a ritual hole in the ground dug to give infernal deities or spirits of the deceased access to the upper world for a brief interval of time."[63] He explores the various characteristics that constitute the *modus operandi* of *ābi* sacrifices, including the time of day for these sacrifices (when mentioned, they are performed at night), the propitious placement of the pit, and other characteristics of the offerings.[64] As such, the use of the *ābi* appears to have been largely restricted to sacrifice to chthonian deities.[65]

Germane to the present topic is the text KUB 10.63 (CTH 715), which describes the winter festival to IŠTAR (probably Hurrian Šauška) of Nineveh.[66] Early in the text (i 17–28), the focus is on an *ābi* sacrifice for ^{d}U *ma-ra-ap-ši*, who is either the Storm-god Teššub with the epithet *marapši* or one of his hypostases.[67] The text reads as follows:

> The diviner opens up an *ābi* before the Storm god *marapši*. The AZU priest offers one sheep to the Storm god *marapši*. The AZU priest slaughters it down into the *ābi*. He lets flow the blood down into a cup. He places it (i.e., the cup) on the ground before (the pit of?) the Storm god *marapši*. The AZU priest (moves on) to the raw intestines and heart. He cuts a little (off) and he takes a little blood. He places them (i.e., the cut meat and blood)

62. On the use of the divine determinative that sometimes appears before the word, see H. A. Hoffner Jr., "Second Millennium Antecedents to the Hebrew ʾÔḇ," *JBL* 86 (1967) 388. The likely Hurrian-derived *ābi* is possibly synonymous with Hittite *ḫatteššar* and *patteššar*. Other terms for pits used in ritual are *wappu-* for clay pits and ARÀḪ, "storage pit" (Billie Jean Collins, "Necromancy, Fertility and the Dark Earth: The Use of Ritual Pits in Hittite Cult," in *Magic and Ritual in the Ancient World* [ed. Paul Mirecki and Marvin Meyer; Religions in the Graeco-Roman World 141; Leiden: Brill, 2002] 225). See also Johannes Friedrich and Annelies Kammenhuber, *Hethitisches Handworterbuch* (2nd ed.; Heidelburg: Carl Winter, 1978) 181–83, sub "*api*"; Jan Puhvel, *Hittite Etymological Dictionary* (Berlin: Mouton, 1984) 99–102.

63. Hoffner, "Second Millennium Antecedents to the Hebrew ʾÔḇ," 401.

64. Ibid. 393–400.

65. See also Bryce, *Life and Society*, 185; Piotr Taracha (*Religions of Second Millennium Anatolia* [Dresdener Beihefte zur Hethitologie 27; Wiesbaden: Harrassowitz, 2009] 155) states that the pits are things "through which contact with the netherworld took place."

66. On Ištar of Nineveh, see Ilse Wegner, *Gestalt und Kult der Ištar-Šawuška in Kleinasien: Hurritologische Studien III* (AOAT 36; Kevelaer: Butzon & Bercker / Neukirchen-Vluyn: Neukirchener Verlag, 1981) 11.

67. Van Gessel, *Onomasticon*, 2:787; Haas, *Geschichte der hethitischen Religion*, 657 n. 158: "'Teššop (des) marapše' vgl. noch KBo 33.163 Vs. 11." The form *marapši* appears to be built on the root *mar-* of uncertain meaning and the derivational morpheme *≈apš-* also of uncertain function. On *≈apš-*, see Wilhelm, "Hurrian," 102; Wegner, *Hurritisch*, 88.

down in the *ābi*. He closes the *ābi* up with thick bread. They carry forth the (slaughtered) sheep, and the temple personnel cut it up.[68]

The sacrifice to the Storm-god *marapši* involves two acts that are characteristic of chthonic ritual sacrifice: the creation of an *ābi* pit and the offering of blood down into the pit. Blood is used in different ways in Hittite ritual, but it typically appears in conjunction with offerings to the underworld deities. The blood offering to the Storm-god *marapši*, including the act of slaughtering the sacrificial animal down into the pit (i.e., in such a way as to make the blood pour directly down into the pit from the animal), indicates that this particular hypostasis of the Storm god has certain chthonic associations. Since the ideogram for the Storm god, [d]U, is followed by a Hurrian epithet(?), and since the ritual is for *IŠTAR* of Nineveh, who is probably Hurrian Šauška, it is likely that we are dealing specifically with either Teššub himself or a hypostasis of the god.

Teššub, by his nature as a Storm god, is a celestial deity. This characteristic is reinforced by his status as son of Anu. Just like Zeus, however, the Hurrian Storm god is not simply of the heavenly realm but contains certain aspects that are chthonian in nature. Just as Zeus Meilichios and Polieus are associated with the earth and therefore receive certain chthonian ritual offerings, Teššub *marapši* is offered blood and meat sacrifices through the medium of the *abi* pit, a ritual hole with clear chthonian connections. I argue here that this dual nature of Teššub is not simply reflected in the ritual texts of the Hittites and Hurrians but is contained within the very story of his genesis. As the son of both heavenly Anu and earthly Kumarbi, Teššub represents the union of these two separate lines of gods.

Conclusion

I have taken here a literal approach to understanding Teššub's connection to Anu and Kumarbi in the Hurrian Theogony. The Storm god's creation in this text is the result of an unusual act when Kumarbi bites off Anu's penis. As Anu makes clear, this initially emasculating act will actually be Kumarbi's downfall. Through the consumption of Anu's penis and sperm, despite having spit some out, Kumarbi has not just become a carrier for Anu's seed but has actually become impregnated. Teššub is not simply the child of Anu but the

68. Hoffner, "Second Millennium Antecedents to the Hebrew ʾÔḇ," 391; Haas, *Geschichte der hethitischen Religion*, 657; Wegner, *Hurritische Opferlisten aus hethitischen Festbeschreibungen*, vol. 1: *Das Glossar* (Corpus der hurritischen Sprachdenkmäler 1: Abteilung: Texte aus Boğazköy 3/1; Rome: LoGisma, 1995) 164–66 (as ChS 1/3 1, no. 38); Collins, "Necromancy," 231

child of both divinities, as Anu's analogy to bronze makes clear. This has the dual result of creating a Storm god who has certain chthonic characteristics and transforming an otherwise male deity, Kumarbi, into a mother.

Zeus gains duality when he swallows his wife Metis. The power of the feminine to create offspring to challenge him has been negated. Furthermore, Zeus undergoes the integration of *bie*, "violence," and *metis*, "cunning," a characteristic that no other male god possesses. Kumarbi's duality is different. Through the swallowing of the male reproductive organ, he gains the female power of reproduction (although this is not a quality that he desires to possess). In Hesiod's *Theogony*, Zeus's swallowing of Metis negates the female, uniting it with the male. In the Hurrian Theogony, Kumarbi's swallowing of Anu's penis creates the female by transforming Kumarbi into the mother of gods.

Why the Hurrian Theogony fills the role of the female creator with the male Kumarbi is unclear. Gaia and Rhea give birth to successive generations of gods who challenge and ultimately replace their forefathers in Hesiod's *Theogony*. In the Phoenician *Theogony* by Philo of Byblos, Berouth is the woman who gives birth to Ouranos, the "Terrestrial Native," who follows Elioun as king of the gods. Ouranos marries his sister Earth, who then gives birth to Kronos, who eventually drives Ouranos from heaven and assumes the role of king. Demarous, the adopted son of Kronos's brother Dagon and his eventual successor is the offspring of Ouranos with a concubine.[69] Kronos's castration of Ouranos is a secondary act that plays no role in the actual succession of gods. That the Hurrian version transforms Kumarbi into the mother goddess through his swallowing of Anu's penis and semen is exceptional among these three preserved myths. What I propose here is that, by eliminating the female and by forcing Kumarbi into this position, the Hurrian Theogony has created a tighter union between the celestial (Anu) and the chthonic (Kumarbi) in the form of the Storm-god Teššub.

69. On this, see López-Ruiz, *When the Gods Were Born*, 95–101.

Creation in the Bible and the Ancient Near East

W. G. LAMBERT†

Birmingham

Serious comparisons should begin, of course, with full understanding of the matters being compared, but in a brief essay such as this, shortcuts must be taken. However, the author has himself done some necessary homework, the results of which lie behind much of the presentation here.[1]

Biblical creation material comes from three main sources: the first is Gen 1:1–2:3: the six days of God's creation followed by a day of rest. Second comes Gen 2:4–3:24: the story of Adam and Eve in the garden. Third, there are poetic allusions to battles between God and monsters and to creation scattered widely in Hebrew poetry. Hermann Gunkel collected and studied this material in his *Schöpfung und Chaos in Urzeit und Endzeit* (1895), the *Endzeit* coming in the New Testament Revelation. As it happened, a young American scholar, G. A. Barton, had made a presentation to the American Oriental Society in the previous year with exactly these points. Gunkel compared the Hebrew allusions to the so-called Babylonian epic of creation and other Babylonian texts and claimed to find parallels. The Babylonian Tiʾāmat was a dragon-monster like Leviathan. The Hebrew *tehōm*, which is certainly etymologically cognate with the Babylonian Tiʾāmat, was drawn into the picture, and so Genesis 1 was fully involved.

This approach is now completely discredited. Ancient Near Eastern parallels to the Hebrew poetic allusions do indeed exist in literary form in the Ugaritic tablets, and artistic depictions also exist, as I demonstrated in "Leviathan in Ancient Art."[2] And I know of no single occurrence of the word or concept *chaos* in any Sumerian or Babylonian creation material. The second biblical source, the Garden of Eden, is not so far paralleled in anything ancient Near

1. Unfortunately, Prof. Lambert died before he could provide the footnotes to this paper. For the references and a much-expanded exposition of his views, see now W. G. Lambert, *Babylonian Creation Myths* (MC 16; Winona Lake, IN: Eisenbrauns, forthcoming).

2. In *Shlomo: Studies in Epigraphy, Iconography, History and Archaeology in Honor of Shlomo Moussaieff* (ed. Robert Deutsch; Tel-Aviv: Archaeological Center, 2003) 147–54.

Eastern (or elsewhere). This then leaves the seven days of creation. The motive behind the account is of course the Hebrew Sabbath, and the various creative acts spread over the six days have not been shown to depend on anything ancient Near Eastern. However, there is something in the opening passus that is an exception.

First, a correct translation is essential. While the traditional rendering, "In the beginning God created the heavens and the earth," has antiquity and popularity behind it, it gives no sense in the context. It reads like a formal summary of the whole process, but it creates some chaos of its own. As written and so translated, the creation of earth is an initial act, but the parallel heaven is then created a second time on Day two. Biblical harmonizers can of course bring gallons of gloss to heal over the breach, but the alternatives must be considered first. Rashi, it seems, first proposed the translation:

> When God began to create the heavens and the earth—the earth was formless(?), there was darkness on the face of the deep, and the spirit of God hovered over the surface of the waters—then God said, "Let there be light," etc., etc.

The two obvious advantages of this rendering are that it avoids the double creation of heaven, and it admirably fits the end of the narrative: "God completed the work he had done on the seventh [2:1, sixth] day" (Gen 2:2).

Grammar can be raised as an objection to this translation. One can of course ignore the pointing as medieval, but *brʾ* is not. However, there is one parallel to a preterite in such a context: Isa 29:1: *qiryat hanâ Dāvid.* Here too a preterite follows a construct noun. Incidentally, *brʾ* is used in pre-Islamic Arabic for human building and suchlike, so the restriction to God's activity is clearly a Hebrew development.

With this scholarly rendering, serious comparison with ancient Near Eastern material can begin. Genesis 1 begins with earth and cosmic water existing. Their origin is neither explained nor sought after. The same situation prevailed in much of the ancient Near East. Sumerians and Babylonians similarly began their cosmologies with basic matter, the origin of which is neither explained nor sought. Here we must cast our net widely and cease supposing that what is commonly called "The Babylonian Epic of Creation" [*Enūma Eliš*] is a standard and norm for that civilization. It is a lengthy composition for its civilization that most likely originated at the end of the second millennium B.C., and its main purpose is to explain how Marduk, the city god of Babylon, came to head the pantheon. Creation is incidental to this and occupies not much of the total. There is plenty of other material, though commonly in allusions rather than detailed accounts. However, it goes back in preserved written form to the middle of the third millennium B.C. Here "creation" began with pre-existing gods performing the necessary acts, or with these gods themselves being part of the process. One of the most senior, or even THE most senior Sumerian god was Enlil, with spouse Ninlil. En and nin mean 'lord' and 'lady'. The meaning of lil is not really clear. There is such a Sumerian word with the meaning 'breath' or 'vapor', but Sumerian scribes generally did not go into the meaning of this name, perhaps to avoid the common noun as unbefitting their chief god. Cosmology at this point consists of tracing back the ancestry of the pair Enlil and Ninlil to their ultimate forbears: a theogony. This is well known in list form in copies from ca. 2500 to 200 B.C. Regularly, the lists begin with Enki and Ninki, but there is no general agreement about the intervening pairs, who can vary from 2 to 23! The intervening pairs seem to have no other purpose than to put time between the original pair Enki and Ninki and the then-worshiped pair, Enlil and Ninlil. This Enki is entirely different from the well-known god of the town of Eridu, Enki(g), whose wife was never called Ninki(g). Ki in Sumerian is the common noun 'earth', so according to this theogony everything began with earth, a not unnatural conclusion for landlocked Mesopotamia. But since creativity was understood from human, animal, and some plant life to be by necessity a bisexual affair, Earth has been turned into a lord and lady pair: Enki and Ninki.

So here a Sumero-Babylonian concept of ultimate beginnings agrees with something in Genesis 1. The cosmic water of Genesis 1 can also be found in Babylonian myth. The so-called Epic of Creation (*Enūma Eliš*) begins with a theogony, leading up to Marduk. It is, like Enlil's ancestry, bisexual for the most part. It begins with Tiʾāmat and Apsû, Tiʾāmat being a feminine Babylonian noun 'sea', and Apsû referring to the body of subterranean water conceived as existing beneath the surface of the earth, from which all springs draw their supplies, and grammatically a masculine noun. So the text begins with male and female cosmic water. Line 5 explains that "they mixed their waters together," referring to Tiʾāmat and Apsû, with the result in line 9: "gods were born of them" (i.e., the mixed waters). As with Enki and Ninki, the basic element has to appear in a bisexual pair. And note that there is no chaos here: everything is peaceful and purposeful, and the narrative goes on to explain the births of gods actually worshiped in the author's time and, in due course, the creation of the human race.

While the pair Enki and Ninki are well documented in list form because the theogony was incorporated into cultic texts, the background of the Babylonian Tiʾāmat is totally obscure. A few scattered occurrences are known, but nothing from which to form a cultural history. There have been attempts to make Tiʾāmat a loan in Babylonia from outside; for example, the Ugaritic Yam

'Sea' has been compared, but Yam is male. I assume that there was a background in Babylonia, but so far it is unknown.

So we have one conclusion to advance: earth and "the deep" in Genesis 1 are paralleled in Mesopotamian sources. Since the general story of Genesis 1–10—from Adam to the flood—is generally accepted to have a Babylonian background, it is no surprise to note another matter with the same background. The time and method of the migration of these matters from Babylonia to Palestine is of course open to discussion; the fact of influence is surely not in doubt.

Searching for Meaning in Genesis 1:2

Purposeful Creation out of Chaos *without* Kampf

JoAnn Scurlock

Elmhurst College (retired)

It has often been argued that there is a close relationship between the first Genesis creation account and the Babylonian creation epic *Enūma eliš*, extending even to the order in which the various elements of the universe were created.[1] Many scholars who make arguments of this sort wish to use them as a means of importing the *Chaoskampf* motif into Genesis[2] and, correspondingly,

Author's note: This is a revised version of a paper read at the 218th meeting of the American Oriental Society (Chicago, 2008). I would like to thank Dennis Pardee, Steven Holloway, Michael Murrin, K. Lawson Younger, and Richard Beal for reading earlier drafts of this essay and making many helpful suggestions. Any errors that remain are, of course, my own.

1. For an argument for an intimate relationship between the Babylonian creation epic *Enūma eliš* and Genesis 1ff., see most fervently Hermann Gunkel, *Creation and Chaos in the Primeval Era and the Eschaton: A Religio-Historical Study of Genesis 1 and Revelation 12* (trans. K. William Whitney Jr.; Grand Rapids, MI: Eerdmans, 2006) 78–111; cf. E. A. Speiser, *Genesis* (AB 1; Garden City, NY: Doubleday, 1964) 8–13; and Kenton L. Sparks, "*Enūma eliš* and Priestly Mimesis: Elite Emulation in Nascent Judaism," *JBL* 126 (2007) 629–32. W. G. Lambert ("A New Look at the Babylonian Background of Genesis," *JTS* n.s. 16/1 [1965] 287–300) accepts a connection between biblical and Mesopotamian accounts of creation but argues that divine combat between Marduk and Tiʾāmat that precedes creation in the *Enūma eliš* should not be included among the common elements; cf. Claus Westermann, *Genesis 1–11* (trans. John J. Scullion; Minneapolis: Fortress, 1984) 28–33. For a willingness to see any culture but Babylonia as influencing the biblical account, see V. P. Hamilton, *The Book of Genesis: Chapters 1–17* (NICOT; Grand Rapids, MI: Eerdmans, 1990) 110–11. For claims of a mythological underpinning that is exclusively "Canaanite" with nothing to do with Babylonia, see John Day, *God's Conflict with the Dragon and the Sea: Echoes of a Canaanite Myth in the Old Testament* (Cambridge: Cambridge University Press, 1985); and for claims by Egyptologists for the direct cultural influence of Egypt on Gen1.2, see the discussion in Oswald Loretz, "Gen. 1.2 als Fragment aus einem amurritisch-kanaanäischen Schöpfungsmythos in neurer ägyptozentrischer Deutung," *UF* 33 (2002) 387–401. For a more neutral approach that neither accepts nor quite refuses a connection between Babylonia and the Bible, see Alexander Heidel, *The Babylonian Genesis* (Chicago: University of Chicago Press, 1942) 82–140.

2. Such as, for example, Stephen A. Geller, "God, Humanity and Nature," in *Gazing on the Deep: Ancient Near Eastern and Other Studies in Honor of Tzvi Abusch* (ed. Jeffrey Stackert, Barbara Nevling Porter, and David P. Wright; Bethesda, MD: CDL, 2010) 432.

scholars who wish to distance the two accounts often do so out of a desire to be rid of Gunkel's hypothesis altogether.[3] As I have argued elsewhere in this volume, however, regarding Gen 1:1–2:3 as a response to the *Enūma eliš* by no means requires placing God in the role of Marduk defeating primordial Chaos. Instead, it provides an opportunity to discern the nature of God as Creator as this was understood by the authors of the Genesis narrative.

To begin, so to speak, at the beginning, even with every trace of divine combat extirpated from the narrative of *Enūma eliš*, Marduk will have created the world by consecutive acts of separation using what might, with justice, be described as primordial Chaos as raw material. At the exact other end of the spectrum, Christian doctrine understands creation as having been by word and *ex nihilo*, period, end of sentence.[4]

This places Western observers in an awkward position viz-à-viz the ancient text of Gen 1:1–2:3. And, not surprisingly, there is considerable resistance to using the word "creation" when Sumerian gods or Marduk or, for that matter, Yahweh separate out and assign functions to things that already exist.

It is usually assumed[5] that creation by word and *ex nihilo* must have been an invention of Greek philosophy, sorting with a "rational" view of God. In fact, it is Jewish writers of the Hellenistic Age (2 Macc 7:28) and not Greek philosophers who are the source of the Christian doctrine of creation by word *ex nihilo* (Rom 4:17; Heb 11:3). The Greco-Roman philosophical axiom was that *ex nihilo nihil fit* ("nothing was made from nothing") and that the *demiourgos* was a Father and Maker—that is, both a procreator and a creator by deed,

3. Such as, for example, Rebecca S. Watson, *Chaos Uncreated: A Reassessment of the Theme of "Chaos" in the Hebrew Bible* (BZAW 341; Berlin: de Gruyter, 2005) 58–59.

4. So, for example, John H. Walton (*Ancient Near Eastern Thought and the Old Testament* [Grand Rapids, MI: Eerdmans, 2006] 181–95) argues that a conceptualization of "creation" as separation reflects an ancient Mesopotamian (and Hebrew) incapacity for or general disinclination toward abstract or rational thought. It follows, as argued in John H. Walton, *Ancient Israelite Literature in Its Cultural Context* ([Grand Rapids, MI: Eerdmans, 1989] 19–44) that Hebrew ברא does not mean to "create," or at least not as we would understand creation. For Walton, when God creates, he does so through the spoken word, as in the Egyptian Memphite theology. Compare also Westermann (*Genesis 1–11*, 108–10), although for him, the innate Oriental failure of abstraction remedied only by the arrival on the scene of rational beings (Greeks) was not whether creation was *ex nihilo* or whether it presumed already-preexisting material but the ability to pose such a question in the first place. It should be noted that, in John H. Walton, *Genesis 1 as Ancient Cosmology* (Winona Lake, IN: Eisenbrauns, 2011), the rational/irrational dichotomy has been abandoned in favor of a much more useful (and interesting) distinction between materiality and functionality—that is, between the disenchanted and essentially meaningless material world of modern science and the spirited and meaningful "functional" world of ancient texts.

5. See above, n. 4.

and surprisingly limited in his powers.[6] It would, then, be more accurate to say that the doctrine of *ex nihilo* creation by word was a reaction to the "rational" view of God.

At the time when Gen 1:1–2:3 was written, creation by word and *ex nihilo* versus creation by deed from primordial Chaos as a philosophy-versus-religion issue was not yet even a glimmer in the eye of controversy. It is thus hardly surprising that no fuss was made about it. Nor was fuss necessary, since ancient Near Eastern conceptualizations of creation were not in binary-opposition mode. Akkadian *banû*, the term used for Marduk's creative activities, is used to describe processes—such as fashioning a building or work of art, constructing a geometric figure, producing abstract concepts, and forming the cosmos[7]—that would also be appropriate to describe as "creation" in English. The word's range is broad with regard to the method employed, including everything from creation by word and *ex nihilo* through human procreation to destruction, separation, and rearrangement.

Ancient Mesopotamians, moreover, understood creation not as a one-off event but as a continuing process that has taken place and still takes place by various methods and at various times by various actors, including not only gods and men but also human mothers. Although Marduk is most famous for his acts of separative creation by deed, he was perfectly capable of creation by word alone: *iq-bi-ma i-na pi-i-šu uʾ-a-bit lu-ma-šu i-tur iq-bi-šum-ma lu-ma-šu it-tab-ni*, "(Marduk) spoke and, he destroyed the star with his mouth. He spoke again to it and, as a result, the star was created."[8]

In Gen 1:1, 1:21 and 1:27, Yahweh's creative acts are described using the Hebrew verb ברא. This verb is used only of God, but there is no particular reason that this functional equivalent of Akkadian *banû* cannot also include more than one type of "creation" and, indeed, if Hebrew ברא meant only one type of creation, it would hardly have been necessary to specify the exact method of creation at every point in the narrative.[9]

6. For references, see David T. Runia, *On the Creation of the Cosmos according to Moses: Introduction, Translation and Commentary* (Philo of Alexandria Commentary Series 1; Leiden: Brill, 2001) 113–14, 119, 137–41, 145–49, 151–53, 175.

7. For references, see *CAD* B 83–90.

8. *Enūma eliš* IV 25–26.

9. For Hebrew ברא, see BDB 135.

According to Ellen van Wolde, Hebrew ברא means exclusively "to separate" and, therefore, the translation "to create" is inappropriate (Ellen van Wolde, "Why Does the Verb ברא Not Mean 'To Create' in Genesis 1.1–2.4a?" *JSOT* 34 [2009] 3–23). She bases her argument on "cognate literature," by which she means Sumerian. However, texts written in Sumerian (which died out in the early second millennium at the very latest) are hardly "cognate" with a passage written in a Semitic language that most scholars now date to the exilic period. In any case, BAD is not the word for "to create" in Sumerian (which is DÍM). Neither is it the

In the biblical account, creation was arguably not *ex nihilo*[10] but used the primordial waters (תהום) as material.[11] Parts of the creative process are also explicitly described as separation.[12]

One could, of course, argue that, as often happens, a term could be used as a catchall but still have a specific base meaning. Thus, in Gen 1:1, Hebrew ברא would be used generically and the other two times be used with its more specific meaning. Interesting, then, is the fact that, in Gen 1:21 and Gen 1:27, the two times that Hebrew ברא is actually used to designate a single creative

---

normal way of rendering "to separate" (which is KUD, Akk. *parāsu*). It literally means "to distance" (Akk. *nesû*). In the majority of instances, BAD is used to describe not deliberate but spontaneous separation, which is rendered in Akkadian (in the *Enūma eliš*) by the use of the N-stem of *banû*. See Joan Goodnick Westenholz, "Heaven and Earth: Asexual Monad and Bisexual Dyad," in *Gazing on the Deep: Ancient Near Eastern and other Studies in Honor of Tzvi Abusch* (ed. Jeffrey Stackert et al.; Bethesda, MD: CDL, 2010) 306–7.

Walton (*Ancient Cosmology*, 127–33) agrees with van Wolde that the basic meaning of Hebrew ברא is "to separate" (based on Hebrew etymologies, not misinterpreted Sumerian literature) but still argues that it should be translated "bring (something) into existence" and not simply and in all contexts as "to separate."

10. That is, except by implication, meaning that the chaotic waters were themselves ultimately created by God.

> Everything that exists under the sun or above was not made from non-existence at the outset. Instead He brought forth from total and absolute nothing a very thin substance devoid of corporeality but having a power of potency, fit to assume form and to proceed from potentiality into reality. This was the primary matter created by G-d. . . . He did not create anything, but He formed and made things with it, and from this (primary matter) He brought everything into existence and clothed the forms and put them into a finished condition. (Ramban [Nachmanides], *Commentary on the Torah: Translated and Annotated with Index by Rabbi Charles B. Chavel*, vol. *Genesis* [New York: Shilo, 1999] 23)

By contrast, 2 Macc 7:28, the Samaritans, and the Karaites take creation as *ex nihilo* (see ShaDal [= Samuel David Luzzatto], *The Book of Genesis: A Commentary by ShaDal* [trans. Daniel A. Klein; Northvale, NJ: Jason Aronson, 1998] 3–4). For a discussion of this problem, see Cuthbert A. Simpson, *Genesis* (Interpreters Bible 1; Nashville: Abingdon-Cokesbury, 1952) 466–68; Westermann, *Genesis 1–11*, 108–10; cf. Heidel, *Babylonian Genesis*, 89–96. Nahum M. Sarna (*Genesis* [JPS Torah Commentary; Philadelphia: Jewish Publication Society, 1989] 5) also acknowledges that this is not creation *ex nihilo* but argues that there is an "intimation" of the concept. Mark S. Smith (*The Priestly Vision of Genesis 1* [Minneapolis: Fortress, 2010] 49–59) discusses the issue and concludes that Genesis 1 explicitly describes the "divine transformation of preexistent water and other elements" (p. 51).

11. For a discussion of this term, see John Skinner, *A Critical and Exegetical Commentary on Genesis* (ICC; New York: Scribner, 1910) 17 with note, 19; Westermann, *Genesis 1–11*, 104–6.

12. See Westermann, ibid., 33–35; cf. Heidel, *Babylonian Genesis*, 114–16. For the centrality of the concept of separation to God's creation in Genesis 1, see Smith, *Priestly Vision*, 79–80, 90–92. Similarly, Ovid's description of creation mentions speech acts ("commands") but foregrounds separation as the key element in creation (Ovid, *Met.* 1.5–9, 21–23).

act, the act is quite specifically creation by deed.[13] As I said, this was a non-issue at the time, and even procreation as a Godly power gets a nod in the phrase: "These are the generations of heaven and earth."[14]

But if the notion that creation was *ex nihilo* is anachronistic, is the notion that God is a divine intellect also an anachronistic introduction of the Hellenistic age? Or, to put it differently, is creation, when it involves physically separating or rearranging things that already exist, whether by Marduk or Yahweh, a purely mechanical process, without thought or reflection, as one might separate the yolk of an egg from its white in order to make pudding?

Philo of Alexandria tells us that Hellenistic Jewish exegetes understood Gen 1:1–5 to mean that God formed a plan for the creation of the cosmos before he created it.[15] Moreover, it was a characteristic of the intellect in general and of the mind of God in particular to open up "a vast network of paths, all of them highways, and passes through land and sea, investigating what is present in both realms,"[16] or, as *4 Ezra* 16:62–63 puts it: "search out hidden things in hidden places." This is all very well, but where does one find evidence for this searching divine intellect in the actual text of Gen 1:1–5?

One of the interpretational cruxes of Genesis 1 is the difficult Gen 1:2, which mentions that the spirit of God or, alternatively, a wind from God is engaged in some activity rendered by the root רחף. The dictionaries translate רחף "to tremble," "to hover," and "to tremble and hover" (*HALOT*) and "to hover" (BDB).[17] The root רחף has altogether three references: Gen 1:2, Deut 32:11, and Jer 23:9. BDB splits these references into two separate roots, one of which would mean "to grow soft or relax" and would appear in Jer 23:9. That there is more than one root involved here is certainly plausible, since Jer 23:9 describes something done by a person's bones. However, bones do not temporarily "grow soft," and the *HALOT* translation of "tremble," which follows the Septuagint's σαλεύω, "to shake, toss (of ships)," makes perfect sense in this context and is supported by Akkadian *ra'ābu*, "to tremble (in fever)," as well as Arabic *raḥafa*, "to quake (of the earth), tremble (of an old man)." This having been said, the remaining two references and their cognates/irregular correspondents—Syriac *reḥep* and Ugaritic *rḫp*—can only with difficulty be fitted into the concept of *tremulo* required by *ra'ābu/raḥafa*. Neither is it im-

13. These are the great sea monsters and mankind, one of whom at least was formed of clay "in the image" of God. See Geller, "God, Humanity and Nature," 432–33.

14. See ibid., 423–24.

15. Philo, *Opif.* §§16–20. For a translation of this text with extensive commentary, see Runia, *On the Creation of the Cosmos according to Moses*, 50–51, 135–43. Note also the Memphite theology, apud S. Geller, "God, Humanity and Nature," 432.

16. Philo, *Opif.* §69.

17. *HALOT* 3:1219–20; BDB 934.

mediately obvious that they are related to each other. Indeed, the Septuagint translates all three references from context and makes no attempt to relate one passage to the others.

Deut 32:11 refers to a male eagle teaching his fledglings to fly. The NAB translates this: "As an eagle incites its nestlings forth by **hovering** over its brood, So he spread his wings to receive them and bore them up on his pinions." The Septuagint translates from context ἐπιποθέω, "to yearn after, " implying that the father is rather sad to have them go. It should probably be related to Syriac *reḥep* instead: "to brood, incubate; to shade, protect," and, indeed, the Peshiṭta uses this Syriac root to render both Deut 32:11 and Gen 1:2. In any case, the verb in the passage can only with difficulty be connected with "trembling" or "hovering" or "like a bird, that moves its wings back and forth,"[18] which is a rather forced way of reconciling Deut 32:11 and Jer 23:9 with the restless movement required by Gen 1:2. Whatever it would be that a father eagle would do to encourage his brood to climb on top of his wings for launching from the nest, hovering far above them would not be it.

On the other hand, the irregularly corresponding Ugaritic *rḫp* refers to Anat in a context very similar to Gen 1:2: *ʿnt di dit rḫpt [b šm]m rmm* ("Anat, who is winged and flies, *rḫp*'s [in] the highest [he]avens").[19] In this passage, she is winged and in motion, so "hovering" might be appropriate. This parallel is quite compelling, particularly from a grammatical point of view. Since it is the spirit of God that is the subject of the verb in Gen 1:2, what appears there is the feminine participle of the Piel: **מרחפת**.

The spirit of God is presumably being imagined, if not actually as a bird, as birdlike (i.e., both moving and sentient). But is this birdlike spirit of God indeed "hovering," that is to say, flying but in such a way as to remain consistently in one spot? Apparently not. The Septuagint translates, yet again from context, with the passive of ἐπιφέρω, which means literally, "to be borne along." This is the way in which Ionian Greek philosophers characterized the natural motion allegedly characteristic of perfect astral bodies as in the "moving gods" (οἱ φερόμενοι θεοί) of Plotinus (2.3.9). This interpretation would make the precreative act a physical process involving innate and/or essentially purposeless movement.[20]

18. M. Grünbaum, "Über Schem hammephorasch als Nachbildung eines aramäischen Ausdrucks und über sprachliche Nachbildungen überhaupt," *ZDMG* 39 (1885) 607, apud *HALOT* 3:1219.

19. KTU 1.108; see Manfred Dietrich and Oswald Loretz, "Baal *rpu* in KTU 1.108, 1.113 und nach 1.17 vi 25–33," *UF* 12 (1980) 174, 176.

20. Following the Septuagint, Luther's Bible has "und der Geist Gottes schwebete auf dem Wasser"; the KJV has: "And the spirit of God moved upon the face of the waters"; and the RSV has "And the spirit of God was moving over the face of the waters."

It is perhaps for this reason that the targums prefer to interpret the ambiguous רוח (*ruaḥ*) = πνεῦμα in this passage as a "wind" or "wind-like (i.e., moving but mindless) spirit" sent by the Lord rather than the Lord's own "spirit,"[21] thus avoiding compromising in any way the wisdom of God.[22] *Targum Onqelos* (Grossfeld trans.) has "Now the earth was [desolate and empty] and darkness <was> on the face of the deep [and a wind] from before the Lord was **blowing** on the surface of the water." *Targum Neofiti* (McNamara trans.) reads: "And the earth was waste and unformed, desolate of man and beast, empty of plant cultivation and of trees, and darkness was spread over the face of the abyss; and a spirit of mercy from before the Lord was **blowing** over the surface of the waters." *Targum Pseudo-Jonathan* (Maher trans.) renders: "The earth was without form and void, desolate of people and empty of all animals; darkness was upon the surface of the deep and a merciful wind from before God was **blowing** over the surface of the water."[23] Taken in this way, the mysterious wind of Gen 1:2 would be literally whipping the primordial waters into shape, a last vestige of the motif of God as storm in divine combat with the sea, allegedly borrowed from ancient Mesopotamia.[24]

Although frequently influenced by the targums, here the Latin Vulgate has an almost direct translation of the Septuagint: *spiritus Dei (super) ferebatur*. As is clear from the *Quaestiones*, however, Jerome did not interpret this as

21. Winds "blow"; hence *Tg. Onq.*'s מנשבא instead of מרחפת.

22. On this point, see *ShaDal*, 5–6.

23. Compare also rabbinic tradition: see Dirk U. Rottzoll, *Rabbinischer Kommentar zum Buch Genesis* (Studia Judaica 14; Berlin: de Gruyter, 1994) 30, 35–37. In this, the rabbis are followed by Speiser, *Genesis*, 3, 5; and by Sarna, *Genesis*, 6–7. In general, Jewish scholars favor this interpretation of the verse. Indeed, Harry M. Orlinsky ("Wanted: A New English Translation of the Bible for the Jewish People," *Essays in Biblical Culture and Bible Translation* [New York: Ktav, 1974] 361) condemns the translation "Spirit" rather than "wind" as "christological interpretation," unsuitable in a work intended for Jewish readers. Actually, Rashi favored the "spirit" interpretation for Gen 1:2: "'The Throne of Glory' was standing in the air, hovering above the waters (suspended there) by the breath of God's mouth and by His command—as a dove hovers above its nest" (*Gen. Rab.* 2; *b. Ḥag.* 15a, apud Pinhas Doron, *Rashi's Torah Commentary: Religious, Philosophical, Ethical, and Educational Insights* [Northvale, NJ: Jason Aronson, 2000] 4). The interpretation "wind" was introduced by Rashbam, who differs with Rashi on this point, perhaps to ward off Christian interpretation of the phrase as referring to the Holy Spirit. For a discussion, see Martin I. Lockshin, *Rabbi Samuel Ben Meir's Commentary on Genesis: An Annotated Translation* (Jewish Studies 5; Lewiston, NY: Edwin Mellen, 1989). Equally committed to the interpretation of this passage as "wind" are (perhaps ironically) all of the greatest Syriac Christian commentators—this on the authority of Mar Ephrem (Edward G. Mathews Jr., "The Armenian Commentary on Genesis Attributed to Ephrem the Syrian," in *The Book of Genesis in Jewish and Oriental Christian Interpretation* [ed. Judith Frishman and Lucus van Rompay; Traditio exegitica Graeca 5; Louvain: Peeters, 1997] 147, 153–57).

24. See Geller, "God, Humanity and Nature," 432.

"moving about aimlessly" but, on the contrary, as an act both unmoving and purposeful. That is, we may imagine the Spirit of the Lord *incubabat sive confouebat in similtudinem volucris ova calore animantis*, "lying over or tending, like a bird animating eggs with heat." By this interpretation, the Spirit of God is "brooding (and fertilizing)"[25] the primordial waters (תהום) over which it is "hovering."

The issue has theological implications for Christians, because Matt 3:16 and Mark 1:10–11 appear to contain explicit references to Gen 1:2. The passages in question describe the baptism of Jesus by John the Baptist: "After Jesus was baptized, he came directly out of the water. Suddenly, the sky opened and he saw the Spirit of God descend like a dove and hover over him. With that, a voice from the heavens said, 'This is my beloved Son. My favor rests on him.'"[26] The association between Gen 1:2 and the Baptism of Jesus is found already in the first-known commentary on the Gospel of Mark.[27] It appears in nineteenth-century classics[28] and continues to be cited in modern commentaries.[29] By this interpretation, baptism would not merely represent a rebirth but an actual re-creation of the individual.

In this case, Gen 1:2 must, obviously, be talking about the Holy Spirit and not a "wind" sent by God to blow over the formless waste. But we are ignoring the fact that the Holy Spirit in this passage is moving rather than stationary. What is worse, are we really to believe that the Spirit of God is not simply birdlike but is an actual giant bird that laid and then hatched the egg that became the universe?[30] Was creation, in fact, a procreative act?

25. BDB 934.

26. Note also Vardan's *Commentary on Genesis* which, putting the cart before the horse, insists on the interpretation of Gen 1:2 as the Spirit of God brooding over the waters and takes it as a reference to "the mystery of the font of baptism" (Mathews, "Armenian Commentary," 154–55).

27. Michael Cahill, *The First Commentary on Mark: An Annotated Translation* (Oxford: Oxford University Press, 1998) 33 ad Mark 1:8.

28. As, for example, Franz Delitzsch, *New Commentary on Genesis* (trans. Sophia Taylor; 2 vols.; Clark's Foreign Theological Library n.s. 36–37; Edinburgh: T. & T. Clark, 1888–89) 1:81.

29. As, for example, Joel Marcus, *Mark 1–8* (AB 27A; Garden City, NY: Doubleday, 2000) 165.

30. Simpson, *Genesis*, 466: "The chaos has the underlying idea of a cosmic egg which was hatched by the brooding Spirit, as by a bird, to produce the universe." Similarly, Skinner, *Commentary on Genesis*, 17–18 with note: "The Spirit of God was brooding not, as has sometimes been supposed, a wind sent from God to dry up the waters." Already, Delitzsch referred to this as the "world egg" (ᾠόν) and related it to the Finnish epic *Kalewala* and the Indian *Mahabharata* (Delitzsch, *Genesis*, 62; cf. pp. 77, 81 [quoting also Milton: "Dove-like sat'st brooding on the vast abyss"]).

Indeed, the incongruity of this image has led not a few Protestant and Catholic scholars to follow the targums and to understand Gen 1:2 as a wind blowing over the formless waste, preferring to sacrifice a possible connection between Gen 1:2 and Mark 1:10–11 to taking the risk of making a mockery of God.[31] Alternatively, with Odil Hannes Steck[32] and Victor P. Hamilton,[33] one can simply show that the proper translation of רוח in this passage is not "wind" but "spirit" and leave it at that.[34]

Less than a handful of references, counting both Hebrew and Ugaritic, seem a rather slim basis for hazarding any interpretation of רחף. However, the range of meaning involved is quite unusual. What we are looking for is a common thread between an activity typically engaged in by father birds vis-à-vis their hatchlings, by astral divinities such as Anat, and by the Creator on the eve of creation. It does not seem likely that there would be more than one way, if that, of reconciling these three apparently disparate activities.

Fortunately, we do have available to us one way of reconciling them. Before creating the visible heavens, Marduk does something that the Akkadian verb *ḫiāṭu* is used to describe.[35] What is this precreative process exactly, and what does it tell us about the ancient Mesopotamians' understanding of the process of creation?

On the one hand, *ḫiāṭu* means "to watch over, to take care of,"[36] and may be used to describe a father's tutelary relationship to his children: "Do not keep him (the boy) from going to school; watch over (*ḫi-iṭ-ma*) his hand(writing) and help him."[37] On the other hand, *ḫiāṭu*, which can appear in the D-stem, means "to explore, penetrate into, survey, examine, investigate, search."

31. Scholars who have embraced this interpretation include G. von Rad, B. Vawter, and R. K. Harrison. For bibliographical references, see Hamilton, *Genesis 1–17*, 111. Westermann (*Genesis 1–11*, 76, 106–8) gives a full argument for this interpretation, citing previous work on the subject (pp. 74–76). The NAB (Catholic) has: "While a mighty wind swept over the waters"; and the NEB (Protestant) has: "And a mighty wind that swept over the surface of the waters"; as, of course, does the NJPS translation: "A wind from God sweeping over the water."

32. Odil Hannes Steck, *Der Schöpfungsbericht der Priesterschrift* (FRLANT 115; Göttingen: Vandenhoeck & Ruprecht, 1975) 233–37.

33. See Hamilton, *Genesis 1–17*, 111–17 (with a full discussion and previous works on both sides of the issue).

34. See also Ellen van Wolde, *Stories of the Beginning: Genesis 1–11 and Other Creation Stories* (trans. John Bowden; London: SCM, 1996) 21–22. Smith (*Priestly Vision*, 53–57) retains the "wind" translation but tries to inject into this "wind" some idea of soul or life-force as well.

35. *Enūma eliš* IV 135–V 22. For a translation and discussion of this passage, see Heidel, *Babylonian Genesis*, 42–45.

36. CAD Ḫ 159a.

37. CT 2.11 30.

The meanings of *ḫiāṭu* "are dominated by the concept of watching carefully (not in order to protect, as *naṣāru*, but) with the purpose of understanding and penetrating."[38] So, the father is not just protecting his children but seeing to their education and development—one might say engaged in the process of separating good from bad behavior and creating/molding mature adults from the children before him. In order to do this, he must observe the child with a view to the final product, formulate a plan of action, and periodically assess the progress being made, as when Michelangelo studied a block of stone before he began to carve it. The father need not himself be his child's teacher/molder, but the child's education/molding must be both planned and supervised. In short, what is contemplated in this situation is not *ex-nihilo* creation but a rearrangement of elements that are already present. Nonetheless, cognition forms the essential basis for action.

Astral bodies that regularly cross the heavens, such as the sun, moon, and stars, are said to explore the furthest reaches of the heavens:

> (Ningal, wife of the moon god) explorer of the heavens (*mu-ḫa-i-ṭa-at šá-ma-mi*). (ND 2480:5)[39]
>
> She (Ištar) explores (*ta-ḫi-ṭa*) the ends of heaven and earth alike, like Šamaš (the sungod). (AKA 206 i 2)

Although motion is certainly implied (*ḫā'iṭu* means "night watchman"), *ḫiāṭu* refers to an essentially cognitive process: "You (Šamaš) explore (*ta-ḫa-ṭa*) all the lands with your light as one would cuneiform signs."[40] Cuneiform signs are pretty to look at, but understanding them requires far more than simply allowing your eyes to wander over them. Similarly, the job of a night watchman is not simply to move about but to poke his nose into every dark corner, to detect any sign of suspicious behavior, and to keep his ears pricked for every untoward sound.

Apart from exploring distant and unfamiliar territory,[41] *ḫiāṭu* is used to describe what we might term "searching the hearts of men" or "wringing every last drop of meaning from difficult texts," even "looking before you leap."

> (I, Nabonidus, am) one who investigates carefully whatever he does, examining its consequences (*ar-kat-su ḫi-i-ṭa*).[42]

38. *CAD* Ḫ 159a, 162a.

39. See H. W. F. Saggs, "A Hymn," in *Studi sul vicino oriente antico dedicata alla memoria di L. Cagni* (ed. Simonetta Grazianni; Naples: Istituto Universitario Orientale, 2000) 907.

40. KAR 361:3.

41. ARM 3.17: 23; AKA 271: 51; 3R 8:71.

42. Hanspeter Schaudig, *Die Inschriften Nabonids von Babylon und Kyros' des Großen* (AOAT 256; Münster: Ugarit-Verlag, 2001) no. 2.8 i 11.

I (Ashurbanipal) examined (*a-ḫi-iṭ*) the contents of all (the works of) the scribal art, the teachings of all the masters.[43]

I (Ištar) look around and listen, seeking out (*ú-ḫa-a-a-ṭa*) the disloyal and putting them into the hands of my king.[44]

You (Gilgameš, judge of the Netherworld) question, investigate (*ta-ḫa-ṭi*), judge, review and bring things to proper conclusion.[45]

(Šamaš, god of justice) who searches (*ḫa-ʾ-iṭ*) the hearts of men. (VAB 4.254 i 12)

I (Esarhaddon) searched out (*a-ḫi-iṭ-ma*) all of the guilty persons . . . every one of them and punished them severely. (Esarhaddon 1 ii 10)[46]

Since *ḫiāṭu* also means "to weigh out (with a balance)," judgment is implied in these last passages.

All-powerful gods such as Marduk are said to survey all of creation:

(I am Marduk) who has surveyed (*ḫi-i-ṭu*) the height of the remotest heaven. . . . I know the depth of the gaping Abyss.[47]

He (Marduk) who surveys (*i-ḫa-ṭu*) what is in front and behind, right and left, above and below. (ABL 1240:12)

Of the usurper, Irra, it is said:

Sweep on like the wind and survey (*ḫi-i-ṭa*) the circles (of heaven and earth). (KAR 168 i 34)

Before creation is possible, the Creator must have some idea of what he is to do and, before that, he must take a very close look at the raw materials with which he plans to work. Or to paraphrase Marduk's Address to the Demons: "(Marduk) who has surveyed (*ḫa-ʾ-iṭ*) the Abyss, made plans."[48] Returning to the *Enūma eliš*, where we began, before Marduk created the visible heavens as a counterpart to the Abyss, he "crossed the sky and surveyed (*i-ḫi-ṭam-ma*) the sacred (i.e., hidden or secret) places."[49]

43. Maximilian Streck, *Assurbanipal* (VAB 7; Leipzig: Hinrichs, 1916) 4 i 33.

44. Stephen H. Langdon, *Tammuz and Ishtar: A Monograph upon Babylonian Religion and Theology* (Oxford: Clarendon, 1914) pl. 2 ii 32.

45. Paul Haupt, *Das babylonische Nimrodepos* (Assyriologische Bibliothek 3; Leipzig: Hinrichs, 1884–91) no. 53:7.

46. Erle Leichty, *The Royal Inscriptions of Esarhaddon, King of Assyria (680–669* BC*)* (RINAP 4; Winona Lake, IN: Eisenbrauns, 2011) 14.

47. W. G. Lambert, "An Address of Marduk to the Demons," *AfO* 17 (1954–56) 312/316 A 8–9.

48. Lambert, "Address," 313/317 C 11.

49. *Enūma eliš* IV 141 (Philippe Talon, *The Standard Babylonian Creation Myth: Enuma Eliš* [SAA Cuneiform Texts 4; Helsinki: Helsinki University Press, 2005] 56). The Akkadian word for "places" (*ašrātu*) can refer specifically to temples, that is, "sacred places."

In sum, there is no question that Marduk created the cosmos out of something—namely, the dismembered corpse of Tiʾāmat. Nonetheless, for Mesopotamians as for us, creation was not mere mechanical separation but a process requiring a cognitive, pre- or para-creative act, just like Michelangelo with his block of stone. Thus, we have in Akkadian *ḫiāṭu* the **exact** same range of meaning as in our troublesome verbs.

It is difficult, then, not to think that we have discovered a functional equivalent[50] of Hebrew רחף and Ugaritic *rḫp*. Applying this bonanza of new references to our old, barely attested verbs allows us to understand that the father eagle of Deut 32:11 was "watching over" his young, and Anat was "exploring" the heavens. In support of our interpretation of the Ugaritic root as referring to purposeful movement, in the ʾAqhatu Legend, Anat takes her revenge on the son of Daniʾilu by attacking him on the wing. In Dennis Pardee's translation: "The hawks **soared (*rḫp*)** above him, the flock of birds surveyed (*bṣr*) the scene. ʿAnatu **soared (*rḫp*)** amongst the hawks."[51] The second verb is, as noted, *bṣr*, meaning something like "to look at, keep an eye on"; it is related to Arabic *baṣara* and has a Hebrew cognate, בצר, which can also mean "to examine."[52]

Frequently also, in Akkadian, when more than one thing is to be investigated, *ḫiāṭu* is used of one thing, and a second verb—which also means something like "to look upon, to keep an eye on, to watch over, to inspect, to observe," namely *barû*[53]—is used of the other. So, for example, "Marduk, my lord, examines (*i-ḫa-ṭu*) the word (and) inspects (*i-ba-ar-ri*) the heart."[54] The difference between the two Akkadian verbs has less to do with the meaning as such than with the idea of activity implied by *ḫiātu*. One "inspects" (*barû*) the exta by standing over them and looking down upon them; one "explores" (*ḫiātu*) distant regions by going about in them or, in the case of astral divinities, by

For Mesopotamians, "sacred places" were, by definition, places of highly restricted access. In the Creation Epic, Marduk's survey takes place at a point at which the heavens are not yet "sacred places," in the sense that they have been sacralized, as they will eventually be by Marduk for the use of the other gods. What they are is "sacred places" in the sense that nobody but Marduk currently has access to them. This is closer to the English notion of a "secret place" than a "sacred" place.

50. This is not, obviously, a cognate, since we are clearly dealing with a separate root. However, it is not uncommon to find two Semitic languages expressing what is clearly the same concept using two different roots. This situation is what I mean by "functional equivalent."

51. Dennis Pardee, "The ʾAqhatu Legend (1.103)," COS 1:349, 350.

52. *HALOT* 1:148.

53. Interestingly, Akkadian *barû* appears to be a formal cognate of Hebrew ברא, although, in meaning, the Hebrew root is closer to Akkakian *banû*.

54. Langdon, VAB 4.68:35. For other references, see *CAD* B 115–18 and Ḫ 159–62.

flying over them. Assuming that the alternation of Ugaritic verbs is not simply poetic, what would be meant is that Anat and the birds first sought out their victim, and then the birds looked on while Anat closed in for the kill.

In other words, Ugaritic *rḫp*, like Hebrew רחף and Akkadian *ḫiātu*, implies purposeful movement, whereas Syriac *reḥep* retains the idea of purposeful activity (and indeed the same type of purposeful activity is contemplated) but is not specific as to whether or not movement is involved. Thus, in the Syriac Bible, Elisha would be "devoting his full attention to" the dead child and the angels "watching over" the dying Virgin.[55] Since, moreover, it is a precreative act that we are potentially describing with this root, the additional implication in both cases would be that Elisha's attentions to the child and the angels' attentions to the Virgin were a necessary prelude to revival/translation, understood as literal recreation.

Similarly, the father eagle of Deut 32:11 (God) is "devoting his attention to" his brood (Israel) with a view to separating them from other nations (32:8) and, in so doing, creating/molding them as a people (32:12).[56] That is, God played the father eagle's role of tutor, separating good from bad behavior and creating/molding mature eagles from the eaglets before him in accordance with a predetermined plan.

In sum, the use of רחף for the Creator in Gen 1:2 would imply movement, making "hovering" or "brooding" (both of which are stationary activities) inappropriate translations of the Hebrew text. Furthermore, the passage deals not with a restlessly moving and mindless "wind" but with the birdlike soul-spirit of an all-knowing and all-wise God.[57] In the context of Gen 1:2, רחף would specifically represent that necessary intimate knowledge of raw materials, which for both Mesopotamians and Hebrews must precede the formative process of creation.

55. See Skinner, *Commentary on Genesis*, 18 note.

56. This appears to confirm Jeffrey Tigay's insight:

> The Torah sees 'setting apart', or differentiation, as the characteristic activity by which God created and organized the world. According to the first chapter of Genesis, God separated light from darkness, the upper waters from the lower waters, the oceans from the dry land, and the day from the night. By these acts of separation He created an orderly world out of chaos. Later, He separated humanity into different nations, separated Israel from other peoples, and separated the Levites from the rest of Israel. All of this indicates that God created order in the world by establishing distinctions, and that Israel emulates His acts as creator by respecting the distinctions He established between the pure and impure. (Jeffrey H. Tigay, *Deuteronomy* [JPS Torah Commentary; Philadelphia: Jewish Publication Society, 1996] 137)

57. For more arguments in support of an interpretation as "Spirit," see Walton, *Genesis 1 as Ancient Cosmology*, 146–52.

If, then, we have understood correctly, the verse should be translated: "With darkness over the face of the Abyss and the spirit of God **surveying**[58] the face of the waters," thus preserving the possibility of connection with Mark 1:10–11 and making God a thoughtful creator, as already understood by Philo of Alexandria. With this translation, moreover, the last possible vestigial remnant of *Chaoskampf* before creation is extirpated from the narrative while strengthening, and not diminishing, the correspondence between Gen 1:1–2:3 and the *Enūma eliš*.

58. The Hebrew has "**over** the face of the waters"; we might think of the English expression "to run something over in one's mind."

Part 2

Monster-Bashing Myths

The Fifth Day of Creation in Ancient Syrian and Neo-Hittite Art

Douglas Frayne

University of Toronto

1. *The Fifth Day of Creation: The Day Sea and Bird Monsters Were Fashioned*

In the Priestly account of the creation story found in Gen 1:1–2:3, God brings forth from the seas a myriad of creatures, both fish and sea creatures, some of whom, as we learn from other sources, were monsters. Gen 1:20–21 reads as follows:

> [20] And God said, "Let the waters bring forth swarms of living creatures, and let birds fly above the earth across the firmament of the heavens."
>
> [21] So God created the great sea monsters and every living creature that moves, with which the waters swarm, according to their kinds, and every winged bird according to its kind. And God saw that it was good.

1.1. Views on Genesis 1:20–21 in Rabbinic Sources

The passage from Genesis cited above is laconic in the extreme. One might well ask the question: to what did the great sea creatures of v. 21 refer? An answer, although from much later sources, is found in rabbinic and pseudepigraphic texts. Rabbi Johanan, for example, taught that the words "and God created the great sea-monsters" in Gen 1:21 referred to the Leviathan that is also referred to in Isa 27:1.[1]

Rashi's commentary on Gen 1:21 repeats the tradition: "God created the great sea monsters" and, in its explanation of *tananim*:[2]

> *hatananim*THE HUGE CREATURES—the large fishes that are in the sea; and according to the statement of the Agada (B. Bath. 74b) it means here the Leviathan and its consort which He created male and female. He, however, killed the female and preserved in salt for the benefit of the righteous in the time to come, for had they been permitted to be fruitful and multiply the world could not have endured because of them.

In the Syriac *Apocalypse of Baruch*, the following is noted about Behemoth (*2 Bar*. 29:4):[3]

> And Behemoth shall be revealed from his place and Leviathan shall ascend from the sea, those two great monsters which I created on the fifth day of creation, and shall have kept until that time; and then they shall be for food for all that are left.

1.2. Scriptural Evidence for Yahweh's Battle with Leviathan at the Time of Creation

According to J. Day,[4] some biblical passages refer to Leviathan's defeat in a clear world-creation context. Ps 74:12–17, for example, indicates that Leviathan was created when the world came into being. The biblical passage reads as follows:

> [12] Yet God my King is **from of old**,
> working salvation in the earth.
> [13] You divided the sea by your might;
> you broke the heads of the dragons in the waters.
> [14] You crushed the heads of Leviathan;
> you gave him as food for the creatures of the wilderness.
> [15] You cut openings for springs and torrents;
> you dried up ever-flowing streams.
> [16] Yours is the day, yours also the night;
> you established the luminaries and the sun.

1. *B. B. Bat*. 74b; cited in M. Rosenbaum and A. M. Silbermann in collaboration with A. Blashki and L. Joseph, *Pentateuch with Targum Onkelos, Haphtaroth and Rashi's Commentary* (New York: Hebrew Publishing, 1935) 5–6.

2. Rashi, *Commentary on Genesis*, at v. 21 (translation mine).

3. A. F. J. Klijn, "2 (Syriac Apocalypse of) Baruch," in *The Old Testament Pseudepigrapha* (ed. James H. Charlesworth; Garden City, NY: Doubleday, 1983) 630.

4. John Day, "Leviathan," *ABD* 4:294.

[17] **You have fixed all the bounds of the earth;**
you made summer and winter. (NRSV)

A similar account of the subduing of a sea monsters is found in Ps 89:9–12, where the monster bears the name Rahab. Rahab is probably another name that refers to Leviathan.

[9] You rule the raging of the sea;
when its waves rise, you still them.
[10] You crushed Rahab like a carcass;
you scattered your enemies with your mighty arm.
[11] The heavens are yours, the earth also is yours;
the world and all that is in it—you have founded them.
[12] The north and the south—you created them.

2. *Extrabiblical References to the Cosmic Battle against a Sea Monster*

2.1. *Early Dynastic Ebla Sources*

In his recent exhaustive study of the weather god in ancient Mesopotamian and North Syrian cuneiform literature, D. Schwemer, following the work of P. Fronzaroli,[5] pointed out three incantations from ED IIIb period Ebla (ARET 5 4; 5 16 V 5–VI 4; and 5 2+ obv. II 8–III 2)[6] that refer to an attack by Hadda (Adad) on an obscure enemy-being, who the texts indicate was bound with seven weapons.[7] A fourth incantation (ARET 5 1 obv. II 11–III),[8] while it does not mention Hadda by name, is similar to the other three texts, and its evidence should be taken into account in any discussion of the material. The nature of the weapons wielded by Hadda is disputed by scholars, with translations "hoe" and "lance" being two renditions given.[9] Fronzaroli used these references to seven weapons to conjecture that Hadda was attacking a monster with seven heads,[10] an idea that Schwemer believes to be stretching

5. Pelio Fronzaroli, "Les combat de Hadda dans les texts d'Ebla," *MARI* 8 (1997) 283–90.

6. See Dietz-Otto Edzard, *Hymnen, Beschwörungen und Verwandtes aus dem Archiv L. 2769* (ARET 5; Rome: Missione Archeologica Italiana in Siria, 1984) for first editions of these texts. They have also been treated in Manfred Krebernik, *Die Beschwörungen aus Fara und Ebla: Untersuchungen zur ältesten keilschriftlichen Beschwörungsliteratur* (Hildesheim: Olms, 1984).

7. Daniel Schwemer, *Die Wettergottgestalten Mesopotamiens und Nordsyriens im Zeitalter der Keilschriftkulturen: Materialien und Studien nach den schriftlichen Quellen* (Wiesbaden: Harrassowitz, 2001) 116–19.

8. Ibid., 117.

9. Ibid., 188 n. 817.

10. Fronzaroli, "Les combat de Hadda," 286.

the evidence.[11] In two incantations, an apparent second deity (or epithet of a deity) is mentioned that is written *du-na-an* or [d][*d*]*u-na-nu*. Rather than seeing this as an epithet of Hadda, meaning "strong," from the root DNN, as Schwemer suggests,[12] I prefer to take the name to be a writing of the later Ugaritic god Tunnanu, who appears as a snake-like dragon-monster from the sea in texts from Ugarit. He appears in the Ugaritic corpus eight times as a helper of the sea, being one of the monsters defeated by the goddess Anat or the god Baʿal. In the Hebrew Bible an equivalent monster, Tannin, who usually appears as a serpentine cosmic monster is defeated by Yahweh, as we read in Isa 51:9:

עורי עורי לבשי־עז זרוע יהוה עורי כימי קדם דרות עולמים
הלוא את־היא המחצבת רהב מחוללת תנין

> Awake, awake, put on strength, O arm of the Lord; awake, as in the days of old, the generations of long ago! Was it not you who cut Rahab in pieces, who pierced the dragon?

Heider gives details about the nature of the *Tannîn*:

> Related to the issue of etymology [of *Tannîn*] is the question of the history of the form, *tannîn*. A Ugaritic polyglot text writes the word as *tu-un-na-nu* = /*tunnanu*/ or /*tunnānu*/ (Ugaritica V [1968] 137:1:8, pp. 240–41). J. Huehnergard suggests that "the word is probably a D verbal adjective in origin, although the etymology remains obscure." . . . The change in vocalization from Ugaritic *tunnanu* to Hebrew *tannîn* may be according to the development *quttal* > *qattil* known from Arabic, or it may have happened by analogy (or even confusion) with *tan* ("jackal"), as evidenced by the occurrence of *tannîn* in Lam 4:3 for *tannîm* ("jackals") and the reverse in Ezek 29:3 and 32:2 for "dragon" (or "crocodile") (so Loewenstamm 1975: 22).[13]

Schwemer notes the antiquity of the mythological motif of the *Chaoskampf* as illustrated by the Ebla incantations:

> P. Fronzaroli deutet diese Beschwörungspassagen als früheste Bezeugungen für den mythischen Kampf des Wettergottes gegen das im Meer behauste Schlangenwesen, der uns seit der altakkadischen Zeit in unterschiedlichen Ausformungen begegnet, Chaosbekampfer-Mythologem . . . Wir dürfen für dieses weit verbreitete mythische Motiv ein hohes Alter voraussetzen; überlieferungsgeschichtlich läß sich nachweisen, daß es im nordwestlichen Syrien eine alte, eigenständige Tradition gab, die dieses Mythologem verar-

11. Schwemer, *Wettergottgestalten*, 188 n. 817.
12. Ibid., 118.
13. George Heider, "Tannin," *DDD* 1579–84.

> beitete. . . . Es ist also von vornherein wahrscheinlich, daß der Mythos in Ebla und im zeitgenossischen Halab bekannt war.[14]

While the incantations noted above come from the city of Ebla, Fronzaroli points out that the most important sanctuary of the god Adad in the time of the Ebla archive was at Aleppo.[15] It may be that the incantations dealing with Adda from Ebla are to be set in the geographical setting of the Aleppo countryside. Schwemer[16] and Haas[17] have noted that some of the incantations mention a certain god Amarig, whom Haas pointed out appears in an economic text from Ebla.[18] He perceptively noted that this same divine name appears in much later Hurrian/Hittite sources from Bogazköy.[19] Another divine name in these Ebla incantations is the god Ardawan, apparently connected with a mountain that was the nesting ground of eagles. Haas notes in this connection that the mountain-god Kuwari appears in connection with eagles and, furthermore, that one Hittite text names this god Kuwari in connection with Mount Ammarikki.[20]

Haas also indicates that a Hittite historical fragment, tentatively identified by Tischler and Del Monte as being an account of a border dispute of King Šarri-kušuḫ of Carchemish, mentions a triad of apparently conjoining place-names that are relevant to this discussion. They are the town of Gadamana, the land of Mukiš, and Mount Ammari[k].[21] Haas proposed a location of Ammarig in the valley of the ʿAfrin River at modern Mount Simʿan.[22] If one examines the modern topographical map of this particular district, one sees that three modern toponyms can plausibly be linked to the ancient place-names. Two of these have a *ba-* prefix, which is probably a reduced form of a Semitic (Aramaic) word for "house." The first is modern Baqdîna < *Ba+qdîna, to be connected with the place-name Gadamana in the Hittite text. It lies a mere 14 km southeast of modern Jebel Simʿan, Haas's posited location for Mount Amarig,[23] and a mere 18 km northwest of Aleppo. Ammarig, in turn, can plausibly be located at the modern town of ʿAnjara (through metathesis) that lies a mere 3 km southeast of Baqdîna.

14. Schwemer, *Wettergottgestalten*, 118–19.
15. Fronzaroli, "Les combat de Hadda," 286–88.
16. Schwemer, *Wettergottgestalten*, 118.
17. Volkert Haas, "Zwei Gottheiten aus Eblaisch- hethitischer Überlieferung," *Oriens Antiquus* 20 (1981) 251–57.
18. Ibid., 251.
19. Ibid., 252–53.
20. Ibid., 254.
21. Ibid., 252.
22. Ibid., 253.
23. Ibid.

The ancient place-name Ardawan, in turn, can be linked to modern Basratun < *Ba+ratun, which lies a mere 3 km southwest of ʿAnjara. These towns all lie about 18 km northwest of Aleppo.

Hadda's attack on the serpentine monster apparently alluded to in the Ebla ED IIIb texts is almost certainly an early example of the motif of the struggle against the monsters found in the later Marduk theology of *Enūma eliš*. Marduk slays the sea-goddess Tiʾāmat and creates the universe from her body. It is well known that *Enūma eliš* was recited on the fourth day of the Akitu Festival at Babylon and that Marduk and his entourage made a pilgrimage on the seventh day of the festival to an Akitu house located south of the city. We are grateful to Pongratz-Leisten[24] for describing in detail the various Akitu processionals in Babylonian and Assyrian sources.[25] Relevant to our discussion are the comments of George in a review of Pongratz-Leisten's book. He writes:

> Pongratz-Leisten's study of her subject begins with a discussion of the nature of space, the point of which is to demonstrate the different significance of the city, on the one hand, and the countryside outside, on the other. . . . . . the processions of the *akitu* festivals, which typically move from city to countryside and back again. The city is seen as a place of ritual, the countryside a place of myth.[26]

The dichotomy between the city and countryside is further seen in the concept that a central city such as Babylon was considered to be the navel of the world, as Maul has pointed out in his important article entitled "Die altorientalische Hauptstadt: Abbild und Nabel der Welt."[27] As one progressed out from the order of the capital city at the safe navel of the world, one proceeded from a zone of civilization and just rule to the outer fringes of the world, where barbarians, enemy forces, witches, and monstrous men and animals held sway. Wiggermann notes:

> The peripheral world of the right hand column [Periphery] can be defined as the shadow side of the familiar world in the left hand column [Centre]. The

24. Beate Pongratz-Leisten, *Ina šulmi īrub: Die kulttopographische und ideologische Programmatik der akītu-Prozession in Babylonien und Assyrien im 1. Jahrtausend v. Chr.* (Baghdader Forschungen 16; Mainz am Rhein: von Zabern, 1994) 37–84.

25. Ibid., 60–64.

26. Andrew George, "Studies in Cultic Topography and Ideology," *BO* 53 (1996) 364.

27. Stefan Maul, "Die altorientalische Hauptstadt: Abbild und Nabel der Welt," in *Die Orientalische Stadt: Kontinuitat, Wandel, Bruch. 1. Internationales Colloquium der Deutschen Orient-Gesellschaft. 9.–10. Mai 1996 in Halle/Saale* (ed. Gernot Wilhelm; Colloquien der Deutschen Orient-Gesellschaft 1; Saarbrücken: Saarbrücker Verlag, 1997) 109–24; ET: http://prelectur.stanford.edu/lecturers/maul/capitalsnotes.html.

> two spheres do not normally intermingle, and enemies, wild animal spirits, demons, or monsters—infringing upon the civilized world are regarded as signs of divine displeasure with a king or with individual citizens. The fact that peripheral elements can and do infringe upon civilization shows that there is no impassable boundary between the two spheres.[28]

In view of our tentative locations of the ancient towns of Ammarig and Ardawan just northwest of Aleppo, it may be that these two small towns were connected with a divine procession of Hadda of Aleppo, but this is uncertain.

2.2. Old Akkadian Period Ešnunna Sources

In 1974, A. Westenholz provided an edition of a school text from Tell Asmar, earlier mentioned by Gelb, which mentioned Tiʾāmtum in a title of the god Tišpak: "steward of Tiʾāmat."[29] Westeholz notes that according to Lambert this is clearly an early reference to the mythological being Tiʾāmat who is also referred to by the Old Assyrian personal name Puzur-Tiʾāmtim. Unfortunately, the Ešnunna text is so brief that it tells us little about the relationship between Tiʾāmat and Tišpak.[30]

On this text, Schwemer notes further:[31]

> Daß in Nordbabylonien schon früh das wahrscheinlich aus dem ostlichen Mittelmeerraum stammende Motiv des Meeresbekämpfers mit Ninurta-Traditionen verknüpft wurde, zeigt die erstmals in einem altakkadischen Schultext bezeugte, aus dein Labbu-Mythos besser bekannte Tradition von Eshnuna, die den Gott Tišpak als Bekämpfer des Meeres und des Meerungeheuers vorstellt.

It should be pointed out in this context that the possible relationship of this text to the Labbu myth may be seen pictorially in an Old Akkadian period seal from Ešnunna that was described by Frankfort in the following manner (see fig. 1):

> Two gods spearing four-legged, seven headed Hydra; six tongues of flame arise from back; two worshippers; star in field.[32]

28. F. A. M. Wiggermann, "Scenes from the Shadow Side," in *Mesopotamian Poetic Language: Sumerian and Akkadian* (ed. M. E. Vogelzang and H. Vanstiphout; Cuneiform Monograph 2; Groningen: Styx, 1996) 211.

29. Aage Westenholz, "Old Akkadian School Texts: Some Goals of Sargonic Scribal Education," *AfO* 25 (1974–77) 102; I. J. Gelb, *Sargonic Texts from the Diyala Region* (MAD 1; Chicago: University of Chicago Press, 1952) 101.

30. The text is discussed in Schwemer, *Wettergottgestalten*, 229.

31. Ibid.

32. Henri Frankfort, *Stratified Cylinder Seals from the Diyala Region* (OIP 72; Chicago: University of Chicago Press, 1955) pl. 45 no. 478.

Fig. 1. Seven-headed hydra-like monster being attacked by two figures. After Frankfort, *Stratified Cylinder Seals from the Diyala Region*, pl. 45 no. 478. Reproduced by permission of the Oriental Institute, University of Chicago.

The depiction of seven heads on the hydra in this seal probably bears some relationship to the number seven, which occurs repeatedly in the Ebla incantations in connection with Adda's struggles against the forces of chaos.[33]

2.3. Ur III Sources

In 1984, in a study of the Sumerian verb lu(g), P. Steinkeller referred to a line from an unpublished Ur III incantation that read: pirig muš-huš ab-šag$_4$-ga lu$_5$-ga, which he translated "the lion, *mušḫuššu* dragon which lives in the midst of the sea."[34] Steinkeller's translation with the singular verb "lives" reveals that he took the terms pirig and muš-huš to be in apposition to each other, with the ancient author indicating that here we had an instance of a *Mischwesen* who was part lion and part serpent. This unpublished Ur III incantation is not the only Ur III period source to mention a chaos-monster as a *Mischwesen*. Cunnigham notes other Ur III incantations that are relevant to the present discussion:[35]

> Three chaos-monsters are described causing suffering in the incantations: samana in Texts 59 and 71 and the šegbar and ušumgal in Text 58. In addition Text 63 is concerned with a chaos-monster but it is less clear which—in line 2 it refers to the pirig (lion) and in its last line to the ušumgal. Pos-

33. See lastly Schwemer, *Wettergottgestalten*, 116–19.

34. Piotr Steinkeller, "The Sumerian verb lug$_x$ (LUL)," *Studi epigrafici e lingistici sul Vicino Oriente antico* 1 (1984) 6.

35. Graham Cunningham, *'Deliver Me from Evil': Mesopotamian Incantations, 2500–1500* BC (Studia Pohl: Series Maior 17; Rome: Pontifical Biblical Institute, 1997) 89.

sibly the two are complementary given that an unpublished contemporary incantation associates the lion with a different type of mythical snake: "The lion, the fearsome snake which lives in the centre of the sea" (pirig muš-huš ab-šà-ga-lu$_5$-ga . . .).

The iconographic evidence from Aleppo and Carchemish analyzed below in this essay indicates that this understanding of the last monster to be a *Mischwesen* is indeed correct. The Aleppo and Carchemish iconographic material reveals that the Leviathan figure in some cases had both a human and lion head, along with the tail of a snake

2.4. *Old Babylonian Mari Sources*

In 1993, J.-M. Durand published a Mari letter, A. 1968, in which a Mari envoy to the city of Aleppo named Nūr-Sîn reports to Zimrī-Līm about an oracular pronouncement from the god Addu of Aleppo. It reads as follows:[36]

> Thus (speaks) Addu: I have given the whole land to Iahdun-Līm and (because of) my weapons, he had no rival. I have returned you to the t[hrone of the house of your father]. **I have given you the weapon[s] with which I smote the Sea.** With the oil of my . . . , I have anointed you. Nobody stands before (= against) you.

As Schwemer has pointed out, the attack on the Sea by Addu in this text should almost certainly be related to the much later Babylonian accounts of the chaos struggles of Marduk found in *Enūma eliš* as well as Babylonian texts dealing with the exploits of the warrior-gods Ninurta-Ningirsu, Iškur, Tišpak, and Nergal.[37]

2.5. *Middle Bronze Art from Ebla*

In two articles published in 1987, P. Matthiae described the finds of the 1983–86 excavation seasons at Ebla.[38] Of importance for this study was the discovery of a small sanctuary labeled G3 (since it lay in area G in the archaeological field zones of Ebla), which Matthiae indicates, with some imprecision, dates to the Middle Bronze period, ca. 1800 B.C.E. The sanctuary was found in the sacred precinct adjacent to Temple D and lay a mere 50 m east of the MB "Western Palace" in area Q (see fig. 2). On the left side of the entrance to the

36. The letter is edited in Jean-Marie Durand, "Le combat entre le Dieu de l'orage et la Mer," *MARI* 7 (1993) 43–46.

37. Schwemer, *Wettergottgestalten*, 229.

38. Paolo Matthiae, "Les dernières découvertes d'Ébla en 1983–1986," *CRAIBL* (1987) 135–61; idem, "Una stele paleosyriana da Ebla e la cultura figurative della Siria altorno al 1800 A.C.," *Scienze dell'Antichità* 1 (1987) 497–95.

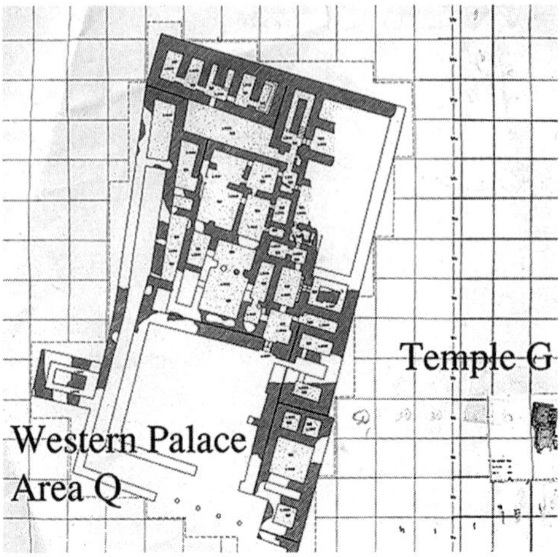

Fig. 2. Location of Temple G3 just east of the MB "Western Palace" in area Q. Image reproduced with the kind permission of the Missione Archeologica a Ebla, Sapienza University, Rome.

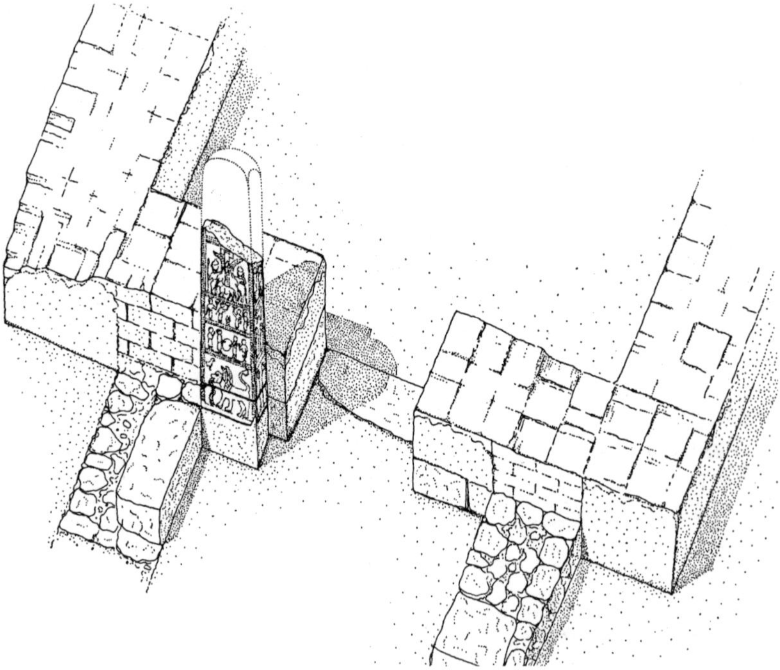

Fig. 3. Entrance to Temple G3, showing stele on the left side of the entrance. Image reproduced with the kind permission of the Missione Archeologica a Ebla, Sapienza University, Rome.

sanctuary, the base of a basalt stele was found in situ. Later, two pieces of the same monument were found at other locations in the area of Palace E. The reconstructed stele at present has a height of 1.72 m with an estimated original height of 2.30 m (see fig. 3). The iconography of the stele was discussed in detail by Matthiae in an article in a volume honoring Finet. Matthiae writes:[39]

> L'iconographie de la déesse debout a l'intérieur du temple ailé sur le dos d'un taureau est très rare dans la glyptique paléosyrienne, mais un cylindre avec cette image de la collection Poche doit être daté de la première moitié du XVIIIe siècle av. J.C. . . . Un deuxième sceau avec Ia même iconographic divine a l'intérieur d'un édicule dépourvu d'ailes . . . conserve dans la collection Moore, est peut-être de peu plus ancien. La déesse nue érigée dans le naos ailé sur un taureau abattu par un hèros est le theme principal du célèbre sceau de Samiya gravé vers 1775 av. J.C. alors qu'un cylindre palèosyrien archaïque provincial, peut-être du premier quart du XVIIIe siècle av. J.C., représente la déesse nue dans l'édicule sans ailes sur un taureau . . . en face d'un roi ayant la tiare a comes des souverains contemporains d'Ebla. La déesse en nudité sur le taureau dans un édicule ailé composé d'une guilloche, évoquant certainernent les eaux de la fécondité, est sûrement une variante de la même iconographie divine, documentée par deux cylindres paléosyriens de peu plus tardifs de la Morgan Library et du British Museum.

It should be noted that the Paleo-Syrian motifs found on various cylinder seals discussed by Matthiae also have a clear forerunner in the *Geflügte Tempel* motif commonly found in seals of Old Akkadian date, a motif that has been analyzed by M. Boehmer in his comprehensive study of the development of Old Akkadian glyptic.[40] While Matthiae is almost certainly correct that the large female figure in the winged temple depicted on the stele is a representation of the goddess Ištar, it is by no means certain that this proves that the sanctuary G3 as a whole was dedicated to this goddess. Ištar is only one of many beings depicted on the stele. Indeed, the shrine is quite small, and we might expect a larger temple for such an important goddess as Ištar, whom texts tell us was an important deity at Ebla.

39. Paolo Matthiae, "Le temple ailé et le taureau," in *Reflets des deux fleuves: Volume de mélanges offerts à André Finet* (ed. Marc Lebeau and Philippe Talon; Akkadica Supplementum 6; Leuven: Peeters, 1989) 127.

40. Rainer Michael Boehmer, *Die Entwicklung der Glyptik während der Akkad-Zeit* (Untersuchungen zur Assyriologie und vorderasiatischen Archäologie 4; Berlin: de Gruyter, 1965) 105–9.

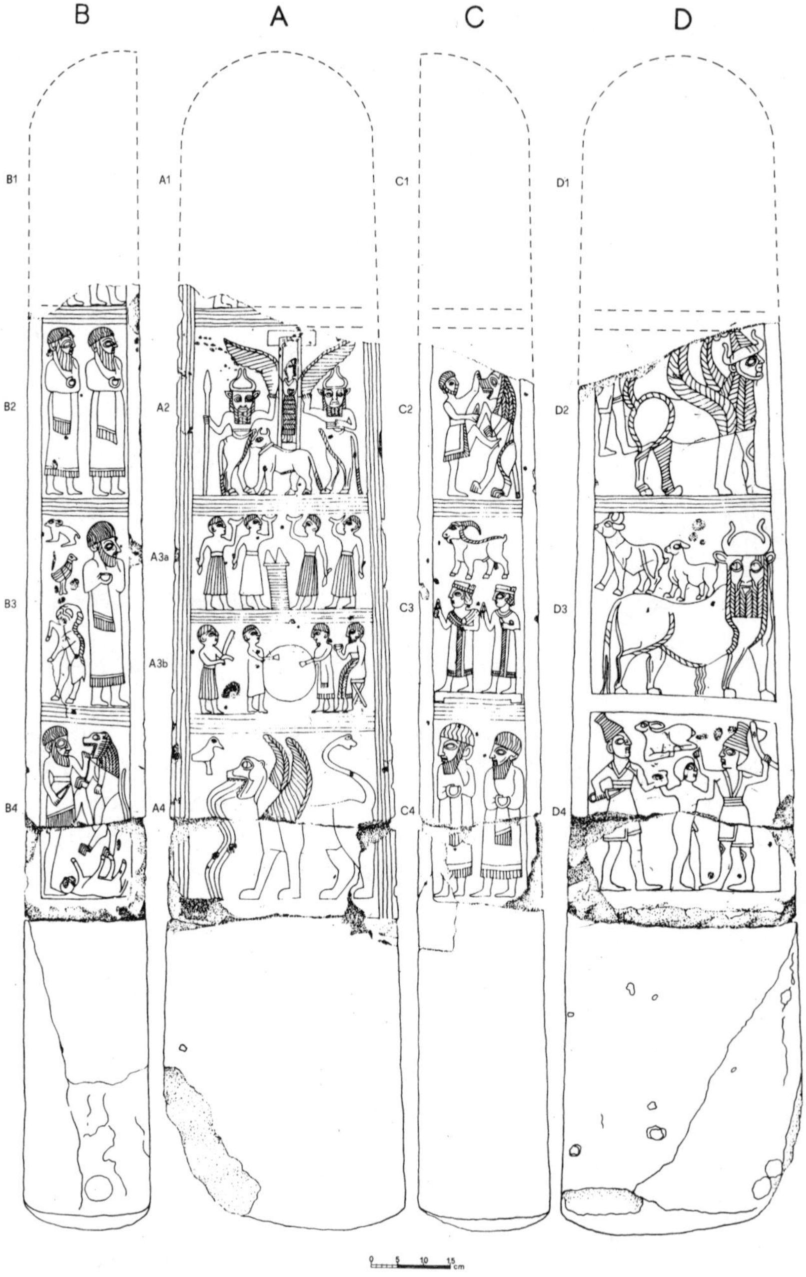

Fig. 4. Stele found at the entrance to Temple G3 at Ebla. Image reproduced with the kind permission of the Missione Archeologica a Ebla, Sapienza University, Rome.

Table 1. The Ebla G3 Monument and Babylonian Constellations
(see fig. 4)

Register Number according to Matthiae, Pinnock, Matthiae, Ebla, *390–91*	*Description of Figure on Stele*	*Constellation in* MUL.APIN *Name and Tablet Number*	*Constellations in OB Star Lists (Horowitz,* "Some Thoughts")	*Modern Constellation*
A1	missing	—		—
A2	Ištar/Anunītu	Anunītu I i 42 *kakkabu ša arki ikî anunītu*, "The Star Which Is behind the Field: Anunītu"	^{d}nin-si$_{4}$-ab-na(?), "the russet lady of heaven"	Andromeda
A2	The Rectangular Temple	Ikû I I 42 *kakkabu ša arki ikî anunītu*, "The Star Which Is behind the Field: Anunītu"	*ikû*, "the (rectangular) field"	Great Square of Pegasus
A2	The Bull of Heaven	Alû I ii 1 *alû is lê agê Ani*, "The Bull of Heaven, the Jaw of the Bull, the crown of Anu"	gu$_{4}$-an-na, "The Bull of Heaven"	Taurus
A3a	Four Male Figures Holding up the Sky	SIPA.ZI.AN.NA I ii 2 *šidalu* ^{d}*pap-sukkal sukal* ^{d}*a-nim u* INNIN, "The True Shepherd of Anu, Papsukal, the Messenger of Anu and Inanna"	sipa-zi-an-na	Orion
A3b	Banquet Scene, Man with Cup, Harp, and Drum	—	balag^{a}	Crater Lyra
A4	Leonine/Snake Creature = Leviathan Bird	MUŠ I ii 8 *Niraḫ Ningizzida, bēl erṣeti*, "Nirah, Ningišzida, Lord of the Netherworld" Āribu I ii 9 *āribu kakkab Adad*, "The Raven star of Adad"	muš uga^{mušen}	Hydra Corvus

B1	Missing	—	—	—
B2	Lustration figure	Dumuzi I i 43 *kakkabu ša arkišu izzazzu agru dumuzi*, "The Star Which Stands behind It Is the Hired Man Dumuzi"	lú-ḫun-gá	Aries
B3	Lustration figure Hare[b] Bird	Dumuzi I i 43 *kakkabu ša arkišu izzazzu agru dumuzi*, "the star which stands behind it is the hired man Dumuzi" — Šinunūtu i I 41 *kakkabu ša ina meḫret ikî izzazzu šinunūtu*, "The Star Which Stands Opposite the Field: the Swallow"	lú-ḫun-gá	Aries Lepus —
B4	Lion	Nēšu II iii 30 *šumma Nēšu kakkabūšu iltappû*, "If the stars of the Lion . . ."	ur-maḫ	Leo
C1	Missing	—	—	—
C2	Lion	Nēšu II II iii 30 *šumma Nēšu kakkabūšu iltappû*, "If the stars of the Lion . . ."	ur-maḫ	Leo
C3	She-goat triangle[c] (musical instrument)	Enzu I I 24 *enzu Gula*, "The She-Goat: Gula"	ùz, "She-goat" sag-dù-a[d], "triangle"	Lyra Triangulum
C4	Lustration figures	Dumuzi I i 43 *kakkabu ša arkišu izzazzu agru dumuzi*, "The Star Which Stands behind It Is the Hired Man Dumuzi"	lú-ḫun-gá	Aries
D1	Missing	—	—	—
D2	?			
D3	Human-headed bull	Kusarikku	—	Centaurus

D4	Gilgamesh and Enkidu slaying Huwawa	Šību I I 3 Šību Enmešarra, "The Old man, Enmešara"	šu-gi	Perseus

a. For the constellation balag, "harp" or "drum," in OB god lists, see Horowitz, "Some Thoughts on Sumerian Star-Names," 166, line 404.

b. There is no ancient Mesopotamian constellation "Hare" known to me, but the depiction on the Ebla stele is clear. Lepus was one of the 48 constellations listed by the second-century astronomer Ptolemy, and it remains one of the 88 modern constellations.

c. The triangle may be a symbol of the divine musician Geštin-ana. For Geštin-ana as divine musician, see Bendt Alster, "Geštinanna as Singer and the Chorus of Uruk and Zabalam: UET 6/1 22," *JCS* 37 (1985) 219–28. If Geštin-ana had a stellar equivalent, it may have been the constellation Triangulum, since its shape (like a grape leaf) resembles a triangle, and the constellation is located immediately beside that of Aries, the star group connected with her brother Dumuzi.

d. For the constellation sag-dù, "triangle," in OB god lists, see Horowitz, "Some Thoughts on Sumerian Star-Names," 166, line 402.

3. *The Ebla Stele from Area G3: A Uranographic Monument?*

A careful study of the various motifs found on the basalt stele from Ebla reveals that it portrays a strange mixture of exotic monsters and human figures. In many cases, the representations of the mythological beings can be linked to ancient Mesopotamian constellations. However, we should preface the discussion with the remarks of Horowitz about our relative paucity of knowledge about ancient Sumerian astronomy. He writes:

> That the Sumerians of the third and fourth millennia had no formal written discipline of astronomy or astrology that can be compared to that in Akkadian in the second and first millennia, nor can we fully assess what the Sumerians did or did not know about the skies above them on the basis of what has come down to us in written form. . . . However, on the other hand, we do have anecdotal evidence for a practical and even academic Sumerian astronomical tradition (the Šulgi passage), as well as the Sumerian star-names themselves, which remained in use down to the death of the cuneiform writing system. . . . What then is the source of all these Sumerian star-names known from the second and first millennia, which so far exceed the forty or so known from Sumerian sources and the star-lists of the forerunners to Urra = hubullu . . . ? The present author surmises that most are genuine Sumerian-language names that were in use in third-millennium Sumer and Akkad, just as we Assyriologists suppose that the vast majority of the Sumerian vocabulary known to us from the Old Babylonian period is genuinely Sumerian.[41]

41. Wayne Horowitz, "Some Thoughts on Sumerian Star-Names and Sumerian Astronomy," in *An Experienced Scribe Who Neglects Nothing: Ancient Near Eastern Studies in Honor of Jacob Klein* (ed. Yitschak Sefati et al.; Bethesda, MD: CDL, 2005) 177–78.

Although the evidence from MUL.APIN is a much later than the evidence provided by both the Ebla stele and the OB star lists, I have used this later work as a frame for the discussion, since it is the basis of our most complete understanding of ancient Babylonian astronomy.

4. Other Depictions of Leviathan in Ancient Syrian and Neo-Hittite Art

4.1. *What Did Leviathan Look Like?*

Before I begin the discussion of Leviathan in ancient art, we should examine a passage from the book of Job in the Bible for textual material to compare to the iconographic evidence. We read in Job 41:

> [1] Can you draw out Leviathan with an fishhook, or press down its tongue with a cord?
> [2] Can you put an rope in its nose, or pierce its jaw with a hook?
> [3] Will it make many supplications to you? Will it speak soft words to you?
> [4] Will it make a covenant with you to be taken as your servant forever?
> [5] Will you play with it as with a bird, or will you put it on leash for your girls?
> [6] Will traders bargain over it? Will they divide it up among the merchants?
> [7] Can you fill its skin with harpoons, or its head with fishing spears?
> [8] Lay hands on it; think of the battle; you will not do it again!
> [9] Any hope of catching it will be disappointed; were not even the gods overwhelmed at the sight of it?
> [10] No one is so fierce as to dare stir it up. Who can confront it and be safe?—under the whole heaven, who?

The passage describes a monstrous creature that we know from comparative material was a snaky creature, which could be captured using a hook in its nose and a cord or reed in its tongue or jaw. Pope notes that the Qumran targum for v. 2 reads as follows:

> *ntšwʾ zmm bʾaph*
> *wbhrtk tqwb lsth*

> Can you put a ring in his nose.
> Or with your gimlet pierce his cheek?[42]

42. Marvin Pope, *Job* (AB 15; Garden City, NY: Doubleday, 1973) 332.

Pope notes that the word *zmm* can be read as *zemām* and translated "muzzle," and the iconographic evidence examined below supports this reading.

Fig. 5. Detail of stele found at the entrance to Temple G3 at Ebla, showing a Leviathan-like monster. Image reproduced with the kind permission of the Missione Archeologica a Ebla, Sapienza University, Rome.

4.2. A Depiction of Leviathan in Middle Bronze Ebla

As noted above on p. 75, in Register A4 of the stele from Ebla, a *Mischwesen* is depicted that is characterized as having four legs, a leonine head, a mouth from which water is streaming, two upright wings attached at the beast's shoulders, and a snaky tale that coils up in a characteristic curl (see fig. 5). This last feature is found in all depictions of the creature, and it is the most distinctive characteristic of this monster. The distinctive curl in the tail may be connected to the name Leviathan itself, since the proper name is derived from the Semitic root *lwy*, "to twist" or "to coil." If my identification is correct, this is the earliest depiction of Leviathan in Syrian monumental art. It dates roughly to the same time as Mari letter A. 1968, which, as noted, refers to the god Addu's battle against the Sea.

4.3. Depictions of Leviathan in Neo-Hittite Art

4.3.1. Aleppo

In 2000, Kohlmeyer published a book entitled *Der Tempel des Wettergottes von Aleppo* in which he described the results of his excavations of a temple located on the citadel of Aleppo, the remains of which date from the EB to Neo-Hittite period. An overview of the finds has been provided in an account directed to a popular audience by Andrew Lawler that is worth repeating here:[43]

> A massive citadel built atop a 150-foot-tall hill of solid rock looms over Aleppo's old quarter. Fortresses have risen above this northern Syrian city since Roman times. But at the heart of the citadel, amid ruins of Ottoman palaces and hidden behind high walls that date to the Crusader era, a team of German and Syrian archaeologists is clearing debris from a large pit that shows this hilltop was significant long before the Romans arrived. Here, amid clouds of dust, a battered basalt sphinx and a lion—both standing seven feet tall—guard the entrance to one of the great religious centers of ancient times, the sanctuary of the storm god Adda.

43. Andrew Lawler, "Temple of the Storm God," *Archaeology* 62 (2009) 20.

> Kay Kohlmeyer, an archaeologist at Berlin's University of Applied Sciences and the excavation co-director, has spent more than 10 years peeling away the layers of rubble that conceal the rich history of this temple. . . .
>
> On a hot April morning, Kohlmeyer welcomes me into the shade of the corrugated roof that now covers Adda's sanctuary. As my eyes adjust to the sudden gloom, I spy a row of stone friezes of gods and mythical creatures still standing in a neat row at the far end of the temple.

The ancient structure was situated beneath a mosque at the top of the citadel. The walls of the entrance to the temple and the temple walls themselves were adorned with a long series of stunning stone orthostats depicting various mythological figures.

Of importance to the present discussion is the fact that the 17th and 18th blocks in the row of temple reliefs from the Adad Temple in Aleppo clearly depict two Leviathan-like figures very similar to those found in the MB stele from Ebla.[44] They are winged monsters with the combination of a human head, wings, and serpentine tail. Another example of a Leviathan figure is found on block 4 in the row of temple reliefs.[45]

We may note in passing that this particular Leviathan *Mischwesen* recalls the classic description of the Greek sphinx, which is depicted in ancient Greek art as a monster with the head of a woman, the body of a lion, the wings of an eagle, and a snake-headed tail. Both the Syrian-Neo-Hittite Leviathans described in this study and the sphinxes acted as merciless guardians of gateways. Indeed, as we shall see below, representations of Leviathans are found on either side of the entrance to the palace at the Neo-Hittite site of Sakçagözü.

4.3.2. Carchemish

In his study of Neo-Hittite art, Orthmann referred to a basalt orthostat from Carchemish, from the so-called Herald's wall, to which he gave the siglum Karkemish E/8.[46] The orthostat provides us with the clearest and most detailed depiction of a Leviathan-like creature in Neo-Hitite art (see fig. 6). The animal in question wears a crown, has a human face, and a lion head protrudes from its breast/neck area. The monster is further adorned with two wings at the shoulders and has a tail turned up in a distinctive s-shaped curl.

A second basalt orthostat from Carchemish was assigned the siglum Karkemish H/4 by Orthmann, but it is not as well preserved as Karkemish E/8.[47]

44. Kay Kohlmeyer, *Der Tempel des Wettergottes von Aleppo* (Münster: Rhema, 2000) 106, figs. 148–49.

45. Ibid., 96, fig. 133.

46. Winfried Orthmann, *Untersuchungen zur späthethitischen Kunst* (Bonn: Habelt, 1971) 504–5 and pl 27b.

47. Ibid., 611 and pl. 33b.

4.3.3. Tell Halaf

Two orthostats from Tell Halaf given the siglum A3/151 and A3/152 by Orthmann[48] show a crowned *Mischwesen* with human faces that are adorned with two wings at the shoulders and with tails turned up in the distinctive s-curl. They are clearly depictions of a Leviathan. Of interest is the fact that A/3 152 shows a lion head emerging from the neck or breast of the beast as we have seen in some other (but not all) depictions of Leviathans.

Fig. 6. Figure of a Leviathan monster from Carchemish. After Orthmann, *Untersuchungen zur späthethitischen Kunst*, pl. 27b. Reproduced courtesy of the Chair for Pre- and Protohistory and Near Eastern Archaeology of the Saarland University.

4.3.4. Karatepe

Additional examples of Leviathan-like creatures are depicted in two stone monuments from Karatepe: Karatepe A/9 and A/30.[49] The monsters face each other across the entrance passage to the North Gate of the town of Karatepe. The *Mischwesen* have human heads, four legs, and two wings. Unfortunately, the published photos of the beasts are of poor quality, so not all of the details can be determined from them.

4.3.5. Sakçagözü

Three basalt blocks designated Sakçagözü A4, A8, and A12 by Orthmann[50] were set up in a row facing each other at the entrance to the palace at Sakçagözü. The monsters in all cases have a human head, four legs, and two wings, with erect tails ending in the distinctive s-curl.

4.3.6. Zincirli

Another interesting example of a Leviathan figure is found on a basalt orthostat at Zincirli; it was given the siglum Zincirli B/22 by Orthmann.[51] This Leviathan creature appears to have a human head, a crown, a noose around its neck, two wings, and a tail turned up in the characteristic s-curl. The beast is shown being pursued by a human figure who holds some sort of noose or lasso in his hand. As noted above, this noose is possibly connected with the Hebrew word *zemām* found in the Qumran targum on Job 41 dealing with Leviathan.

48. Ibid., pl. 11g–h.
49. Ibid., 490 and pl. 15g; 490 and pl. 17i.
50. Ibid., pls. 50–51.
51. Ibid., 542 and pl. 59d.

A clear companion piece to the preceding orthostat is a similar basalt orthostat, which Orthmann designated Zincirli B/21.[52] It stands immediately beside the previously described piece. The orthostat depicts a beast similar to Zincirli B/22, but this time the Leviathan creature is shown with his tail hanging down, not in it usual erect position. This may be a pose indicating some distress on the beast's part. We also note that in this second depiction the beast's headgear has been removed, and the noose that in B/22 was shown hanging loosely around his head has now been gripped tightly shut by a male figure who now stands in front of the beast instead of behind him. My interpretation is that B/22 and B/21 are consecutive scenes showing the pursuit and capture of Leviathan by a human figure. The identity of the captor is unclear.

A third example of a Leviathan creature from Zincirli is depicted on a basalt block denoted Zincirli B/31 by Orthmann.[53] It depicts a warrior with a spear pointed toward a four-legged, human-faced, leonine, winged creature with a serpentine tail. I understand the warrior figure that stands beside the Leviathan-like creature to be another example of the human figure discussed in the previous example.

A fourth example of a Leviathan-like creature at Zincirli is found in block A/5,[54] which shows one Leviathan standing on another, an arrangement that recalls the 17th and 18th blocks at Aleppo.[55]

5. *Depictions of Leviathan from Other Areas*

5.1. Megiddo

An important additional source on Leviathans is a Hittite ivory from Megiddo.[56] About its discovery, Alexander writes:

> Excavations in 1937 at Megiddo in Palestine revealed a cache of ivories that included a small plaque of great interest to Hittitologists. . . . Although its subject matter and style immediately linked it with the Hittite world, discovery in an area outside Hittite rule provoked serious questions concerning its artistic as well as geographical origins.[57]

---

52. Ibid., 542 and pl. 59f.
53. Ibid., 543 and pl. 61c.
54. Ibid., 538 and pl. 55c.
55. Kohlmeyer, *Der Tempel des Wettergottes*, 106, figs. 148–49.
56. See Robert Alexander, "Šaušga and the Hittite Ivory from Megiddo," *JNES* 50 (1991) 163 for a drawing of the plaque.
57. Ibid., 161.

Of note is the appearance of two Leviathan figures on the extreme left and right sides of the third register from the top of the plaque. Regarding these depictions, Alexander writes:

> Perhaps the most individual of these images is the winged two-headed lion, so striking an image that it survived with little change through the Neo-Hittite centuries. A composite beast, its basis is the body of a lion with its head held low (markedly different from the type with elongated neck and leonine head held high). The addition of wings parallels Near Eastern use of wings on the sphinx acquired from Egypt and makes the animal more than an ordinary lion. Above the neck is added a divinizing element, the human head with the tall, conical, Hittite tiara. Representations from later centuries stress the continuity of the body, neck, and animal head, and show that the divine head was understood as an addition either by its relation to the contour of the neck or by its placement on the animal (occasionally above the head).[58]

Additional examples of Leviathan figures are found on a gold ring from Konya, on a gem in the State Hermitage, and on a powder box from Mahmudiye, all discussed by Danmanville.[59]

6. *Behemoth in Ancient Syrian and Neo-Hittite Art*

6.1. *What Did Behemoth Look Like?*

Before we begin an investigation into possible representations of Behemoth in ancient Syrian and Neo-Hittite art, we should examine the literary description of the beast that is found in the book of Job 40:

> [15] Look at behemoth, which I just as I made you; it eats grass like an ox.
> [16] Its strength is in its loins, and its power in the muscles of its belly.
> [17] It makes its tail stiff like a cedar; the sinews of its thighs are knit together.
> [18] Its bones are tubes of bronze; its limbs like bars of iron.
> [19] It is the first of the great acts of God—only its Maker can approach it with the sword.
> [20] For the mountains yield food for it where all the wild animals play.
> [21] Under the lotus plants it lies, in the covert of the reeds and in the marsh.
> [22] The lotus trees cover it for shade; the willows of the wadi surround it.

58. Ibid., 165.

59. Jenny Danmanville, "Iconographie d'Ištar-Šaušga en Anatolie ancienne," *RA* 61 (1962) 122–29.

Fig. 7. Detail of stele found at the entrance to Temple G3 at Ebla, showing a Behemoth-like monster. Image reproduced with the kind permission of the Missione Archeologica a Ebla, Sapienza University, Rome.

[23] Even if the river is turbulent, it is not frightened; it is confident though Jordan rushes against its mouth.
[24] Can one take it with hooks or pierce its nose with a snare?

6.2. Behemoth at Middle Bronze Ebla

We have seen that literary allusions in incantations to the combat by the storm god against the sea probably date all the way back to ED IIIB Ebla. In addition, a depiction of a Leviathan-like creature is found on a MB stele that once stood at the entrance to temple G3 in the same city. We might expect, then, that the mythological figure of Behemoth found in the Bible will also appear in ancient Syrian art. In the biblical passage from the book of Job noted above, Behemoth is described as being an ox-like creature that feeds on grass. The biblical account also relates that the creature's "power is in the muscles of its belly."

Now, if we examine register D3 of the MB stele from Temple G3 at Ebla, we see that it depicts a large, recumbent, horned, human-headed, pot-bellied bovine creature (see fig. 7). A study of the iconography indicates that this large bovine is almost certainly to be connected with the creature known in Akkadian as *kusarikku* and *ditānu*. In my understanding, this particular *Mischwesen* appears in register D3. It is of particular interest that, in a Hittite lexical text, in its Akkadian column, there is an equation of Sumerian a l i m (which corresponds to Akkadian *kusarikku* and *ditānu*) with the Akkadian word *karšānu*, "big-bellied," an apt description of the biblical Behemoth.

We may note that the image in the MB Ebla stele of a human-headed bovine creature immediately brings to mind another artifact from ancient Ebla—that is, a beautiful wooden, gold, and steatite-plated statuette depict-

Table 2. Sources for Sumerian and Akkadian Equivalences

giš-gu_4-[alim]	[*a-lim-bu-ú*]	Hh VIIB 84
[kuš]-alim	MIN (*ma-šak*) *di-ta-nu*	Hh XI 32
[gu_4-al]im-kù-GI	*ku-s*[*a-rik-ku*]	Hh XII 344
gu_4-alim	MIN = *a-lim-bu-ú*	Hh XIII 301
gu_4-alim	*ku-sa-rik-kum*	Hh XIII 310
alim	*di-ta-nu*	Hh XIV 144a

ing a recumbent, human-headed bull; it was found in the ED IIIb palace.[60] All commentators have agreed that this Ebla statuette is a depiction of the *kusarikku*, a mythical beast that is often depicted in ancient Near Eastern art.[61] Of further interest to the discussion is a passage in the Epic of Anzû that deals with Ninurta's slaying of the *kusarikku* beast "in the midst of the sea." It is noteworthy, in this connection, that the Ebla stele depicts wavy lines extending from the belly of the stout bovine creature: they probably represent a stream of water—that is, the big-bellied beast has been placed in a riverine setting.

6.3. *Behemoth as* Kusarikku: *Behemoth as a Centaur*

As noted, the large bovine, human-headed creature depicted in register D3 in the Ebla stele can be identified as the Sumerian creature denoted an alim, or gu_4-alim. It is rendered in Akkadian as *kusarikku* or *ditānu*. The lexical sources for these equations are provided in table 2.

Note the fact that Hh XI 32 and Hh XIV 144 indicate that Sumerian alim is sometimes equated with Akkadian *ditānu*. On this latter term, we may note the comments of the *CAD*:[62]

> The animal *ditānu* (*didānu*) is attested only in lex. texts and in the Etana passage quoted sub. Mng. 1. . . . Sum. alim (Akk. *karšānu*, big-bellied) is

60. For images and discussion, see Paolo Matthiae, Frances Pinnock, and Gabriella Scandone Matthiae, *Ebla: Alle origini della civiltà urbana—trent anni di scavi in Siria dell'Università di Roma "La Sapienza"* (Milan: Electa, 1995) 329 and 139. Other *kusarikkus* are shown on pp. 305 snd 306 of the same book.

61. See Boehmer, *Die Entwicklung der Glyptik*.

62. *CAD* D 165.

> rendered in Hittite (MSL 3 64:11, Sa Voc. from Bogh.) by the hapax *ti-ša-nu-uš*, which points definitely to Heb. *dīšōn*.

A study of the biblical form Dedan, cognate with Akkadian *ditānu*, is informative. In the discussion of Dedan in the *DDD*, Spronk notes:

> This status [of *ditānu*] be it historical or mythical, accords well with the prominent place he [*ditānu*] takes in some Ugaritic ritual texts related to the cult of the dead. In KTU 1.161 the spirits of the royal ancestors ("the Rephaim of the earth") are called "the assembly of Dedan." The parallelism between "Rephaim of the earth (i.e., the netherworld)" and "the assembly of Dedan" indicates that Dedan was regarded as the first of the deified royal ancestors. In this text the names of the deceased kings are called one by one to receive sacrifices. In return they are asked to hail the living king and his city.[63]

6.4. *Behemoth as Enkidu and the Centaur Chiron*

The figure on the MB stele from Ebla that we have identified as being Behemoth is a bovine creature with a human head. In this respect, he reminds us of the figure of Enkidu, who similarly was a creature that was a bull-man capable of human speech.

Now, George, in his superlative edition of the *Gilgameš Epic* found in his *Babylonian Gilgamesh Epic* provides a detailed discussion of the character of Enkidu. He notes:

> The name of Gilgameš's bosom friend, [is] written en-ki-dùg. . . . The name means "lord (of) the pleasant place."[64]

Here I take the expression "pleasant place" to be a euphemism for "the Underworld." This blessed Netherworld could possibly refer to a concept similar to the Elysian Fields. Enkidu by this understanding would be an immortalized dead hero.

George points out that Enkidu played a special role in the epic as a mentor and confidant for Gilgamesh. George notes:

> As Gilgameš's most intimate companion he was naturally also his confidant. A more thought-provoking (but anachronistic) view is that 'Enkidu, sent by the gods to match and reform Gilgameš, is the partner of Gilgameš in the Manichaean sense of a spiritual counterpart, a divine twin sent by God to convey noble counsel'. However that may be, in Enkidu's role as Gilgameš counsellor lies the probable solution to the strange equation a.rá.imin =

63. Klaas Spronk, "Dedan," *DDD* 440.

64. Andrew George, *The Babylonian Gilgamesh Epic: Introduction, Critical Edition and Cuneiform Texts* (Oxford: Oxford University Press, 2003) 138.

> Enkidu in the group vocabulary quoted in Chapter 3. The word a.rá, 'way, behaviour', can have overtones of 'good counsel', to the extent that it was sometimes interpreted by Babylonian scholars as *māliku*, "counsellor." Perhaps, then, a.rá.imin was meant by the list's composer to convey the notion "counsellor *par excellence*."[65]

If we turn to the evidence of comparative mythology to try better to understand the nature of the bull-man Enkidu, we note that a possible parallel to him can be seen in the Greek centaur named Chiron, who, like Enkidu was the "counselor par excellence." Unlike the other wild and uncontrollable centaurs, Chiron was intelligent, civilized, and kind, and he was known for his knowledge and skill with medicine. For example, Homer notes an address of Eurypylos to Patroklos in which the medical skills of Chiron are lauded:

> Cut the arrow out of my thigh . . . and put kind medicines on it, good ones, which they say you have been told of by Achilleus, since Kheiron (Chiron), most righteous of the Kentauroi (Centaurs), told him about them.[66]

It is of interest, then, that Enkidu's connection with the healing arts for children is alluded to in a Mesopotamian work—that is, a baby incantation edited by Farber. The relevant section is provided using Farber's English translation:

> [1–4] You there, baby, human offspring: you have indeed come forth, have indeed seen the sun, the li[ght].
>
> [5–10] Did you never treat your mother like this in the womb?
>
> Instead of being nice to your father, (and) letting your mother lead a normal life, you have frightened the nursemaid, you have disturbed the wet-nurse.
>
> [11–14] As a result of your crying, the god of the house cannot sleep, sleep does not overcome the goddess of the house.
>
> Whom should I send to Enkidu, who established the number of three for the night watches . . . ?[67]

The connection of Enkidu and Chiron with medical skill is interesting in view of Spronk's remarks in connection with the healing arts of the Dedan: "According to KTU 1.124 Ditan could be called upon to help a sick child."[68] We should bear in mind, in this connection, that Chiron was the son of Kronos and that Kronos, in turn, is said to be a Titan. The appearance of the term

65. Ibid., 143, with internal quotation from Stephanie Dalley, "Gilgamesh and Manichaean Themes," *Aram* 3 (1991) 28.

66. *Iliad* 11.832ff.; following the translation of Lattimore.

67. Walter Farber, *Schlaf, Kindchen, Schlaf! Mesopotamische Baby-Beschwörungen und -Rituale* (Mesopotamian Civilizations 2; Winona Lake, IN: Eisenbrauns, 1989) 34–37.

68. Spronk, "Dedan," 440.

"Titan" prompts us to ask the question whether there is some connection between the Syrian Didanu/Dedan and Greek Titan. The comments of Bremmer are relevant:

> He [Burkert] also draws attention to the fact that the mythical ancestor of the kings in Ugarit is called Ditanu. Subsequent research has pointed out that Ditanu seems to refer to a mythical group, the mythical royal ancestors. Given the eventual origin of the Titans from North Syria. an etymological connection with these Ditanu is not impossible even though there is very little known about these royal ancestors.[69]

The possible connection between Syrian ditānu, Biblical Dedan and Greek Titan warrants further study.

6.5. *The Astral Connections of the Kusarikku*

Various cuneiform sources indicate that *the kusarriku*, in addition to being a mythical beast, was also an ancient Babylonian constellation.[70] While it does not appear in any extant section of the star list MUL.APIN,[71] it is mentioned in the OB "Hymns to the Gods of the Night" in a section dealing with the stars Gibil, Erra, the Elamite bow, the Pleiades, Orion, the Chariot, the She-goat.[72]

Since the *kusarikku* was a Mischwesen, being part man and part bull, cross-cultural evidence would suggest a possible identification of the Mesopotamian bull-man with the ancient Greek figure of titan Centaurus, who was half man and half horse. Most Babylonian constellations have later Greek counterparts, and the case of the star group *kusarikku* may be another case. If the connection is true, then the example would add one more couplet to corresponding Babylonian and ancient Greek constellations. The various correlations have been noted by Bobrova and Militarev,[73] and the data are summarized in table 3.

Of relevance to the discussion is the observation of Hunger and Pingree that the stars listed in MUL.APIN move in three separate paths that circumscribe different regions of the sky and cosmos:

---

69. Jan Bremmer, "Remember the Titans!" in *The Fall of the Angels* (ed. Christoph Auffarth and Loren Stuckenbruck; Leiden: Brill, 2004) 48.

70. For references, see *CAD* K 584.

71. There is no appearance of the term *Kusarikku* in Hermann Hunger and David Pingree, *MUL.APIN: An Astronomical Compendium in Cuneiform* (AfO Beiheft 24; Horn, Austria: Berger, 1989).

72. See *CAD* K 584.

73. Larissa Bobrova and Alexander Militarev, "From Mesopotamia to Greece: On the Origin of Semitic and Greek Star Names," in *Die Rolle der Astronomie in den Kulturen Mesopotamiens: Beiträge zu 3. Grazer Morgenländischen Symposion (23.–27. September 1991)* (ed. Hannes Galter; Graz: Graz Kult, 1993) 307–29.

Table 3. Corresponding Babylonian and Greek Constellations

Star in MUL.APIN	*Ancient Greek Constellation*
1. MUL.MUL, "The Star Cluster" or "Star of Stars"	Pleiades
2. GU_4.AN.NA, "The Steer of Heaven"	Taurus
3. SIPA.ZI.AN.NA, "The Loyal Shepherd of Heaven"	Orion
4. ŠU.GI, "The Old One"	Perseus
5. ZUBI, "The Scimitar"	Auriga
6. MAŠ.TAB.BA.GAL.GAL, "The Great Twins"	Gemini
7. AL.LUL, "The Crayfish"	Cancer
8. UR.GU.LA, "The Lion"	Leo
9. AB.SÍN, "The Seed-Furrow"	Virgo
10. ZIB.BA.AN.NA, "The Scales"	Libra
11. GÍR.TAB, "The Scorpion"	Scorpio
12. PA.BIL.SAG	Sagittarius
13. SUḪUR.MAŠ.KU_6, "The Goat-Fish"	Capricorn
14. GU.LA, "The Great One"	Aquarius
15. KUN.MEŠ, "The Tails"	Pisces
16. SIM.MAḪ, "The Great Swallow"	SW Pisces
17. A-nu-ni-tum	Andromeda
18. LÚ.ḪUN.GA, "The Agrarian Worker"	Aries

> For the constellations that pass through the northernmost gates belong to the path of Enlil, those that pass through the central gates belong to the path of Anu, and those that pass through the southernmost gates belong to the path of Ea, though it is absolutely clear that there are no fixed boundaries.[74]

In this scheme, the northern path of Enlil contains 33 stars or constellations, the presumably equatorial path of Anu contains 23 stars or constellations, and the southern path of Ea contains 15 stars or constellations.

Now, in the Ugaritic sources mentioned above, we noted the connection of the *kusarikku/ditānu* with the cult of the dead heroic kings. The position of the star connected with the dead heroes in the lowest part of the sky would fit well with the Babylonian idea of the various strata of star circles that made up the universe.

74. Hunger and Pingree, *MUL.APIN*, 139.

6.6. *Behemoth in Neo-Hittite Art*

While representations of Leviathan-like creatures are commonly attested in Neo-Hittite art, the identification of Behemoth-like creatures is a more difficult proposition. We have seen that in stele G3 from MB Ebla, there is a depiction of a human-headed, bearded bull-man that is likely to be identified with the Mesopotamian *kusarikku* and, in turn, the Syrian *ditānu*.

Orthmann has discussed the various representations of the *Stiermensch* or "Bull-man" in Neo-Hittite art.[75] He notes:

> Als Stiermensch wird em Mischwesen bezeichnet, das seit sehr früher Zeit in Mesopotamien vorkommt und aus dem Hinterkörper eines Stieres und dem Oberkörper eines Menschen zusammengesetzt ist. Diese beiden Bestandteile der Figur werden kaum abgewandelt, sodaß die Unterschiede im Erscheinungsbild zwischen den Darstellungen der verschiedensten Epochen nur Einzelheiten betreffen.[76]

The representations of the *Stiermenschen* noted by Orthmann generally depict a pair of bearded bull-men shown facing each other and holding long staffs in their hands, apparently because of these demons' function of guarding gates. A similar disposition is found for the *laḫmu* figures, who resemble *kusarikku*'s in many ways, but who are fully human and clearly not *Mischwesen*. Of interest is Wiggermann's demonstration that the name *laḫmu* means "hairy ones."[77] Now, I have suggested on p. **88** that the *kusarrikku* constellation is to be identified with the ancient Greek constellation of Centaurus. According to Hunger and Pingree,[78] the modern constellation of Centaurus is to be equated with ancient Babylonian star group EN.TE.NA.BAR.ḪUM = *ḫabiṣirānu*. In the Sumerian name, the element EN.TE.NA means "winter," and the element BAR.ḪUM, "hairy." The Sumerian element meaning "hairy" is possibly connected to the hairy nature of both the *laḫmu* and *kusarikku* creatures, although this is uncertain. The Akkadian word *ḫabiṣirānu*, which is of unknown etymology, denotes "mouse," but it may originally have meant "hairy." If this understanding is true, then the term would have been used to refer to a particularly hairy creature—namely, the mouse.

---

75. Orthmann, *Späthethitischen Kunst*, 306–10.

76. Ibid., 307.

77. F. A. M. Wiggermann, *Babylonian Prophylactic Figures: The Ritual Texts* (Amsterdam: Free University, 1986) 286.

78. Hunger and Pingree, MUL.APIN, 138.

7. *Representations of Bird Monsters in Neo-Hittite Art*

7.1. Bird Monsters in Middle Bronze Ebla

At Ebla, we have seen that a bird figure appears in Register A4 of the MB stele from area G3, notably in the same register that shows a Leviathan-like figure. The juxtaposition is noteworthy and important to this discussion. I have pointed out above that the Ebla stele appears to be an Uranographic monument and, if this is true, then the bird figure we find there should be connected to a constellation. The most likely candidate for this star group would be the Sumerian constellation of the *uga* bird "crow, raven," which equates to the Akkadian term *āribu*. As is well known, the Babylonian constellation of the crow was borrowed into ancient Greek astronomy from Mesopotamia as *korax*, Latin *Corvus*, and our modern Corvus, the crow.

The modern constellation of Corvus lies in the vicinity of two other notable constellations that figure in ancient myths. We may note Crater, "The Cup," and Hydra, "The Water Snake." The constellation of the cup can clearly be linked to the cup that appears in the Ebla stele in register A3, where it stands as the focal point of what appears to be a banquet scene.

It is of interest and relevant to this discussion of constellations that the ancient Greeks had a second designation for the constellation we call the Crater, namely, *Argeion hudrion*, "The Water Bucket." It is also noteworthy that the constellation of the water bucket can be linked all the way back to an ancient Sumerian myth, Inanna and Šukaletuda. A passage in this myth mentions four discrete elements, the god Enki, a crow, a date palm, and a water bucket. The meaning of the passage as a whole is enigmatic, and I give an English translation below:

> [48] Full of wisdom, he (Enki) adds the following words:
> [49] "Raven, I shall give you instructions. Pay attention to my instructions.
> [50] Raven, in the shrine I shall give you instructions. Pay attention to my instructions.
> [51] First, chop up (?) and chew (?) the kohl for the incantation priests of Eridu
> [52] with the oil and water which are to be found in a lapis lazuli bowl and are placed
> [53] in the back-room of the shrine.
> [54] It chopped up (?) and chewed (?)
> [55] Then plant them in a trench for leeks in a vegetable plot;
> [56] Then you should pull out (?). . . ."

Table 4. Astronomical Correlations

Element in Sumerian Myth	*Babylonian Constellation*	*Greek Constellation*	*Modern Constellation*
Enki	Gula	Υδροχοος, "Water Carrier"	Aquarius "Water Carrier"
Uga bird	Crow	Κοραξ, "Crow"	Corvus "Crow"
Date palm	Date palm frond of Er	Κορη, "Maiden"	Virgo[a] "Maiden"
Shaduf or Water Bucket	—	Αργειον ὑδριον, "Water bucket"	Crater "Cup"

a. Inanna's connection with the date palm is well known.

[57] Now, what did one say to another?
[58] What further did one add to the other in detail?[79]

The text tells us that the raven paid attention carefully to the instructions of Enki and then performed the deed exactly as he had been ordered. It seems to be some kind of cultic act:

[69] That a bird like the raven, performing the work of man,
[70] should make the counterweight blocks of the shadouf bump up and settle down;
[71] that it should make the counterweight blocks of the shadouf bump down and rise up—who had ever seen such a thing before?
[72] Then the raven rose up from this oddity,
[73] and climbed up it—a date palm!—with a harness.
[74] It rubbed off the kohl (?) . . . which it had stuffed into its beak onto the pistils (?).
[75] . . . just as with a date palm, which . . . ,
[77] a tree growing forever—who has ever seen such a thing before?
[78] Its scaly leaves surround its palm heart.
[79] Its dried palm-fronds serve as weaving material.
[80] Its shoots are like a surveyor's gleaming line;
[81] they are fit for the king's fields.
[82] Its (?) branches are used in the king's palace for cleaning.

79. Konrad Volk, *Inanna und Šukaletuda: Zur historisch-politischen Deutung eines sumerischen Litaraturwerkes* (Santag 7; Wiesbaden: Harrassowitz, 1995) 48. The English translation is from Jeremy A. Black, *The Literature of Ancient Sumer* (Oxford: Oxford University Press, 2004) 199..

Table 5. Cross-Cultural Parallels

Sumerian Myth Inanna and Šukaletuda	*Greek Tale*	*Modern Constellation*
Enki	—	Aquarius
Uga bird	Raven	Corvus
Date palm	Fig tree	Virgo
Shaduf or Water-bucket	Cup	Crater
—	Water snake	Hydra

> [83] Its dates, which are piled up near purified barley,
> [84] are fit for the temples of the great gods.
> [85] That a bird like the raven, performing the work of man,
> [86] makes the counterweight blocks of the shadouf bump up and settle down;
> [87] that it makes the counterweight blocks of the shadouf bump down and rise up—who had ever seen such a thing before?
> [88] At his master's command, the raven stepped into the Abzu.[80]

It is of interest that the actions of the *uga* bird here are paralleled by modern date pollinators as Campbell Thompson describes:[81]

> The word for the rope used by the man who climbs the palm to fertilize the [female flowers] is *tubalû* / . . . . I have seen him, carrying the pollen in a little muslin bag, as he climbs the palm with both hands and feet, having the rope in a loop round himself and the tree to support him, exactly as described in Pliny Natural History xiii.

In the Sumerian myth Inanna and Šukaletuda, astronomical correlations can be made as in table 4. A similar cast of characters is found in an ancient Greek tale that recounts that the figures of the raven, cup, and hydra were cast into the sky because of the god Apollo's anger at the crow's tardiness in carrying out a mission to bring the god some figs. The cross-cultural parallels are presented in table 5.

The cumulative data assembled here suggest that the bird that appears in register A4 of the Ebla stele is a representation of a crow or raven.

80. Volk, *Inanna und Šukaletuda*, 119. The translation is from Black, *Literature of Sumer*.
81. Reginald Campbell Thompson, *A Dictionary of Assyrian Botany* (London: British Academy, 1949) 310.

7.2. Representations in Neo-Hittite Art of a Bird Genius Holding a Bucket and "Cone"

7.2.1. Aleppo

Block 9 found in the Adad Temple at Aleppo shown in Kohlmeyer's book[82] depicts a winged *Mischwesen* with a avian head, who is shown holding what looks like a cone in his left hand and a bucket in his right. Kohlmeyer points out that this equipment is shown later in Neo-Assyrian reliefs depicting a bird-headed *Mischwesen* possibly performing the pollination of the "Sacred Tree,"[83] as for example, in the reliefs of the palace of Ashurnasirpal II at Nimrud.

Block 11 at Aleppo[84] similarly depicts a winged *Mischwesen*, but this time he has a a leonine head; the genius holds a "cone" in his left hand, and in his right hand a bucket.

7.2.2. Sakçagözü

Sakçagözü A2 depicts a winged *Mischwesen*, probably with a bird head, although the photo is unclear. He is holding a bucket in his right hand. Since the published photo is poor, it is hard to determine what he holds in his other hand. It clearly corresponds to Block 11 at Aleppo, discussed above.

Sakçagözü A10 similarly depicts a winged *Mischwesen* that holds a "cone" in his left hand and a bucket in his right hand, so it is comparable with Block 9 at Aleppo.

One might be tempted to identify this pollinating bird in the reliefs with the great Ziz bird that appears in much later Jewish folklore. The Ziz was a giant griffin-like bird said to be large enough to be able to block out the sun with its great wingspan. It has been described in great detail in a recent article by Wazana, who compares it to the famous Anzu bird of Sumerian and Babylonian tradition.[85] In the summary of her work she writes:

> This study will attempt to add another member to the group of creatures belonging to the sphere of combat myths. Anzu, a mythic Mesopotamian bird, left its talon prints in the Bible. As in the cases of Leviathan and Behemoth, traditions regarding Anzu are hinted at in the Bible and more fully developed in post-biblical literature. Furthermore, this discussion has

82. Kohlmeyer, *Der Tempel des Wettergottes*, 100 and fig. 139.

83. Whether or not this is a pollinating scene has been hotly debated by scholars. For a complete discussion of the issue, see Mariana Giovino, *The Assyrian Sacred Tree: A History of Interpretations* (OBO 230; Fribourg: Academic Press / Göttingen: Vandenhoeck & Ruprecht, 2007).

84. Kohlmeyer, *Der Tempel des Wettergottes*, 101, fig. 141.

85. Nili Wazana, "Anzu and Ziz: Great Mythical Birds in Ancient Near Eastern, Biblical, and Rabbinic Tradition," *JANESCU* 31(2009) 111–35.

Table 6. Banquet Scenes in Neo-Hittite Art That Are Juxtaposed with Chaos Monsters

Site	*Orthmann Sigla*	*Description*
Carchemish	Ab/4[a]	Seated male figure (ruler) holding a cup before a table loaded with food; musician
Carchemish	F/5[b]	Male musicians facing right
Carchemish	F/7a[c]	Male musicians facing right
Carchemish	F/8–12[d]	Female musicians (sistrum players) facing left
Carchemish	F/13–16[e]	Attendants bringing food
Tell Halaf	A/3/171[f]	Solitary seated male figure (ruler) with cup beside two bull-men holding up a sun disk
Karatepe	A/16–20[g]	Procession of figures bearing food before seated male figure (ruler)
Karatepe	B/1[h]	Procession of figures bearing food; musicians
Karatepe	B/2[i]	Standing figures before seated male figure (ruler)
Sakçagözü	A/5[j]	Standing figure with cup (ruler)
Sakçagözü	A/6–7[k]	Attendants to standing figure (ruler; one has a fly wisk, the other is a falconer)
Sakçagözü	A/13[l]	Depiction of a ruler
Zincirli	A/6[m]	Two standing figures with cups
Zincirli	B/3[n]	Two seated figures with cups; one male, one female
Zincirli	B/15[o]	Seated figure
Zincirli	B/18[p]	Musicians
Zincirli	F/5–8[q]	Musicians

a. Orthmann, *Späthethitischen Kunst*, 498 and pl. 21c.
b. Ibid., 507 and pl. 29c.
c. Ibid., 507–8 and pl. 29 d, f.
d. Ibid., 508 and pls. 29–30.
e. Ibid., 508–9 and pl. 30.
f. Ibid., pl. 10g.
g. Ibid., 491 and pls. 16–17.
h. Ibid., 494 and pls. 18c, 76a.
i. Ibid., 494 and pls. 18d, 76e.
j. Ibid., 530and pls. 49d and 73d.
k. Ibid., 530 and pl. 50a.
l. Ibid., 532 and pl. 51a.
m. Ibid., 538 and pl. 56a.
n. Ibid., 539 and pl. 57c.
o. Ibid., 541 and pl. 59c.
p. Ibid., 541 and pl. 59e.
q. Ibid., 546 and pls. 63g, 63f, and 64a.

> consequences for the reconstruction of the general course of transmission and change that mythical traditions have undergone from ancient Near Eastern traditions to the Bible and to classical rabbinic sources.[86]

If Wazana is correct that Ziz is a later form of the Babylonian Anzu bird, then Ziz would clearly not be connected with the crow figure that we find depicted in Register A4 of the MB Ebla stele.

8. *The Celebratory Banquet after the Defeat of the Chaos Monsters*

As noted above, at both MB Ebla and at Sakçagözü, we find depictions on monumental art of a banquet scene right next to representations of mythical chaos monsters, one of which can be identified with the figure of Leviathan. This particular grouping is striking, and surely it is not merely coincidental. It leads to the conclusion that the banquet scenes found in MB Eblaite and Neo-Hittite art are representations of a celebratory banquet comparable with the banquet described in the epic *Enūma eliš*, when Marduk holds a joyous feast to celebrate his victory over Tiʾāmat. As Maul indicates:

> Every year during the new-years celebration, Marduk's battle against the forces of chaos, the triumphal victory of the gods and the ordering act of creation, was re-enacted. As described in the myth Enūma eliš, the Babylonian gods assembled every year for this occasion. Their cultic images traveled in celebratory processions from Babylonian cities to this event. These (cultic images of the) Gods were assembled on the pedestal called the "sacred hill" in order to give up their power to Marduk, king of the gods, so that he could (as described in the myth) go into battle against those forces, embodied by Marduk's opponent Tiamat, which threatened the continued existence of the world.[87]

There are several depictions of banquet scenes in Neo-Hittite art that are juxtaposed with depictions of chaos monsters. The evidence is summarized in table 6.

9. *Conclusion*

In his article "Leviathan, Behemoth and Ziz: Jewish Messianic Symbols in Art," Gutman makes the following observations:

86. Ibid., 113.
87. Cited from Maul, http://prelectur.stanford.edu/lecturers/maul/capitalsnotes.html.

> Leviathan and Behemoth, the legendary monsters of the Bible, most probably belonged to an Ancient Near Eastern mythological context, but they assume a new symbolic meaning in the late classical period. The transformation may be due to the revolutionary changes introduced into Judaism under Pharisaic leadership when prime emphasis came to be placed on personal, individual salvation in the world to come. Hence, we find for the first time in the apocryphal-pseudepigraphal and the later rabbinic literature that these mythical beasts are destined for the meal of the righteous in the world to come.[88]

The idea that the "celebratory banquet" motif is a late innovation is also echoed in remarks by Gaster:

> At the end of the present era, Behemoth, like Leviathan, will challenge God, but will suffer defeat. His carcass will then be served as food to the righteous (B.B. 740; Palestinian Targ. Nom. 9:26). This is probably a Jewish version of the Iranian myth concerning the ultimate defeat of the mythical ox Hudhayaos, for whom a similar fate is said to be reserved.[89]

Additionally, Wazana notes that the issue of whether or not rabbinic sources were dependent on ancient Near Eastern traditions is a very thorny question. She writes:

> Studies dealing with mythic traditions in rabbinic literature have asked whether they are the recurrent remains of older traditions or inner-Jewish developments, namely, memory or interpretation. When trying to reconstruct the original Israelite epic, Cassuto claimed that midrashic mythical motifs fed on an ancient Near Eastern heritage, growing from traditions current among the people and renewed in rabbinic literature. . . . Daniel Boyarin . . . called Cassuto's claim that mythic materials were preserved in folk tradition till later periods "naive and unnecessary."[90]

The art-historical and textual evidence assembled in this essay clearly indicates that the motif of a celebratory banquet apparently held after the defeat of chaos monsters has deep roots in ancient Near Eastern mythology and that it can be traced all the way back in Syrian art to MB Ebla, as evidenced by a stele found in temple G3, which, in two adjacent panels, depicts both a Leviathan creature and a celebratory banquet scene. The same motifs are frequently attested in later Neo-Hittite art in similar juxtapositions.

88. Joseph Gutman, "Leviathan, Behemoth and Ziz: Jewish Messianic Symbols in Art," *HUCA* 38 (1968) 224.

89. Theodor Gaster, "Behemoth," *IDB* 376.

90. Wazana, "Anzu and Ziz," 129.

Once upon a Time in Kiškiluša

The Dragon-Slayer Myth in Central Anatolia

Amir Gilan

Tel Aviv University

From Hittite Illuyanka to Harry Potter's Hungarian Horntail, dragon-snakes are part of humanity itself. "An adequate account of the development of the dragon-legend," writes G. Elliot Smith,[1] one of the pioneers of comparative dragonology, "would represent the history of the expression of mankind's aspirations and fears during the past fifty centuries or more. For the dragon was evolved along with civilization itself." Almost as popular as the dragon himself are stories about the dragon-slayer, the hero that overcomes the monster.[2] Many of the dragon-slayer stories follow a relatively constant narratological structure[3] but could be applied to convey different meanings. Most of the heroes must kill the dragon in order to prevent a catastrophe of some sort. Only a few of them get the monster at the first attempt. The hero often fails miserably at first and manages to slay the dragon only with helpers and the special weapons that they provide. Many of these monsters have in common a strong affinity to water—an ambivalent element in itself.[4] "The fundamental element in the dragon's power," adds G. Elliot Smith,[5] writing on the Egyptian mythological lore, "is the control of water. Both in its beneficent and destructive aspects, water was regarded as animated by the dragon."

Author's note: This essay is a revised translation of my German article "Das Huhn, das Ei und die Schlange: Mythos und Ritual im Illuyanka-Text," in *Hethitische Literatur* (ed. M. Hutter and S. Hutter-Braunsar; AOAT 391; Münster: Ugarit-Verlag, 2011) 99–114.

1. G. Elliot Smith, *The Evolution of the Dragon* (Manchester: Manchester University Press, 1919) 76.

2. Joseph Fontenrose, *Python: A Study of Delphic Myth and Its Origins* (Berkeley: University of California Press, 1959); Qiguang Zhao, *A Study of Dragons, East and West* (Asian Thought and Culture 11; New York: Peter Lang, 1992) 119–41; Calvert Watkins, *How to Kill a Dragon* (Oxford: Oxford University Press, 1995).

3. Vladimir Propp, *The Morphology of the Folktale* (trans. Laurence Scott; Austin: University of Texas Press, 1968); Neil Forsyth, *The Old Enemy: Satan and the Combat Myth* (Princeton: Princeton University Press, 1987).

4. Zhao, *Study of Dragons*, 113–14.

5. G. E. Smith, *The Evolution of the Dragon*, 103.

In the ancient Near East, the story can be traced to the third millennium B.C.E.[6] Tišpak of Ešnunna fought a dragon (*labbu*) of immense magnitude.[7] In the Syrian-Hittite world, we first encounter the mythological combat between the Storm god and the sea in the Old Babylonian period in a letter, published by Jean-Marie Durand, in which Addu of Aleppo reminds King Zimri-Lim of Mari that it was with the Addu's weapons that Zimri-Lim had won back his father's kingdom—weapons that he, Addu, had used to fight against *têmtum*.[8] The weapons of the Storm god are likewise mentioned in a very fragmentary mythological text written in Hittite, the Bišaiša-Text (CTH 350.3). In the fragment of the story that survives, the mountain Bišaiša attempts to persuade the goddess Ištar/Šaoška to spare his life—after he has raped the sleeping goddess—by offering her a valuable piece of information: the whereabouts of the weapons of the Storm god, with which he overcame the sea.[9] Allusions to this story can also be found, in my opinion, in the so-called Puḫānu-Text.[10]

The conflict between the Storm god and the sea is also featured in the Hurro-Hittite *Kumarbi Cycle*. Many of the opponents created by Kumarbi in order to regain the kingship over the gods are closely related to water.

The Song of the Sea, found in Hittite and in Hurrian fragments documents the battle fought between Teššop and the Sea. The composition was sung, according to the colophons of the texts, during a festival in honor of Mount Ḫazzi (Zaphon, Kasion, the Keldağ by the Bay of İskenderun, the scene of many dragon-slayer stories).[11]

6. Jean-Marie Durand, "Le mythologème du combat entre le dieu de l'orage et la mer en Mésopotamie," *MARI* 7 (1993) 143; Nicholas Wyatt, "Arms and the King: The Earliest Allusions to the Chaoskampf Motif and Their Implications for the Interpretation of the Ugaritic and Biblical Traditions," in *There's Such Divinity Doth Hedge a King: Selected Essays of Nicolas Wyatt on Royal Ideology in Ugaritic and Old Testament Literature* (Burlington, VT: Ashgate, 2005) 152–53.

7. F. A. M. Wiggermann, "Tišpak, His Seal, and the Dragon mušḫuššu," in *To the Euphrates and Beyond: Archaeological Studies in Honour of Maurits N. van Loon* (ed. Odette M. Haex, Hans H. Curvers, and Peter M. M. G. Akkermans; Rotterdam: Balkema, 1989) 117–33; Wyatt, "Arms and the King," 153–55.

8. Durand, "Le dieu de l'orage et la mer," 41–61; Daniel Schwemer, *Die Wettergottgestalten Mesopotamiens und Nordsyriens im Zeitalter der Keilschriftkulturen: Materialien und Studien nach den schriftlichen Quellen* (Wiesbaden: Harrassowitz, 2001) 226–32.

9. KUB 33.108. Schwemer, ibid., 233; Volkert Haas, *Die hethitische Literatur* (Berlin: de Gruyter, 2006) 212–13.

10. Amir Gilan, "Der Puḫānu-Text: Theologischer Streit und politische Opposition in der althethitischen Literatur," *AoF* 31 (2004) 277–79.

11. Franca Pecchioli Daddi and Anna Maria Polvani, *La mitologia ittita* (Testi del Vicino Oriente antico; Brescia: Paideia, 1990) 147; Daniel Schwemer, "The Storm-Gods of the Ancient Near East: Summary, Synthesis, Recent Studies, Part 2," *JANER* 8 (2008) 25; Jürgen Lorenz and Elisabeth Rieken, "Überlegungen zur Verwendung mythologischer Texte bei den Hethitern," in *Festschrift für Gernot Wilhelm anlässlich seines 65. Geburtstages am*

Another opponent of Teššop was Ḫedammu, a snake-like monster of huge proportions that Kumarbi bore with the daughter of the sea.[12] Ḫedammu was about to destroy the world but was stopped with the help of the goddess Ištar/Šaoška. The goddess and her two handmaidens bathed on the beach, seduced the monster, and caused Ḫedammu to become so excited that he came out of the water, where he met his end. The story shows many parallels with the first *Illuyanka* story.[13] Ullikummi, a giant stone tower that was created by Kumarbi's ejaculating his sperm on a rock in the middle of a lake, is likewise closely connected to water.[14]

The best-known Hittite versions of the *Drachentöter* tradition are found in the so-called *Illuyanka* text (CTH 321), one of the better-known Hittite compositions. The text recounts two battles between the Storm god of the Sky and the serpent (^{MUŠ}*illuyanka-*, ^{MUŠ}*elliyanku-*).[15] The text was edited already in the 1920s by Archibald Sayce.[16] The close parallels to Greek mythological lore, especially to the Typhon traditions, were noted only a few years later, by

28. Januar 2010 (ed. Jeanette C. Fincke; Dresden: ISLET, 2010) 229–30; Robin Lane Fox, *Travelling Heroes: Greeks and Their Myths in the Epic Age of Homer* (New York: Random, 2010) 242–301.

12. Beatrice André-Salvini and Mirjo Salvini, "Un nouveau vocabulaire trilingue sumérien-akkadien-hourrite de Ras Shamra," in *General Studies and Excavations at Nuzi 10/2* (SCCNH 9; Bethesda, MD: CDL, 1998) 9–10; Meindert Dijkstra, "The Myth of the *apsi* 'the (Sea)Dragon' in the Hurrian Tradition: A New Join (KBo 27,180)," *UF* 37 (2005) 315–28.

13. See most recently Harry A. Hoffner Jr., "A Brief Commentary on the Hittite Illuyanka Myth (CTH 321)," in *Studies Presented to Robert D. Biggs: June 4, 2004* (ed. Martha Roth et al.; AS 27; Chicago: Oriental Institute, 2007) 125.

14. Translations of these myths are offered by H. A. Hoffner Jr., *Hittite Myths* (2nd ed.; SBLWAW 2; Atlanta: Scholars Press, 1998). See now also the online editions in http://www.hethport.uni-wuerzburg.de/txhet_myth/textindex.php?g=myth&x=x.

15. Scholars disagree on the etymology of the word. Whereas some scholars postulate a non-Indo-European, Ḫattian, origin (most recently, Alwin Kloekhorst, *Etymological Dictionary of the Hittite Inherited Lexicon* [Leiden Indo-European Etymological Dictionary Series 5; Leiden: Brill, 2008] 384), others suggest an Indo-European etymology. According to Joshua T. Katz ("How to Be a Dragon in Indo-European: Hittite *illuyankaš* and Its Linguistic and Cultural Congeners in Latin, Greek, and Germanic," in *Mír Curad: Studies in Honor of Calvert Watkins* [ed. Jay Jassanoff, H. Craig Melchert, and Lisi Oliver; Innsbrücker Beiträge zur Sprachwissen 92; Innsbrück: Institut für Sprachwissenschaft der Universität Innsbruck, 1998] 317–34), the word is constructed from *illi/u*, "eel," and *anga, "snake." See now Norbert Oettinger ("Nochmals hethitisch illuyanka," *Investigationes Anatolicae: Gedenkschrift für Erich Neu* [ed. Jörg Klinger, Elisabeth Rieken, and Christel Rüster; Studien zu den Boğazköy-Texten 52; Wiesbaden: Harrassowitz, 2010] 189–96), who translates the first element, *illi/u*, as "dragon," which he relates to ^{NA_4}*elluešar*, "dragon's den"; cf. idem, "Die indogermanischen Wörter für 'Schlange'," in *Ex Anatolia Lux: Anatolian and Indo-European Studies in Honor of H. Craig Melchert* (ed. Ronald Kim et al.; Ann Arbor, MI: Beech Stave, 2010) 278–84.

16. Archibald Sayce, "Hittite Legend of the War with the Great Serpent," *Journal of the Royal Asiatic Society* (1922) 177–90.

Walter Porzig (1930).[17] Since then, the text has appeared in several editions and various translations and has been studied from different perspectives in numerous articles offering a wide range of interpretations.[18]

The *Illuyanka* text owes its popularity to its ostensible antiquity and its evident resemblance to other dragon-slayer stories. As was shown by Calvert Watkins,[19] many dragon-slayer stories share poetic forms found already in the *Illuyanka* stories. Moreover, the story is offered in two, structurally very similar versions, both appearing in one and the same composition.[20] Last but not least, the stories, especially the first one, seem to be embedded in ritual action—an assumption that has heavily influenced its interpretation. This essay will be dedicated to this last aspect, which is indeed essential to the interpretation of the myths. In the following pages, therefore, I will take a closer look at the ways that the *Illuyanka* stories are embedded in the text. On the way, some of the interpretations that have been offered so far in modern Hittittological scholarship concerning these stories will be challenged, and new ones will be offered.

Perhaps the most well-accepted notion about the *Illuyanka* stories concerns the context of their performance. The *Illuyanka* stories are embedded in what is usually considered to be a description of a festival, usually identified as the *Purulli* festival. According to most scholars, the myths were performed during this festival, whereas the first myth even serves clearly as an etiology, explaining why the festival was celebrated. The *Illuyanka* text became, therefore, a prime example in modern scholarship of a cosmological myth embedded in ritual practice in Hittite religious literature.[21] Before we take a closer look at these claims, some notes on the relations between myth and ritual are in order.

17. Walter Porzig, "Illuyankas und Typhon," *Kleinasiatische Forschung* 1 (1930) 379–86. For comparisons with other traditions, see Volkert Haas, "Medea und Jason im Lichte hethitischer Quellen," *Acta Antiqua Academiae Scientiarum Hungaricae* 26 (1978) 241–53; and Jan N. Bremmer, "The Myth of the Golden Fleece," *JANER* 6 (2006) 9–39. See also Robin Lane Fox, *Travelling Heroes in the Epic Age of Homer* (New York: Vintage, 2009) 280–301.

18. Gary Beckman, "The Anatolian Myth of Illuyanka," *JANES(CU)* 14 (1982) 11–25; José García Trabazo, *Textos religiosos hititas: Mitos, plegarias y rituales* (Madrid: Trotta, 2002) 75–103; Elisabeth Rieken et al., eds., hethiter.net/: CTH 321 (INTR 2010–11–23). A recent, critical overview of all these studies is offered in Hoffner, "Brief Commentary on the Hittite Illuyanka Myth."

19. Watkins, *How to Kill a Dragon*.

20. See Hoffner, "Brief Commentary on the Hittite Illuyanka Myth," 123–30 for an overview of the different story elements found in the *Illuyanka* stories and their interpretation.

21. Beckman, "Illuyanka," 24; Erich Neu, "Der alte Orient: Mythen der Hethiter," *Bochumer Altertumswissenschaftliches Colloquium* 2 (1990) 103; Haas, *Die hethitische Literatur*, 97; Schwemer, "Storm-Gods 2," 24; Piotr Taracha, *Religions of Second Millennium Anatolia* (Dresdener Beiträge zur Hethitologie 27; Wiesbaden: Harrassowitz, 2009) 137; Franca

The ties between myth and ritual have strongly preoccupied the modern study of religions, especially in the first half of the twentieth century.[22] The myth-ritual theory is connected to scholars such as William Robertson Smith, who first worked out the dependence of myth on ritual. Sir James Frazer expanded and modified the theory in the different editions of his monumental work *The Golden Bough.*[23] Frazer studied various vegetation deities, such as Adonis, Attis, Demeter, Tammuz, Osiris, and Dionysus, whose death and rebirth were celebrated ritualistically during the New Year Festival in order to guarantee, according to Frazer, nature's coming back to life. "Under the names of Osiris, Tammuz, Adonis, and Attis," writes Gaster in the *New Golden Bough*, "the people of Egypt and western Asia represented the yearly decay and revival of life, especially of vegetable life, which they personified as a god who annually died and rose again from the dead. In name and detail the rites varied from place to place: in substance they were the same."[24] The meaning of myth to ritual was, for Frazer, fundamental. Segal puts it this way: "Myth gives ritual its original and soul meaning. Without the myth of the death and rebirth of that god, the death and rebirth of the god of vegetation would scarcely be ritualistically enacted."[25]

The biblical scholar Samuel Henry Hooke studied ancient Near Eastern religions and managed to reconstruct cult patterns that are quite similar to Frazer's drama of death and rebirth.[26] Hooke could identify in many New Year, as well as other central calendric festivals, the same elements. These include a dramatic representation of the death and resurrection of the god; the recitation or symbolic representation of the myth of creation; a ritual combat in

Pecchioli Daddi, "Connections between KI.LAM and the *Tetešḫapi* Festival: The Expressions *ḫalukan tarnanzi* and *ḫeun tarnanzi*," in *Pax Hethitica: Studies on the Hittites and Their Neighbours in Honour of Itamar Singer* (ed. Yoram Cohen, Amir Gilan, and Jared L. Miller; Studien zu den Boğazköy Texten 51; Wiesbaden: Harrassowitz, 2010) 264, to name but a few examples.

22. Henk S. Versnel, "What's Sauce for the Goose Is Sauce for the Gander: Myth and Ritual, Old and New," in *Approaches to Greek Myth* (ed. Lowell Edmunds; Baltimore: Johns Hopkins University Press, 1990) 25–90; Kathrin Bell, *Ritual: Perspectives and Dimensions* (New York: Oxford University Press, 1997) 3–22; Robert A. Segal, *The Myth and Ritual Theory: An Anthology* (Malden, MA: Blackwell, 1998) 1–13; idem, *Myth: A Very Short Introduction* (Oxford: Oxford University Press, 2004) 61–78. A more elaborate overview on the myth and ritual theory in the context of the *Illuyanka* stories is found now in my article "Das Huhn, das Ei und die Schlange: Mythos und Ritual im Illuyanka-Text." I will return to this subject in greater detail elsewhere.

23. James George Frazer, *The Golden Bough: A Study in Magic and Religion* (3rd ed.; 12 vols.; New York: MacMillan, 1910–15).

24. Theodore Gaster, ed., *The New Golden Bough: A New Abridgement of the Classic Work* (New York: Criterion, 1961) 164.

25. Segal, *Myth: A Very Short Introduction*, 66.

26. Versnel, "What's Sauce for the Goose Is Sauce for the Gander," 35–38.

which the triumph of the god over his enemies was depicted; sacred marriage; a triumphal procession in which the king played the part of the god followed by a procession of lesser gods or visiting deities.[27]

Central for the myth and ritual theory was the Babylonian Akītu-Festival.[28] Scenes such as the humiliation of the king in the Esagila, the recitation of the *Enūma eliš* within the festival, and the so-called Marduk Ordeal all provided the myth and ritual theorists with perfect materials concerning the relations between deity and king, myth and ritual.

Hooke's work was further developed by Theodor Herzl Gaster in his book *Thespis* (1950).[29] For Gaster too, myths were real myths only if they were performed in ritual. Only the performance of myth in ritual could create cultic drama. In his book, Gaster presented several ancient Near Eastern myths that demonstrate the seasonal pattern, among them several Anatolian myths such as the Telipinu- and other disappearance myths, the mythos of the Frost *ḫaḫḫima*, as well as the story he called the "Snaring of the Dragon"—the *Illuyanka* text, performed during the *Purulli* festival.[30]

Today, the cultic drama of parallel mythic and ritualistic death and rebirth seems almost obsolete.[31] It seems now that myths and rituals could relate in numerous ways to each other, or not relate at all. Myths could be adapted in many different cultic contexts, for example, or in none.[32] Critics, such as Fontenrose[33] and J. Z. Smith[34] have shown that Frazer's work included many mistakes and inaccuracies. In this manner, the myth and ritual interpretation

27. Samuel Henry Hooke, "The Myth and Ritual Pattern of the Ancient Near East" = chap. 1 in idem, *Myth and Ritual: Essays on the Myth and Ritual of the Hebrews in Relation to the Cultures of the Ancient Near East* (London: Oxford University Press, 1933) apud Segal, *The Myth and Ritual Theory*, 88–89.

28. Jonathan Zittel Smith, *Imagining Religion: From Babylon to Jonestown* (Chicago: University of Chicago Press, 1982) 91; Versnel, "Sauce for the Goose," 36; Bell, *Ritual: Perspectives and Dimensions*, 17–20. On the festival, see Julye Bidmead, *The Akitu Festival: Religious Continuity and Royal Legitimation in Mesopotamia* (Piscataway, NJ: Gorgias, 2002).

29. Theodor Herzl Gaster, *Thespis: Ritual, Myth and Drama in the Ancient Near East* (New York: Schuman, 1950).

30. See, however, the very critical review of the book by Albrecht Goetze, "Review of Th. H. Gaster: *Thespis: Ritual, Myth and Drama in the Ancient Near East*," *JCS* 6 (1952) 99–102.

31. J. Z. Smith, *Imagining Religion*, 91; Versnel, "Sauce for the Goose," 44

32. Walter Burkert, *Homo necans* (Berlin: de Gruyter, 1972) 39–44; Greg S. Kirk, *The Nature of Greek Myths* (Harmondsworth, Middlesex: Penguin, 1974) 31–37; Jan N. Bremmer, *Götter, Mythen und Heiligtümer im antiken Griechenland* (Berlin: Ullstein, 1998) 74.

33. Joseph Fontenrose, *The Ritual Theory of Myth* (Folklore Studies 18; Berkeley: University of California Press, 1966).

34. Jonathan Zittel Smith, "When the Bough Breaks," *HR* 12 (1973) 342–71; idem, *Imagining Religion*, 157.

of the Akītu-Festival was refuted in Assyriological studies.[35] The studies of the myth and ritual school, concludes Catherine Bell, almost became myths themselves.[36] However, in the Hittitological interpretations of the *Illuyanka* myths, this strand of interpretation is still alive and kicking.

A strong Frazerian interpretation of the *Illuyanka* stories is offered by Volkert Haas in various publications:

> Mit dem Illuyanka-Text liegt ein jahreszeitlicher Mythos vor, indem sich im kultischen Nachvollzug des Urzeitgeschehens die Ordnung und die Kräfte des Kosmos erneuern. Der Mythos ist in zwei Fassungen überliefert. Am Ende des landwirtschaftlichen Jahres im Herbst nach der Ernte besiegt der hethitische Python Illuyanka, die Personifikation des Winters, den die Kräfte des Frühlings verkörpernden Wettergott Tarhunta, der nun außer Funktion getreten ist und sich während der Wintermonate in der Gewalt des Illuyanka befindet.
>
> Zu Beginn des Frühlings, mit dem Erwachen der Wachstumskräfte, folgt ein zweiter Kampf, in dem der Wettergott mit der Hilfe seines Sohnes bzw. des Menschen Hupašiya den Illuyanka besiegt. Der Mythos, der Teil des althethitischen Neujahrsfestrituals ist, endet mit der Ätiologie des sakralen Königtums. Wahrscheinlich wurde er auch mimisch dargestellt.[37]

The elements of Frazer's cultic drama here are obvious: cosmic drama, order and chaos, renewal of the vegetation, the role of the king, and the performance in ritual. Some of these elements were not accepted by other, more-skeptical scholars.[38] For example, the identification of the *Purulli* festival as the Old Hittite New Year festival did not find many supporters.[39] Other myth and ritual elements are, however, widely accepted. Three central elements are given here:

1. The myths were performed during the *Purulli* festival. "The Text," notes for example Hans Gustav Güterbock "states expressly that the story was recited at the *Purulli* festival of the Storm god, one of the great yearly cult ceremonies."[40] This, as far as I can see, is accepted by everyone. In fact, the *Illuyanka* text

35. Wolfram von Soden, "Gibt es ein Zeugnis dafür, dass die Babylonier an die Wiederauferstehung Marduks geglaubt haben?" ZA 51 (1955) 130–66; Jeremy A. Black, "The New Year Ceremonies in Ancient Babylon: 'Taking Bel by the Hand' and a Cultic Picnic," *Religion* 11 (1981) 39–59.

36. Bell, *Ritual: Perspectives and Dimensions*, 21.

37. Volkert Haas, *Hethitische Berggötter und hurritische Steindämonen: Riten, Kulte und Mythen* (Mainz: von Zabern, 1982) 45–46; idem, *Die hethitische Literatur*, 97, cited below.

38. See, for example, Hoffner, *Hittite Myths*, 11.

39. *CHD* P 392b; Piotr Taracha, *Religions of Second Millennium Anatolia* (Dresdener Beiträge zur Hethitologie 27; Wiesbaden Harrassowitz, 2009) 136.

40. Hans Gustav Güterbock, "Hittite Mythology," in *Mythologies of the Ancient World* (ed. Samuel N. Kramer; Garden City, NY: Doubleday, 1961) 150–51.

(CTH 321) became a prime example in modern scholarship of a local Anatolian myth embedded in ritual practice in Hittite religious literature.[41] Some scholars even follow Gaster[42] in suggesting that the myth was not only recited during the festival but also staged there.[43] This assumption is based on the appearance of one figure from the second myth, the "Daughter of the Poor Man," in the cult of the goddess Tetešḫabi. However, it is not clear whether or not the Tetešḫabi cult belonged to the *Purulli* festival in the first place.[44]

2. The *Illuyanka* stories are calendrical in nature, symbolizing, if not helping to bring about the regeneration of nature in spring. According to this interpretation, shared by many scholars, the defeat of the Storm god—symbolizing the rain[45]—endangers the forces of nature,[46] whereas the Storm god's final victory rejuvenates these forces in spring.[47] Scholars disagree, however, about the meaning of the snake. Suggestions include chaos and evil,[48] winter,[49] the Kaška tribes,[50] and the lord of the underground waters.[51]
3. Most scholars agree that the *Illuyanka* stories are closely related to the Old Hittite ideology of kingship. "The mythic Story about the dragon Illuyanka," writes, for example, Klinger,[52] "could be interpreted as an etiological legitimation of the invention of kingship . . . very secure are the close ties between the Hittite kings and the festival respectively the place where the mythological drama is located—namely the city of Nerik." The importance of the text to Hittite kingship is based on its location, the city of Nerik,[53] a major Hittite cultic center, but also on the identification of Ḫupašiya, the

41. Beckman, "Illuyanka," 24; Erich Neu, "Der alte Orient: Mythen der Hethiter," *Bochumer Altertumswissenschaftliches Colloquium* 2 (1990) 103; Haas, *Die hethitische Literatur*, 97; Schwemer, "Storm-Gods 2," 24; Taracha, *Religions*, 137; Pecchioli Daddi, "Connections between KI.LAM and the Tetešḫapi Festival," 264; Lorenz and Rieken, "Verwendung mythologischer Texte," to name but a few examples.

42. Gaster, *Thespis*.

43. Franca Pecchioli Daddi, "Aspects du culte de la divinité hattie Tetešḫapi," *Hethitica* 8 (1987) 361–79; eadem, "KI.LAM and Tetešḫapi," 261. Goetze, in his review of Gaster's books (p. 99) was rather critical of this possibility. Gaster's answer to those critical remarks is found in Gaster, "Myth and Story," *Numen* 1 (1954) 210–11.

44. Taracha, *Religions*, 136.

45. Volkert Haas, *Geschichte der hethitischen Religion* (HO 1/15; Leiden: Brill, 1994) 325; Hoffner, "Brief Commentary on the Hittite Illuyanka Myth," 124; Pecchioli Daddi, "KI.LAM and the Tetešḫapi," 264–69.

46. Hoffner, "Brief Commentary on the Hittite Illuyanka Myth," 124.

47. Schwemer, "Storm-Gods 2," 24.

48. Birgit Christiansen, "Seil und Schnur. B. Bei den Hethitern," *RlA* 12:360.

49. Neu, "Mythen der Hethiter," 103; Haas, *Die hethitische Literatur*, 97.

50. Hatice Gonnet, "Institution d'un culte chez les Hittites," *Anatolica* 14 (1987) 93–95.

51. Hoffner, "Brief Commentary on the Hittite Illuyanka Myth," 124.

52. Jörg Klinger, "The Cult of Nerik: Revisited," in *Central-North Anatolia in the Hittite Period: New Perspectives in Light of Recent Research* (ed. Franca Pecchioli Daddi, Giulia Torri, and Carlo Corti; Studia Asiana 5; Rome: Herder, 2009) 99.

53. For this city, see Volkert Haas, *Der Kult von Nerik: Ein Beitrag zur hethitischen Religionsgeschichte* (Studia Pohl 4; Rome: Pontifical Biblical Institute, 1970); and Klinger, "The Cult of Nerik: Revisited," 97–107.

> man who helped the Storm god to slay the snake in the first *Illuyanka* story, as an archaic king. The role of the goddess Inara as the titulary deity of Ḫattuša also supports this assumption.[54] In this aspect, the story fits well within other ancient Near Eastern *Chaoskampf* traditions, such as the Marian and the Ugaritic versions, which are closely linked to concepts of the royal ideology of kingship.[55]

But can the *Illuyanka* text fulfill all these expectations? The text (CTH 321) is available in eight or nine empire-period copies[56] but contains linguistic archaisms that suggest that it is based on an older composition. Hoffner notes the relatively low number of archaisms,[57] which according to Klinger show "the characteristic features of a moderately modernized text of the typical process of copying an older tablet."[58]

The text presents itself as the words of Kella, the GUDU$_{12}$-priest of the Storm god of Nerik. The GUDU$_{12}$-priest usually belonged to the local Anatolian, Hittite-Hattian tradition and was active in the cult as an incantation and evocation priest.[59] However, the *Illuyanka* text is rather unique in that it represents a speech or a report of a GUDU$_{12}$-priest. Unlike other mythological texts of the local Anatolian tradition, no gods are evoked or mollified,[60] and as I shall presently claim, no real ritual practices are described[61]—in fact, the text is quite unique, a fact that has rarely been commentated on by modern scholars.

This is how the text begins (KBo 3.7 i 1–11, with duplicate KBo 12.83):

> [U]MMA ^{m}*Kell[a* ^{LÚ}GUDU$_{12}$] ŠA ^{d}10 ^{URU}*Nerik nepišaš* ^{d}I[ŠKUR-*ḫ*]*u-*[*n*]*a*$^{?}$ *purulliyaš uttar nu mān kiššan taranzi*
>
> *utne≈***wa** *māu šešdu nu≈***wa** *utnē paḫšanuwan ēšdu nu mān māi šešzi nu* EZEN$_4$ *purulliyaš iyanzi*
>
> *mān* ^{d}IŠKUR-*aš* ^{MUŠ}*Illuyankašš≈a* INA ^{URU}*Kiškiluša argatiēr nu≈za* ^{MUŠ}*illuyankaš* ^{d}IŠKUR-*an taraḫta*

54. Hoffner, "Brief Commentary on the Hittite Illuyanka Myth," 126–28. For Inara, see now Taracha, *Religions*, 42–43, with ample bibliography.

55. Wyatt, "Arms and the King."

56. The affiliation of duplicate J (KUB 36.53) to the composition is now contested in Košak's concordance.

57. Hoffner, "Brief Commentary on the Hittite Illuyanka Myth," 122.

58. Klinger, "The Cult of Nerik: Revisited," 100.

59. Ada Taggar-Cohen, *Hittite Priesthood* (Texte der Hethiter 26; Heidelberg: Carl Winter, 2006) 229–78; Taracha, *Religions*, 66.

60. Maria Lepši, "'Wort(e) des Kella': Erzählen im altanatolischen 'Illuyanka-Mythos,'" in *Modi des Erzählens in nicht-abendländlichen Texten* (ed. Stephan Conermann; Berlin: EB-Verlag, 2009) 23.

61. As claimed by most commentators on the text; see most recently Lorenz and Rieken, "Verwendung mythologischer Texte," 219.

> Thus speaks Kell[a, the $GUDU_{12}$-priest] of the Storm God of Nerik: this is the matter of the *Purulli* festival of the s[torm go]d of heaven. When they speak thus:
>
> "Let the land prosper and thrive, and let the land be protected"—and when it prospers and thrives they perform the *Purulli* festival.
>
> When the Storm God and the serpent fought each other in Kiškiluša, the serpent defeated the Storm God.

The story goes on and recounts how the goddess Inara, with the help of the man Ḫupašiya, helped the Storm God to defeat the serpent. The story does not end, however, with the serpent's defeat. The larger portion of the story concentrates on Inara and Ḫupašiya and their failed relationship. For the purpose of the current discussion, the last paragraph of the story is of great importance (KBo 3.7 ii 15′–20′):

> ^{d}*Inaraš INA* ^{URU}*Kiškil[ušša wit]* É-*ŠU ḫunḫuwanašš[≈a* ÍD *ANA*] *QATI* LUGAL *mān dāi[š] ḫa[nt]ezziyan purull[iyan] kuit iyaueni Ù QAT* [LUGAL É-*er*] ^{d}*Inaraš ḫunḫuwanašš≈a* ÍD [. . .]
>
> Inara [went] to Kiškil[ušša] and put her house [as well as the river] of the watery abyss [into] the hand of the king. Because of that (or since then) we are celebrating the **first** Purulli festival—May the hand of the [king . . . the house] of Inara as well as the river of the watery abyss.

This is as far as the first *Illuyanka* story goes. The text continues abruptly with an unfortunately-fragmentary but completely different narrative concerning the deified mountain Zaliyanu and the issue of rain in the city of Nerik (KBo 3.7 ii 21′–25′):

> The (mountain) Zaliyanu is the **fir[st]** among all. When it rains in Nerik, the herald brings forth thick bread from Nerik. He had asked Zaliyanu for rain.

A closer look at the beginning of the text, however, reveals that nowhere is it specifically said that the *Illuyanka* story was recited during the *Purulli* festival. At first, Kella informs his audience what the *Purulli* festival is, a spring festival that is celebrated when (or perhaps: so that)[62] the land prospers and thrives. The passage given in direct speech (cited "direct from the cult") includes only the first sentence in the second paragraph, as the use of the direct speech marker *-wa* (marked in bold letters above) clearly demonstrates.

62. As recently suggested by H. Craig Melchert, "Motivations for Hittite Mythological Texts," in *Writing Down the Myths: The Construction of Mythology in Classical and Medieval Traditions* (ed. Joseph Nagy and Kendra Willson; Turnhout: Brepols, forthcoming), reviving an older proposal by Stefanini (apud Pecchioli Daddi and Polvani, *La mitologia ittita*, 50).

The function of the first *Illuyanka* story is clearly given at the end of the narrative, cited above. It explains why the first ("foremost," "original") *Purulli* festival was celebrated in Kiškiluša or in Nerik. The audience of the text is not the congregation celebrating the festival but the recipients of the text in Ḫattuša, whom Kella seeks to inform about the meaning and history of a specific *Purulli* festival, originating in Kiškiluša and celebrated probably in Nerik. It is well known that the *Purulli* festival has archaic, local, north-central roots.[63] It was celebrated in several towns for several deities.[64] Spring festivals were, however, integral parts of the cultic calendar in many Anatolian towns and villages. With his etiology of the *Purulli* festival in Kiškiluša, Kella tries therefore, to "sell" the importance of this specific cult foundation to the authorities in Ḫattuša.

It seems, therefore, that there is not much in the text itself that supports the myth and ritual notion that the myth was performed during the *Purulli* festival itself. Could it be only a projection of the myth and ritual theory, inspired perhaps by the Babylonian *Akītu* festival?

In fact, a closer look at the story weakens the calendrical interpretation of it as well. As we have seen, the *Illuyanka* stories are, according to this interpretation, calendrical in nature, symbolizing if not helping to bring about the regeneration of the forces of nature in the springtime. However, as Hoffner[65] rightly observes, "Unlike the so-called Disappearing Deities Myths, the text does not elaborate the natural catastrophes that must have followed from the Storm-god's disablement." It seems that Kella is not at all interested in a cosmic drama that modern scholars believe to have discovered in the myth. Instead, he tells a story of a much humbler, local scope concerning Inara and Ḫupašiya, the house that the goddess built in Tarukka, and the river of the underground waters in Kiškiluša. As Beckman rightly notes,[66] the story serves as an etiological myth for the establishment of royal cult in Kiškiluša. Kella, in my opinion, only tries here to emphasize the meaning of this cult by stating its antiquity or importance—by relating it to the famous *Chaoskampf* and to the celebration of the "first" *Purulli* festival. Striking features in the local landscape or prominent ruins in the area may have given support to his claim.[67]

63. Galina Kellerman, "Towards the Further Interpretation of the Purulli-Festival," *Slavica Hierosolymitana* 5–6 (1981) 35–46; Volkert Haas, "Betrachtungen zur Rekonstruktion des hethitischen Frühjahresfestes (EZEN *purulliyaš*)," ZA 78 (1988) 284–98; idem, *Geschichte der hethitischen Religion* (HO 1/15; Leiden: Brill, 1994) 696–747; Klinger, "The Cult of Nerik: Revisited," 99–101; Pecchioli Daddi, "KI.LAM and the Tetešḫapi," 262.

64. See the *CHD* P 392a for the attestations.

65. Hoffner, "Brief Commentary on the Hittite Illuyanka Myth," 129.

66. Beckman, "Illuyanka," 24.

67. As suggested by Hoffner, "Brief Commentary on the Hittite Illuyanka Myth," 126–27.

But the often assumed close ties with the Hittite institute of kingship could be questioned on a closer inspection as well. In comparison with other Hittite texts pertaining to the cult,[68] the king plays here a surprisingly minor role, appearing only twice, both times in connection with royal cult foundations. Compared with the numerous invocations and benedictions embedded in local Anatolian cult that present the king as the governor of the whole land or as a son of the royal couple of the Hittite pantheon (the Storm God and the Sun Goddess of Arinna), the endowment of the house and the river of underground waters in Kiškiluša seems rather modest in scope. But the proposed connection between Ḫupašiya and Hittite kingship also fails to convince. The story itself offers no hints about a connection between Ḫupašiya and the king.[69] In fact, I am not aware of any evidence in the entire Hittite tradition so far that supports the thesis that Ḫupašiya was ever viewed as an ancient ancestral king or associated with the royal Hittite family in any other way.

In conclusion so far: according to the interpretation presented here, Kella simply recounts the first *Illuyanka* story in order to inform the central authorities in Ḫattuša of the importance of the "first" *Purulli* festival and to convince them also to support the royal cult institution in Kiškiluša that is related to it. The myth is told by Kella, not to the congregation of celebrators during the festival, but to the recipients of the text in Ḫattuša. It is noteworthy that both Kiškiluša and Tarukka are hardly attested in other Hittite sources.[70]

Additional support for this interpretation may be found in the second (and by far the lesser-known) part of the text. However, some short remarks on the second *Illuyanka* story are in order first.

Seen from a structural point of view, the second serpent story is similar to the first one, with the "son of the weather god" in the role of Ḫupašiya as the human character in the story, who finds his death as a result of the *Drachenkampf*. The story shares many parallels with the mythological story about Telipinu and the daughter of the sea[71] as well as with the Typhon story in the *Bibliotheca* of Pseudo-Apollodorus.[72] In both,[73] a marriage and the social and financial obligations that are involved in it play a vital role in the story. Even more than in the first serpent story, the Storm God is shown here in a very

68. A collection of these is offered by Alfonso Archi, "Auguri per il Labarna," in *Studia Mediterranea Piero Meriggi dicata* (Studia Mediterranea 1; Pavia: Aurora, 1979) 27–51.

69. Hoffner, *Hittite Myths*, 11. See also idem, "Brief Commentary on the Hittite Illuyanka Myth," 126–27 for a balanced overview of the different opinions.

70. As already noted by Hoffner in ibid., 131.

71. Idem, *Hittite Myths*, 26–28; Haas, *Die hethitische Literatur*, 115–17.

72. Neu, "Mythen der Hethiter," 103–4.

73. The second *Illuyanka* story shares the motif of marriage, etc., with only the Telepinu myth. It shares other motifs (the stolen organs) with the Typhon story.

negative light, sacrificing his son for his own salvation. This time, the story connects the serpent to the sea, explicitly, but other geographical details are completely missing. Unfortunately, due to the fact that both the beginning and the end of the story are broken, it is impossible to reconstruct the way in which it connects to the first *Illuyanka* story or to the "ritual" narratives that surround it. The context in which this story was presented by Kella remains a puzzle as well.

Immediately following the story, however, is the introduction of a new speech by Kella (Copy A: KBo 3.7 iii 34′–35′). This is followed by the fragmentary and by now controversial copy J, which does not offer any new information to the understanding of the composition anyway. The tradition improves considerably with copy D, but the content becomes even more puzzling. Here, Kella recounts an enigmatic mythical scene that took place in the city of Nerik, featuring a dialogue between the deities and another $GUDU_{12}$-priest by the name of Taḫurpili on matters of rank among the deities. Here we encounter again the mountain-god Zaliyanu, this time in the company of his consort Zašḫapuna and his concubine Tazzuwašši (KBo 34.33 + KUB 12.66 iv 1′–10′; with KBo 3.7 iv 1′–6′ and KUB 17.6 iv 1–4):

> [And] in front/for the $GUDU_{12}$-priest they made the **[fir]st** gods the last, and the last they made the **first** gods.
>
> The cult delivery of Zali(ya)nu is **great**. But (the cult delivery of) Zali(ya)nu's wife, Zašhapuna, is **greater** than the Storm god of Nerik.
>
> The gods speak to the $GUDU_{12}$-priest Taḫpurili as follows: "When we go to Nerik (KBo 3.7 iv 5′: to the Storm god of Nerik), where shall we sit?"

The question is settled by the casting of lots, and a decision is reached about the rank and sitting order of the deities around the spring in Nerik. However, just like the first *Illuyanka* story, this narrative also seems to necessitate a royal cult endowment. Here, toward the very end of the text, the Hittite king makes his second and final appearance. This also is in the context of a cult foundation. This royal endowment secures the cult needs of the three deities—Zaliyanu, his consort Zašḫapuna, and his concubine Tazzuwašši—or their priests in the town of Tanipiya. Like the serpent myth, this mythological/ritual narrative serves as an etiology for a royal cult foundation. The parallels between the two cases can hardly be overlooked. In both, Kella provides mythological narratives to justify the importance of local cult institutions.

The parallels between the two scenes are hard to miss. In both, Kella attempts to convey the importance of local cult institutions and to convince his audience of their importance. Instead of narrating a central cosmic drama, a major narrative that concerns the rejuvenation of nature, the fight between order and chaos, or the origins of kingship, Kella is merely attempting to convince his audience—probably the central administration in Ḫattuša—of the importance of local, provincial cult institutions that he is describing. His goal is most likely to secure their maintenance. Therefore, he claims that the *Purulli* festival in Kiškiluša is the first/original *Purulli* and explains the religious roots of the royal cult donation in Tanipiya. That is why throughout the text he is so preoccupied with rank, describing the *Purulli* festival in Kiškiluša or the mountain Zaliyanu as the foremost, the cult rations of Zaliyanu or Tašḫapuna as big and biggest, or the episode about the rank of the deities and their seating order over the spring in Nerik.

Thus, according to the interpretation I am suggesting, Kella offers with the *Illuyanka* stories neither a calendrical myth of cosmological dimensions nor a central myth legitimizing the institution of Old Hittite kingship. Rather, in "his" composition, presumably a compilation of several mythological etiologies, Kella tries to stake and to substantiate religious claims. I therefore venture to term this unique text a "mythological cult inventory."[74] Embedding his story within the framework of the famous battle between the Storm god and the serpent, he invested his local cult with importance. The *Illuyanka* text shows that the myth of the dragon-slayer was indeed known in north-central Anatolia, perhaps as early as the Old Hittite period. Unfortunately, it does not give us any clues about the meaning that Kella, the recipients of "his" text in Ḫattuša, or the festival participants in Nerik ascribed to this mythological combat. We can only continue to speculate about that.

74. For the Hittite cult inventories, see Joost Hazenbos, *The Organization of the Anatolian Local Cults during the Thirteenth Century* B.C. (Cuneiform Monographs 21; Leiden: Brill-Styx, 2003).

The Northwest Semitic Conflict Myth and Egyptian Sources from the Middle and New Kingdoms

Joanna Töyräänvuori

University of Helsinki

Versions or traditions of the conflict myth are known from ancient Egyptian sources, and they have often been connected to or compared with the Ugaritic *Baʿal Cycle*, which together with the Babylonian *Enūma eliš* are probably the best known examples of such a myth. Although Wyatt has stated that no specific *Chaoskampf* myth existed in Egypt,[1] Malamat went so far as to claim that, together with the Hebrew Bible, the Egyptian sources display the closest affinity to the texts from Ugarit.[2] Many of the Egyptian myths describe battles between at least partially anthropomorphized or even fully humanized incarnations of the gods. A famous myth featuring the sun-god Re's battle against the serpent Apep also has somewhat of a maritime connection, a feature of the eastern Mediterranean and Mesopotamian myths. According to Wyatt, it is the myth of Re and Apep that would offer the nearest parallel to the conflict myth in Egyptian sources, at least in conceptual terms.[3] It must be noted, however, that in Egyptian myths it is the sun god who plays the part of the warrior, not a storm or a weather god, as in the Northwest Semitic traditions.[4]

Northwest Semitic influence flowed into Egyptian culture following the period of the rule of the Asiatic Hyksos in the 15th Dynasty.[5] Contact between

1. Nicholas Wyatt, "*There's Such Divinity Doth Hedge a King*": *Selected Essays of Nicholas Wyatt on Royal Ideology in Ugaritic and Old Testament Literature* (Aldershot: Ashgate, 2005) 163.

2. Abraham Malamat, *Mari and the Bible* (Leiden: Brill, 1998) 29.

3. In political terms, he sees the myth of Horus and Seth as the nearest parallel (Wyatt, "*There's Such Divinity*," 163).

4. Donald B. Redford, *Egypt, Canaan, and Israel in Ancient Times* (Princeton, NJ: Princeton University Press, 1992) 46. However, it must be pointed out that the sun god also played the part of the divine warrior in some Sumerian and Sumero-Babylonian myths.

5. The Hyksos were "speakers of the West Semitic tongue" (Redford, ibid., 100).

Egypt and the eastern Mediterranean had naturally existed prior to this, and there had been a sizable Asiatic population in Egypt during the 12th and 13th Dynasties. But relations between Egypt and Levantine cities outside of Byblos had not been particularly warm.[6] A second period of close contact between Egypt and the Levant followed during the time of the New Kingdom with the spreading of the Egyptian empire into Asia, a period that lasted from the time of King Ahmose of the 18th Dynasty to the middle of the 20th Dynasty (ca. 1550–1120 B.C.).[7] A garrison was assigned to Ugarit in the fifteenth century B.C., during the reign of Amenophis II or Thutmose III.[8] During this time of close contact, several Northwest Semitic divinities, such as Anat, Ashtart, and Resheph were adopted into the Egyptian pantheon,[9] and other Semitic divinities were given Egyptian equivalents. For example, the storm-god Baʿal was called Seth in Egyptian texts.[10] While these Semitic deities were given Egyptianizing iconographies, their characteristics and natures stayed more or less intact.[11]

According to Wyatt, the independence of the Egyptian renderings of the conflict myth serves to highlight the homogeneity, coherence, and continuity of the traditions in the "western Asiatic world,"[12] but the degree to which the Egyptian traditions had an independent genesis is an open question. On the contrary, it is more than possible that the Egyptian stories borrowed from the "western Asiatic" narratives.

The Egyptian story that has been most often connected with the conflict myth is the story of the sun-god Re's journey to the underworld, where daily he had to battle the monstrous serpent, Apep (*ʿȝpp*).[13] Apep, or Apophis, as

6. Ibid., 81, 101–2. An "urban but thoroughly Middle Bronze Canaanite" population existed, especially on the major sites of Tell el-Dabʾa, Tell el-Yehudiyeh, and Tell el-Maskhuta.

7. Ibid., 140. See pp. 148–60 for the creation of the Egyptian empire.

8. Ibid., 160.

9. Stephanie L. Budin, "A Reconsideration of the Aphrodite-Ashtart Syncretism," *Numen* 51 (2004) 100. Redford (*Israel, Canaan, and Israel*, 43) writes that, while "an occasional Asiatic deity may turn up in the Egyptian pantheon, consciously 'borrowed' and partly 'Egyptianized' like Hathor of Byblos, for the most part the cults, pantheons, and mythologies of Egypt and western Asia remained distinct in outward expression." He holds that the mythologies sprang out of specific landscapes and climates, the cults arising from markedly different societies.

10. Raymond O. Faulkner, Edward F. Wente, and William Kelly Simpson, *The Literature of Ancient Egypt: An Anthology of Stories, Instructions, and Poetry* (New Haven, CT: Yale University Press, 1973) 77.

11. Budin, "Aphrodite-Ashtart," 100.

12. Wyatt, "*There's Such Divinity*," 164.

13. John A. Wilson, "The Repulsing of the Dragon and the Creation," *ANET* 6–7. For a newer translation, see Erik Hornung, *The Valley of the Kings: Horizon of Eternity* (New

the creature is known in Greek sources, was depicted as a giant serpent. For example, the Middle Kingdom text on *Not Dying Because of a Snake* describes Re's enemy as a 50-foot or 30-cubit-long serpent, albeit the name Apep is not mentioned in the text (the name of the serpent is "He-on-the-mountain-that-he-must-overthrow"). Ludvig Morenz described Apep as an impressive supernatural figure, an enemy of order, and an "anti-god." Apep was not known in Old Kingdom sources but seems to have made its appearance during the 9th Dynasty of the First Intermediate Period, ca. twentieth century B.C. The first-known mention of the name Apep is in the tomb inscription of nomarch Ankhtifi of Moᶜalla, which pessimistically describes the world as *tz pn n ᶜȝpp*, "this sandbank of Apep" (Moᶜalla 4:10).[14] This may invoke Apep as the world-encircling sea or river.

The figure of Apep featured more frequently in the Coffin Texts of Middle Kingdom times, where Apep was described as a water-dwelling enemy of the sun-god Re, attacking his solar bark.[15] The narrative was also popular during the New Kingdom, from the 18th to 21st Dynasties, and is featured in the tombs of the Valley of Kings, in many of which the giant serpent encircles the entire burial chamber, thus making Apep one of the main features of Re's journey into the underworld. The confrontation between Re and Apep was featured as a part of the Amduat, a funerary text painted on the inside walls of burial chambers, taking place at its seventh hour. But, at least in some iterations of the myth, it is actually the god Seth standing on Re's solar bark that confronts Apep with a curse, because Seth was the only one of the sun god's entourage that Apep did not manage to hypnotize.[16] Apep is then bound, speared, dismembered with hot knives, roasted, and burned nightly.[17]

During the period of the New Kingdom, Apep was featured in Underworld books, or the so-called *Apophisbücher*, featuring magical spells against the serpent.[18] There is also a text called "The Names of Apep Which Shall Not Be" (Papyrus Bremner-Rhind 32:13–32:42), featuring a litany of negative epithets of Apep.[19] The same papyrus, dating to the Ptolemaic period

York: Timken, 1990) 103–13. First published by E. A. Wallis Budge in *Facsimiles of Egyptian Hieratic Papyri in the British Museum, First Series* (London: British Museum, 1910).

14. Ludwig D. Morenz, "Apophis: On the Origin, Name, and Nature of an Ancient Egyptian Anti-God," *JNES* 63 (2004) 201.

15. Ibid., 203. The barks were actually two: *matet*, or "strengthening," for the morning and *semket*, or "weakening," for the evening.

16. Redford, *Egypt, Canaan, and Israel*, 47.

17. Robert A. Armour, *Gods and Myths of Ancient Egypt* (Cairo: American University in Cairo Press, 2001) 61.

18. Morenz, "Apophis," 203.

19. Ibid., 205.

but containing much older material, also features "The Beginning of the Book of Overthrowing Apophis, the Enemy of Re and the Enemy of the King" (25:21–28:18), a text also known by the name of "The Repulsing of the Dragon."[20] This text is a first-person monologue by Re on the events featured in the Amduat. The Apophis described in these texts is extremely animal-like, having next to no anthropomorphic characteristics. Since the creature is also vanquished daily, almost as a matter of course ("I have consumed his bones, I have annihilated his soul during every day, I have cut up the vertebrae of his back"), he does not even seem to present a proper threat to the sun god. It is only when this natural order of things is disrupted that the figure of Apep becomes horrific.

The story of Apep and Re was also a popular motif in Egyptian iconography. A Theban tomb (of an official by the name of Iner-Kha) also featured a fairly well-known image of Re in the form of a white cat (which, adorned with the Amun crown, bears a striking resemblance to a hare) impaling the serpent Apep.[21] This scene is also featured in the Papyrus of Hunefer rendition of the Book of the Dead, dating to the 19th Dynasty. Apep was not depicted as a serpent only in the iconography of the Amduat. Its name was also written with the determinative for a snake, although from the Coffin Texts onward the determinative was apparently mutilated, according to Morenz, for euphemistic reasons.[22] In Coffin Text 5:224a, we also have a form in which the name has both the determinative for a snake and a determinative for a person, which may indicate that Apep was conceived of at least partially anthropomorphically. An alternative image of Apep depicted the creature as a turtle, albeit this was far less common than its depiction as a snake.[23] Because natural order, the order of the world was a major concern of ancient Egyptians, it may indeed be justified to describe Apep as an agent of Chaos, a role that has often also been thrust upon the Ugaritic Yamm, possibly in part due to the association of the two. In Egyptian sources, Apep was never given the designation *nṯr*, "god." Apep also never received his own cult, nor was he depicted in statues.[24] These are factors that have often been suggested were also shared by the Ugaritic Yamm, but it is rather unclear whether or not Yamm was featured as a divine recipient of offerings in the cult of Ugarit. Morenz suggested that Apep might

20. Raymond O. Faulkner, *The Papyrus Bremner-Rhind* (Bibliotheca Aegyptiaca 3; Brussels: Édition de la Fondation égyptologique Reine Élisabeth, 1933).

21. *ANEP* 218 (fig. 669).

22. Morenz, "Apophis," 202.

23. Ibid.

24. Ibid.

originally have been a figure of popular religion and therefore is missing from the "elite" sources that have survived from Old Kingdom times.[25]

A connection between creation and the subduing of a water monster (or "the greed of the waters," *snk n mw*)[26] has also been found in the Middle Egyptian text *Teaching for King Merykara*. According to Redford, the hero-monster motif is here concealed in the substratum of mythological thought underlying more popular myths.[27] *The Teaching for King Merykara* is a didactic text, not a myth. If indeed the subduing of a water monster was meant by the term, then it would indicate that this sort of mythological thinking was not unfamiliar to the ancient Egyptian. But one can hardly assume that this singular mention would have been affected by Northwest Semitic conceptions, because during the purported time of the writing of the text there were few connections between Egypt and the Levant.[28] Redford is correct in pointing out that ancient Egyptian creation accounts did not commonly make use of the creation battle motif. Unlike in the Northwest Semitic world, in Egypt this motif was, according to him, a rationalization of the solar eclipse.[29]

Another Middle Egyptian story that has sometimes been linked with the conflict myth, "The Story of the Shipwrecked Sailor,"[30] seems upon closer inspection to hold very little relevance to a study of the conflict myth. Dated to the 11th Dynasty or the early Middle Kingdom,[31] the literary text features a sailor, shipwrecked on a magical island ("island of the *kꜣ*"), full of fruit trees and all good things. This island is inhabited by a serpent creature, who relays to the sailor the story of his entire brood's being burned and killed by a falling meteorite. The story has been interpreted as an instruction or teaching

25. Ibid. There may even exist a connection between the name of the monster Apep and the Hyksos pharaoh Apepi.

26. Sometimes also translated as the "submerger of the waters."

27. Redford, *Egypt, Canaan, and Israel*, 46. Redford dates the text to the 21st century B.C., apparently regarding it as contemporary to King Merikare's reign (and on pp. 67–68 suggests that it would have been authored by Merikare's father, King Akhtoy III), King Merikare being regarded as the last ruler of the somewhat obscure 10th Dynasty. The dating seems early, considering the fact that the language of the text is Middle Egyptian, and this would make the text one of the first ever to be written in Middle Egyptian. The principal sources for the text, namely, the Hermitage and Carlsberg papyri, date to the 18th dynasty in the New Kingdom. Translation and transliteration of the text in Stephen Quirke, *Egyptian Literature 1800 B.C.: Questions and Readings* (London: Golden House, 2004) 112–20.

28. Redford, *Egypt, Canaan, and Israel*, 69.

29. Ibid., 47.

30. For example, Günter Lanczkowski ("Die Geschichte des Schiffbrüchigen," *ZDMG* 103 [1953] 363–68), who associates the serpent and the sea with the notion of the primal ocean.

31. Faulkner, Wente, and Simpson, *Literature*, 50.

disguised as narrative, expressing cultural virtues of the time.[32] The serpent then sends the sailor back home with his ship full of all the good things of the island, and while the sailor promises to report to his king of the magnificence of the island, the serpent tells the sailor that he will not be able to return, because the island will have disappeared. The narrative does not seem to have much bearing on the conflict myth, because it features no battle, and the serpent creature, while frightening, is in no way malevolent. Despite the fact that the serpent Apep in the Re narrative is an adversary of the sun god, in ancient Egypt snakes and serpents were not considered evil creatures but symbols of protection.[33] This may be seen most readily in the fact that the pharaoh's crown featured a cobra ready to attack the enemies of the king. Because the motif of conflict is absent, the serpent is not malevolent, and only tenuous links between the adversary of the Northwest Semitic conflict myth and the serpent have been made to begin with, it appears that this narrative has little to offer in the way of understanding the *Chaoskampf*.

While the sea in the narrative is called the "Great Green" (*wꜣḏ-wr*), a designation usually connected with the Mediterranean, the fact that the serpent calls himself "the lord of Punt" (line 151) is cause enough to suspect that the island was believed to have been located in the Red Sea.[34] The Semitic word *yam*, on the other hand, is used of the sea instead of the "Great Green" in the New Kingdom text that is dated to ca. the thirteenth century B.C., *The Story of Two Brothers*.[35] In this text, the sea takes a lock of hair from the unnamed wife of one of the brothers in what appears to be a location in Lebanon or its vicinity ("Valley of the Cedar"). Because the names of both of the brothers, Anubis and Bata, were known as gods, it has been suggested that the story may have had a mythological setting.[36] Malamat suggests that this Egyptian tale was influenced by Canaanite mythology, as does Redford, who connects it with the motif of the goddess and the "lascivious sea monster."[37] But apart from the Semitic name of the creature, there seems little to connect the incident in the tale with the Yamm of the Ugaritic myth. It is noteworthy, however, that in

32. Ibid., 6.

33. Harry A. Hoffner Jr., *Hittite Myths* ([2nd ed.; SBLWAW 2; Atlanta: Scholars Press, 1998] 11) agrees that in Egypt reptiles could be symbols of protection but continues that "clearly in Hittite culture, as in Babylonia and ancient Israel, serpents usually represented evil."

34. Faulkner, Wente, and Simpson, *Literature*, 51.

35. Papyrus D'Orbiney. Facsimile in Georg Möller, *Hieratische Lesestücke 2* (Leipzig: Hinrichs, 1927).

36. John A. Wilson, "The Story of Two Brothers," *ANET* 23.

37. Malamat, *Mari and the Bible*, 30; Redford, *Egypt, Canaan, and Israel*, 234.

this story, as in the older New Kingdom text the Astarte papyrus, the sea is clearly personified.[38]

The Astarte papyrus, also known by the name "Astarte and the Tribute of the Sea" (PAmherst 19–21), features a myth that has much more relevance to the topic at hand. The badly damaged Astarte papyrus, published by Gardiner in 1932,[39] is dated to the 18th or 19th Dynasty (Late Bronze in the Levant), ca. 1300 B.C.[40] Gardiner held that the story, the oldest of the known Late-Egyptian tales, was of cosmogonic character, and he still likened the myth to the Babylonian creation epic *Enūma eliš* rather than to the newly discovered Ugaritic texts. He writes that "in the Ramesside age Babylonian literature did exercise some second-hand influence upon the literature of the Egyptians."[41]

Sayce, on the other hand, connected the story of the papyrus to a fragmentary Hittite text, referred to by Sayce as KUB 12.49. He called the Hittite legend a "very remarkable parallel" to the Egyptian text. The text translated by Sayce, featuring Kumarbi and the sea, is actually KUB 12.65 iii, a portion of the Song of Hedammu. The Song of Hedammu,[42] part of the *Kumarbi Cycle* of myths of probable Hurrian origin, shows that the sea was conceived of as a

38. Alan H. Gardiner, "The Astarte Papyrus," in *Studies Presented to F. L. Griffith* (London: Egypt Exploration Society, 1932) 77. On p. 78, he also describes the sea of the Tale of Two Brothers as a "predatory being" grabbing at the woman, "perhaps a reminiscence of Astarte herself." It should be emphasized that this motif of the sea's abduction of a woman is found nowhere in the Ugaritic texts and may represent a native Egyptian or southern Levantine theme. See Donald B. Redford, "The Sea and the Goddess," in *Studies in Egyptology Presented to Miriam Lichtheim* (ed. Sarah Israelit-Groll; Jerusalem: Magnes, 1990) 830–35.

39. Photographs or collotype plates of the papyrus had already been published by Percy E. Newberry in *The Amherst Papyri* (London: Quaritch, 1899), although, according to Gardiner ("Astarte Papyrus," 75), H. Ibscher of the Staatliche Museen zu Berlin was the first to position the fragments at his behest. On the publication history of the papyrus, see Gardiner, "Astarte Papyrus," 77. Lord Armherst of Hackney must have obtained the papyrus prior to 1871, when it was, according to Gardiner ("Astarte Papyrus," 74), first called attention to by Samuel Birch in "Varia," ZÄS 9 (1871) 119.

40. Archibald H. Sayce, "The Astarte Papyrus and the Legend of the Sea," *JEA* 19 (1933) 56; Malamat, *Mari and the Bible*, 30. The papyrus was formerly a part of the Amherst collection but now belongs to the collection of the Pierpont Morgan Library in New York. See Wilson, "Ashtarte," 17.

41. Gardiner, "Astarte Papyrus," 74, 81.

42. Since Sayce, the tablet KUB 12.65 (KUB 12.49 in Sayce, "Astarte Papyrus") has been joined to KBo 26.71, and four more duplicates have been found. These are edited by Jana Siegelová, *Appu-Märchen und Hedammu-Mythus* (Studien zu den Boğazöy-Texten 14; Wiesbaden: Harrassowitz, 1971) 35–88; translation in Hoffner, *Hittite Myths*, 50–55; and Franca Pecchioli Daddi and Anna Maria Polvani, *La mitologia ittita* (Brescia: Paideia, 1990) 140–41.

human-like or anthropomorphic character in certain Hittite texts.[43] But unlike Kumarbi (*ᵈKu-mar-bi-ya-as*), the sea (*a-ru-na-as*) does not receive the divine determinative in the text.[44] Another interesting detail of the Hittite text is that the sea is seated on a throne (KUB 12.65 iii 16). The motif of cleaving may also be present in the text, although unlike in Babylonian myth, in the Hittite myth it is the universe that, in Sayce's translation, is broken in two.[45] According to Sayce, like the Astarte papyrus, the Hittite text also relates to the concept of the deified sea.[46] For Sayce, the Astarte papyrus conveyed an epic in which the sea appears in mythological form and takes "his place by the side of the other deities of the Egyptian Pantheon."[47]

The story of the Astarte papyrus was finally connected to the Ugaritic mythos by Gaster in his 1952 article entitled, "The Egyptian 'Story of Astarte' and the Ugaritic poem of Baal."[48] Gaster suggested that the entire background of Baʿal's struggle with Yamm could be explained through this Egyptian story, in which Astarte is given as a bride to appease the sea, which had gained supremacy over the gods. Gaster claimed that the general situation of the Egyptian tale accorded "perfectly with that implied in the Ugaritic poem."[49] The Astarte papyrus was connected by Gaster especially to cols. I and IV of *KTU* 1.2.[50] Malamat also insisted that the Astarte papyrus "consists of an actual Canaanite myth" and that in this myth the sea god, who holds dominion over the earth and the other gods, is entrapped by the beauty of the nude Astarte sitting by the seashore and is subsequently brought into conflict with the goddess's consort, of whom there is no mention in the extant text. He

---

43. Note also the Hittite myth "Telipinu and the Daughter of the Sea God," in which it is the daughter of the sea that is whisked away from her father. See Hoffner, *Hittite Myths*, 26–27.

44. Although according to Sayce ("Astarte Papyrus," 59), it does feature the determinative, for example, in KUB 20.1. See also B. H. L. van Gessel, *Onomasticon of the Hittite Pantheon* (HO 1/33; Leiden: Brill, 1998) 48 with syllabic writing *Aruna-* and p. 605 with Sumerographic writing A.AB.BA. The serpent Hedammu, being the offspring of the god Kumarbi and the daughter of the sea god, also does not receive the divine determinative.

45. Hoffner's translation (in *Hittite Myths*, 53), on the other hand, makes no mention of this, opting for "He traversed (the distance) in one (stage)"; similarly Siegelová, *Appu-Märchen und Hedammu-Mythos*, 51 ("Es legte [die Strecke] auf einmal zurück"); Pecchioli Daddi and Polvani, *La mitologia ittita*, 141 ("Egli coprì il percorso in un sol balzo") and *CHD* Š 238, s.v. *šarra-* D 3 g.

46. Sayce, "Astarte Papyrus," 56.

47. Ibid., 56.

48. Theodor H. Gaster, "The Egyptian 'Story of Astarte' and the Ugaritic Poem of Baal," *BO* 9 (1952) 81–85.

49. Ibid., 82.

50. Ibid., 82–85. Also W. F. Albright, *Yahweh and the Gods of Canaan* (London: Athlone, 1968; repr. Winona Lake, IN: Eisenbrauns, 1990) 116.

further remarks that the myth reflects the violent power of the sea, threatening mariners and coastal inhabitants.[51]

In the Astarte papyrus, the sea (*ym*) demands tribute from the other gods[52] or else he will cover the earth and the mountains (14, *y*). The tribute, which

51. Malamat, *Mari and the Bible*, 30.

52. It should be noted that the interpretation that it is the sea demanding tribute of the other gods is based on Gardiner's interpretation of the text. Prior to his reconstruction of the events (in Gardiner, "Astarte Papyrus," 77–78), there was some confusion about who was the recipient and who was the giver of the tribute. Gardiner based his hypothesis at least partly on the Tale of the Two Brothers ("though in still more masterful and tyrannical a fashion"), which is a later text. On p. 81, he also points out that this interpretation "would be quite a new departure in Egyptian fiction." The romantic or erotic tension between Astarte and the sea is also based on Gardiner's interpretation and was not present in the previous interpretations that revolved around Astarte's coming to Egypt. This is an important thing to consider, because this interpretation has also had its effect on the interpretation of the Ugaritic myth. For example, Redford (*Egypt, Canaan, and Israel*, 44) writes of Yamm as "the avaricious monster who lords it over the gods and lusts after the beautiful goddess Astarte." Also see Redford, "The Sea and the Goddess" (pp. 831–33), where he states that the goddess is "beset by the water monster" in Levantine versions of the myth, from which the Egyptian story of Astarte was translated. This fits Gardiner's interpretation of the Egyptian myth to a T but seems poorly supported by the Ugaritic material. This interpretation was later followed, for example, by Mark S. Smith (*The Ugaritic Baʿal Cycle, Volume I: Introduction with Text, Translation and Commentary of KTU 1.1–1.2* [VTSup 55; Leiden: Brill, 1994] 23), who lists five motifs shared by the Astarte papyrus and the Ugaritic text:

1. claim of tribute by the sea,
2. the payment of tribute,
3. the initiative against the sea,
4. the response of Baʿal to fight against the sea,
5. the sea's title "ruler."

Most of these points of contact seem somewhat contentious. There may exist some broad similarities in motif, but points (1) and (2) are rather poorly attested in the Ugaritic texts ("tribute," *ʾargm*, is mentioned by El in *KTU* 1.2 I 38 as something that Baʿal should deliver to Yamm, but it is not claimed by Yamm; Yamm's claims are not well understood). Tribute ([ṯ]y) is mentioned in association with the sea or Yamm in the tablet RIH 78/3+30:14′–16′, which reads:

[*w*]*yirš.snp.ln.dym.hw*	And he demands 2/3 from us, that of the Sea it (is)
[ṯ]*y.ugrtym.hw.*	tribute of the Ugarititians, it (is)
[*ks*]*p.hw.dym.hw.d.ugrtym*	silver it (is), that of the Sea it (is), that of the Ugaritians

The passage is difficult to interpret, but because its context seems to be Pharaoh Setnakhte demanding from the Ugaritian King Ammurapi the return of payments made by Setnakhte's predecessor to the Ugaritians in exchange for their support, the implication of the passage may be simply that the funds have been spent and are no more: they have been transformed into ships, grain, and *hacksilber*. Johannes C. de Moor ("Egypt, Ugarit and the Exodus," in *Ugarit—Religion and Culture: Essays present in Honour of Professor John C. L. Gibson* [ed. Nicholas Wyatt, Wilfred G. E. Watson, and Jeffery B. Lloyd; UBL 12; Münster: Ugarit-Verlag, 1996] 232), however, suggests that the "money" had been donated to the sea-god Yamm by the people of Ugarit, who "mockingly identified YHWH with Yammu." Why an Egyptian pharaoh should care about the replacement of the name of a Semitic deity with another for the purposes of mockery of one of them is anyone's guess). Point 4) can scarcely be

included gold, silver, and lapis lazuli is initially to be delivered by a goddess named Renut (Renutet), who seems to function as a messenger of some sort (1, x+ 12).[53] Renenut, however, sends a bird to find Astarte, who was possibly requested by the sea to be the one to bring his booty. Astarte is sent to represent the gods, and the sea demands the goddess be given to him as wife along with the tribute. The sea, who is called "the ruler" (2, x+ 6),[54] sees the "furious and tempestuous" goddess sitting by the shore of the sea apparently in torn clothes, singing and laughing at the sea,[55] and the two exchange words (2, x+ 18–3, I). Because the sea solicits the Ennead of the gods for Astarte to be given as his wife, Astarte seems to be awarded a throne and made a part of the Ennead (3, y).[56] The gods of the Ennead must strip off their jewelry to make up the weight of the tribute on the scales. The rest of the papyrus is broken, and it is difficult to say how the story would have progressed apart from the fact that it seemed to go on for quite a bit.[57]

---

found in the Egyptian text, and with regard to point [5]), there exists no etymological connection between the Ugaritic *zbl* and the Egyptian *ḥqȝ*, which is found inside a cartouche in 1 x +8. The word was not an unusual title for villains in Egyptian texts and was given, for example, to Anubis in PT 805.

On pp. 45–46, Redford (*Egypt, Canaan, and Israel*) suggests that the sea's lust for the goddess is somehow more rooted in the mythologies of cities south of Byblos. It must be stated that the sources he quotes are not from the Late Bronze Age but date to the Hellenistic era.

53. While messenger divinities are a staple of Ugaritic myths, they usually seem to come in pairs.

54. At least according to Gardiner, "Astarte Papyrus," 78–79.

55. Wolfgang Helck ("Zur Herkunft der Erzählung des sog. 'Astartepapyrus,'" in *Fontes atque pontes: Eine Festgabe für Hellmut Brunner* [ed. Manfred Görg; Ägypten und Altes Testament 5; Wiesbaden: Harrassowitz, 1983] 220) suggests that she is attempting to beguile ("zu betören") the sea with music and her nudity. It must be noted that it is not expressly stated in the text that the goddess is nude, but this is implied by the torn state of her clothes. Gardiner ("Astarte Papyrus," 79) interpreted the scene so that the goddess was in tears because she found her task disagreeable. I suggest that the disheveled state of the goddess's clothes instead reflects her having traveled extensively: between her dominion and that of the gods as well as between the dominion of the gods and the human world—whether in search of the Sea or in flight from him—or even in flight from the other gods and their demands.

56. So Wilson, "The Repulsing of the Dragon and the Creation," 18; Gardiner, "Astarte Papyrus," 80. Helck ("Astartepapyrus," 222) thinks that these gestures are merely a part of normal polite conduct among the gods.

57. Only 2 of the proposed 15 columns (according to Gardiner, the papyrus consisted of 15 pages on the *obverse* side and 5–6 on the *reverse*) remain, and only a few of the sentences are preserved whole, mostly on pp. 1–2 (Gardiner, "Astarte Papyrus," 74–75; Helck, "Astartepapyrus," 220). The extant columns are from the beginning of the text, because there are merely 7 lines ("and probably more than this") missing from the top of the papyrus. Alan H. Gardiner, *Late-Egyptian Stories* (Brussels: Édition de la Fondation égyptologiques, 1981) 76a, 81.

On line 4, 15, y, the god Seth, which the Egyptians likened to the Northwest Semitic Baʿal, is mentioned.[58] It appears that Seth is unimpressed by the sea's threats (he "seated himself calmly"). It is possible that the sea and Seth battled later on,[59] but no evidence of this remains. This interpretation could be informed by Seth's role as the slayer of Apep, or both of these roles of Seth may have been informed by his association with the Northwest Semitic Baʿal.[60] Some support for the interpretation has also been found in one of the remedies of the Hearst medical papyrus. PHearst 170 (11.13)[61] features a spell against a "*Tnt-amw* disease," in which we find the lines "As Seth fended off[62] the Sea (*wȝḏ-wr*), so will Seth fend off you, O *Tnt-amw*." But ultimately, we do not know what became of the relationship between Astarte and the sea in the Astarte papyrus. Gardiner suggests that the sea was conciliated rather than conquered, although there is no hint about how the story of the Astarte papyrus would have ended.[63]

It is difficult to ascertain how the ancient Egyptians interpreted or received the story, but it does not seem as though they were greatly concerned about the awesome and mythicized power of the sea. It has also been noted that, during the Ramesside period, to which the text dates, certain texts were copied so carelessly that it seems their respective scribes had not fully understood the context of their exercises.[64] It is possible that there is some kind of connection between the Ugaritic and the Egyptian texts, as Northwest Semitic mythos was somewhat popular in Egypt during the late Middle and early New Kingdom. It is also noteworthy that the papyrus was connected to the Babylonian *Enūma eliš* by Gardiner and to the Hittite Legend of the Sea by Sayce before the Ugaritic texts had yet become widely available.

According to Ritner, Astarte had been adopted into the cult and mythology of Egypt by the beginning of the New Kingdom. Ritner holds that the

58. Robert K. Ritner, "The Legend of Astarte and the Tribute to the Sea," COS 1:35; Helck ("Astartepapyrus," 217) calls it the *interpretatio aegyptiaca* of the weather god's name. Also Redford, *Egypt, Canaan, and Israel*, 117.

59. So Ritner ("Legend of Astarte," 35), according to whom, from "other sources, it appears that the Sea is ultimately vanquished in the combat by Seth."

60. For example, the Berlin Medical Papyrus 189 mentions the sea (*ym*) hearing the voice of Seth.

61. Walter Wreszinski, *Der Londoner medizinische Papyrus (und der Papyrus Hearst)* (Leipzig: Hinrichs, 1912).

62. Or "charmed."

63. Gardiner, "Astarte Papyrus," 81. On an interesting note, the Song of Hedammu also breaks off at a point where the goddess Sauska and Hedammu, the serpent converse, the goddess having gone to seduce the monster with her nudity (§§12.1–15.2 in Hoffner, *Hittite Myths*).

64. Faulkner, Wente, and Simpson, *Literature*, 10.

story has an indigenous Egyptian setting, even though it is parallel to the Ugaritic myth.[65] Helck suggests that, while it may be futile to look for the text's Vorlage, the cultural sphere in which the myth was formed should be more easily traced. He comes to the conclusion that neither the topic of the text nor its details are Egyptian but, rather, North Syrian and Hittite.[66] Redford, on the other hand, suggests that the origin of the hero-monster motif featuring the lecherous sea, while belonging to the same tradition as the Ugaritic myth, arose in the cities south of Byblos, examples of which he recounts from Aphek, Tyre, Joppa, Ashkelon, and Gaza.[67] It has also been suggested that the papyrus contains a cult legend for Astarte of Memphis.[68] Stadelmann, for instance, saw in the text a Memphite creation myth.[69]

Egyptian religious conceptions were heavily influenced by eastern Mediterranean or Northwest Semitic ideas in the Late Bronze Age. Many Northwest Semitic gods familiar from the Ugaritic pantheon were adopted into Egyptian religion, some associated with native Egyptian gods (for example, Baʿal with Seth), and some worshiped by their Semitic names, such as Anat and Qudshu.[70] The so-called Winchester relief portraying a goddess bearing the names Qudshu-Astarte-Anat has been dated to the time of the 19th or 20th Dynasty, which may have been during the reign of Ramesses III and was in roughly the same period as the Astarte papyrus.[71]

Whether or not there is a relation between this Egyptian tale and the epic myths from Ugarit, note that what we have at the beginning of the Astarte papyrus is what appears to be a cosmogonic myth. In it, the union of sea and earth produces "the four regions of the earth" (I, x+ 6–7). The creation of the world preceding the *Chaoskampf* is something that has not been found in the Ugaritic texts, despite numerous attempts to locate (or presuppose) it. The existence of the Egyptian text does not allow us to postulate the existence of a

65. Ritner, "Legend of Astarte," 35.

66. Helck, "Astartepapyrus," 216, 223.

67. Redford, *Egypt, Canaan, and Israel,* 45–46.

68. Helck, "Astartepapyrus," 215.

69. Rainer Stadelmann, *Syrisch-palästinensische Gottheiten in Ägypten* (Probleme der Ägyptologie 5; Leiden: Brill, 1967) 509.

70. Northwest Semitic influence can be seen, for example, in Ramesses II's naming of one of his daughters Bint-Anat, "Daughter-of-Anat," and his weapon "Anat-is-victorious." Names bearing the theophoric element *Anat* had started appearing in Egyptian scarab inscriptions during the 15th Dynasty, some centuries after the first attestations of Anat as a theophoric element in the Old Babylonian period in Mari and Babylon. See Redford, *Egypt, Canaan, and Israel,* 110; Alberto R. W. Green, *The Storm-God in the Ancient Near East* (Biblical and Judaic Studies from the University of California, San Diego 8; Winona Lake, IN: Eisenbrauns, 2003) 201–2.

71. I. E. S. Edwards, "A Relief of Qudshu-Astarte-Anat in the Winchester College Collection," *JNES* 14 (1955) 51.

cosmogonic myth preceding the battle of Yamm and Baʿal in the *Baʿal Cycle*, but it does give room for some speculation. But what does require emphasis is the seeming direction of influence. The Northwest Semitic or Canaanite milieu has traditionally been seen as the borrower of Egyptian and other surrounding influences,[72] but it is quite clear that, when it comes to the conflict myth, it was the Egyptians who did much of the borrowing during the time of the writing of these stories.

Here, I should also mention an El-Amarna literary or scholarly text, EA 340[73] from the "Canaanite group," which seems to refer to a similar theme. The New Kingdom text dating roughly to the fourteenth century is short and fragmentary, but line 6 features the word "sea," A.AB.BA. Reference is also made to a king LUGAL/*šarru*, a chariot, and clouds in heaven (*er-pe-ti eš-tu* AN). Line 3 may refer to Lebanon or Laban (*ki la-ba-ni* URU.KI). Unfortunately, only eight lines of the text have been partially preserved, so it is difficult to tell whether it is the conflict myth that is being referenced here. Because the Amarna letters famously contain exchanges between the Thutmosid administration of the 18th Dynasty and their eastern Mediterranean correspondents, however, it is entirely possible that this text relates to or references for the Egyptians the myth that was so popular with the Northwest Semites at the time.

While inarguably a myth of conflict, the New Kingdom story from the time of the 20th Dynasty, *The Contendings of Horus and Seth* (P. Chester Beatty I), on the other hand, has seldom been compared with the Northwest Semitic conflict myth. There is no mention of an aqueous foe in the story, but it does bear at least some affinity to the struggle between Baʿal and Yamm because, in it, Horus and Seth contend for kingship. It is Horus, not Seth(-Baʿal) who eventually becomes the king of Egypt, which in itself might serve as a vague reference to the Asiatic myth. Seth's role had become increasingly adversarial in Egyptian mythos following the end of the Hyksos reign, although references to the conflict between the two gods do go back to Old Kingdom times. Seth, whom the Hyksos had worshiped as Baʿal, later became associated with Apep and the Greek Typhon, essentially becoming his own worst enemy. Baʿal became Yamm.

Subduing chaos by establishing and maintaining order and permanence was one of the primary and fundamental ideological functions of the Egyptian

72. For example, Wyatt, "*There's Such Divinity*," 19: "Suffice to say that there is undoubtedly contact between the Egyptian and Sumero-Akkadian traditions, and with the Canaanite world lying between the two cultural matrices, it should occasion no surprise to find traces of the same tradition."

73. J. A. Knudzon, *Die El-Amarna Tafeln* (VAB 2; Leipzig: Hinrichs, 1907–15).

king. One of the ways in which this function was presented was by the king's conquering of an enemy, which was a general theological statement of his efficacy in the role of a king.[74] While it may be that maintaining ordered society is the staple of any ruler, it seems that this Egyptian conception of divine kingship is often projected onto the Northwest Semitic idea of kingship, and the Northwest Semitic king is also seen as the conqueror of chaos. But there were differences in the legitimation of kingship between the ancient Egyptians and the ancient Northwest Semitic peoples. The main difference was that the Northwest Semitic king was not considered divine, and his power was not legitimated by divine birth. An Egyptian king's kingship was legitimated by his participation in the cycle of divine birth; the Northwest Semitic king's by his ability to combat his enemies. And these different ideologies for the establishment of kingship require different myths for their legitimation. For the ancient Egyptian, the conquering of chaos was a special concern, in that chaos was the opposite of *maʾat*, a concept of extreme significance. Every king's duty was to reestablish *maʾat* in the land, to reintroduce order, truth, and justice into nature as well as human society.[75] This is actually said in so many words in royal inscriptions: "The King Pepi II has put *maʾat* in the place of *isfet*."

All in all, there seem to be very few instances of a conflict myth, let alone the Northwest Semitic conflict myth, to be found in ancient Egyptian mythology. This may be due to the fact that myths of conflict in ancient Egypt were presented not in actual mythology of creation and divine beings but in the person of the pharaoh. The focus was on historical, political myths. The pharaoh was the hero-warrior, the conqueror of the "seven bows," whose triumphs were told again and again (often using the very same words and phrases copied from earlier tombs and monuments) of pharaoh after pharaoh. These conquest narratives may have had some historical basis on some occasions, but often they exemplified idealized political mythology, an imagined history that became a reality because it was so written. The creation of the ancient Egyptian world was not the result of conflict, but the creation of the united Egyptian state under the legendary King Narmer in the Early Dynastic period was—or so goes the legend.

The Northwest Semitic king's power sought its legitimacy from participation in the warrior god's conquest of his mythicized foe; in Egypt, the pharaoh, the son of Re, played the part of the warrior god, conquering Egypt's actual

74. Mary Wright and Dennis Pardee, "Literary Sources for the History of Palestine and Syria: Contacts between Egypt and Syro-Palestine during the Old Kingdom," *BA* 51 (1988) 156; Henri Frankfort, *Ancient Egyptian Religion: An Interpretation* (New York: Columbia University Press, 1948) 49.

75. Redford, *Egypt, Canaan, and Israel*, 74.

(although, in number and iconography, at least partially mythicized) foes. There also seems to have been no real connection of mythical foes to the concept of the sea in Egyptian mythology, despite the battle of Re and Apep taking place in it since, due to the influence of the Nile on Egyptian society, the Mediterranean sea, although an important trade-route to the Cypro-Levantine world, was of relatively little significance to the ancient Egyptian.[76]

The references to the conflict myth and the conquering of the sea that we find in Egyptian texts may date to the 15th Dynasty of the Middle Kingdom, because the Hyksos, the "foreign rulers," are proposed to have been of Amorite stock.[77] It would make sense for some Amorite myths or legends to have circulated in Egypt during their reign, and indeed to have influenced the genesis of the Egyptian and Egyptianizing traditions of the conflict myth. What remains is that it is extremely doubtful that any *indigenously* Egyptian myth would have influenced the Northwest Semitic conflict myth, except to provide a thin veneer of stylistic, iconographic influence, bringing in Egyptian color and fashion to the narrative, for example, in the form of the Memphite smith.

76. Which is not to suggest that ancient Egyptians were not a maritime people, as is sometimes claimed. During the time of the Egyptian empire of the early New Kingdom, the Mediterranean coast up to the river Orontes belonged to the Egyptian sphere of influence, maintained through its naval power (Redford, *Egypt, Canaan, and Israel*, 167).

77. Ibid., 107. De Moor ("Egypt, Ugarit and the Exodus," 227) also suggests that both the Ugaritic ruling class and the proto-Israelites were of Amorite extraction.

Yamm as the Personification of Chaos?

A Linguistic and Literary Argument for a Case of Mistaken Identity

Brendon C. Benz

William Jewell College

Introduction

The battle between Baʿl and Yamm in *KTU* 1.2 IV is often regarded as reflecting aspects of Gunkel's *Chaoskampf* motif, in which a divine hero confronts and defeats the elements of chaos that threaten to disrupt the established order. Some, therefore, have maintained that Yamm is the personification of these chaotic forces or, at the very least, the inimical cosmic enemy of the pantheon.[1] Textual support for this claim is largely drawn from *KTU* 1.3 III 38–46, a litany of victory sung by Anat:

38. *lu maḫaštu mêdada ʾili yamma*	Indeed I smote Yamm, the beloved of El
39. *lu kallêtu nahara ʾila rabbama*	Indeed I annihilated Naharu, the great god
40. *lu ʾištabim tunnāna ištm*[ ]*h*	Indeed I bound Tunnan . . .
41. *maḫaštu baṯna ʿaqallatāna*	I smote the twisty serpent
42. *šalyaṭa dā šabʿati raʾašīma*	The tyrant of seven heads
43. *maḫaštu mêdada ʾilima ʾāriša*	I smote the beloved of El, Desire
44. *ṣamattu ʾigla ʾili ʿātika*	I destroyed Rebel, the Calf of El
45. *maḫaštu kalbata ʾilima ʾišata*	I smote Fire, the Dog of El
46. *kallêtu bitta ʾili ḏabūba*	I annihilated Flame, the daughter of El

In her recent analysis of this passage, Aicha Rahmouni contends that the epithet "the dragon of the two flames," which she reads at the end of line 40,

1. So Arvid Schou Kapelrud, *Baal in the Ras Shamra Texts* (Copenhagen: Gad, 1952) 101–2; Pierre Bordreuil and Dennis Pardee, "Le combat de *Baʿlu* avec *Yammu* d'après les textes ougaritiques," *MARI* 7 (1993) 70; Wayne Pitard, "The Binding of Yamm: A New Edition of the Ugaritic Text KTU 1.83," *JNES* 57 (1998) 273–80; Marc Van de Mieroop, *A History of the Ancient Near East* (Malden: Blackwell, 2007) 168. *Contra* Frank Moore Cross, *Canaanite Myth and Hebrew Epic* (Cambridge: Harvard University Press, 1973) 118–20; Elizabeth Williams-Forte, "The Snake and the Tree in the Iconography and Texts of Syria during the Bronze Age," in *Ancient Seals and the Bible* (ed. Leonard Gorelick and Elizabeth Williams-Forte; Malibu, CA: Undena, 1983) 18–43.

"refers to Yammu, the god of the sea."[2] In this way, she identifies Yamm with Tunnan, the serpentine enemy of the created order.[3]

A reevaluation of the syntax, semantics, and structure of this text, however, suggests an alternative reading. By highlighting the temporal function of *w-* as it operates in the epic poetry of Ugarit and examining the poetic structure of the passage at hand, I argue that Yamm should not be equated with Tunnan. Instead, Tunnan should be identified with "the twisty serpent" // "the tyrant with seven heads" in the lines that follow, epithets that are used elsewhere to describe Lītān. Read in this way, Yamm represents one of a number of figures, *including* Tunnan and/or Lītān, with whom Anat did battle and defeated. This reading calls into question the textual support for necessarily identifying Yamm as the personification of the powers of chaos, compelling us to reconsider the nature of his conflict with Baʿl.

As is indicated by the incomplete translation of *KTU* 1.3 III 38–46 provided above, the primary crux of this passage is located in line 40. There, a small break has left a gap at the end of the final phrase. According to Dennis Pardee's epigraphic analysis, the restoration of a /d/ or an /l/ is the most likely reconstruction, both letters being equally plausible.[4] This allows for two possible readings of this broken phrase. The following is an evaluation of the merits and drawbacks of each of these reconstructions. After selecting the most likely option and analyzing its role in the passage, I conclude with a few suggestions about how this text should inform our understanding of the identity of Yamm and his contextual companions.

Restoring a /d/: "Indeed I bound Tunnan and Destroyed Him"

Beginning with Pardee's initial suggestion, restoring a /d/ at the end of line 40 produces a first-person common singular *yaqtulu* verb from the root *šmd*, plus the third-person masculine singular suffix *-hū*. The resulting line is commonly

2. Aicha Rahmouni, *Divine Epithets in the Ugaritic Alphabetic Texts* (trans. J. N. Ford; HO 1/93; Leiden: Brill, 2008) 310.

3. This reading is echoed in Gregorio del Olmo Lete and Joaquín Sanmartín, *A Dictionary of the Ugaritic Language in the Alphabetic Tradition* (trans. Wilfred G. E. Watson; HO 1/67; Leiden: Brill, 2003) 873: "DN, 'dragon' *ym*'s primordial ally or double."

4. According to Pardee, the break could have contained . . . either two narrow signs or one wide one. The traces which remain are: the upper left corner of a vertical wedge on the left side of the break and the tip of what is probably another vertical wedge on the right side of the break. . . . As for the trace on the right side, it is high on the plane of writing, with no trace of another tip below it, so is probably the upper right corner of a vertical wedge rather than the tip of an horizontal one—the very bottom of the plane of the writing is damaged and one cannot, therefore, determine whether or not there is another tip there. Thus Herdner's /l/ in the slot is perfectly plausible, but /d/ is equally so ("Will the Dragon Never Be Muzzled?" *UF* 16 [1984] 253).

rendered, "Indeed I bound Tunnan and destroyed him." This reconstruction is, however, problematic on several levels. Semantically, though the root *šmd* is known from Biblical Hebrew, Aramaic, and Akkadian,[5] it is not attested elsewhere in the Ugaritic corpus. Moreover, in Biblical Hebrew it is only attested in the Niphal ("to be exterminated") and the Hiphil ("to annihilate, exterminate"), and in Akkadian, the word *šamādu* has the meaning "to apply, inlay (ornaments)."[6]

On the syntactical level, we must determine how one is to read the phenomenon of two finite verbs appearing in a single line as this reconstruction suggests. Though multiple finite verbs do not regularly appear in a single line in the epic poetry from Ugarit, this construction is not unknown. It occurs approximately 150 times in the texts of *Aqhat*, *Kirta*, and *The Baʿal Cycle* (see appendix 1). These examples fall into two general categories. The largest consists of poetic lines containing verbs that are linked by the particle *w-*.[7] The other consists of lines in which the verbs are not linked by a *w-*.

With regard to the first category, the examples therein are subdivided into three classes. The first and smallest of these includes two parallel examples in which the two verbs involved are linked by a *disjunctive w-*.[8] The second and third categories are related in that the verbs in each line are linked by a *conjunctive w-*. While the first of these subgroups consists of formulaic phrases, the second contains lines that are not formulaic. In spite of this distinction, the function of the conjunctive *w-* is the same. In both cases, the second verb is semantically and therefore temporally dependent on the first. Accordingly, the *w-* functions as a marker indicating that each verb within the line denotes a different poetic moment or temporal frame within the sequential progression of the narrative.

This phenomenon is clearly illustrated in *KTU* 1.19. The third column of this tablet describes the actions of Danil as he searches for the corpse of his son, which has been devoured by birds. After asking Baʿl three times to break the wings of the potential culprits flying above, Danil articulates his plan and carries it out when his request is fulfilled. This plan consists of four successive actions described in two separate lines. The temporal progression in these lines is indicated by both the semantic range of the individual verbs and the presence of a conjunctive *w-* separating them. When the birds are brought down before Danil, "he splits their bellies *and then* he looks" (*ʾibkʿ kbdthm*

5. Pardee, "Dragon," 254.

6. *CAD* Š/1 288.

7. The sole exception to this rule is *KTU* 1.4 IV 35, where the two imperatives *lḥm*, "eat," and *štym*, "drink," are linked by the particle *hm*.

8. *KTU* 1.1 IV 18 // 1.3 IV 33, *ʿatm. bštm. wan. šnt.*, "You delay, but I depart."

w'aḥd, lines 3–4, 10, 18–19, 24, 32–33, 38). Upon discovering evidence of Aqhat's corpse, "he weeps *and then* he buries him" (*'abky waqbrnh*, lines 5, 20, 34, 40). In both cases, the verbs involved represent two different actions carried out successively.

Another group of examples reflecting this construction appears in *KTU* 1.3 I. Lines 4–5, 8–9, and 18 are syntactically parallel. Each begins with a participle that sets the general *a-temporal* narrative stage for the two finite verbs that follow,[9] both of which mark discrete temporal frames in the progression of the narrative. In lines 4–5, while standing, the actor prepares (*ytʿr*) *and then* gives Baʿl food (*w-yšlḥmnh*). Similarly, in lines 8–9, while moving about (*ndd*), the actor invites (*yʿšr*) *and then* offers Baʿl a drink (*w-yšqnh*). Finally, in line 18 the actor, who remains standing, intones a song (*ybd*) *and then* sings (*w-yšr*).

Though it could be argued from a modern semantic perspective that the act of "intoning" takes place during the same poetic moment as "singing a song," another more common formulaic phrase suggests the opposite point of view for the ancient. More often than not, direct discourse in Ugaritic poetry is introduced with a variation of the phrase "She raised her voice *and then* she declared" (*tšu gh wtṣḥ*).[10] This formula suggests that the lifting of the voice is a preparatory act that temporally precedes the act of speaking. By analogy, so too is the act of intoning a prerequisite for the act of singing. In each of these cases, the chronological progression of the passage requires the first verb to precede the second.[11] This precedence is formally marked by the presence of the *w-* and the intervening role it plays in the phrase. A comparable formula is

9. See also *KTU* 1.10 II 25. Reading *qm* as a participle runs contrary to Josef Tropper's analysis of the form (*Ugaritische Grammatik* [AOAT 273; Münster: Ugarit-Verlag, 2000] 648–49). However, Sanmartín, *Dictionary of the Ugaritic Language*, 702 lists it as the form of both the perfect and the ms participle. The same phenomenon is seen in Biblical Hebrew, where קם functions as both the ms participle and the 3ms Qal perfect. In addition, *KTU* 1.2 II 31; 1.15 II 18–19; 1.19 II 8–10 and 1.16 I 13–14 all represent cases in which participles are used to establish the narrative frame in which the action of the verb that follows is carried out. For example, according to *KTU* 1.19 II 8–9, *while* Paghit wept, she led the donkey (*bkm.tmdln.ʿr*). Compare this text especially with 1.16 VI 4, a line that begins with the contracted form of the feminine-singular participle *bky* and is followed by two finite verbs separated by the temporal *w-*: *bkt. tgly. wtb'u*, "As she was crying, she presented herself *and then* she entered." A similar phenomenon takes place when a line is fronted by an infinitive. In these examples, the action of the infinitive sets the temporal frame in which the action of the finite verb that follows takes place (see *KTU* 1.14 I 31; 1.17 V 9; 1.19 I 28; II 27; III 56; 1.4 II 12).

10. *KTU* 1.1 V [17]; 1.3 III 36; 1.4 IV 30, V 25–26, VII 22; 1.5 II 17, 21, VI [3], 22; 1.6 I 39, II 11–12, III 17, IV 9; 1.14 IV [2], 38–39; 1.15 III 27; 1.16 IV 15–16, 40–41; 1.17 II 11–12; VI 15, 53; 1.18 I 23; IV 6–7; 1.19 II 47–48; III 1, 11–12, 16, 25–26, 30, 42, 51; IV 2–3, 19–20).

11. Other examples that fall within this category include *KTU* 1.1 IV 16; 1.2 IV 27; 1.3 I 4, 8, 18, II 38, III 21–22, IV 21, 42, V [4]; 1.4 III 12, 13, [33], [34], V 46–47; 1.6 I 16, III 18.

found in the common Akkadian phrase *pâšu īpušamma*, "to work the mouth," followed by *issaqaram*, "to speak," as in the phrase *Etana pâšu īpušamma ana erîmma issaqaršu*, "Etana worked his mouth *and then* said to the eagle."[12] Here, the temporal priority of "opening" or "working" the mouth is specifically marked by the suffix *-ma* appended to the verb *epēšum*.[13]

This phenomenon stands in sharp contrast to the examples that fall into the second category mentioned above. In these cases, though a single line contains multiple verbs, they are *not* separated by the conjunction *w-*. This construction, in combination with the nature of the verbs employed, suggests that the actions of the verbs are being executed during the *same* poetic moment. In other words, such a sequence of verbs marks cases of internal verbal parallelism occurring within a single poetic line. For example, in lines 4 and 9 of *KTU* 1.4 IV, Qudshu wa-Amrar, the servant of Athirat, prepares Athirat's donkey//mule (*ʿr // pḥl*) in order that she might travel to El. In the process of these preparations, Qudshu wa-Amrar "tied the donkey—bound the mule" (*mdl ʿr ṣmd pḥl*).[14] The actions of these verbs are clearly temporally

12. See *CAD* Z 21.

13. John Huehnergard offers the following description of the semantic nuance of the coordination *-ma*, which stands in contrast with the coordinating *-u*:

> Clauses connected with *u* bear equal semantic or thought stress, and are reversible; that is, the classes could be reversed without altering their essential meaning or relationship to each other. When clauses are connected with *-ma*, the main thought stress, the emphasis, lies with the last clause. Further, clauses connected with *-ma* may not be reversed without changing the meaning. Clauses connected with *-ma* are logically related in some way. The first clause normally presents the conditions that result in the action of the second clause. The first clause may be said to be "logically subordinate" to the second. (John Huehnergard, A *Grammar of Akkadian* [Winona Lake, IN: Eisenbrauns, 2005] 49–50)

Huehnergard continues with the following example from Akkadian: *ilū šarram ul iškunū-ma mātum iḫliq*, "The gods did not install a king, and so (or and then) the land perished" (p. 50). Another formulaic phrase that follows this pattern is the description of obeisance that is offered from an inferior to his or her superior before the delivery of a message. This formula consists of three lines. The first two lines are syntactically parallel in that they each contain two verbs describing some act of deference separated by a conjunctive *w-*. In the first line, the inferior is to "bow down *and then* fall" (*hbr wql*), and in the second he is to "prostrate himself *and then* give honor" (*tšt ḥwy wkbd*). Though the semantics of the opening verb in both lines is not entirely clear, the temporal progression suggested by the sequence is evident. This sequence is brought to a close temporally in the third and final line, which *begins* with a conjunctive *w-* followed by the verb "to speak" (*rgm*, *KTU* 1.1 IV [24]–[25], V [15]–16; 1.2 I 15–[16]; 1.3 VI 19–21; 1.4 IV 25–26, VIII 26–29; 1.6 I 36–38; 1.17 VI 50–51). Two additional formulaic statements that indicate a progression in the narrative line by means of the conjunctive *w-* include the announcement of the arrival of a character at a particular location and the less common description of laughter. In the first example, the formula indicates that a character "comes" (*gly*) to a particular location "*and then* enters" (*wt/ybu*; *KTU* 1.3 V 7; 1.4 IV 23; 1.5 VI [1]). In the second example, the character first "unknit the brow *and then* laughed" (*yprq lsb wyshq*; *KTU* 1.4 IV 28; 1.6 III 16; 1.17 II 10).

14. See also the parallel passage in *KTU* 1.19 II 3–5, 8–9.

synonymous and are meant to be read as parallel statements describing a single act. As lines 14–15 indicate, the donkey//mule refer to the same beast upon which Qudshu wa-Amrar sets Athirat.[15]

The unique temporal nature of this construction is underscored by examples in which the verbal sequence is preceded by a temporal particle that demarcates a single chronological frame in which the actions that follow commonly operate. One instance of this occurs in the description of Baʿl's divine banquet in *KTU* 1.4 VI.[16] In line 55, the general chronological stage is set by the introductory particle *ʿd*, "as": *ʿd. lḥm. šty. ʾilm*. The fact that the two verbs that follow are operating within the same poetic moment is indicated by the following line, which, by means of a conjunctive *w-*, *interrupts* the poetic moment of the first line: *wpqmrǵṯm. ṯd.* In spite of this interruption, the nuance of the introductory particle *ʿd* allows for the two poetic moments to overlap. Understood thus, a wooden rendering of this passage reads as follows: "In the midst of the time frame in which the gods both ate and drank // (*then*) animals that suckle on the breast were provided."[17]

Returning to line 40 of *KTU* 1.3 III, if indeed a /d/ is to be reconstructed in the break, one would expect a conjunctive *w-* intervening between the initial verbal phrase *lu ʾištabim*, "indeed I bound," and the resulting verbal phrase *ʾištamid-hū*, "I destroyed him," on the basis of the temporal sequence of these two actions. As such, the line would read, "Surely I bound Tunnan *and then* I destroyed him." Its absence, along with the aforementioned semantic difficulties revolving around the root *šmd* suggest that we should evaluate the merits of the alternative reconstruction proposed by Pardee and followed by Rahmouni.

15. Compare with Zech 9:9. Another version of this construction is found in the rhetorical question posed to Baʿl and Anat by Athirat in *KTU* 1.4 II 24–25. There she asks her divine children, "Would you murder me or would you murder my sons?" (*mḫṣyhm*[*.m*] *ḫṣ* / *bny*). As in the example above, this sequence of verbs is not meant to represent two sequential events but to create a general, temporally synonymous context that underscores the eradication of the family in general rather than its members in particular.

16. See also the very broken but parallel passage in *KTU* 1.5 IV 12–14.

17. Note the parallel phrase in *KTU* 1.15 VI 2–3, which carries the same nuance: *ʿdm.* <*t*>[*lḥ*]*m. tšty* / *wtʿn. mṯt ḥry*. A similar construction is found in *KTU* 1.5 I 1–4 // 27–31. There, the general chronological frame of the verbs that follow is set by the introductory particle *k*, "as, when." In contrast to 1.4 VI 55–56, however, this sequence of verbs is not interrupted by a conjunctive *w-*. This indicates that all of these actions occur in the same temporal frame. Thus at the very moment in which Baʿl killed Lītān (*ktmḫṣ ltn*), "the heavens grew hot, they melted" (*ṯṯkḥ ttrp šmm*).

Restoring an /l/: "Indeed I bound Tunnan—the Two Flames That Belong to Him"

In contrast to the verbal phrase rendered by the reconstruction of a */d/*, reading an */l/* in the break produces a clause that consists of the noun *ʾišatêmi*, "the two flames," followed by the asyndetic relative clause *le-hū*, "that belong to him." The resulting line consists of two balanced clauses. While the first is a general statement regarding the "binding" of Tunnan, the second narrows the focus of what Anat "bound" through the elision of the opening verb:[18]

lu ʾištabim tunnāna	Indeed I bound Tunnan
ʾišatêmi le-hū	(I bound) the two flames that belong to him

This proposal solves the semantic and syntactic difficulties posed by the first reconstruction. However, before we can accept it and evaluate its implications, we must scrutinize it with similar rigor.

The most obvious question that arises when considering this reading is whether or not possession is rendered with the preposition *l-* in an asyndetic relative phrase elsewhere in the poetic corpus from Ugarit. In fact, there are five examples of this structure from the *Baʿl Cycle* alone. Three of them indicate something that a character is lacking. For example, in *KTU* 1.4 IV 50–51, Athirat delivers the following complaint to El: "There is not a house that belongs to Baʿl like the gods" (*wn. ʾin. bt. lbʿl / km. ilm*).[19] Conversely, the fourth instance indicates what belongs to a character. In *KTU* 1.3 III 20–21, Baʿl announces to Anat via his messengers, "Behold, there is a message that belongs to me and I will tell you" (*dm. rgm / ʾiṯ. ly. w. ʾargmk*). The final example comes from a broken context in which Anat is apparently referred to as "the in-law that belongs to the gods" (*ybm. lʾilm, KTU* 1.6 I 31).[20]

Based on the above evaluation of both possible reconstructions, I consider it best to accept the latter, reading "Indeed I bound Tunnan // (I bound) the two flames that belong to him." With this conclusion at hand, we can now begin the process of determining the relationship between Yamm and Tunnan.

---

18. For other examples of elision or gapping that occurs in Ugaritic poetry, see Wilfred G. E. Watson, *Classical Hebrew Poetry* (JSOTSup 26; Sheffield: JSOT Press, 1986) 174–75.

19. See also 1.2 I 19, "There is not a house that belongs to me like the gods" (*ank.ʾin. bt*[*.l*]*y* [*km. i*]*lm*), and *KTU* 1.2 I 22, "But there is not a wife that belongs to you" (*wn*[.] *ʾin. aṯt*[*. l*]*k*).

20. Other examples of this construction in poetic texts include *KTU* 1.13 7, "bind the heads that belong to your warriors" (*ʿtk. rʾiš*[*t.*] *lmhrk*); *KTU* 1.17 I 20, "There is not a son that belongs to him like his brothers" (*bl. iṯ. bn. lh. <k><<w>>m. aḫh*); and *KTU* 1.82 2: "Already, the curse is not belonging to me" (*ʾidy. ʾalt. ʾin ly*). Examples from nonpoetic texts include *KTU* 4.422 1, "cattle that belong to them" (*alpm lhm*), and *KTU* 4.339 17, "people who belong to the king" (*bnšn dt lmlk*).

In order to do this, we must first determine the relationship between line 40 and the lines that precede and follow it.

The Poetic Logic of KTU 1.3 III 38–46

As I indicated at the outset of this study, Rahmouni concludes that "the epithet *tnn ʾištm lh* 'the dragon of the two flames' . . . *refers to Yammu, the god of the sea*."[21] Read in this way, line 40 constitutes the final line of a tricolon that begins in line 38. The result is that Tunnan of line 40 is identified with *ym* // *nhr* in lines 38 and 39, respectively.[22] There are, however, several problems that arise from this reading. If line 40 is indeed the third of a tricolon, it disrupts the poetic logic of both the individual unit and the entire passage in which it is embedded. In line 38, Anat proclaims that she "smote" (*mḫṣ*) Yamm. This statement is followed by the parallel claim that she "put an end" (*klt*) to the River, an epithet elsewhere attributed to Yamm. The narrative current of these two lines is clear. Depicting the events of a battle as they would have occurred, the scene moves from smiting to annihilating. This same dramatic depiction is employed in lines 43–44 and 45–46, both of which form two sets of parallel lines. If line 40 is the third line of a tricolon, it reverses this logic. Rather than continuing her litany of victory after noting her annihilation of Yamm, Anat reverts to the pre-death activity of binding him (*tnn*) and then annihilates him again after she had *already* annihilated him in line 39.

This complication is resolved if lines 38–39 are read as a bicolon followed by a tricolon consisting of lines 40–42. Read in this way, the activities depicted in lines 40–42 are distinguished from those in lines 38–39. It is equally significant that this alteration results in a uniform progression of syntactic parallelism throughout the entire passage that ultimately demarcates its independent units (see table 1).

As this lineation indicates, the passage consists of four distinct episodes, each of which contain two verbs (V), two modifiers (M), and two objects (O). In the final two (lines 43–44 and 45–46), these grammatical elements parallel one another (V-M-O // V′-M′-O′). In lines 38–39, the order of the modifier and object of the second line are reversed, forming a partial chiasm within the unit (V-M-O // V′-O′-M′).[23] The final division is unique in that it consists of three lines (40–42). Nevertheless, it is constructed according to the same

21. Rahmouni, *Divine Epithets*, 310; emphasis mine. Though he follows the alternative reconstruction, Pardee ("Dragon," 251–53) arrives at the same conclusion in his own structural analysis of this passage.

22. See Sanmartín, *Dictionary of the Ugaritic Language*, 873.

23. For more examples of chiasmus in Ugaritic poetry, see John W. Welch, "Chiasmus in Ugaritic," in *Chiasmus in Antiquity* (ed. John W. Welch; Champaign, IL: Research Press, 1998) 36–49; Watson, *Classical Hebrew Poetry*, 202.

Table 1. KTU 1.3 III 38–46

38	V-M-O *lu maḫaštu–mêdada ʾili–yamma*	Indeed I smote Yamm, the beloved of El
39	V′-O′-M′ *lu kallêtu–nahara–ʾila rabbama*	Indeed I annihilated River, the great god
40	V-O-M *lu ʾištabim–tunnāna–ʾišatêmi le-hū*	Indeed I bound Tunnan, his two flames
41	V′-O′ *maḫaštu–batna ʿaqallatāna*	I smote the twisty serpent
42	M′ *šalyaṭa dī šabʿati raʾašīma*	the tyrant of seven heads
43	V-M-O *maḫaštu–mêdada ʾilima–ʾāriša*	I smote Desire, the beloved of El
44	V′-M′-O′ *ṣamattu–ʾigla ʾili–ʿātika*	I destroyed Rebel, the Calf of El
45	V-M-O *maḫaštu–kalbata ʾilima–ʾišata*	I smote Fire, the Dog of El
46	V′-M′-O′ *kallêtu–bitta ʾili–dabūba*	I annihilated Flame, the daughter of El

general pattern as its counterparts with the verb and object of the first line paralleled in the second, and the modifier paralleled in the third (V-O-M // V′-O′/-M′).

The independent integrity of lines 40–42 is confirmed in the textual parallels located in *KTU* 1.5 I 1–3 and 1.5 I 27–30. There, Mot makes the following announcement:

kī timḫaṣ lîtāna baṯna barīḥa	When you killed Lītān, the fleeing serpent
takalliyu baṯn ʿaqalatāna	Annihilated the twisty serpent
šilyaṭa dī šabʿati riʾašīma	the tyrant with seven heads

As in the proposed reconstruction of *KTU* 1.3 III 40–42 above, the battle with the divine enemy to which Mot refers consists of three lines, two of which employ the same epithets to refer to this enemy. In addition, these passages share the same grammatical parallelism. As in *KTU* 1.3 III 40–42, the three lines in 1.5 I 1–3 // 27–30 are structured as follows:

line 1: V-O-M
line 2: V′-O′
line 3: -M′

The weight of these observations indicates that *KTU* 1.3 III 40–42 is a single unit that refers to a single divine enemy who is set apart from those that precede and follow him.

Conclusion: The Identity of Yamm and His Contextual Companions

The above evidence strongly suggests that, rather than being an epithet for Yamm, the title *tunnāna ʾišatêmi le-hū* belongs to a different character altogether. Read as a single unit, lines 40–42 refer to Tunnan as the "twisty serpent" (*bṯn. ʿqltn*), the "potentate with seven heads" (*šlyt. d. šbʿt. rašm*).[24] In *KTU* 1.5 I 1–3, these epithets also belong to Lītān, suggesting that Lītān and Tunnan are the same character.[25] Support for this identification is found in Isa 27:1, where the biblical Leviathan is set parallel to and thereby identified with the *tannīn*.[26] Moreover, later Mandaic literature not only associates Leviathan (*lywyʾtyn*) with the "dragon" (*tʾnyn*) but also refers to this dragon as one that has "seven heads."[27]

The identification of Tunnan with Lītān in cooperation with a body of textual and iconographic evidence from the wider ancient Near East ultimately helps to clarify the meaning of the proposed reconstruction of *KTU* 1.3 III 40. In Job 41, Yahweh provides a detailed description of Leviathan. In v. 11 [ET: 21], he indicates that "torches go forth from his mouth" along with "sparks of fire" (מפיו לפידים יהלכו כידודי אש יתמלטו).[28] This description is illustrated and illuminated by iconography that depicts dragon-like figures breathing forth flames. For example, a cylinder seal from the Akkadian period depicts a winged monster pulling a divine chariot. From its mouth, this creature belches forth what appears to be two flames, which are reminiscent of a forked tongue.[29] From the Neo-Babylonian period, the famous serpent-dragon *or mušḫuššu* is repeatedly depicted on the Ištar gate and the Processional Way at Babylon. It

24. *Contra* Wilfred G. Lambert, "Trees, Snakes and Gods in Ancient Syria and Anatolia," *BSOAS* 48 (1985) 444.

25. So John Day, *God's Conflict with the Dragon and the Sea: Echoes of a Canaanite Myth in the Old Testament* (Cambridge: Cambridge University Press, 1985) 13.

26. See also Isa 51:9; Job 7:12; Ezek 29:3, 32:2; Jer 51:34; Ps 74:12–13; Day, *God's Conflict with the Dragon*, 5, 13–15, 24, 34, 41, 45. Contra Mark S. Smith, *The Origins of Biblical Monotheism* (Oxford: Oxford University Press, 2001) 36.

27. See Rahmouni, *Divine Epithets*, 304 n. 15; Ethel S. Drower and Rudolf Macuch, *A Mandaic Dictionary* (Oxford: Clarendon, 1963) 480. See also Isa 27:1, in which *tannîn* is set parallel to *liwyātān*.

28. Compare with 2 Sam 22:9 // Ps 18:9, where a consuming fire is said to come forth from the mouth of Yahweh (ואש מיפיו תאכל).

29. Reproduced in Jeremy Black and Anthony Green, *Gods, Demons and Symbols of Ancient Mesopotamia* (Austin: University of Texas Press, 1992) 52.

also possesses a forked tongue, the tip of which resembles two flames.[30] Read in light of this evidence, the image depicted in *KTU* 1.3 III 40 becomes clear. Anat did not merely bind Tunnan//Lītān but, more specifically, "*muzzled*" his mouth and thereby bound the flames//the forked tongue that issued from it.[31] It was only after she subdued him that she was able to smite him. Returning to Job, in 40:25 [ET 41:1], Yahweh rhetorically asks Job, "Can anyone subdue his (Leviathan's) tongue with a rope?" (ובחבל תשקיע לשנו). Apparently Anat can.

The foregoing evidence argues against identification of Yamm with Tunnan. Yamm is simply one of a number of figures including Tunnan or Lītān that

30. Ibid., 166. For additional examples, see Othmar Keel, *The Symbolism of the Biblical World* (trans. Timothy J. Hallett; New York: Seabury, 1978; repr. Winona Lake, IN: Eisenbrauns, 1997) 50–53. In her analysis of ancient Near Eastern Ivories in the British Museum, Edith Porada provides further clarification with regard to this imagery: "[The] parallelisms between griffin and winged lion-dragon suggest a relationship between the monsters both composed of lion and eagle; they indicate furthermore that if the lion-dragon is associated with the fire which he vomits, the griffin would probably share such an association and be correctly identified as a 'burning creature'." According to Porada, the description of characters as "fiery creatures" is often a reference to the tongue-like fires that they emit from their mouths (Porada, "Review of A *Catalogue of the Nimrud Ivories with Other Examples of Ancient Near Eastern Ivories in the British Museum* by Richard D. Barnett," *AJA* 63 [1959] 92–94). See also *KTU* 1.83 5–7, where *tnn* is the most likely source of the tongues that "lick the heavens" (*lšnm. tlḥk. šmm*) and tails that "roil/rend (?) the sea" (*ṯṯrp ym . ḏnbtm*). In opposition to this reading, Pitard contends that this is a description of Anat rather than Tunnan ("The Binding of Yamm," 275–76). This conclusion is based on his contention that *ym* in line 7 is a reference to "the god Yamm" rather "than a generic reference to the sea" (p. 276). Accordingly, the actor of this passage must be the opponent of Yamm, since the action is being taken against him. Because Pitard identifies Yamm with Tunnan, the possibility of the latter being the actor is also eliminated. However, according to his lineation of this passage (p. 273), *ym* is set parallel with *šmm*, "heavens," which he regards as an impersonal noun. Taking this parallelism seriously, I find it preferable to regard the heavens (*šmm*) and the sea (*ym*) as constituting a natural merism meant to depict the overwhelming size of the character whose tongues lick and roil/rend (?) them. A similar metaphor is used for Mot in *KTU* 1.5 II 2–3 ("[a lip to the ea]rth and a lip to the heavens") and Shahar and Shalim in *KTU* 1.23 61–62 ("a lip to earth, a lip to the heavens"). In both of these examples, the earth and the heavens are clearly impersonal nouns set in opposition in order to illustrate the scope of the divine attributes in question. Contrast this with the parallel reference to Yamm/Nahar in lines 11–12. The use of the title Nahar in this context clearly indicates that reference is being made to the god Yamm. Informed by these observations and our reading of *KTU* 1.3 III 40, we will find it most plausible to identify Tunnan as the actor in *KTU* 1.83 5–7 (see n. 33 below).

31. For a review of the debate revolving around the nuance of the verb *šbm*, "to bind/to muzzle," see Pitard, "The Binding of Yamm," 276–77. In support of the reading "to muzzle," Loewenstamm cites a passage from *Ludlul bēl nēmeqi* that depicts Marduk as placing a muzzle on the mouth of a lion who is about to devour the protagonist (*i-na pi-i gir-ra akili-a id-di nap-sa-ma* ^d^*Marduk*). According to Loewenstamm, "This Akkadian text combines the conceptions of beating and muzzling in a way analogous to" *KTU* 1.83 3–10 (Samuel E. Loewenstamm, "ʿAnat's Victory over the Tunnanu," *JSS* 20 [1975] 23).

Anat defeated.[32] This reconstruction finds support in the fact that Yamm is never directly identified with Tunnan or Lītān in the rest of the textual corpus from Ugarit.[33] As we saw above, Yamm is absent from Mot's litany in *KTU* 1.5 I 1–3 // 27–30. In addition, the *Baʿl Cycle* concludes with the statement that *ʾarš* and Tunnan are *in* the sea (*bym*), thereby distinguishing both characters *from* the sea. Finally, in *KTU* 1.82,[34] a magical incantation text in which the speaker invokes the aid of Baʿl and Anat in order that they might ward off malevolent spirits and monsters of every sort,[35] Yamm is never mentioned.[36]

Resolving this case of misidentification should cause us to take pause and reconsider the common characterization of Yamm. Is he indeed the personification of the powers of disorder, or does he simply have the capacity to wreak havoc when necessary, much in the same way that Baʿl does when he finds it appropriate? If the latter option is accepted, we must also reconsider the nature of the conflict between Baʿl and Yamm in *KTU* 1.2 IV. Is it truly representative of a *Chaoskampf* or simply the struggle between two equally legitimate candidates vying against one another to fill the role of king over the divine assembly? Because these two are the representatives of the two opposing sources of water flowing from the base of El's mountain, both of whom are

32. Frank Moore Cross makes a similar distinction in his analysis of this passage: "ʿAnat defeats the dragon and Yamm among others in CTA 3.3.35–43. The description of Baʿl killing the dragon (*tnn*) is found in PRU 2.1.1 and [*KTU* 1.5.I 1–5]" (*Canaanite Myth*, 149 n. 12).

33. See Day, *God's Conflict with the Dragon*, 14–15. According to Pitard's new edition of *KTU* 1.83, reference is made to both Yamm and Tunnan in the preserved lines of this short text (see n. 30 above). As with our analysis of *KTU* 1.3 III 38–46, however, their presence in the same text does not imply their identification, particularly when the actions taken against them are in no way paralleled. Following Pitard's translation A, which he considers to be "the most likely one," rather than Yamm's being bound and set on the heights of Lebanon, a very different fate is envisioned for him. He is scattered toward the desert, toward the multitude of *ḫt*. This reading is strengthened by the above observation that the personified character Yamm is not introduced until line 11. Again, Tunnan and Yamm here appear as two separate characters. Though they may be closely associated with one another, they should not be identified as the same figure.

34. Charles Virolleaud, *Textes en cunéiformes alphabétiques des archives est, ouest et centrales* (PRU 2; Paris: Imprimerie Nationale, 1957) no. 1; Johannes C. de Moor and Klaas Spronk, "More on Demons in Ugarit," *UF* 16 (1984) 237–49.

35. These include *tnn* (line 1), *ršp* (line 3), *mt* (line 5), *bṯnm*/*bṯnt* (lines 6, 35), *bnt*. *ḥ*[*rn*] (line 13), ʿ[*gl*.ʾ*l*] (line 14), *bnt ṣʿṣ*, "creatures of Agitation" (lines 18, 41), *bnt ḫrp* (line 18), *bn ḥtt* (line 23), *llm*, "night-demons" (line 33), *brḥ*, "fleeing (serpent)" (line 38; see *KTU* 1.5 I 1 above), *bnt mʿmʿ*, "creatures of intestinal trouble" (line 41), and *ʿbd ḥrn*, "servant of Horon" (line 41).

36. In fact, in lines 25–30, when the demons are commanded to return to their original domains, not only is Yamm absent, but so is any reference to *ym* the sea. Instead, the term *mdb*, "flood" is used (line 27). See David Toshio Tsumura, *Creation and Destruction* (Winona Lake, IN: Eisenbrauns, 2005) 179–81.

referred to as "judge" (*ṯāpiṭu*) when they occupy the throne, the latter option seems most viable.[37]

37. The fact that Baʿl is able to usurp Yamm's position reflects Ugarit's environment. As the *Hymn to Aten* indicates, this region relied primarily on the "upper Nile" for its source of rain. Thus, the storm god would most certainly have taken precedence over the personification of the river/*nhr* (see Smith, *The Origins of Biblical Monotheism*, 65).

Appendix 1. The Temporal Function of w- *in the Epic Poetry from Ugarit*

A. Examples of Internal Poetic Parallelism

KTU	*Transliteration*	*Translation*
1.1 IV 10	*ḥšk. ʿṣk. ʿ[bṣk]*	Hasten! Hurry! Rush!
1.2 II 19	*tbʿ. ġlmm. lyṯb*	The lads hasten—they do not dwell
1.2 IV 25–26	*yprsḥ. ym. yql lʾarṣ*	Yamm collapsed—He fell to the earth
1.3 III 18	*ḥšk. ʿṣk. ʿbṣk*	Hasten! Hurry! Rush!
1.3 III 46–47	*ʾimtḫṣ. ksp ʾitrṯ. ḫrṣ*	I fought for silver—I took possession of gold
1.3 IV 11	*[ḥ]šk. ʿṣk. ʿbṣk*	Hasten! Hurry! Rush!
1.3 IV 32	*lk. lk. ʿnn. ʾilm*	Go! Go! O servants of the gods
1.4 I 25–26	*yṣq. ksp. yšlḥ ḫrṣ*	He casts silver—He pours out gold
1.4 II 24–25	*mḫṣy hm [.m]ḫṣ bny*	Would you murder me or murder my sons
1.4 III 40–42	*[ʿd tl]ḥm. tšty [ʾilm]* *[wtp]q .mrġtm. [ṭd.]*	As the gods both ate and drank Then animals that suckle on the breast were provided
1.4 IV 4–5	*[mdl. ʿr] ṣmd. pḥl*	Tie the donkey—bind the mule
1.4 IV 9	*mdl. ʿr ṣmd. pḥl*	Tie the donkey—bind the mule
1.4 VI 55–56	*ʿd tlḥm. tšty ʾilm* *wpq mrġtm. ṭd.*	As the gods both ate and drank Then animals that suckle on the breast were provided
1.5 I 4	*ṯṯkḥ. ttrp. šmm.*	The heavens grew hot—they withered
1.5 I 30–31	*ttkḥ. [ttrp. šmm.]*	The heavens grew hot—they withered
1.15 III 16–17	*ṣġrthn. ʾabkrn/ʾabrkn tbrk*	The youngest of them I shall name firstborn—she shall be blessed
1.15 VI 2–3	*ʿdm. <t>[lḥ]m. tšty* *wtʿn. mtṯ ḥry*	As they ate and they drank Then Lady Huraya spoke

1.15 VI 6–7	*km rgm. ṯrm [.] rgm*	As the captains spoke and conversed
1.16 I 43	*lk. šr. ʿl ṣrrt*	Go sing upon the heights
1.16 II 26	*tṣr. trm. tnq[t]*	She wails—she raises a cry
1.16 II 34	*tṣr. trm [.t]nqt*	She wails—she raises a cry
1.16 III 2	*ʿn. tr. ʾarṣ. wšmm*	Search—scout the earth and the heavens
1.17 V 19–20	*šlḥm. ššqy ʾilm*	Dine and wine the gods
1.17 V 20	*sʾad. kbd. hmt*	Uphold—honor them
1.17 V 29	*tšlḥm. tššqy ʾilm*	She dines—she wines the gods
1.17 V 30	*tsʾad. tkbd. hmt*	She upholds—she honors them
1.17 VI 30	*kbʿl. kyḥwy. yʿšr*	Like Baʿl: *When* he revives he invites
1.19 II 3–4	*mdl. ʿr ṣmd. pḥl*	Tie the donkey—bind the mule

B. *Examples of Sequential Temporal Action Marked by an Intervening w-*

1. *Formulaic Clauses*

Speech Formula

KTU	*Transliteration*	*Translation*
1.1 V 17	*[yšʾu. ghm. wy]ṣḥ*	They raised their voice *and then* they declared
1.3 III 35–36	*tšʾu gh. wtṣḥ*	She raised her voice *and then* she declared
1.4 IV 30	*yšʾu. gh. wyṣ[ḥ]*	He raised his voice *and then* he declared
1.4 V 25–26	*tšʾu gh. wtṣḥ*	She raised her voice *and then* she declared
1.4 VII 22	*yšʾu [.] gh[.] wyṣḥ*	He raised his voice *and then* he declared
1.5 II 16–17	*tšʾa ghm. wtṣḥ*	They raised their voices *and then* they declared
1.5 II 21	*[yšʾu] gh. wyṣḥ*	He raised his voice *and then* he declared
1.5 VI 3	*[tšʾa. ghm. wtṣ]ḥ*	They raised their voices *and then* they declared
1.5 VI 22	*yšʾu. gh [.] wyṣḥ*	He raised his voice *and then* he declared
1.6 I 39	*tšʾu. gh. wtṣḥ*	She raised her voice *and then* she declared
1.6 II 11–12	*tšʾu. gh. w[tṣ]ḥ*	She raised her voice *and then* she declared
1.6 III 17	*yšʾu. gh. wyṣḥ*	He raised his voice *and then* he declared
1.6 IV 9	*tšʾu. gh. wtṣḥ*	She raised her voice *and then* she declared
1.14 VI 2	*tšʾa[n. ghm. wtṣḥn]*	They raised their voices *and then* they declared
1.14 VI 38–39	*tšʾan ghm. wtṣḥn*	They raised their voices *and then* they declared
1.15 III 27	*wtšʾu. gh. w[tṣḥ]*	Then she raised her voice *and then* she declared
1.16 VI 15–16	*yšʾu. gh wyṣḥ.*	He raised his voice *and then* he declared

1.16 VI 40–41	*yšʾu. gh wyṣḥ.*	He raised his voice *and then* he declared
1.17 II 11–12	*yšʾu. gh wyṣḥ.*	He raised his voice *and then* he declared
1.17 VI 15	*[tšʾu gh] wtṣḥ*	She raised her voice *and then* she declared
1.17 VI 53	*[tšʾu] gh. wtṣḥ.*	She raised her voice *and then* she declared
1.18 I 23	*[tšʾu] gh. wtṣḥ.*	She raised her voice *and then* she declared
1.18 IV 6–7	*[tšʾu gh] wtṣḥ.*	She raised her voice *and then* she declared
1.19 II 47–48	*[yšʾu gh] wyṣ[ḥ]*	He raised his voice *and then* he declared
1.19 III 1	*[yšʾu gh] wyṣ[ḥ]*	He raised his voice *and then* he declared
1.19 III 11–12	*yšʾu. gh wyṣḥ.*	He raised his voice *and then* he declared
1.19 III 16	*yšʾu. gh. wyṣḥ.*	He raised his voice *and then* he declared
1.19 III 25–26	*yšʾu. gh wyṣḥ.*	He raised his voice *and then* he declared
1.19 III 30	*yšʾu. gh. wyṣḥ.*	He raised his voice *and then* he declared
1.19 III 42	*yšʾu. gh. wyṣḥ.*	He raised his voice *and then* he declared
1.19 III 51	*yšʾu. gh. wyṣḥ.*	He raised his voice *and then* he declared
1.19 IV 2–3	*yšʾu. gh wyṣḥ.*	He raised his voice *and then* he declared
1.19 IV 19–20	*[y]šʾu gh. wyṣḥ*	He raised his voice *and then* he declared

Obeisance Formula

KTU	*Transliteration*	*Translation*
1.1 IV 24–25	*l[pʿn. ʾil. yhbr.* *wql]* *yštḥwy [.wykbdnh]*	At the feet of El he bows *and then* falls down He prostrates himself *and then* honors him
1.1 V 15–17	*[lpʿ]n. ʿnt [yhbr.* *wql.]* *[yšt]ḥwyn.* *wy[kbnh.]*	At the feet of Anat they bow *and then* they fall down They prostrate themselves *and then* they honor her
1.2 I 5–6	*[lpʿn. ʾil. yhbr.]* *wyql[.]* *[y]štḥw[y .]* *wykb[dnh]*	At the feet of El he bows *and then* falls down He prostrates himself *and then* honors him
1.3 III 9–10	*lpʿn. ʿnt. hbr. wql.* *tštḥwy. <w>kbdhyt*	At the feet of Anat bow *and then* fall down Prostrate yourselves <*and then*> honor her
1.3 VI 18–20	*lpʿn. kṯ<r> hbr. wql* *tštḥwy. wkbdhwt*	At the feet of Kothar bow *and then* fall down Prostrate yourself *and then* honor him
1.4 IV 25–26	*lpʿn. ʾil. thbr. wtql* *tšḥwy. wtkbdh*	At the feet of El she bowed *and then* she fell down She prostrated herself *and then* she honored him

1.4 VIII 26–29	*lpʿn.mt hbr. wql tšthwy. wkbdhwt*	At the feet of Mot bow *and then* fall down Prostrate yourself *and then* honor him
1.6 I 36–38	*lpʿn ʾil. thbr. wtql tšthwy. wtkbdnh*	At the feet of El she bowed *and then* she fell down She prostrated herself *and then* she honored him
1.17 VI 50–51	*[lpʿn ʾil t]hbr. wtql tšth[wy wtkbd]nh*	At the feet of El she bowed *and then* she fell down She prostrated herself *and then* she honored him

Approach and Entry Formula

KTU	*Transliteration*	*Translation*
1.3 V 7	*tgl. ḏ[d.] ʾil[.] wtbʾu*	She came to the mountain of El *and then* she entered
1.4 IV 23	*tgly. ḏd. ʾil. wtbʾu*	She came to the mountain of El *and then* she entered
1.5 VI 1	*[tgly. ḏd. ʾil. w] tb[ʾa]*	They came to the mountain of El *and then* they entered
1.6 I 34–35	*tgly. ḏd ʾil. wtbʾu*	She came to the mountain of El *and then* she entered

Laugh Formula

KTU	*Transliteration*	*Translation*
1.4 IV 28	*yprq. lṣb. wyṣḥq*	He unknit the brow *and then* he laughed
1.6 III 16	*wyprq. lṣb wyṣḥq*	Then he unknit the brow *and then* he laughed
1.17 II 10	*yprq. lṣb. wyṣḥq*	He unknit the brow *and then* he laughed

2. *Nonformulaic Clauses*

KTU	*Transliteration*	*Translation*
1.2 IV 26	*tnġṣn. pnth. wydlp. tmnh*	His joints shake *and then* his form collapses
1.2 IV 27	*yqṯ bʿl. wyšt. ym*	Baʿl drags *and then* dismembers/pours out Yamm
1.3 I 4–5	*qm. yṯʿr w.yšlḥmnh*	While standing, he prepares *and then* offers Baʿl food
1.3 I 8–9	*ndd yʿšr. wyšqynh*	While moving about, he serves *and then* offers Baʿl drink

1.3 I 18	*qm. ybd. wyšr*	While standing, he intones a song *and then* sings (see 1.17 VI 31)
1.3 II 23	*mʾid. tmtḫṣn. wtʿn*	She fights hard *and then* she looks about
1.3 II 24	*tḫtṣb. wthdy. ʿnt*	She does battle *and then* Anat surveys
1.3 IV 42	*tḥspn. mh. wtrḥṣ*	She draws water *and then* she washes
1.3 V 4–5	*[tdʿṣ. p] ʿn [wtr.] ʾarṣ*	She thrust her feet *and then* the earth trembled
1.4 III 12	*[ ]. ydd. wqlṣn*	. . . he stood up *and then* he abased me
1.4 III 13	yqm. wywpṯn	He arose *and then* he spat on me
1.4 V 20	*tdʿṣ. pʿnm wtr. ʾarṣ*	She thrust her feet *and then* the earth trembled
1.4 V 46–47	*tʿdb. ksʾu wyṯṯb*	A throne is set up *and then* he is seated
1.6 I 16–17	*tbkynh wtqbrnh*	She bewailed him *and then* she buried him
1.6 III 18	*ʾaṯbn. ʾank. wanḫn*	I shall sit *and then* I shall rest (see 1.17 II 12–13)
1.14 I 14	*ʾatṯ. trḫ. wtbʿt*	He wed a wife *and then* she departed
1.14 I 33–34	*šnt. tlʾuʾan wyškb*	Sleep overwhelmed him *and then* he lay down
1.14 II 9	*trtḥṣ. wtʾadm*	Wash yourself *and then* rouge
1.14 II 32	*ʿdn [.] ngb. wyṣʾi*	May the troop be supplied *and then* let it go forth
1.14 III 52	*yrtḥṣ. wyʾadm*	He washes himself *and then* he rouges
1.14 IV 13	*ʿdn. ngb. w[yṣʾi.]*	The troop is supplied *and then* it goes forth
1.16 I 12–13	*ybky wyšnn*	He cried *and then* he fell asleep
1.16 II 35	*tbky. wtšnn*	She cried *and then* she fell asleep
1.16 VI 4	*bkt. tgly. wtbʾu*	As she was crying, she presented herself *and then* she entered
1.17 I 3–4	*yd [ṣth. yʿl.] wyškb*	Removing his garment, he ascended and then he laid down
1.17 I 14	*yd. ṣth. yʿl. wyškb*	Removing his garment, he ascended and then he lay down
1.17 II 12–13	*ʾaṯbn. ʾank wanḫn*	I shall sit *and then* I shall rest (see 1.6 III 18)
1.17 II 32–34	*yšlḥm kṯrt. wyššq bnt. hll snnt.*	He dines the Katharat *and then* wines the moon's radiant daughters
1.17 VI 30–31	*ḥwy. yʿšr. wy[š] qnh*	The revived one he invites *and then* he causes him to drink
1.17 VI 31	*ybd. wyšr. ʿlh*	He intones a song *and then* he sings over him (see 1.3 I 18)
1.19 II 14–15	*bṣql. yḥbq wynšq.*	The stalks he embraces *and then* he kisses
1.19 II 21–22	*šblt. yḥ[bq] wynšq*	The ears he embraces *and then* he kisses

1.19 III 3–4	*ʾibq[ʿ kbdthm w] ʾaḥd*	I shall split their bellies *and then* I shall look
1.19 III 5	*ʾabk!y.w. ʾaqbrnh*	I shall weep *and then* I shall bury him
1.19 III 10	*ybqʿ. kbdthm. [wyḥd]*	He split their bellies *and then* he looked
1.19 III 18–19	*ʾbqʿ kbdt[h] wʾaḥd*	I shall split his belly *and then* I shall look
1.19 III 20	*ʾabky wʾaqbrn.*	I shall weep *and then* I shall bury (him)
1.19 III 24	*ybqʿ. kbdth. wyḥd*	He split his belly *and then* he looked
1.19 III 32–33	*ʾibqʿ kbdth. wʾaḥd*	I shall split her belly *and then* I shall look
1.19 III 34	*ʾabky. wʾaqbrnh*	I shall weep *and then* I shall bury him
1.19 III 38	*ybqʿ. kbdth. wyḥd*	He split her belly *and then* he looked
1.19 III 40	*ybky. wyqbr*	He wept *and then* he buried (him)
1.19 IV 54–55	*[t]qḥ. pġt. wtšqynh.*	Paghit takes *and then* she drinks it

3. *Miscellaneous*

Injunctive Clauses

KTU	*Transliteration*	*Translation*
	Clauses with an Intervening w-	
1.1 IV 16	*ʾat. w. ʾank. ʾibġ[yh]*	Come in order that I might *then* reveal it
1.2 II 18	*tn. bʿl[. wʿnnh]*	Give up Baʿl in order that I might *then* humble him
1.2 II 35	*tn. bʿl. wʿnnh*	Give up Baʿl in order that I might *then* humble him
1.3 III 28–29	*ʾatm. wʾank ʾibġyh*	Come in order that I might *then* reveal it
1.16 I 30	*tbkn. wtdm. ly*	Let her cry in order that she might *then* shed tears for me
1.16 V 25–26	*ʾank ʾiḥtrš. wʾaškn*	I shall make an incantation in order that I might *then* create
1.17 VI 17	*[ʾi]rš. ksp. wʾatnk*	Ask for silver in order that I might *then* give it to you
1.17 VI 27	*ʾirš. ḥym. wʾatnk*	Ask for life in order that I might *then* give it to you
1.19 III 13–14	*nšrm tpr. wdʾu.*	O birds, take flight in order that you might *then* fly
1.19 IV 53	*qḥn. wtšqyn. yn*	Take in order that you might *then* drink the wine

Clauses without an Intervening w-		
1.5 I 26	*pnšt. bʿl. [ṭ]ʿn. ʾiṭʿnk*	Let us drink, O Baʿl—I shall pierce you
1.6 I 45–46	*tn ʾaḥd. b. bnk[.] am<<.>>lkn*	Give one of your sons—I shall make him king
1.6 V 19–21	*tn. ʾaḥd bʾaḫk. ʾispʾa*	Give one of your brothers—I shall eat (him)
1.16 VI 37	*rd. lmlk. ʾamlk*	Step down as king—I shall reign
1.16 VI 52–53	*rd. lmlk ʾamlk*	Step down as king—I shall reign

Disjunctive Clauses

KTU	*Transliteration*	*Translation*
1.1 IV 18	*ʾatm. bštm. wʾan[. šnt]*	You delay, but I depart
1.3 IV 33	*ʾatm. bštm. wʾan. šnt*	You delay, but I depart

Explanatory Clauses

KTU	*Transliteration*	*Translation*
1.4 IV 33	*rġb. rġbt. wtġt[ ]*	Surely you are tired because you have traveled
1.4 IV 34	*hm. ġmʾu. ġmʾit. wʿs [ ]*	Or surely you are thirsty because you have journeyed

Part 3

Gunkel and His Times

Chaos and Creation

Hermann Gunkel between Establishing the "History of Religions School," Acknowledging Assyriology, and Defending the Faith

Steven Lundström

Ludwig-Maximilians Universität, Munich

1. *Chaos and Creation: The Dawn of a New Discipline*

In the year 1856, the Royal Asiatic Society initiated a competition regarding the successful decipherment of cuneiform script. And the results, delivered by Rev. Edward Hincks (1792–1866), Sir Henry Creswicke Rawlinson (1810–95), William Henry Fox Talbot (1800–1877), and Julius Oppert (1825–1905) proved successful. Henceforth, scholars spared no efforts in publishing the finds and written records discovered at the ancient sites of Nineveh, Nimrud, and Dur Sharrukin. And the public took great interest in their work as the parallels between Mesopotamian cultures and ancient Israel became more and more evident literally every day. A new discipline came into being; museums and collections dedicated to Assyria and Babylonia were founded. The time of ancient Near Eastern artifacts' being restricted to curiousty shops and *Kuriositätenkabinette* ("curiosity cabinets") of European potentates came to an end.

All the more was this true when, in the year 1874, George Smith (1840–76) drew attention to four fragments that he had discovered among the cuneiform tablets of the British Museum unearthed by Sir Austen Henry Layard

(1817–94) in Ashurbanipal's palace in Kuyunjik/Nineveh. These texts (fragmentary as they were at that time) presented an account of the world's creation and at the same time gave rise to an intense and controversial discussion of the historical and cultural background and the connections among ancient Israel, the Bible, and ancient Near Eastern cultures. His work, *The Chaldean Account of Genesis* published in 1875, was not merely a landmark in the vast fields covered by Oriental studies. It contributed significantly to the acceptance of Assyriology in general and may have helped to establish this new discipline in Germany in particular.

Although the basic principles of deciphering cuneiform script and, therefore, the foundations of Assyriology were widely recognized in Great Britain, France, and the United States from the days of the great competition on, German academics remained skeptical and neglectful (see below).[1]

The Arabist Justus Olshausen (1800–1882) and the theologian Eberhard Schrader (1836–1908) were among the first to argue in favor of Assyriology and its methodological basis in the 1860s and 1870s.[2] On behalf of the Deutsche Morgenländische Gesellschaft, Schrader published a study in the year 1872 in which he proved the accuracy of his system of deciphering, and thereby hoped to provoke some sort of reaction and counterargument, since Olshausen's and his own earlier contributions had subsequently been ignored.[3] Until then—long after Paul-Émile Botta (1802–70) and Sir Austen Henry Layard had made their discoveries—the ancient Near Eastern cultural remains seemed only good enough to inspire artists, for example, to attach a cuneiform inscription to the mantelpiece of a chimney in Weimar castle.[4]

Additionally, Schrader shared a part in directing a young scholar toward Assyriology. In 1873, this young man was sent by Hermann Brockhaus (1806–77)

1. Johannes Renger, "Die Geschichte der Altorientalistik und der vorderasiatischen Archäologie in Berlin von 1875–1945," in *Berlin und die Antike: Aufsätze* (ed. Willmuth Arenhövel and Christa Schreiber; Berlin: Wasmuth, 1979) 151–52; and Claus Wilcke, "Statt eines Vorwortes: Altorientalistische Jubiläen in Leipzig," in *Das geistige Erfassen der Welt im Alten Orient: Sprache, Religion, Kultur und Gesellschaft* (ed. Claus Wilcke; Wiesbaden: Harrassowitz, 2007) 8–9.

2. Justus Olshausen, *Prüfung des Charakters der in den assyrischen Keilinschriften enthaltenen semitischen Sprache* (Abhandlungen der Königlichen Akademie der Wissenschaften, Ph.-Hist. Klasse 49; Berlin: Königliche Akademie der Wissenschaften, 1864) and Eberhard Schrader, "Die Basis der Entzifferung der assyrisch-babylonischen Keilinschriften, geprüft von Eberhard Schrader," ZDMG 23 (1869) 337–74.

3. "[S]chon früher haben wir diese vielleicht brennendste Frage der altorientalischen Wissenschaft einer Prüfung unterstellt in der Erwartung, daß durch diesselbe die Gegner der Entzifferung sich zu einer wissenschaftlichen Formulierung und Begründung ihrer Zweifel möchten veranlaßt sehen. Diese Erwartung ist leider unerfüllt geblieben" (idem, "Die assyrisch-babylonischen Keilinschriften," ZDMG 26 [1872] 2).

4. See www.klassik-stiftung.de/fileadmin/. . ./schloss.pdf.

of Leipzig to Jena and told to pay a visit to Schrader in order to investigate whether the "decipherment of the Assyrian-Babylonian cuneiform script was accomplished successfully or not."[5] Obviously, Schrader was most persuasive, because this scholar was none other than Friedrich Delitzsch (1850–1922), who was then habilitated as lecturer of Assyriology in Leipzig in 1874.[6]

In the three decades to come, Assyriology was established at German universities and academies and, just as importantly, a great majority of the public and the scholarly community took great interest in the new discipline, its research and discussions and, not least, the activities of its representatives.[7] Toward the end of the nineteenth century, it even became part of Germany's struggle to close the gap in its rivalry with France, the British Empire, and the United States, not only in political and economic power, colonies, and military strength, but also in science.[8]

To name but a few historical benchmarks, there are Schrader's appointment as Professor of Semitic Studies (Berlin) in 1875, Delitzsch's and Zimmern's appointments as professors of Assyriology (Leipzig) in 1878/1900, the foundation of several associations such as the Orient Comité in 1887,[9] the Vorderasiatische Gesellschaft in 1895 and the Deutsche Orient-Gesellschaft in 1898[10] as well as the launch of periodicals and series such as the *Wiener*

---

5. Friedrich Delitzsch, "Mein Lebenslauf," *Reclam Universum* 47 (1920) 242–43.

6. Renger, "Geschichte der Altorientalistik," 152; Joachim Oelsner, "Altorientalistik in Jena 1," MDOG 139 (2007) 73–74; and Wilcke, "Statt eines Vorwortes," 6, 8–9.

7. For the history of Assyriology at German and Austrian universities, see Renger, "Geschichte der Altorientalistik," 151–92 (Berlin from 1875 to 1945); Hermann Hunger, "Geschichte der Altorientalistik in Wien," in *Euphrat und Tigris: Österreichische Forschungen zum Alten Orient* (ed. Friedrich Schipper; Wiener Offene Orientalistik 3; Vienna: LIT, 2004) 19–22 (Vienna from 1884 to the 1970s); Oelsner, "Altorientalistik in Jena 1," 71–81; idem, "Altorientalistik in Jena: Teil 2," MDOG 140 (2008) 75–88; idem, "Altorientalistik in Jena: Teil 3 (Schluss)," MDOG 141 (2009) 21–43 (Jena from 1872 to 2002); and Wilcke, "Statt eines Vorwortes," 7–16 (Leipzig 1874 to 2006).

8. Olaf Matthes, "Der Aufruf zur Gründung der Deutschen Orient-Gesellschaft vom November 1897," MDOG 130 (1998) 9–16; Olaf Matthes, and Johannes Althoff, "Die 'Königliche Kommission zur Erforschung der Euphrat- und Tigrisländer," MDOG 130 (1998) 241–54; Gernot Wilhelm, "Vorwort; Einführung: 100 Jahre Ausgrabungen der Deutschen Orient-Gesellschaft," in *Zwischen Tigris und Nil: 100 Jahre Ausgrabungen der Deutschen Orient-Gesellschaft in Vorderasien und Ägypten* (ed. Gernot Wilhelm; Mainz am Rhein: von Zabern, 1998) 3, 5–13; Nicola Crüsemann, *Vom Zweistromland zum Kupfergraben: Vorgeschichte und Entstehungsjahre (1899–1918) der vorderasiatischen Abteilung der Berliner Museen vor fach- und kulturpolitischem Hintergrund* (Jahrbuch der Berliner Museen Beiheft 42; Berlin: Mann, 2000) 60–63, 109–37.

9. Nicola Crüsemann, "Ein Vorläufer der DOG: Das Orient-Comité," in *Zwischen Tigris und Nil: 100 Jahre Ausgrabungen der Deutschen Orient-Gesellschaft in Vorderasien und Ägypten* (ed. Gernot Wilhelm; Mainz am Rhein: von Zabern, 1998) 13; and Crüsemann, *Vom Zweistromland*, 87–97.

10. Matthes, "Der Aufruf," 9–16; Crüsemann, *Vom Zweistromland*, 126–32.

Zeitschrift für die Kunde des Morgenlandes in 1887, the *Keilinschriftliche Bibliothek* in 1889 and the *Orientalistische Literaturzeitung* in 1898.

Among the numerous books, articles, pamphlets, and papers that had been published in these years, the translation of George Smith's book *The Chaldean Account of Genesis* (1876) and, especially, Schrader's book *Die Keilinschriften und das Alte Testament*[11] (1872) surely had the greatest effect on perceptions about ancient Near Eastern discoveries and their impact on biblical studies and theology in Germany.

2. *Defending the History of Religions School and Assyriology's Turn to* Eigenbegrifflichkeit

2.1. Establishing the History of Religions School and Acknowledging Assyriology

In the very same year that Friedrich Delitzsch turned to Assyriology, Schrader published his *Keilinschriften*, in which he gathered and commented on all the textual evidence that underlines the connections between Assyrian-Babylonian literature and the Old Testament. According to Schrader: "The time has come . . . to bring in the harvest" because "this harvest is rich, full of surprises, especially with regard to cultural history and history. . . . It is clear that the lion's share of these discoveries refers to the Old Testament; the analysis of the results based on the decipherment of the cuneiform script must begin."[12] In the preface to his *Keilinschriften*, he also set forth the reason that the cuneiform texts should be studied: to him—and to many theologians who agreed with him—doing Assyriology meant arriving at a better understanding of Israel's history and its religion.[13]

11. Eberhard Schrader, *Die Keilinschriften und das Alte Testament* (Giessen: Ricker, 1872); 2nd rev., extended ed. with a contribution by Paul Haupt published in 1883 (Giessen: Ricker); and George Smith, *The Chaldean Account of Genesis, Containing the Description of the Creation, the Fall of Man, the Deluge of the Partiarchs, the Fall of Men, the Deluge, the Tower of Babel, the Times of the Patriarchs, and Nimrod; Babylonian Fables and Legends of the Gods; from the Cuneiform Inscriptions* (London: Low, Marston, Searle, and Rivington, 1876) translated into German on behalf of Friedrich Delitzsch as *George Smith's Chaldaische Genesis: Keilinschriftliche Berichte über Schöpfung, Sündenfall, Sinthflut etc. Autorisierte Übersetzung von Hermann Delitzsch* (Leipzig: Hinrichs, 1876).

12. "Der Zeitpunkt dürfte gekommen sein, da man . . . die reife Aerndte einsammeln soll. Diese Aerndte ist eine selten reiche, überraschende, vor allem in culturhistorischer und historischer Beziehung. . . . Es ist begreiflich, dass der Löwenantheil dieser Entdeckungen dem Alten Testament zufällt; eine Verwerthung der Ergebnisse der Keilschritentzifferung für dasselbe hat zu beginnen" (see Schrader, *Die Keilinschriften und das Alte Testament*, iii–iv; English translations of German quotations in this essay are mine unless otherwise indicated).

13. See ibid.; and, e.g., Mark W. Chavalas, "Assyriology and Biblical Studies: A Century and a Half of Tension," in *Mesopotamia and the Bible: Comparative Explanations* (ed.

In the following two decades, biblical scholars and Orientalists like Schrader, Jeremias, and their students such as Delitzsch presented studies dealing with the connections between "Babylon" and ancient Israel. Theology gradually became more open to the idea of relating Israelite history, culture, and religion to "Babylon." Even adversaries such as Franz Delitzsch, one of the most eminent conservative biblical scholars, eventually acknowledegd the importance of ancient Near Eastern cultures and discoveries and their impact on ancient Israel and the Bible.[14] At the same time, source criticism (*literarhistorische Schule*) based on a historical-critical analysis of the Old Testament and a historical understanding of revelation was established.[15]

In the 1880s, some biblical scholars who were also inspired by the new discoveries and Schrader's work started to question source criticism, claiming that the history of "biblical religion" cannot be reconstructed by concentrating on the written sources alone. To them, the oral traditions were *preliminary to the written form* and therefore crucial to the understanding and reconstruction of the Old Testament and Israelite religion. In fact, they developed a new approach, form critcism (*Formgeschichte*), on the basis of which they analyzed the Old Testament in its cultural environment. Relating biblical traditions to other Oriental cultures and religions was to lead to a better understanding of the distinctives that set the Bible, ancient Israel, and Christianity apart from the ancient Near East. This group of scholars, mainly situated in Göttingen at this time, was made up of Paul de Lagarde (1827–91), Albert Eichhorn (1856–1926), and several students, among whom Hermann Gunkel (1862–1932) would play an eminent part in the years to come.[16]

Though Gunkel's *Schöpfung und Chaos* (*Chaos and Creation*), published in 1895, was not the first study of the relations between the Old Testament and Babylonian textual traditions, it was certainly the most influential study together with Schrader's aforementioned *Keilinschriften*. In his work, Gunkel claimed that Genesis 1 was not the *freie Konstruktion des Verfassers* or merely

Mark W. Chavalas and K. Lawson Younger Jr.; JSOTSup 341; Sheffield: Sheffield Academic Press, 2002) 21–35.

14. Klaus Johanning, *Der Bibel-Babel-Streit: Eine forschungsgeschichtliche Studie* (Europäische Hochschulschriften Reihe 23; Theologie 343; Frankfurt a. M.: Peter Lang, 1988) 87 (with additional references).

15. Of the answers given by the conservatives, the *Heilsgeschichte* approach of Johann C. K. von Hofmann (1810–77) should probably be considered most influential. Acccording to Hofmann, history is focused on Jesus Christ the Saviour, inspired by God, with the Holy Scriptures picturing the life and the transfiguration of Christ the redeemer. The Old Testament (and therefore the history of ancient Israel) prepares the advent of Christ. This approach formed the basis of other schools as well; see Johanning, *Der Bibel-Babel-Streit*, 85–87 (with additional bibliography).

16. Ibid., 168–71.

the *literarische Rezeption des Stoffes* but comprised texts that reflect a long oral tradition that is embedded within ancient Near Eastern creation myths, among which was the Babylonian *Enūma eliš*, which provides the closest parallels. Through this study, Gunkel sought to point out the charactistics of Israelite history and religion that were not isolated but were part of a larger cultural area. Thus, he refused the conservative approach to the *Heilsgeschichte*, which sets ancient Israel apart from any other culture. Furthermore, like many theologians, he thought of the Old Testament as a preliminary stage that led directly to Christianity and redemption in Jesus Christ. But in contrast to conservatives, Gunkel and others required every culture's history and religion to originate with God's revelation, not just the Old Testament and Israelite history, thus forming a "necessary phase of religious beliefs" that prepared the ground for the True Faith.

He cooperated closely with Heinrich Zimmern (1862–1931),[17] who contributed to *Chaos and Creation* with his Assyriological expertise by commenting on Gunkel's interpretation of the relationship between the Old Testament's Genesis and Babylonia's mythological literature, focusing on *Enūma eliš*, and providing a translation of this myth.[18]

2.2. *Defending the Faith: The* Babel-Bibel-Streit *and Its Impact on German Assyriology and Theology*

So far, theological and Assyriological debates had confined themselves to the academic world. Thus, the research had little impact on the public perception and intepretation of the Old Testament and its relationship to the New Testament. The lack of impact was also due to the education and training of clerics.[19] But it is often stated that the reason the public took no notice was because German scholars had no suitable artifacts to spark interest in the ancient Near East and the consequences of its discovery.[20] Although this was certainly one reason, the main reason was that biblical scholars never went public with their research. In order to put things right, the members of the History of Religions School began to produce more-accessible works for a

17. Doris Prechel, "Heinrich Zimmerns Beiträge zur Kenntnis der babylonischen Religion," in *Das geistige Erfassen der Welt im Alten Orient: Sprache, Religion, Kultur und Gesellschaft* (ed. Claus Wilcke; Wiesbaden: Harrassowitz, 2007) 117–24.

18. Hermann Gunkel, *Schöpfung und Chaos in Urzeit und Endzeit: Eine religionsgeschichtliche Untersuchung über* Gen 1 und Ap Joh 12, *mit Beiträgen von Heinrich Zimmern* (Göttingen: Vandenhoeck & Ruprecht, 1895) v–ix, 399–428.

19. Idem, *Israel und Babylonien: Der Einfluss Babyloniens auf die israelitische Religion* (Göttingen: Vandenhoeck & Ruprecht, 1903) 3–4.

20. Renger, "Geschichte der Altorientalistik," 151–52; and Wilcke, "Statt eines Vorwortes," 8–9.

wider audience.[21] The idea proved to be highly successful. From then on, the struggle between conservatives holding onto the *Offenbarungscharakter* of the Old Testament and liberals claiming that only literary and historical analysis can prove the divine nature of the biblical texts was no longer confined to the academic world. The breakthrough came when Delitzsch presented the first of his three Babel-Bibel lectures in 1902. In 1903–4, he held the second and third lectures, and several other publications on this subject followed until 1921, just a year before his death.

There are many reasons why Delitzsch presented his first Babel-Bibel lecture in 1902, as well as for the way he presented it.[22] The timing was perfect. In the late 1890s and early 1900s, the Deutsches Reich, German society, and the scholarly community put a great deal of effort into acquiring ancient Near Eastern artifacts and obtaining excavation licenses. A few years before, in 1897, excavations in ancient Babylon had begun and resulted in important finds. But Robert Koldewey, Friedrich Delitzsch, and Leopold Messerschmidt (1870–1911) were already working toward a second excavation project. Again, they focused on a central Mesopotamian location: the site of Tell Qalaʿat Shirqat—the ancient capital of Assyria—the city of Aššur. The Deutsche Orient-Gesellschaft, which was responsible for planning and carrying out such projects, and its representatives had the best of relations with the emperor, as society's protector, and with the government, as well as the financial and industrial sectors. And they knew how to make use of it.[23] The emperor was present when Delitzsch held his most famous lecture.

Regarding his personal point of view, Delitzsch stated:

---

21. As Gunkel insisted on in his *Israel und Babylonien*, 20–21.

22. See, e.g., Daniel D. Luckenbill, "German Freedom," *The Biblical World* 52 (1918) 177–85; Johanning, *Der Bibel-Babel-Streit*; Reinhard G. Lehmann, *Friedrich Delitzsch und der Babel-Bibel-Streit* (OBO 133; Freiburg: Universitätsverlag / Göttingen: Vandenhoeck & Ruprecht, 1994); Mogens Trolle Larsen, "The 'Babel/Bible' Controversy and Its Aftermath," CANE 1:95–106; Reinhard G. Lehmann, "Der Babel-Bibel-Streit: Ein kulturpolitisches Wetterleuchten," in *Babylon: Focus mesopotamischer Geschichte, Wiege früher Gelehrsamkeit, Mythos der Moderne—2. Internationales Colloquium der Deutschen Orient-Gesellschaft 24.–26. März 1998 in Berlin* (ed. Johannes Renger; Colloquien der Deutschen Orient-Gesellschaft 2. Saarbrücken: SDV, 1999) 505–21; Bill T. Arnold and David B. Weisberg, "A Centennial Review of Friedrich Delitzsch's 'Babel und Bibel' Lectures," *JBL* 121 (2002) 441–57; and Suzanne L. Marchand, *German Orientalism in the Age of Empire: Religion, Race and Scholarship* (Cambridge: Cambridge University Press, 2009), for a thorough discussion of the *Babel-Bibel-Streit*, its historic background, main characters, and so on.

23. A few weeks after his first lecture, Delitzsch sent a memorandum concerning the excavation of Tell Qalaʿat Shirqat to Imperial Chancellor T. von Bethmann-Hollweg (1856–1921), who in turn forwarded it along with a letter of recommendation to the emperor; see Crüsemann, *Vom Zweistromland zum Kupfergraben*, 189–91.

> Babylonia and the Bible—What has been said here displays only a small excerpt of the significance of the excavations in Assyria and Babylonia for the history and progress of humanity. May it help establish the recognition that it was high time for Germany to pitch her tent on the palm-crowned banks of the streams of Paradise! Figure 50 displays the residential premises for members of the expedition dispatched by the German Oriental Society, which works indefatigably there among the ruins of Babylon from morning until evening, in heat and cold, for Germany's honor and for Germany's science. . . . Supported, like the archaeological undertakings of other nations, by the increasing participation of our people and the energetic support of our government, the German Oriental Society . . . will also certainly maintain its glorious place under that sun . . . always inspired afresh by gratitude for the highest personal patronage and warm interest, which His Majesty our King and Emperor has been pleased to bestow to its efforts in a lasting and gracious manner.[24]

Though Delitzsch clearly attached the utmost importance to excavations as scientific endeavors, he thought of them also as patriotic acts neccessary to maintain Germany's place among the nations. In fact, the advancement of science and patriotism were two sides of the same coin to him and most of his colleagues.

But Delitzsch was also driven by the wish to establish Assyriology. His motives have already been discussed by his contemporaries and by later scholars. In this regard, it is important to remember the beginnings of Assyriology, which had been neglected by theologians in the 1850s and 1860s in Germany, theologians who considered it to be a *Hülfswissenschaft* (an auxiliary

---

> 24. Babel und Bibel—das Gesagte stellt nur einen kleinen Ausschnitt dar aus dem, was die Ausgrabungen in Babylonien-Assyrien für Geschichte und Fortschritt der Menschheit bedeuten. Möchte es die Erkenntnis befestigen helfen, dass es für Deutschland höchste Zeit war, auch seinerseits an den palmenbekränzten Ufern des Paradiesesstromes sein Zelt aufzuschlagen! Das Bild 50 zeigt das Wohnhaus der Mitglieder der von der Deutschen Orient-Gesellschaft ausgesandten Expedition, welche drüben auf den Ruinen von Babylon vom Morgen bis zum Abend, bei Hitze und bei Kälte rastlos arbeiten für Deutschlands Ehre und für Deutschlands Wissenschaft. . . . Getragen, gleich den archäologischen Unternehmungen der anderen Nationen, von der wachsenden Teilnahme unseres Volkes und der thatkräftigen Unterstützung unserer Regierung wird die Deutsche Orient-Gesellschaft . . . ihren Platz gewiß ruhmvoll auch an jener Sonne behaupten . . . immer von neuem von Dank beseelt für den Allerhöchsten persönlichen Schutz und die lebendige Teilnahme, welche seine Majestät unser Kaiser und Herr ihren Bestrebungen angedeihen zu lassen huldvollst geruhen.

See Friedrich Delitzsch, *Babel und Bibel. Ein Vortrag: Neue durchgesehene Ausgabe mit Anmerkungen* (Leipzig: Hinrichs, 1903) 51–52; translation from Arnold and Weisberg, "A Centennial Review of Friedrich Delitzsch's 'Babel und Bibel' Lectures," 445.

science).[25] The Babel-Bibel lectures were not his first attempt to change this. In 1874, the very same year as his *habilitation*, he arranged for the German translation of Smith's *Chaldean Genesis*. In the following decades, he dedicated his life and work to providing a sound methodological basis for Assyriology[26] *and* to establishing it in Germany. While many liberal theologians such as his teacher Schrader and Gunkel worked with the new findings and Assyriological research and therefore acknowledged the still-young discipline, most conservatives rejected any impact of Mesopotamian culture on the Old Testament outright. Consequently, the first Babel-Bibel lecture was also his answer to conservatives.[27]

One of his most important points was that ancient Israel depended heavily on Babylonia, because Canaan had been dominated by Babylonian culture when the Israelite tribes took possession of the land. Besides details such as weights and measures, *Opferkult*, and Israelite priesthood,[28] Delitzsch especially referred to biblical texts that were detectable in "a purer and more original form" in Babylonia. In his view, the authors of narratives such as the deluge or creation accounts (Gen 1:1–2:3) were based on cuneiform texts adapted by the biblical authors. But Delitzsch did not confine himself to this. He also insisted that Babylonia had influenced Israel's perception of law and its idea of justice by pointing out parallels between the Decalogue and the Codex of Hammurapi. According to Delitzsch, for both Babylonians and Israelites, breaking the law was a sin that would have the consequences of disease, suffering, and ill fate. Therefore, Delitzsch also considered the fall of mankind as it is reported in Gen 3:15 to be derived from Babylonian traditions. This again was a heavy blow to theologians such as Franz Delitzsch, who thought Gen 3:15 to be the *Proto-Evangelium* and Adam and Eve to be prototypes of the faithful who are justified in Christ.[29]

Naturally, conservatives responded. There were numerous publications and public statements.[30] In contrast, liberals such as Hermann Gunkel remained silent. To them, most of Delitzsch's views were neither new nor especially

25. See Chavalas," Assyriology and Biblical Studies," 21–22, 32–33; and Eva Cancik-Kirschbaum, "Zum wissenschaftlichen Ort einer 'Hülfswissenschaft,'" *MDOG* 142 (2010) 19–25.

26. See, e.g., Renger, "Geschichte der Altorientalistik," 170–71; and Marchand, *German Orientalism*, 197–202.

27. See Johanning, *Der Bibel-Babel-Streit*, 33–43; Lehmann, *Friedrich Delitzsch*, 80–123; Larsen, "'Babel/Bible' Controversy," 99–100; Arnold and Weisberg, "A Centennial Review of Friedrich Delitzsch's 'Babel und Bibel' Lectures," 441–46; and Chavalas, "Assyriology and Biblical Studies," 21, for Delitzsch's first Babel-Bibel lecture.

28. Delitzsch, *Babel und Bibel: Ein Vortrag*, 29.

29. Johanning, *Der Bibel-Babel-Streit*, 36–37.

30. Ibid., 85–136.

disturbing, since they had not only accepted the impact of Mesopotamia on ancient Israel and the Old Testament but had also used the new data to support their own ways of analyzing the Bible and its cultural background.[31]

In his second Babel-Bibel lecture, Delitzsch answered his critics.[32] It was nothing less than a challenge to both conservative and liberal theologians alike, because he demanded no less than the primacy of Babel over Bibel, denying the latter's *Offenbarungscharakter* ("revelatory nature"). In fact, Delitzsch questioned theology's right and even ability to anaylze the Bible and revelation, insisting that Assyriology and ancient Near Eastern archaeology alone were capable of doing so. Then, the liberal theologians joined the discussion, struggling to maintain theology's supremacy for analyzing and interpreting Holy Scripture.

In his second and third Babel-Bibel lectures as well as in his later publications such as *Die große Täuschung* ("The Great Deception"),[33] another of Delitzsch's motives became clear: anti-Semitism. His polemics against Judaism and Jewish culture were anti-Semitic, as Lehmann[34] and Arnold/Weisberg have pointed out.[35] According to Lehmann, Delitzsch's anti-Semitism was mainly based on religious-theological anti-Judaism[36] not identical to the racist-polit-

31. See. e.g. Gunkel, *Israel und Babylonien*, 1–2.

32. Friedrich Delitzsch, *Zweiter Vortrag über Babel und Bibel* (Stuttgart: Deutsche Verlag, 1903).

33. Ibid., Friedrich Delitzsch, *Babel und Bibel. Dritter (Schluss-)Vortrag* (Stuttgart: Deutsche Verlags-Anstalt, 1905), idem, *Mehr Licht. Die bedeutsamen Ergebnisse der babylonisch-assyrischen Grabungen für Geschichte, Kultur und Religion. Ein Vortrag von Friedrich Delitzsch* (Leipzig: J. C. Hinrichs, 1907), idem., *Die Große Täuschung. Kritische Betrachtungen zu den alttestamentlichen Berichten über Israels Eindringen in Kanaan, die Gottesoffenbarung vom Sinai und die Wirksamkeit der Propheten* (Stuttgart/Berlin: Deutsche Verlags-Anstalt, 1920) and idem, *Die Große Täuschung. Zweiter (Schluss-) Teil. Fortgesetzte kritische Betrachtungen zum Alten Testament, vornehmlich den Prophetenschriften und Psalmen, nebst Schlussfolgerungen* (Stuttgart: Deutsche Verlags-Anstalt, 1921).

34. Lehmann, *Friedrich Delitzsch*, 268–271.

35. See Larsen, "'Babel/Bible' Controversy," 103–106 and Arnold and Weisberg, "A Centennial Review of Friedrich Delitzsch's 'Babel und Bibel' Lectures," for a thorough analysis of Delitzsch's Babel-Bible lectures with regard to this topic.

36. Lehmann, *Friedrich Delitzsch*, 268–271 and Arnold and Weisberg, "A Centennial Review of Friedrich Delitzsch's 'Babel und Bibel' Lectures," 446–51. Although Hermann Gunkel certainly is not to be counted among the anti-Judaists or anti-Semites, he, too, refers to Judaism in a non-scientific and somewhat disrespectful way, perceiving it as a preliminary stage to Christianity: "Jewish monotheism . . . is often tainted with hatred . . . of the heathens, which we may understand with regard to the wailful history of a constantly surpressed Judaism, but which we do not want to carry into our religion. . . ./Der jüdische Monotheismus . . . ist vielfach von einem Hass . . . gegen die Heiden befleckt, den man historisch aus den jammervollen Verhältnissen des stets gedrückten Judentums verstehen mag, den wir aber in keinem Fall in unsere Religion mit hineinnehmen wollen . . ." (Gunkel, *Israel und Babylonien*, 32).

ical anti-Semitism which Wilhelm Marr (1819–1904) and Theodor Fritsch (1852–1933) stood for. But then, Delitzsch—being a child of his time—expressed also thoughts shared by many contempories related to the idea of a *völkisches Deutschtum* and containing racist elements.[37] At the same time, he had special bonds with many patriotic Jewish Germans who were equally eager to support Germany's struggle for power and glory. Delitzsch himself strongly felt the need to reject all accusations of being an anti-Semite. The following statement illustrates Delitzsch's contradictory points of view:[38]

> I have never been anti-Semitic in my life in the common sense of the word. In fact I feel connected to a many Jewish men and families, holding them in high regard. Yet, this must not prevent me from helping the public to become acquainted with the influx of data from Near Eastern excavations, even if they change or overturn the views and dogmata based on Israelite literature.[39]

In this regard, it is important to consider Delitzsch's family background: his father, Franz Delitzsch, played an important part in the *Judenmission* to convert Jews to the Christian faith. His father's work and convictions may have had an impact on Friedrich Delitzsch. It remains to be seen whether this actually was the case or not. It may also be that Delitzsch simply was not aware of it, or deliberately concealed it.[40]

In his *Israel und Babylonien: Der Einfluss Babyloniens auf die israelitische Religion* published in 1903, Hermann Gunkel answered Delitzsch. In the beginning, he pointed out that Delitzsch's lectures were but a summary of facts and theories that were already known, meant to be only a comprehensive,

37. Lehmann, *Friedrich Delitzsch*, 271.

38. See the discussion in Lehmann, *Friedrich Delitzsch*, 268–71 and Arnold and Weisberg, "A Centennial Review of Friedrich Delitzsch's 'Babel und Bibel' Lectures," 446–51. In 1918, Luckenbill published a short but quite telling article ("German Freedom," *Biblical World* 52: 177–85) about his "brief summer residence," that he spent in Germany before the First World War in which he also touches upon his encounters with the deep-rooted and thriving German Anti-Semitism of this period.

39. Mein Leben lang war ich kein Antisemit in der üblichen Bedeutung dieses Wortes, vielmehr bin ich zahlreichen jüdischen Männern und Familien in Hochachtung und Zuneigung verbunden. Das darf mich aber nicht daran hindern, die aus den vorderasiatischen Grabungen fortgesetzt zuströmenden neuen Erkenntnisse, auch wenn sie althergebrachte, auf das altisraelitische Schrifttum gegründete Anschauungen und Dogmen modifizieren oder umstoßen, auch der großen Öffentlichkeit zur Kenntnis zu bringen. (Delitzsch, "Mein Lebenslauf," 246).

40. For Franz Delitzsch as a Judaic scholar, the part he played in the missionary movement (*Judenmisson*), and his ambiguous relationship with Jews and Judaism, see the study of Alan Levenson, "Missionary Protestants as Defenders and Detractors of Judaism: Franz Delitzsch and Hermann Strack," *JQR* n.s. 92 (2002) 383–420 (especially pp. 402–12).

vivid overview of what had been achieved by theologians and Assyriologists so far. According to Gunkel, the sudden interest in the Bible and Babylonia was only due to the ways of the press and the way the public's mind works; quite accidentally, the spotlight shone on a lecture that was "attended by the foremost person of our state" (i.e., the emperor). Until then, all attempts to go public with the research had been in vain. The public and the German church were caught offguard, mistaking Delitzsch's presentation for something previously unheard of and for which Delitzsch, in Gunkel's opinion, was taking undeserved credit. But he had caused quite a commotion, and many other theologians, parish priests, and lay people contributed to it with opposing articles, pamphlets, and lectures. The commotion grew even greater when, in his second Babel-Bibel lecture, Delitzsch threw down the gauntlet to the already-overexcited congregation by questioning the *Offenbarungscharakter* of the Old Testament and Israelite religion.[41]

In his *Israel und Babylonien*, Gunkel intended both to answer Delitzsch's theses and to calm the religious public, who were deeply disturbed by the Assyriologist's claims and liberal theology's research. As for the latter, he stated:

> but he [the scientist] also asks the readers, even if they are of another opinion in some aspects, at least to accept that we are seeking the truth with all the strength we can master, and that, in uttering it, . . . we only wish to serve our beloved Evangelical Church.[42]

Although this was aimed at the conservatives' dismissive attitude toward liberal theology,[43] Gunkel highlighted the great opportunities that the ancient Near Eastern written sources offer—which should no longer be applied solely to the biblical sources and the writings of Greek and Roman authors.

One might gain the impression that Gunkel was not merely intending to review Delitzsch's theses critically and to calm conservative theologians and the congregation. It appears that Gunkel was deeply concerned with Delitzsch's move away from theology. He strongly argued in favor of cooperation between theology and Assyriology. Gunkel himself had closely cooperated with Zimmern (see pp. 150–152 above). Thus, he emphasized that analyzing ancient Near Eastern literature had a promising future as long as both

41. See Gunkel, *Israel und Babylonien*, 1–5.

42. "[E]r bittet aber auch die Leser, wenn sie in manchem anderer Meinung sind, uns wenigstens zu glauben, dass wir die Wahrheit aus ganzen Kräften suchen, und dass wir durch ihre Aussprache . . . nur unserer teuren evangelischen Kirche zu dienen wünschen" (ibid., 5–6).

43. See also Gunkel's introductory remarks in *Schöpfung und Chaos*, v–x.

disciplines worked together and held each other in respect.[44] As for Delitzsch, Gunkel understood the way he was responding to his critics:

> It is quite understandable that modern scholars get carried away. . . . And every day new discoveries may come up . . . surely, whole libraries of clay tablets are awaiting their lucky discoverer beneath the surface. . . . So, we can understand when Assyriology . . . encroaches upon all sides, when it examines Greek culture, Roman law, and Israelite religion for a Babylonian basis.[45]

Furthermore, he conceded that Delitzsch was taking a somewhat strident tone due to his critics' offensive attitude.[46] At the same time, Gunkel made perfectly clear that Assyriology should concentrate on gaining mastery of the vast, "almost unmanageable" field of ancient Near Eastern cultures. When it came to theological matters, Assyriologists should seek to cooperate with theologians in order to avoid misunderstandings and mistakes—especially addressing himself to Delitzsch in this regard.[47]

In the following pages, Gunkel argued that ancient Israel was not influenced by Babylonian culture alone but bore the marks of ancient Egypt as well, as the story of Joseph proves. At the same time, Gunkel addresses the question whether a theologian can work with the new Babylonian evidence without questioning the special character of the Old and New Testament witnesses to the revelation and faith. Gunkel's answer was in the affirmative. In his view, it is more than possible, since science can demonstrate that the cultural background and all the similarities that ancient Israel and the Old Testament share especially with Babylonia, but also with other ancient Near Eastern cultures, were but the foundations on which, thanks to God's influence, the true faith was built. God, he argues, revealed himself and his purposes in Israelite history and religion which, again, led directly to the advent of Christ and Christianity. Christian faith and the faithful (including theologians) should

44. See idem, *Israel und Babylonien*, 1–11.

45. "Es ist begreiflich, dass es die modernen Forscher wie ein Rausch überkommt . . . ! Und jeder Tag kann neue Entdeckungen bringen . . . ; noch harren gewiss ganze Bibliotheken von Tontafeln unter der Erde auf den glücklichen Entdecker. . . . So verstehen wir es, wenn die Assyriologie . . . nach allen Seiten hin übergreift, wenn sie auch die griechische Kultur, auch das römische Recht und die israelitische Religion nach babylonischen Grundlagen untersucht (Gunkel, *Israel und Babylonien*, 9).

46. See Gunkel, *Israel und Babylonien*, 32.

47. See Gunkel, *Israel und Babylonien*, 11. Already at the beginning of his article, Gunkel stated that Delitzsch had neglected to acknowledge the fact that the results he had presented were achieved by a whole generation of scholars, see Gunkel, *Israel und Babylonien*, 3.

not fear the truth that research can produce. He explictly referred to his conservative counterparts:[48]

> A faith, we have to say, worthy of its name must be both couragous and brave! What of a faith which fears solid facts, avoids research! If we truly believe in God who revealed himself in history, we must not tell the Most High how events should be . . . but . . . we should praise his doings in history. If we have to change our preception of God's ways in history because we are taught so by solid facts, well then, we simply must relearn! . . . Israelite tradition did not merely borrow Babylonian traditions but changed them—a true miracle in world history—considerably. It turned slag into gold. Shall we Christians not rejoice that we have found a scale in the Babylonian recension [of the Deluge story] to fathom how much closer the God we believe in was to ancient Israel than to the Babylonians![49]

On these grounds, Gunkel rejected Delitzsch's claim that Babylonian culture was superior to ancient Israel. It could not be, because God chose Israel and not Babylonia to prepare the ground for Christianity.

In the last paragraph of *Israel und Babylonien*, Gunkel predicted that neither the public nor the scientific community would remember Delitzsch's Babel-Bibel lectures, because the facts he presented were nothing but old wine in new skins, and his conclusions regarding the Scriptures, Judaism, and Christianity were highly questionable. Nonetheless, Gunkel hoped that some good might come even of Delitzsch's lectures: a permant public interest in Babylonian and biblical research (*babylonische und biblische Forschungen*).[50]

2.3. *Assyriology Turns to* Eigenbegrifflichkeit

The impact that the *Babel-Bibel-Streit* had on theology was rather small. As far as Gunkel was concerned, it was much ado about (almost) nothing since Delitzsch had not come up with anything that was not already known to the

48. See also Gunkel, *Schöpfung und Chaos*, v–x.

49. Ein Glaube, so müssen wir sagen, der seines Namens würdig ist, muss mutig und tapfer sein. Was wäre das für ein Glaube, der sich vor Tatsachen fürchtete, der wissenschaftliche Untersuchung scheute? Glauben wir wirklich an Gott, der sich in der Geschichte offenbart, so haben wir nicht dem Höchsten vorzuschreiben, wie die Ereignisse sein sollen . . . , sondern wir haben . . . sein Walten in der Geschichte zu verehren. Haben wir unsere Anschauungen von Gottes Wegen in der Geschichte zu ändern, weil uns die Tatsachen belehren, nun, so haben wir eben einfach umzulernen! . . . Die israelitische Tradition hat also die babylonische keineswegs einfach übernommen, sondern hat sie—ein wahres Wunder der Weltgeschichte—aufs stärkste umgebildet; sie hat Schlacken in Gold verwandelt. Sollen wir uns also als Christen nicht freuen, dass an jener babylonischen Urrezension ein Maasstab gefunden zu haben, um zu ermessen, wie viel näher der Gott, an den wir glauben, dem alten Israel gewesen ist als den Babyloniern. (Gunkel, *Israel und Babylonien*, 15, 23)

50. See ibid., 40.

scientific community. Delitzsch drew the public's attention to biblical studies and Assyriology—nothing more *and* nothing less.[51] However, things were very different with Assyriology. Apart from his partly questionable goals, Delitzsch's main concern was to establish Assyriology as an independent academic discipline in its own right and to overcome its status as an auxiliary science that was thought to serve the purposes of biblical studies and theology.[52]

In the years to come, Assyriology focused on its "core business"—that is, the publication and edition of great numbers of cuneiform texts preserved on both clay and stone. At the same time, Assyriologists produced several reference works such as dictionaries, grammars, and sign lists.[53] And this is one of the disciplines' main tasks up to the present day.

It was a student of Heinrich Zimmern, Benno Landsberger (1890–1968), who argued in favor of Assyriology's turning to "ancient Mesopotamia's autonomy." In his inaugral lecture *Die Eigenbegrifflichkeit der babylonischen Welt*, presented at Leipzig University in 1926, he opened a new pathway for Assyriology. Basically, he insisted that one should focus on Mesopotamian culture instead of comparing it with other cultures. In any case, one should abandon any framework for the investigation. However, Landsberger also emphasized the need to cooperate with other disciplines.[54]

It has been argued that the *Babel-Bibel-Streit* was only one reason for Assyriology's change to *Eigenbegrifflichkeit* and that it was just as much due to the vast (and still increasing) number of written sources and the rapid progress of Assyriology.[55] Although this is certainly true, it may also be true that the conflicts caused by Delitzsch's nationalistic and sometimes even anti-Semitic statements and theses had their share in Landsberger's programmatic lecture, which referred to ongoing developments in Assyriology.[56] Subsequently, Assyriology's early days almost fell into oblivion and were (and still are) of only minor importance for both Assyriology's *Forschungsgeschichte* and the training of Assyriologists. Nonetheless, the case study presented below may show that Assyriology's origin in theology still has an impact on Assyriological research.

---

51. Ibid., 1–4.

52. See, e.g., Chavalas, "Assyriology and Biblical Studies," 21–22, 32–33.

53. See, e.g., Walter Sallaberger, "Benno Landsbergers 'Eigenbegrifflichkeit,'" in *Das geistige Erfassen der Welt im Alten Orient: Sprache, Religion, Kultur und Gesellschaft* (ed. Claus Wilcke; Wiesbaden: Harrassowitz, 2007) 64 for an overview of the most important works.

54. Ibid., 65–66.

55. Ibid., 64–65 nn. 6 and 8 for additional bibliography and for discussion of the term *Eigenbegrifflichkeit* in English research literature.

56. See, e.g., Chavalas, "Assyriology and Biblical Studies," 35.

3. *The Assyriological Perception of the Underworld and the Afterlife in Mesopotamia: A Case Study*

When it comes to death and the dead, Mesopotamia—like ancient Egypt—has a rich and diverse tradition of both archaeological remains (i.e., many thousands of burials, different types of tombs, grave goods, etc.) and written records. As for the written evidence, there are myths, hymns, and funerary inscriptions as well as a number of diverse sources such as administrative texts and legends on seals.[57] Myths and epics also deliver insight into the Mesopotamian idea of the underworld and the afterlife. It is generally accepted that the Assyrians and Babylonians thought of the underworld as a rather dark and gloomy place. The afterlife was quite a sad affair.[58] Mesopotamia is generally counted among the Mediterranean cultures whose perception of the hereafter is rather hostile to life in contrast to ancient Egypt's or the Hittites' perception.[59] For the sake of argument, usually the following words—attested in the myths *Inanna's/Ištar's Decent to the Netherworld, Nergal and Ereškigal,*[60] and the *Gilgameš Epic*[61]—are cited:

> ^{1}*a-na* KUR.NU.GI$_{4}$.A *qaq-qa-ri l*[*a ta-a-ri* (?)] ^{2} ^{d}INNIN DUMU.MÍ ^{d}30 *ú-zu-un-šá* [*iškun*] ^{3}*iš-kun-ma* DUMU.MÍ ^{d}30 *ú-zu-u*[*n-šá*] ^{4}*a-na* É *e-ṭe-e šu-bat* ^{d}*Ir-*[*kal-la*] ^{5}*a-na* É *ša e-ri-bu-šú la a-ṣu-*[*ú*] ^{6}*a-na ḫar-ra-ni ša a-lak-ta-šá la ta-a-a-*[*rat*] ^{7}*a-na* É *ša e-ri-bu-šú zu-um-mu-ú nu-*[*ú-ra*] ^{8}*a-šar* SAḪAR.ḪÁ *bu-bu-us-su-nu a-kal-šu-nu ṭi-i*[*ṭ-ṭi/ṭu*] ^{9}*nu-ú-ru ul im-ma-ru ina e-ṭu-ti* ^{10}*lab-šu-ma* GIN$_{7}$ *iṣ-ṣu-ri ṣu-bat gap-*[*pi*] ^{11}UGU GIŠ.IG *u* GIŠ.SAG.KUL *šá-bu-uḫ ep-ru*

> ^{1}To *Kurnugia* "the land of no return" ^{2}Ištar, the daughter of Sîn, [set] her mind, ^{3}the daughter of Sîn set her mind ^{4}to the house of darkness, the dwelling place of Ir[kalla]—^{5}(she set her mind) to the house which the ones who

57. See Jean Bottéro, "Les inscriptions cunéiformes funéraires," in *La mort: Les morts dans les sociétés anciennes* (ed. Gherardo Gnoli and Jean-Pierre Vernant; Paris: Maison des sciences de l'homme, 1982) 373–406; and Steven Lundström, "Zur Aussagekraft schriftlicher Quellen hinsichtlich der Vorstellungen vom Leben nach dem Tod in Mesopotamien," *AoF* 30 (2003) 30–50.

58. See, e.g., Bottéro, "Inscriptions . . . funéraires," 374–78; Brigitte Groneberg, "Zu den mesopotamischen Unterweltsvorstellungen: Das Jenseits als Fortsetzung des Diesseits," *AoF* 17 (1990) 259–61; Wolfram von Soden, *Einführung in die Altorientalistik* (2nd ed.; Darmstadt: Wissenschaftliche Buchgesellschaft, 1992), 177–79, 192–93; and Michael Jursa, *Die Babylonier: Geschichte, Gesellschaft, Kultur* (Munich: Beck, 2004) 88–89.

59. Cf., e.g., Groneberg ("Mesopotamischen Unterweltsvorstellungen," 259–61), who refers explictly to Ugarit (p. 260).

60. See Stephanie Dalley, "The Descent of Ishtar to the Underworld," COS 1:381–84; and eadem, "Nergal and Ereshkigal," COS 1:384–90 (with additional bibliographical sources).

61. Cf. Andrew R. George, *The Babylonian Gilgamesh Epic: Introduction, Critical Edition and Cuneiform Texts* (2 vols.; Oxford: Oxford University Press, 2003).

> enter it will not leave, [6](she set her mind) to the road on which the ones who trod it will not return (lit.: the road—its walking is no return), [7](she set her mind) to the house in which the ones who enter it are deprived of light, [8]a place where dust is their sustenance and their food is cl[ay]. [9]Light they do not see there. In darkness [10]they dwell. Like birds (they are clothed with) a winged coat. [11]Over the door and the bolt dust has settled. (*Ištar's Descent to the Underworld*, lines 1–11)[62]

The *Epic of Gilgameš* seems to confirm the idea of the underworld as a miserable place. The hero's mourning for his dead friend Enkidu, his desperate struggle against death, and his search for everlasting life certainly give the impression that the epic's composers and their audience were afraid of death and what comes with it as mortals' inevitable fate. The message of Siduri, the maiden whom Gilgameš met on his journey to Utnapištim, is clear:

> [col. ii 14′]*sa-bi-tum a-na ša-a-šum iz-za-qa-ram a-na* ^{d}GIŠ [col. iii 1] ^{d}GIŠ *e-eš ta-da-a-al* [2]*ba-al-ṭám ša ta-sa-aḫ-ḫu-ru la ut-tu-ta* [3]*i-nu-ma* DINGIR.MEŠ *ib-nu-ú a-wi-lu-tam* [4]*mu-tam iš-ku-nu a-na a-wi-lu-tim* [5]*ba-al-ṭám i-na qá-ti-šu-nu iṣ-ṣa-ab-tu* [6]*at-ta* ^{d}GIŠ *lu ma-li ka-ra-aš-ka* [7]*u-ri ù mu-ši ḫi-ta-ad-dú at-ta* [8]*u_4-mi-ša-am šu-ku-un ḫi-du-tam* [9]*ur-ri ù mu-ši su-ur ù me-li-il*

> [col. ii 14′]The alewife spoke to him, to Gilgameš: [col. iii 1]"Gilgameš, whither you are walking? [2]The life you are looking for, you will not find. [3]When the gods created mankind, [4]they assigned death to mankind, [5]but life they kept in their hands! [6]You, Gilgameš, may your belly be full! [7]Be happy, day and night! [8]Make merry every day! [9]Day and night, dance and play!" (*Epic of Gilgameš*, Old Babylonian Version)[63]

Or to put it differently: enjoy yourself as long as you can; the afterlife is nothing short of sadness. Every mortal may wish to live forever, but the only thing you have to decide is what to do with the time given to you. This view is also held by most Assyriologists up to the present day, though few are aware that it goes back to the beginnings of their discipline, as shown, for example, in the work of Alfred Jeremias, *Die babylonisch-assyrischen Vorstellungen vom Leben nach dem Tode: Mit Berücksichtigung der alttestamentlichen Parallelen*, published in 1887:

> The religion of the people of the Euphrates Valley is practical indeed. Their gods are gods of the living. . . . Dealing with the matters of this world demands all religiousness. There is no time to think and philosophize anxiously

62. Cf. Dalley, "Descent of Ishtar," 381; and Lundström, "Zur Aussagekraft schriftlicher Quellen hinsichtlich der Vorstellungen vom Leben nach dem Tod in Mesopotamien," 41–43 for additional bibliographical references.

63. Cf. George, *Gilgamesh*, 272–76, 278–79, fig. 9, pls. 17–19.

> about the soul's origin and its final destination (lit., the "whereto"), as is characteristic of the people of Egypt—at death, vitality and life are gone, hope and consolation. That is why [Mesopotamian] religion has but a little to do with the image of the underworld [and living therein]. . . . . . . There, they [i.e., the dead who have arrived in the underworld] await the verdict concerning their fate. Namtar, the servant, waits for the orders and lead the doomed on to a place of special inconvenience, be it a place where horrid diseases rob the dead of their remaining strength, or be it the great prison where inedible food, complete darkness, tortures of various kinds await the convict. But the life of those who are not convicted is lacking in peace and is cheerless as well: clay is their food; the light they do not see.[64]

Along with many contemporary theologians of his time, Jeremias was convinced that Israel, Babylonia, and Assyria not only shared the same cultural background but were also of the same origin—with "Abraham, the Babylonian" as the ancestor of the chosen people. All that Israel and Mesopotamia have in common is thus explained. But while, in many ways, Israel prepared the ground for the revelation and appearance of Christ as it is bequeathed in the New Testament, in matters of afterlife old beliefs proved to be quite persistent. Thus Jeremias was convinced that the Old Testament conception derived from Babylonia.[65] In his *Die babylonisch-assyrischen Vorstellungen vom Leben nach dem Tode*, he wrote:

> No wonder, that this was the part [of life and religious beliefs] least touched by the revealed religion (*Offenbarungsreligion*) since it brought about a gradual renouncing of the old traditional Semitic traditions only in an age-long process. . . . According to the Old Testament, good was repaid with health, a blessed and long life, continual descendants; and evil with misfortune,

64. Durch die Religion der Völker im Thale des Euphrat geht ein praktischer Zug. Ihre Götter sind Götter der Lebendigen. . . . Das Auseinandersetzen mit den Erfordernissen der diesseitigen Welt nimmt alles religiöses Interesse in Anspruch. Da bleibt kein Raum für ängstliches Nachdenken und Philosophieren über das Woher? und das Wohin? der Seele, wie es dem Volke der Egypter so charakteristisch ist,—mit dem Tode ist's vorbei mit Kraft und Leben, mit Hoffnung und Trost. Darum hat die Religion als solche mit den Vorstellungen vom Jenseits wenig zu thun. . . . Dort empfangen sie dann den Richterspruch über ihr künftiges Schicksal. Namtar, der Diener, harrt des Befehls und führt die Verdammten an einen Ort besonderer Qual, sei es an den Ort, wo ekelhafte Krankheiten dem Toten den Rest seiner Kraft rauben, sei es in das grosse Gefängnis, wo ungeniessbare Speise, äusserste Finsternis, Qualen der verschiedensten Art des Verurteilten harren. Aber auch das Leben derer, die nicht zu besonderer Strafe verdammt sind, ist fried- und freudelos. Ihre Nahrung ist Lehm, Licht schauen sie nicht. (Alfred Jeremias, *Die babylonisch-assyrischen Vorstellungen vom Leben nach dem Tode: Mit Berücksichtigung der alttestamentlichen Parallelen* [Leipzig: Hinrichs, 1887] 2, 76)

65. Cf. ibid. 106–7.

> sickness, sudden death, and eradication of one's semen. The afterlife remained out of consideration. In this regard, the homeland's folklore had its leeway. Therefore, it is not surprising that we come upon astonishing similarities between Israelite religion and the religious views of its ancestors, the Babylonians.[66]

Having *Innana's/Ištar's Descent* in mind, passages such as Job 10:21–22 seemed sufficient to Jeremias to prove that this was so:[67]

> . . . to the land of gloom and and deep shadow, to the land of deepest night, of deep shadow and disorder, where even the light is like darkness.[68]

However, it seems likely that European-Christian perceptions of the afterlife based on the Old Testmant as well as on ancient Greece affected him more than he was probably aware. Due to his cultural background as a European biblical scholar who knew the classical authors as well as he knew the Old Testament, it appeared evident to him that the underworld as described in the newly discovered Mesopotamian myths was comparable to *Sheol* and *Tartaros*, as he and other theologians (Gunkel included) perceived it.[69] Consequently, they analyzed the fate of certain kings and deities in the underworld as exceptions to the rule that were not the lot of the "men on the street."

> 66. Kein Wunder, denn gerade dieses Gebiet ward von den Konsequenzen der Offenbarungsreligion am wenigisten berührt, da sie auf diesem Gebiete erst in Jahrhunderte langem Prozess die allmählige Loslösung von dem Anschauungskreise des ursemitischen Volkstums bewirkte. . . . Die Vergeltung des Guten besteht auch nach alttestamentlicher Vorstellung in Gesundheit, gesegnetem und langem Leben, dauernder Nachkommenschaft und die Vergeltung des Bösen in Unglück, Krankheit, jähem Tod und Ausrottung seines Samens. Das Jenseits blieb aber ausser Betracht. Hier hatte die Volksvorstellung der alten Heimat freien Spielraum. Darum darf es nicht Wunder nehmen, wenn wir auf diesem Gebiete israelitischer Religion überraschende Paralellen finden mit den Religionsvorstellungen ihrer Stammväter, der Babylonier. (Ibid, 108; references given by Jeremias are omitted.)

67. Compare with ibid., 106–26; and Manfred Görg, *Ein Haus im Totenreich: Jenseitsvorstellungen in Israel und Ägypten* (Düsseldorf: Patmos, 1998) 127–75, for the Old Testament's passages referring to the underworld/the afterlife.

68. See *The Holy Bible: New International Version* (London: Biblica, 1990) 517, translated in German by Jeremias as "Das Land der Finsternis und des Todesschattens, das Land in Dunkelheit gleich Finsternis, des Todesschattens ohne Ordnung, wenn es da aufleuchtet—wie Finsternis ist es" (Jeremias, *Die babylonisch-assyrischen Vorstellungen vom Leben nach dem Tode*, 110).

69. Another quite telling example is Schrader's naming of the myth *Inanna's/Ištar's Descent to the Underworld* as "Die *Höllenfahrt* der Istar," using the term *Hölle* ("hell") to name the Mesopotamian underworld (Eberhard Schrader, *Die Höllenfahrt der Istar* [Gießen: Ricker, 1874]), thus alluding to the underworld as a place of punishment. The title *Ischtars Höllenfahrt* was generally accepted by German Assyriologists and theologians (see Jeremias, *Die babylonisch-assyrischen Vorstellungen vom Leben nach dem Tode*, 4). Recently, it has been replaced by titles such as *Ischtars Gang in die Unterwelt.*

In his first Babel-Bibel lecture, Delitzsch questioned this analysis, insisting that the Mesopotamian view of the afterlife was different from the Old Testament as it was analyzed by theologians:[70]

> The Babylonian image of the underworld is slightly friendlier than that of the Old Testament. The fragmentary preserved twelth tablet of the *Epic of Gilgamesh* contains an exact description of the Babylonian underworld. There we read about a part of the underworld that apparently is intended for the faithful, where "they rest on beds and drink pure water." The *Vorderasiatische Abteilung der Berliner Museen* has lately purchased a clay cone . . . the inscription of which requests in the most moving way that the one who finds this sarcophagus leave it at its place and not damage it. And the short inscription ends with a blessing for the one who does so: "in the upper world, may his name be blessed; in the underworld may his soul drink pure water." Is then the remainder of Sheol for the unfaithful, and not just dusty, but without water or, at best, offering brackish water—in any case, a place of thirst? In the book of Job, which seems familiar with the Babylonian views, we already find (Job 24:18ff.) the hot, waterless desert intended for the evildoer in contrast to the garden with fresh, pure water intended for the faithful.[71]

In his review of Delitzsch's first and second lecture, Gunkel criticized Delitzsch's statement, taking sides with Jeremias:

> What he [Delitzsch] remarked in such a florid manner with regard to the origins of belief in the afterlife is equally highly dubious. Instead, the ancient Babylonians and Hebrews shared the view that, posthumously, the

70. See also Friedrich Delitzsch, *Das Land ohne Heimkehr: Die Gedanken der Babylonier-Assyrer über Tod und Jenseits. Nebst Schlussfolgerungen* (Stuttgart: Deutsche Verlag, 1911).

71. Die babylonische Vorstellung von der Unterwelt ist doch um einen Grad freundlicher als die alttestamentliche. Auf der uns bislang nur erst bruchstückhaft überkommenen zwölften Tafel des Gilgamesch-Epos wird die babylonische Unterwelt auf das genaueste beschrieben. Dort lesen wir von einem Raum innerhalb der Unterwelt, welcher augenscheinlich für die besonders Frommen bestimmt ist, in "welchem sie ruhen auf Ruhelagern und klares Wasser trinken." . . . Die Vorderasiatische Abteilung der Berliner Museen aber hat vor Kurzem einen kleinen Thonkegel erworben, . . . dessen Aufschrift in rührenden Worten bittet, das derjenige, der diesen Sarg finde, ihn an seinem Ort belassen und nicht schädigen möge. Und der kleine Text schliesst mit den Worten des Segens für denjenigen, der solch gutes Werk thue: "auf der Oberwelt bleibe sein Name gesegnet, in der Unterwelt trinke sein abgeschiedener Geist klares Wasser." . . . Hiernach der übrige Scheol doch wohl eigentlich mehr für die Nicht-Frommen und nicht allein staubig, sondern zugleich wasserlos oder höchstens "trübes Wasser" darbietend, jedenfalls ein Ort des Durstes? Im Buche Hiob, welches sich mit babylonischen Anschauungen sehr vertraut zeigt, finden wir (24,18f.) schon den Gegensatz zwischen einer heissen, wasserlosen Wüste, welche für die Frevler, und einem Garten mit frischem klarem Wasser, welcher für die Frommen bestimmt ist. (Delitzsch, *Babel und Bibel: Ein Vortrag*, 38–39)

soul enters the dark underworld, from which there is no escape for the common man.[72]

As one reviews the Assyriological discussion since then, one can detect only minor adjustments. Thus, the idea of a Mesopotamian belief in resurrection brought up by Delitzsch in 1903, Zimmern in 1918, and Langdon in 1923 has been rejected.[73] But, if this vital topic was ever touched upon at all, the overall concept and methodological basis were not questioned. The underworld remained gloomy and dark, and the dead led a passive existence made up of sleeping and waiting to be nourished by their relatives and kinsmen and to be evoked by them from time to time. The picture as a whole is remarkably similiar to Jeremias's statement cited above.[74]

However, considering the archaeological evidence and the information from a great variety of written sources, such as funerary inscriptions or administrative records, we may find that it is time to reconsider the Assyriological perception of the underworld and the life there, which is mainly based on the few mythical passages quoted above. There are several pieces of evidence that may point to a Mesopotamian concept of the afterlife that differs considerably both (1) from Jeremias's idea of the afterlife, based on *his* view of biblical traditions, *and* (2) from the Assyriological perception.

With regard to the written sources, the passages cited above reveal only a portion of what afterlife was like in the underworld. It is from the very same texts that we learn that the fate of heroes, kings, and gods descending into the underworld was quite different, since they did not feast on clay and dust and did not live in complete darkness.[75] According to written sources, myths, and other genres alike, a proper burial, social status, and gifts to present to the gods of the underworld were most important for arriving safely and being welcomed

---

72. Ebenso ist alles, was er über den Ursprung des Glaubens an ein Leben nach dem Tode so blumenreich ausführt, höchst zweifelhaft. Vielmehr stimmen die alten Babylonier und Hebräer in dem Glauben überein, dass die Seele nach dem Tode in die dunkle Unterwelt eingeht, von wannen es für den gewöhnlichen Menschen keine Errettung gibt. (Gunkel, *Israel und Babylonien*, 26–27)

73. See, e.g., Groneberg, "Unterweltsvorstellungen," 259–61, with references to Heinrich Zimmern, *Zum babylonischen Neujahrsfest: Zweiter Beitrag* (Berichte über die Verhandlungen der Sächsichen Gesellschaft der Wissenschaften, phil.-hist. Kl. 70/5; Leipzig: Teubner, 1918) 11–13; and Stephen Langdon, *The Babylonian Epic of Creation* (Oxford: Clarendon, 1923) 32–33.

74. See, e.g., Bottéro, "Inscriptions . . . funéraires," 374–78; Groneberg, "Unterweltsvorstellungen," 259–61; von Soden, *Einführung in die Altorientalistik* (2nd ed.), 177–79, 192–93; and Jursa, *Die Babylonier*, 88–89.

75. See, e.g., my "Zur Aussagekraft schriftlicher Quellen hinsichtlich der Vorstellungen vom Leben nach dem Tod in Mesopotamien."

down there.[76] Having become part of the underworld, the dead led a satisfying life. The counterargument usually brought up here is that myths such as *Inanna's/Ištar's Descent* refer to heroes, kings, and gods but not to the common man. This may be true. However, here may be another explanation.

The "vale of tears" described in the aforementioned passages may refer to the fate of the dead spirits who lack the provisions that their relatives were supposed to give them regularly as part of the ancestor rites (Akkadian *kispu*). These spirits had no choice but to live on clay and brackish water. Perhaps Mesopotamians believed that the "sunny side of the street" trodden by heroes and kings was also for the commoner—that is, that the dead were able to do more than to rest and consume their offerings and libations. Inanna's/Ištar's Descent and the *Epic of Gilgameš* do not resolve this question for certain, although Enkidu's report on the life and fate of, for example, men having two or more sons may point in this direction.[77] In any case, the "vale-of-tears" descriptions refer to a situation in which the living did not or could not take care of their dead any longer.[78] The connection between the welfare of the dead and the *kispu*-rites performed on their behalf, and the ill fate that the neglected dead had to endure is illustrated by Babylonian and Assyrian funerary inscriptions:

> (This is due) forever, for a long time, for the future, in days to come: May the one who sees this tomb not destroy it! May he restore it! The man who sees this shall not mistreat it! May this be what he will say: I will restore this tomb! May the favor he will do be returned to him! Above, may he make a name for himself; below, may his ghost drink pure water! (Old Babylonian funerary inscription)[79]

76. See, e.g., my "'Wenn Du in die Unterwelt hinabsteigen willst . . .': Mesopotamische Vorstellungen von der Ordnung der Unterwelt," in *Kulturgeschichten: Altorientalistische Studien für Volkert Haas zum 65. Geburtstag* (ed. Thomas Richter, Doris Prechel, and Jörg Klinger; Saarbrücken: SDV, 2002) 245–53; idem, "Concerning the Dead: How to Bury an Assyrian King? Possibilities and Limits of the Archaeological and Written Evidence in the 2nd and 1st Millennium BC," in *Proceedings of the Symposium "(Re-)Constructing Funerary Rituals in the Ancient Near East" of the Graduate Center "Symbole der Toten": Universität Tübingen, May 2009* (forthcoming); JoAnn Scurlock, "Soul Emplacements in Ancient Mesopotamian Funerary Rituals," in *Magic and Divination in the Ancient World* (ed. Leda Ciraolo and Jonathan Seidel; Ancient Magic and Divination 3; Leiden: Brill, 2002) 1–6.

77. See George, *Gilgamesh*, 528–30, 732–35.

78. See my "Zur Aussagekraft schriftlicher Quellen hinsichtlich der Vorstellungen vom Leben nach dem Tod in Mesopotamien," 41–44.

79. [1] *a-na ma-ti-ma* [2] *a-na la-ba-ar u_4-mi* [3] *a-na u_4-mi ṣa-a-ti* [4] *a-na u_4-mi ša uḫ-ḫu-ru* [5] KI.MAḪ *a-ni-a-am li-[m]u-ur-ma* [7] *la ú-ša-sa-ak* [8] *a-na áš-ri-šu li-te-ir-šu* [9] *a-wi-lum šu-ú* [10] *ša a-ni-i-ta i-ma-ru-ma* [11] *la i-me-e-šu* [12] *ki-a-am i-qá-ab-bu-ú* [13] KI.MAḪ*-mi a-ni-a-am* [14] *a-na áš-ri-[š]u-mi lu-t[e]-i[r]-šu* [15] *gi-mil i-pu-šu* [16] *li-ir-ti-ib-šu* [17] *i-na e-la-ti šum-šu li-id-mi-iq* [18] *i-na ša-ap-la-ti* [19]

These two different perspectives on the afterlife demonstrate what is most typical of the Mesopotamian view on this matter. There is not just one picture that is valid everywhere and for everyone in every period of Mesoptamian history. There were, for example, many ways to reach the realm of the dead (and many ways to stay in contact), and there was also more than one way to get out of there.[80] If one were to choose catchwords to characterize the Mesopotamian concept of the afterlife, they might be *diversity* and *ambiguity*.

The archaeological evidence mirrors both characteristics perfectly: There are various types of burials (ranging from simple earth pits to brick-work tomb chambers, corpses laid to rest in simple reed mats, as well as in specially manufactured clay sarcophagi).[81] This is *diversity*. Now, if one asks why a sarcophagus burial was chosen for one particular individual, and a person buried next to him or her in the very same house was interred in a plain pit, one is left without a clue. The written sources are of no help in this regard.[82] This is *ambiguity*.

The same is true of the funerary rituals carried out to bury the dead properly—that is, honoring them and ensuring their safe journey to the realm of the dead for the sake of both the dead and the living. Except for a few primary features around which all Mesopotamian funerals were centered, no "textbook" or ritual description of any sort seems to have been in use. Most likely, each funerary ritual was made up specially for each occasion and was therefore as unique as the burial itself.[83] In one important point, however, the archaeological and written sources are clear: except for the amount of wealth spent to prepare and conduct a burial (which in itself resulted in the value of the grave goods used, the choice of a clay or stone sarcophagus, or the size of a tomb), there was no difference between a royal burial and the burial of a common person. Being buried properly and being remembered was of the essence. Social standing and wealth may have had their impact on the deceased person's afterlife, indeed—the higher the standing/the wealthier the dead and his/her family, the better.[84] But at the present, there is no hint whatsoever

e-ṭe-em-mu-šu me-e za-ku-ti [20] *li-il-tu-ú*; see my "'Für die Dauer der Tage . . . für die Tage, die verbleiben' (Standardgrabinschrift, Z. 2–4): Zur Funktion der akkadischen Grabinschriften des 2. und 1. Jts. v. Chr.," *WZKM* 91 (2001) 227–34.

80. See Bottéro, "Inscriptions . . . funéraires"; Groneberg, "Unterweltsvorstellungen," 257–58; and Lundström, "Ordnung der Unterwelt."

81. As for the possiblities and limits of analyzing archaeological data, see, e.g., Diederik J. W. Meijer, "Some Thoughts on Burial Customs," *AoF* 30 (2003) 51–62; and my "Concerning the Dead: How to Bury an Assyrian King?"

82. See ibid.

83. Ibid.

84. See also Alfonso Archi, "The Soul Has to Leave the Land of the Living," *JANER* 7 (2007) 176.

that the commoner's last journey led him/her directly to the sinister outskirts of the underworld, while royalty went directly into the presence of the gods.

All in all, it seems quite reasonable to categorize the terms *diversity* and *ambiguity* under the umbrella term *individuality*. *Individuality* is the most characteristic feature of the Mesopotamian concept of the afterlife. It may be that there were Mesopotamians who thought of the underworld as a dark and cheerless place, just as Jeremias and many contempories understood the term *Sheol* in this way.[85] However, this was only one conception, and others were based on a strong belief in a (more or less) vital existence in the hereafter. This is demonstrated by the fact that Mesopotamians often put considerable effort into burials; by the importance of an unharmed tomb expressed, for example, in the funerary inscriptions; and by the ancestor rites called *kispu* that are well attested in both archaeological and written sources.[86] It has already been pointed out that *Sheol*, as described above, was just one of many concepts about the afterlife in Israel, as Israelite burial customs and other evidence show.[87]

Conclusion

The Holy Bible, theology, and theologians, whatever school they may have belonged to, contributed a great deal to the foundations and development of Assyriology. Biblical scholars such as Schrader were the first Assyriologists, and it was their students, such as Friedrich Delitzsch and Peter Jensen, who turned Assyriology into an independent academic discipline with a sound methodological basis. The *Babel-Bibel-Streit* and pan-Babylonism were but two of many phenomena, developments, events, and discoveries that made the times of Paul-Émile Botta, Sir Austen Henry Layard, George Smith, and Friedrich Delitzsch so exciting. Assyriology owes much to theology in general and to its scholars in particular—conservatives and liberals alike. Their contributions still have a bearing on Assyriology, as the case study demonstrates. The same is true of theology as well, which suddenly had access to a new world that extended both in space and time far beyond the confines of the knowl-

85. S. Lundström, "Zur Aussagekraft schriftlicher Quellen hinsichtlich der Vorstellungen vom Leben nach dem Tod in Mesopotamien," 46–47.

86. Ibid.; see also Caitlín E. Barret ("Was Dust their Food and Clay Their Bread? Grave Goods, the Mesopotamian Afterlife, and the Liminal Role of Inanna/Ishtar," *JANER* 7 [2007] 7–65), who—focusing primarily on the archaeological evidence but also referring to written sources—came to similiar conclusions.

87. See, e.g., Görg, *Ein Haus im Totenreich*; and Thomas Podella, "Totenrituale und Jenseitsbeschreibung zur anamenetischen Struktur der religionsgeschichte Israels," in *Tod, Jenseits und Identität: Perspektiven einer kulturwissenschaften Thanatologie* (ed. Jan Assmann and Rolf Trauzettel; Veröffentlichungen des Institutes für historische Anthropoligie e. V. 7; Freiburg: Alber, 2002) 530–61.

edge of that time. Representatives of both disciplines sometimes showed a strong tendency to neglect or even to diminish the other. But there were also scholars such as George A. Barton,[88] Hermann Gunkel, and Heinrich Zimmern who acknowledged one another and sought to work together. Hermann Gunkel put it this way in *Israel und Babylonien* in answer to Delitzsch's second *Babel-Bibel* lecture (1903):

> May both disciplines—so we wish from the bottom of our heart—come together again for joint projects, holding each other in high respect and being eager to learn from each another.[89]

This is true to the present day and, as many projects successfully accomplished in the last decades show,[90] it is good to remember the history that we share.

---

88. George A. Barton, "Recent German Theories of Foreign Influences in the Bible," *The Biblical World* 31 (1908) 336–47.

89. "Mögen sich—so wünschen wir von Herzen—beide Wissenschaften wiederum die Hand reichen zu gemeinsamer Arbeit, wobei jede die andere achtet und von der anderen zu lernen bestrebt ist" (Gunkel, *Israel und Babylonien*, 11).

90. See Chavalas, "Assyriology and Biblical Studies."

Where Is Eden?

An Analysis of Some of the Mesopotamian Motifs in Primeval J

PETER FEINMAN

Institute of History, Archaeology, and Education

Hermann Gunkel remains a seminal figure in biblical scholarship.[1] The publications of *Schöpfung und Chaos in Urzeit und Endzeit* (*Creation and Chaos in the Primeval Era and the Eschaton*) in 1895[2] and *Genesis* in 1901 changed biblical scholarship. Gunkel's innovation and transformation of Hebrew Bible/ Old Testament study were detailed by Ernest Nicholson in his foreword to a recent reprinting of Gunkel's *Genesis* commentary.[3] These sentiments were echoed in the work of McKenzie: "Hermann Gunkel's treatment of folklore has had such widespread and lasting influence . . . ; his introduction to Genesis has affected all subsequent commentators, whether they accept his proposition or not."[4] In the 80 years since his death and over a century since these publications, the field has undergone tremendous changes in a variety of aspects. This conference provides a welcome opportunity to attempt to bring order to the current chaos that exists and, perhaps, to create a new order out of the deluge of publications that has occurred.

Gunkel's cosmos and chaos analysis addressed the Mesopotamian origins of Genesis 1. My preliminary analysis here will focus on geographic motifs in Gen 2:4b–25 based on Gunkel's *Genesis* commentary as part of a larger study

1. I would like to thank JoAnn Scurlock for the opportunity to participate in this conference and for her dedication and hard work in making this publication possible.

2. H. Gunkel, *Schöpfung und Chaos in Urzeit und Endzeit: Eine religionsgeschichtliche Untersuchung über* Gen 1 und Ap Joh 12 (supplement by Heinrich Zimmern; Göttingen: Vandenhoeck & Ruprecht, 1895; ET: *Creation and Chaos in the Primeval Era and the Eschaton: A Religio-Historical Study of Genesis 1 and Revelation 12* [trans. K. William Whitney Jr.; Grand Rapids, MI: Eerdmans, 2006]).

3. Ernest Nicholson, "Foreword to the English Translation," in Hermann Gunkel, *Genesis* (trans. M. E. Biddle; Macon, GA: Mercer University Press, 1997) 3–4.

4. John L. McKenzie, "The Literary Characteristics of Genesis 2–3," *TS* 15 (1954) 544; repr. in McKenzie's *Myths and Realities: Studies in Biblical Theology* (London: Chapman, 1963) 146–81, 266.

of primeval J. The term *J* is used here in the traditional post-Wellhausen sense. *Primeval* refers to the texts in Genesis 2–11 that are traditionally assigned to the J author, covering the garden, Cain and Abel, the deluge, the Table of Nations, and the Tower of Babel.

To answer the question "Where is Eden?" means determining whether the author meant a real or mythical place. Therefore, Eden, the east, and the four rivers "constitute vital source material in this respect."[5] Once the universe is defined, one can seek the identity of the individual who created order from chaos and established the cosmic center.

The Cosmic Center

> Gen 2:8: And Yahweh God planted a garden *in Eden, in the east*; and there he put the man whom he had formed. (Italicized words represent proposed additions to J.)

"Garden" in the biblical context did not refer simply to the household garden or generic garden of modern usage. On the contrary, the term designated something special in the ancient Near East. Gunkel used the term "holy park" to convey the significance of the term. It is the place where Yahweh was at home, expressed through his strolling through the garden. Gunkel noted that the standard etymology for "garden" is based on the Greek version (LXX), which is rendered into English as "paradise," meaning an "enclosed space," from Persian.[6] This Persian *paradeisos* may be envisioned as a royal hunting park for wild animals and as a place that encompassed the flora and fauna of the universe over which the earthly king ruled.[7] The common conception of *paradise* today, with the lion lying down with the lamb may not be appropriate if one is attempting to understand the meaning of the garden to the original audience of the J narrative.

Various approaches have been taken to understanding the nature of this garden.[8]

1. The garden is the garden of God.[9]

---

5. Terje Stordalen, *Echoes of Eden: Genesis 2–3 and Symbolism of the Eden Garden in Biblical Literature* (Leuven: Peeters, 2000) 256. This quotation ends the section that summarizes the history of biblical research on Eden.

6. Gunkel, *Genesis*, 7.

7. Jan N. Bremmer, "Paradise: From Persia, via Greece, into the Septuagint," in *Paradise Interpreted: Representations of Biblical Paradise in Judaism and Christianity* (ed. Gerard P. Lattikhuizen; Leiden: Brill, 1999) 1–20.

8. See Stordalen, *Echoes of Eden*, 305–17, for a recap of the various approaches.

9. Ed Noort, "Gan-Eden in the Context of the Mythology of the Hebrew Bible," in *Paradise Interpreted: Representations of Biblical Paradise in Judaism and Christianity* (ed. Gerard

2. The location of the garden to the east, *qdm*, which should be interpreted in a temporal sense suggesting a place that exists before time[10] and between the borders of the real world and the divine,[11] a mythic realm perhaps as a utopia,[12] located "nowhere"[13] as a "Never-never land."[14]
3. The garden should be linked to the temple or a sanctuary:

> The connection between temple and garden is quite obvious to the Eastern mind. A temple in the Ancient Near east was not a building, but a sacred enclosure round a (small) shrine. The earliest Semitic sanctuaries were gardens planted in oases where the unexpected fertility of the soil suggested to the Semitic mind the presence of a beneficent deity.[15]

The garden should be understood as being comparable to the antechamber of the holy of holies (Eden) in the cosmic temple,[16] specifically the Solomonic temple in Jerusalem:

> The Solomonic temple preserved the meaning of Eden, the garden sanctuary, for its walls were adorned with figures of guardian cherubim (Gen. 3:24), palm trees and flowers (I Kgs 6:29.32).[17]

The comparison might be negative; the "vision of Jerusalem 'as eden' could be part of a socially repressive elite strategy to enforce boundaries and regulate the Hebrew social universe."[18]

4. The garden should be linked to royal ideology which may or not be connected with a temple. Gardens in particular were associated with Mari, Ugarit, Egypt from the second millennium B.C.E. onward and Assyrian kings from Tiglath-

P. Lattikhuizen; Leiden: Brill, 1999) 22.

10. Ibid.

11. Stordalen, *Echoes of Eden*, 161.

12. Yairah Amit, "Biblical Utopianism: A Mapmakers Guide to Eden," *USQR* 44 (1990) 11–17.

13. Yehuda T. Radday, "The Four Rivers of Paradise," *HS* 23 (1982) 31.

14. McKenzie, "The Literary Characteristics," 555.

15. H. J. van Dijk, *Ezekiel's Prophecy on Tyre (Ez. 26, 1–28, 19): A New Approach* (BibOr 20; Rome: Pontifical Biblical Institute, 1968) 117.

16. John H. Walton, *Ancient Near Eastern Thought and the Old Testament* (Grand Rapids, MI: Baker Academic, 2006) 124–25. See also J. van Ruiten, "Eden and the Temple: The Rewriting of Genesis 2:4–3:24 in the Book of Jubilees," in *Paradise Interpreted: Representations of Biblical Paradise in Judaism and Christianity* (ed. Gerard P. Lattikhuizen; Leiden: Brill, 1999) 75–79; Gordon J. Wenham, "Sanctuary Symbolism in the Garden of Eden," in *"I Studied Inscriptions from before the Flood": Ancient Near Eastern, Literary, and Linguistic Approaches to Genesis 1–11* (ed. Richard S. Hess and David Toshio Tsumura; Winona Lake, IN: Eisenbrauns, 1994) 399–404; repr. from *Proceedings of the Ninth World Congress of Jewish Studies*, Division A: *The Period of the Bible* (Jerusalem: World Union of Jewish Studies, 1986) 19–25.

17. Van Dijk, *Ezekiel's Prophecy on Tyre*, 117. See also Terje Stordalen, "Heaven on Earth—or Not? Jerusalem as Eden in Biblical Literature," in *Beyond Eden: The Biblical Story of Paradise (Genesis 2–3) and Its Reception in History* (ed. Konrad Schmid and Christoph Riedweg; Tübingen: Mohr Siebeck, 2008) 27–57; idem, *Echoes of Eden*, 103; David P. Wright, "Holiness, Sex and Death in the Garden of Eden," *Bib* 77 (1996) 310–11.

18. Stordalen, "Heaven on Earth," 46.

Pileser I through to Ashurbanipal.[19] The concepts of a mythical garden and a royal and/or temple garden are not easily separated:

> The garden was the place of creation from which grew the temple with its vegetal architecture and the habitable world. The pool represents the waters of Nun from which life originally sprang.[20]

This perception of the Egyptian garden posits the garden, and therefore the king's capital and temple, as the cosmic center of the universe in Egypt. This sort of cosmic center or navel of the universe could migrate within a given culture as with Aššur, Calah, Khorsabad, and Nineveh or between cultures with Babylon, Jerusalem, and Rome all demanding central billing at one point. Just as "the light" passed from Luther's Germany to England to Massachusetts' City on a Hill, so also these designations are indicators of shifts in political power and cultural significance. There is a real-world component to understanding the garden that is easy to overlook.

5. The garden has been linked to the specific time of David and Solomon more than to any other kings in Israelite history.[21]

Based on this range of interpretations, the story could be outside the space-time continuum or quite concretely linked to a social-political reality . . . or both. In other words, it is possible for a story, or in this case, a term to originate in an exact moment in time and space with a clear meaning to the original audience that hears it and/or sees the story performed in a ritual. Subsequently, as the original context is forgotten, its meaning and nuances are lost. As a consequence, "[V]arious devices which other scholars have considered literary for the modern, esthetic perspective were actually used for political purposes."[22] Sometimes stories stand the test of time because they lend themselves to

19. Kathryn L. Gleason, "Gardens in Preclassical Times," *OEANE* 2:383–85; A. Leo Oppenheim, "On Royal Gardens in Mesopotamia," *JNES* 24 (1965) 328–33; Stordalen, *Echoes of Eden*, 94–101; David Stronach, "The Garden as a Political Statement: Some Case Studies from the Near East in the First Millennium B.C.," *BAI* 4 (1990) 171–80.

20. Alix Wilkson, "Gardens in Ancient Egypt: Their Locations and Symbolism," *Journal of Garden History* 10 (1990) 202.

21. Walter Brueggemann, "David and His Theologian," *CBQ* 30 (1968) 156–81; idem, "From Dust to Kingship," *ZAW* 84 (1972) 1–18; idem, "Kingship and Chaos: A Study in Tenth Century Theology," *CBQ* 33 (1971) 317–32; Knut Holter, "The Serpent in Eden as a Symbol of Israel's Political Enemies: A Yahwistic Criticism of the Solomonic Foreign Policy," *SJOT* 1 (1990) 106–12; James M. Kennedy, "Peasants in Revolt: Political Allegory in Genesis 2–3," *JSOT* 47 (1990) 3–14; Joel Rosenberg, *King and Kin: Political Allegory in the Hebrew Bible* (Bloomington: Indiana University Press, 1986); Jacques Vermeylen, "Le Récit du paradis et la question des origines du Pentateuque," *Bijdragen Tijdschrift voor Filosofie en Theologie* 41 (1980) 232, 247–48.

22. Marc Brettler, "Biblical Literature as Politics: The Case of Samuel," in *Religion and Politics in the Ancient Near East* (ed. Adele Berlin; Bethesda, MD: University Press of Maryland, 1996) 71.

retelling and acquiring new meaning.[23] The challenge here is to ascertain, if possible, the original intent.

As Gunkel noted, the garden of fertility and plenty contrasted sharply with the harsh reality of the desert steppe. He located this garden east of Canaan, an area that he characterized as a "vast steppe of whose frightful dangers the Canaanite farmer told with horror."[24] According to Gunkel, therefore, the text told a story from the geographical perspective of an audience in the land of Canaan. While speculations about the geographical knowledge of the original audience remain fraught with danger, it is reasonable to conclude that they knew that no such garden of abundance actually existed east of Canaan or even in Mesopotamia at the time, as a place where people actually lived. One thought to keep in mind is that, if people, especially in the land of Canaan, had been asked where in the real world a garden of abundance was located, the most logical answer would have been Egypt (see Gen 13:10), a land with which the West Semitic people of the Levant were very familiar.

Nonetheless, Gunkel asserted: "[I]t is significant that we note no sign of Egyptian influence in the primeval stories."[25] "Despite the proximity to Egypt, Canaan always gravitated more towards Babylonia in its cultural relations."[26] As Naʾaman recently noted, the land of Canaan endured 350 years of Egyptian imperialism whereby many Canaanite people had the opportunity to experience the bounty of Egypt firsthand.[27] Perhaps in Gunkel's time, the absence of Egyptian motifs was a reasonable conclusion to draw. His *Genesis* commentary was published just as the Law Code of Hammurapi was discovered, and the pan-Babylonian escapade was about to begin. Gunkel would issue his own book on that topic.[28] Unfortunately, this perception of the diminution of Egypt's significance for Israel has outlived its usefulness. Nonetheless, it

23. For the retelling and reinterpretation in ancient times, see Eibert J. C. Tigchelaar, "Eden and Paradise: The Garden Motif in Some Early Jewish Texts (I Enoch and Other Texts Found at Qumran)," in *Paradise Interpreted: Representations of Biblical Paradise in Judaism and Christianity* (ed. Gerard P. Lattikhuizen; Leiden: Brill, 1999) 37–62; Stordalen, *Echoes of Eden*, 332–454.

24. Gunkel, *Genesis*, 7.

25. Idem, *The Stories of Genesis* (trans. John J. Scullion; Vallejo, CA: Bibal, 1994) 67 (trans. of *Sagen der Genesis* [Göttingen: Vandenhoeck & Ruprecht, 1901]).

26. Idem, *Genesis*, 88.

27. Nadav Naʾaman, "The Exodus Story: Between Historical Memory and Historiographical Composition," *JANER* 11 (2011) 39–69.

28. Hermann Gunkel, *Israel and Babylon: The Influence of Babylon on the Religion of Israel—A Reply to Delitzsch* (trans. E. S. B.; Philadelphia: McVey, 1904); repr., *Israel and Babylon: The Babylonian Influence on Israelite Religion* (trans. E. S. B and K. C. Hanson; Eugene, OR: Cascade, 2009); original: *Israel und Babylonien: Der Einfluss Babyloniens auf die israelitischen Religion* (Göttingen: Vandenhoeck & Ruprecht, 1903).

continues to challenge Egyptologists who seek to have people look westward instead of eastward.[29]

The Mesopotamian bias of biblical scholarship in general may have prevented the field from recognizing an Egyptian element, even when it was present. Let us suppose for a moment that the original narrative of J contained simply a garden (and a river) that its audience could identify without qualifiers. In this case, the logical referent would have been Egypt. Therefore, any descriptive material or numerical increases beyond that simple garden and river may be supposed to be a later addition to the narrative as a conscious act of will by a second author. To reorient the thinking of the people so that they looked eastward, away from the Egyptian garden, he added both a name and some helpful information to guide/instruct the audience.[30]

The philology of the term *Eden* has been debated. Gunkel related it to the "Babylonian" *edinu*, meaning "steppe."[31] In his *Genesis* commentary, Speiser used "Akkadian" instead of "Babylonian" and pushed it back to its Sumerian root *eden*, an exceedingly common term there, whereas it was more rare in Akkadian.[32] Gunkel concluded that the Garden of Eden originally meant "garden in the steppe, oasis," which he contrasted with the desert. Looking east from Canaan, the biblical author therefore employed a Mesopotamian term to describe this harsh wilderness. This derivation from the "Babylonian" has been challenged.[33] Millard suggested a West Semitic origin based on an Old Aramaic verb cognate meaning "to enrich, make abundant."[34] This meaning would be consistent with the image of the garden and eliminate the search for a geographical place-name. Tsumura elaborated on this understanding to define it as "a place where there is an abundant water supply," which would help determine the physical location of the site.[35] Either way, based on the

29. See John D. Currid, "An Examination of the Egyptian Background of the Genesis Cosmogony," *BZ* 35 (1991) 18–40; J. K. Hoffmeier, "Some Thoughts on Genesis 1 and 2 and Egyptian Cosmology," *JANES* 15 (1983) 39–49.

30. Contra Stordalen, *Echoes of Eden*, 261–70. Hendel regards *qdm* as an example of the *Leitwort* style that helps bind the J narrative together within the primeval history and bind it to the patriarchal history (Ronald Hendel, "*Leitwort* Style and Literary Structure in the J Primeval Narrative," in *Sacred History, Sacred Literature: Essays on Ancient Israel, the Bible, and Religion in Honor of R. E. Friedman on His Sixtieth Birthday* [ed. Shawna Dolansky; Winona Lake, IN: Eisenbrauns, 2008] 93–109).

31. Gunkel, *Genesis*, 7.

32. Ephraim A. Speiser, *Genesis: Introduction, Translation, and Notes* (AB 1; Garden City, NY: Doubleday, 1964) 16–19.

33. Claus Westermann, *Genesis 1–11: A Commentary* (Minneapolis: Augsburg, 1984; repr. 1990) 209–10.

34. Allan R. Millard, "The Etymology of Eden," *VT* 34 (1984) 105.

35. David Toshio Tsumura, "Genesis and Ancient Near Eastern Stories of Creation and Flood," in *"I Studied Inscriptions from before the Flood": Ancient Near Eastern, Literary, and*

premise that the term represents an addition to the narrative by this biblical author, this means that the existing narrative simply used the common noun "garden" for the cosmic center and did not locate this one-river garden in Mesopotamia.

The location of Eden has spawned a cottage industry of its own, while other scholars think the effort is an exercise in futility.[36] The quest has proceeded on both a geographical and mythical basis, with the two being intertwined. A modern breakthrough occurred as archaeology uncovered the buried, previously-unknown texts of the Mesopotamian past—"Mesopotamia" meaning not just the Assyria and Babylonia already known to scholars but Sumer and Akkad as well. The following exchange occurred among scholars after the twentieth-century discovery of the Sumerian myth of *Enki and Ninhursag* and its reference to "Dilmun" as a seeming paradise. It highlights areas of disagreement and sheds light on precisely the sort of exchange in which biblical authors would have operated.

a. Stephen Langdon, an American-born Assyriologist graduate of Union Theological Seminary who became a deacon in the Church of England and a British citizen, authored several publications that claimed a pre-Semitic origin for the stories of paradise, the fall, the flood, and Noah. He located Dilmun on the eastern shore of the Persian Gulf and claimed that the Sumerians originated in central Asia.[37] Reading between the lines, I think he apparently preferred the golden age of the Sumerian world culture to the pessimism of the triumphant Semites expressed in their *Gilgameš Epic*.[38] In a note in the first of these publications, A. H. Sayce praised Langdon for his "discovery of far-reaching importance" and for announcing it via the very society that George Smith had used 41 years earlier for his discovery of the "'Chaldaean Account

Linguistic Approaches to Genesis 1–11 (ed. Richard S. Hess and David Toshio Tsumura; Winona Lake, IN: Eisenbrauns, 1994) 40–41.

36. "[A]ttempts to locate it, even in the author's mind, are futile" (McKenzie, "Literary Characteristics," 555). See also Stordalen, *Echoes of Eden*, 270–80.

37. "Stephen Langdon, Assyriologist, Dies," *New York Times*, May 20, 1937; G. R. Driver, "Langdon, Stephen Herbert (1876–1937)," *Oxford Dictionary of National Biography* (Oxford: Oxford University Press, 2004) 32:477, http://www.oxforddnb.com/view/article/34400 (accessed October 26, 2011).

38. Stephen Langdon, *Tammuz and Ishtar: A Monograph upon Babylonian Religion and Theology* (Oxford: Clarendon, 1914) 8; idem, "A Preliminary Account of a Sumerian Legend of the Flood and the Fall of Man," *PSBA* 36 (1914) 188–96; idem, *Sumerian Epic of Paradise, the Flood and the Fall of Man* (Publications of the Babylonian Section 10/1; Philadelphia: The University Museum, The University of Pennsylvania, 1915); idem, "An Account of the Pre-Semitic Version of the Fall of Man," *PSBA* 36 (1914) 254–256, 263; idem, "Critical Notes Upon the Epic of Paradise," *JAOS* 36 (1916) 145; idem, *Sumerian Liturgical Texts* (PBS 10/2; Philadelphia: The University Museum, 1917).

of the Deluge.'"[39] The headline in the *London Times* on Langdon's discovery read: "Fall and Flood, Pre-Semitic Account Discovered" (June 24, 1914) and one cannot help but wonder about the constant reference to "pre-Semitic."[40] Perhaps the headline in the *New York Times* one month later, "Denies Pre-Semitic Flood" in reference to a response by Samuel Daiches, the Jews' College, London, serves as a reminder of the between-the-lines messages being delivered (*New York Times*, July 24, 1914). The usurpation of the Semitic role by non-Semites paralleled an ancient effort to shortchange the role of Moses. Naturally, it also meant that there would be those who would defend it.

b. Morris Jastrow Jr., the Polish-born son of a rabbi, who almost became a rabbi himself but instead became a professor of Semitics at the University of Pennsylvania,[41] rejected Langdon's translations, interpretations, and conclusions in a series of exchanges in which, just as an article by one author was about to be published, a publication from the other person would arrive. Specifically, Jastrow dismissed the proposed location of Dilmun on the east coast of the Arabian Sea/Persian Gulf, suggesting that Langdon minimized the weight of inscriptional evidence found on one of the Bahrain Islands.[42] Jastrow also perceived an alternative way of understanding the differences between the Semites and the non-Semitic Sumerians that anticipated the clash between the prophets and the Canaanites:

> The differences, then between the early Sumerian and the later Babylonian view may be summed up in the statement that in the Sumerian view the chief factor in the Creation myth is the bringing about of vegetation and fertility, whereas in the Babylonian or Akkadian tale the main stress is laid upon the substitution of law and order for primitive chaos and lawlessness.[43]

Jastrow accepted as a starting point the presumption that the non-Semitic Sumerians arrived in the Euphrates Valley as conquerors bringing their traditions of origins with them.[44] Recent developments in the geology and archaeology of the Persian/Arabian Gulf suggest that the Sumerians may have come from the Gulf, which was flooded post–Ice Age, an event that contributed to the

39. Archibald H. Sayce, "Note," *PSBA* 36 (1914) 196.

40. For the issue of cleansing biblical stories of Semitic taint, see Jerrold S. Cooper, "Posing the Sumerian Question: Race and Scholarship in Early History of Assyriology," *AuOr* 9 (1991) 47–66. For an extreme example of the significance of this sort of cleansing, see Paul Haupt, "The Aryan Ancestry of Jesus," *The Open Court* 23 (1909) 193–204.

41. Harold S. Wechsler, "Pulpit or Professoriate: The Case of Morris Jastrow," *American Jewish History* 74 (1985) 338–55.

42. Morris Jastrow Jr., "Sumerian Myths of Beginnings," *AJSL* 33 (1917) 103–5.

43. Idem, "The Sumerian View of Beginnings," *JAOS* 36 (1916) 131.

44. Idem, "Sumerian and Akkadian Views of the Beginnings," *JAOS* 36 (1916) 274–75.

origin of Sumerian flood stories.[45] If these suggestions prove correct, they will reorient the understanding of both the Sumerian and the biblical flood stories.

c. William Foxwell Albright was born in Chile to Methodist missionaries; was of German, Cornish, Scotch-Irish, and French-Canadian descent and was most closely associated with The Johns Hopkins University, the American Schools of Oriental Research, and the Anchor Bible commentaries, which began with Genesis.[46] He graduated just as this debate was unfolding, having completed *The Assyrian Deluge Epic*, his unpublished dissertation, in 1916. In some of his final publications before he left America at the end of 1919 for the Holy Land, he authored two articles on the subject in which he squarely came down on the side of Jastrow, supporting his position against Langdon on the location of Dilmun.[47] Albright reiterated his position on Dilmun and Bahrain in 1925.[48] He subsequently assisted Kramer in an updated translation of the myth.[49] Prior to its publication but while working on it, Kramer directly addressed some of the issues concerning Dilmun. Kramer strongly advocated Dilmun's location in southwestern Iran, south of Elam.[50]

Thereafter, the translation debate appears to have ebbed as Kramer prevailed. His translation of the myth of Enki and Ninhursag became part of the academic ANE canon.[51] An examination of the myth is outside the scope of this article. However, this review of early twentieth-century scholarship reveals that people of different ethnicities, religions, and agendas brought these differences to their writings even when their affiliations were not specifically identified. They all wrote in standard academic English, an unspoken language except at ritual occasions.

Today it is commonplace to encounter exchanges between writers who quote each other and employ the elaborate footnote referencing system to differentiate one writer's words from another. By contrast, biblical scholars since

45. Douglas J. Kennett and James P. Kennett, "Early State Formation in Southern Mesopotamia: Sea Levels, Shorelines, and Climate Change," *Journal of Island and Coastal Archaeology* 1 (2006) 67–99; Jeffrey I. Rose, "New Light on Human Prehistory in the Arabo-Persian Gulf Oasis," *Current Anthropology* 51 (2010) 849–83.

46. Peter Feinman, *William Foxwell Albright and the Origins of Biblical Archaeology* (Berrien Springs, MI: Andrews University Press, 2004) 31–37; Burke O. Long, *Planting and Reaping Albright: Politics, Ideology, and Interpreting the Bible* (University Park, PA: Pennsylvania University Press, 1997) 59–68.

47. William F. Albright, "Some Cruces in the Langdon Epic," *JAOS* 39 (1919) 65–66, 83; idem, "The Mouth of the Rivers," *AJSL* 35 (1919) 161, 182.

48. Idem, "A Babylonian Geographical Treatise on Sargon of Akkad's Empire," *JAOS* 45 (1925) 237–38.

49. Samuel N. Kramer with William F. Albright, "Enki and Ninhursag: A Sumerian 'Paradise' Myth," *BASOR Supplementary Studies* 1 (1945) 1–45.

50. Samuel N. Kramer, "Dilmun, the Land of the Living," *BASOR* 96 (1944) 18–28.

51. Idem, "Enki and Ninhursag: a Paradise Myth," *ANET* 37–41.

Wellhausen have adopted the Sumerian King List approach to understanding biblical writers: there is only one writer at any given time, and the writers are sequential.[52] This methodology is a construct in biblical writing, just as it was in Sumerian history. An alternative approach to understanding the biblical texts is that the Mesopotamian motifs are the products of writers who were in dialogue with each other, just as Langdon, Jastrow, Albright, and Kramer were in dialogue when they reinterpreted the same texts. The difference is that the biblical writers operated in the political arena and not the ivory tower. Inconsistencies within J, therefore, may reflect the different viewpoints of different contemporary authors.

> One of the principal means of expressing ideas or beliefs in the Bible is through "recycling," i.e., the reuse and remolding of existing material, written or oral. This reworking allowed for the possibility of expressing views which might have been similar, different, or even diametrically opposed to the original meaning of the transmitted material.[53]

In this case, our putative second author would have added the phrase "in Eden, in the east" in order to reorient the audience away from the original location in Egypt to a new location in an eastern Eden. Undoubtedly, the author had a specific location in mind when he used the term. The myth of Enki and Ninhursag is quite specific: the location is Dilmun.[54] Kramer's suggestion of southwestern Iran led to a negative reply by Peter B. Cornwall, who had just written his dissertation entitled *The History of Bahrein Island before Cyrus* (Harvard, 1944) and who had traveled in Bahrain.[55] Perhaps the publication that really put Dilmun on the map was Danish archaeologist Geoffrey Bibby's *Looking for Dilmun: A personal narrative of the discovery of a fifth great ancient civilization, hitherto totally unknown, to rival the 5,000-year-old glories of Egypt, Babylon, Sumer and the Indus Valley*. This 1969 book eventually led to a slew of articles on the subject demonstrating that Bahrain was normally Dilmun but, at times, the adjacent mainland coastal area was also included in that term.[56]

52. Thorkild Jacobsen, *The Sumerian King List* (AS 11; Chicago: University of Chicago Press, 1939); Piotr Michalowski, "History as Charter: Some Observations on the Sumerian King List," *JAOS* 103 (1983) 237–48.

53. Lea Mazor, "The Origin and Evolution of the Curse upon the Rebuilder of Jericho: A Contribution of Textual Criticism to Biblical Historiography," *Textus* 14 (1988) 1.

54. Kramer, "Enki and Ninhursag," 11.

55. Peter Bruce Cornwall, "On the Location of Dilmun," *BASOR* 103 (1946) 3–11.

56. Bendt Alster, "Dilmun, Bahrain, and the Alleged Paradise in Sumerian Myth and Literature," in *Dilmun: New Studies in the Archaeology and Early History of Bahrain* (ed. Daniel T. Potts; Berliner Beiträge zum Vorderen Orient 2; Berlin: Reimer, 1983) 39–75; Daniel T. Potts, "Dilmun: Le paradis et la transgression Flandrienne," *Collected Papers of the Society for Near Eastern Studies* 5 (1998) 21–27.

The location of Dilmun as the Garden of Eden in the ancient Near East is critical for illuminating how this biblical author sought to define his world. It becomes the basis for understanding the subsequent additions to the J narrative. No one then could have found Dilmun on a map in the modern sense, but they would have known that it was in a remote, inaccessible location where the sun rises, closer to Mesopotamia than to Canaan.

This understanding leads to the definition of the universe in the real world anchored at Dilmun.

The Universe

> Gen 2:10–14: [10]A river flowed out *of Eden* to water the garden, *and there it divided and became four rivers.* [11]*The name of the first is Pishon; it is the one which flows around the whole land of Havilah, where there is gold;* [12]*and the gold of that land is good; bdellium and onyx stone are there.* [13]*The name of the second river is Gihon; it is the one which flows around the whole land of Cush.* [14]*And the name of the third river is Tigris, which flows east of Assyria. And the fourth river is the Euphrates.* (Italicized words represent proposed additions to J.)

There was an issue about the authorship of these verses, even though they were all considered to be within the J narrative of the Documentary Hypothesis. Westermann succinctly began his analysis of the text with: "The problem about the passage 2:10–14 has not yet been clarified. Is it originally part of the narrative 2:4b–3:24, or is it a secondary insertion?"[57] One page after asserting, "With the majority of exegetes I accept the story in its present form as the work of one mind, and that mind of no small dimensions," McKenzie acknowledges that Gen 2:10–14 is secondary.[58] Carr concurs that Gen 2:10–14 disrupts the narrative style of the overall story and is only loosely integrated with its context.[59] Noort suggests that it is a mythic-geographical fragment that probably arose as a learned addition to the original text in an attempt partially to localize the garden.[60] Westermann used this dilemma as part of the running comparison between two types of speech within the primeval story: the narrative and the numerative. Here the numeration is geographical, unlike the more common Genesis genealogies, where the numeration is temporal. As a result, he concluded that the information about distant lands

57. Westermann, *Genesis 1–11*, 215.

58. McKenzie, "Literary Characteristics," 553–54.

59. David Carr, "The Politics of Textual Subversion: A Diachronic Perspective on the Garden of Eden Story," *JBL* 112 (1993) 577–78.

60. Noort, "Gan-Eden," 28.

was orally communicated as part on an ongoing tradition that only later was written down as part of this narrative.

According to Gunkel, the narrator of these verses believed these four rivers to comprise all of the earth's major streams. He likened the four-rivers motif to that of the four corners of the world, the four directions of heaven, and the four parts of the earth common in "the ancient Orient."[61] Westermann cited this insight.[62] Gunkel did not specifically identify the "four" motifs as Mesopotamian because he included an Egyptian reference as well. He did, however, state that the Nile was not included in these rivers since, according to him, there were no Egyptian elements in the primeval tradition.[63] Since the city of Aššur was located to the west of the Tigris, he dated the text's origin to pre-1300 B.C.E., when Aššur was the royal capital of Assyria, based on his understanding of Assyrian history. Unlike for Eden, the Pishon, the Gihon, and the Tigris, the biblical author provided no details for the fourth and final river in this insertion. Apparently the Euphrates alone required no descriptive explanation.

Whether or not one should even seek to locate the Pishon and Gihon is itself a source of contention. Gunkel referred to the immaturity of the narrator for his geographical knowledge or lack of knowledge (three times on one page!) and declared it "entirely improper to attempt to reconcile this system of rivers with actual geography."[64] Gunkel asserted that the "(a)uthor's world view rests only partially in reality and partially in traditions whose origins cannot be sought, at any rate, in actual geographical circumstances."[65] Westermann was kinder, referring instead to the "hazy and primitive notions of geography" by the author.[66] He claimed to understand why the names and descriptions of the four rivers were so incomprehensible, so vague. Before tackling the nitty-gritty details of each verse, Westermann plaintively asked:

> One must ask if the extraordinary labor that exegetes have expended to establish the geographical details does not begin from a false presupposition. It does more justice to the text to distinguish clearly what is significant and what is not and to set aside hypotheses that are not soundly based.[67]

Westermann was exactly right. The false presupposition that should be discarded was stated precisely by von Rad:

61. Gunkel, *Genesis*, 8.
62. Westermann, *Genesis 1–11*, 217.
63. Gunkel, *Genesis*, 9.
64. Ibid.
65. Ibid.
66. Westermann, *Genesis 1–11*, 216.
67. Ibid.

> This passage has no significance for the unfolding action, nor are its elements mentioned elsewhere. . . . It must therefore be considered as originally an independent element which was attracted to the story of Paradise but without being able to undergo complete inner assimilation.[68]

Tellingly, von Rad has virtually eliminated the human element from this process of assimilation. "Attracted?" Do texts have magnetic charges? "Inner assimilation?" Are texts independent life forms seeking to be assimilated into the collective myth? The supposition that needs to be dropped is the idea that there was this free-floating, immature, hazy, primitive, oral geographical tradition that somehow of its own accord attached itself to an existing narrative tradition or was grabbed from thin air by an author. Quite the contrary. The contention here is that this passage was created ex nihilo as an act of will by a writer who added it, just as he had "in Eden, in the east," and would add Nimrod and the four kings of chaos (Genesis 14) to change the orientation and meaning of J to fit his political agenda. Therefore, it is quite possible to understand the world view of the author in a specific political context.

In the beginning, a world needed to be created. As proposed here, the author expanded on the J narrative text he had received to describe a world more in tune with the stage on which he wanted Yahweh to operate. The common-noun, one-river garden story, presumably Egypt and the Nile, of the preexisting J narrative became a proper-noun, four-river story anchored in Eden in the east that, as Gunkel noted, encompassed the four quarters of the universe. The author was delivering a message to his audience using a universal four-river scheme. The significance of this point is easy to overlook: the audience of this insertion automatically would have assumed that the four rivers represented *the* rivers of the world, and the audience knew all these rivers. They had no commentaries; they understood the references and allusions communicated to them.

Identifying the four rivers is not the challenge it was once presumed to be. It is inconceivable that a biblical author either in the land of Canaan or in Mesopotamia excluded the Nile River from this four-river world view. An author who excluded the Nile would have forfeited his credibility just as much as he would have if he had left the sun or the moon out of his heavens. Noort succinctly notes, "[W]hen big rivers of antiquity are mentioned, the Nile cannot be missed."[69] Radday wonders, "If Scripture intended to name here great rivers, why is the Nile omitted when Torah elsewhere mentions it no fewer than twenty-eight times?"[70] The Nile must have been part of the four-river,

68. Gerhard von Rad, *Genesis: A Commentary* (rev. ed.; Philadelphia: Westminster, 1972) 79.

69. Noort, "Gan-Eden," 30.

70. Radday, "Four Rivers," 23.

world-encompassing addition to the narrative along with the Tigris and Euphrates. Indeed, it may be said that only a narrowly Meso-centric person, not in Canaan, prior to the Amarna age could have created a four-river world view that excluded the Nile. This biblical author was not such a person. This realization supports the notion that the text was dealing with the real world and not Never-never land. The only issue is which river was the Nile: the Pishon or the Gihon? And if it was the third river, what was the fourth?

The Gihon fits the Nile better than the Pishon. The river that gushes annually and reaches the land of Cush is the best candidate for the Gihon. The effort to link Cush with the Kassites as Speiser did in his *Genesis* commentary is misguided and shortchanges the vision of this author.[71] Similarly, efforts to locate the Gihon in Jerusalem[72] are misguided, based on the mistaken belief that Jerusalem was to be regarded as the cosmic center at creation instead of becoming the center within historical time, with the construction of the temple—the very message that the author of these geographic motifs probably sought to deliver. The selection of the same name for the Egyptian river from the garden as the river in the place where Solomon became king (1 Kgs 1:33) was deliberate.[73] In this manner, the unnamed river of the J narrative has been absorbed into the expanded narrative and used in support of the Davidic monarchy and Jerusalem temple.

Unbeknown to Gunkel and Westermann, but not necessarily to the biblical author and his audience, there was a fourth significant river located in the ancient Near East. This river, recently discovered through satellite imagery, has been dubbed the Kuwait River.[74] In his translation of Gunkel's *Schöpfung und Chaos*, Whitney added a helpful footnote that the four rivers were the Euphrates, Tigris, Nile, and Persian Gulf, with no mention of the Kuwait River.[75] Stordalen "argue(s) for seeing the pericope as symbolic," with the Gihon equaling the Nile but with the Pishon as some combination of the Arabian

71. Speiser, *Genesis*, 20.

72. Contra Lawrence E. Stager, "Jerusalem as Eden," *BAR* 26/3 (2000) 36–47, see Noort, "Gan-Eden," 29, and Stordalen, "Heaven on Earth," 43, for the Gihon as the Nile.

73. Richard Elliott Friedman, *The Hidden Book in the Bible: The Discovery of the First Prose Masterpiece* (New York: HarperCollins, 1998) 295.

74. I first became aware of the Kuwait River through a brief notice in the *New York Times* under "Science Watch," by Walter Sullivan, "Signs of Ancient River" March 30, 1993; see also James A. Sauer, "The River Runs Dry: Creation Story Preserves Historical Memory," *BAR* 22/4 (1996) 52–54, 57, 64; idem, "A New Climate and Archaeological View of the Early Biblical Traditions," in *Scripture and Other Artifacts: Essays on the Bible and Archaeology in Honor of Philip J. King* (ed. Michael D. Coogan, J. Cherry Exum, and Lawrence Stager; Louisville: Westminster, 1994) 381–88; Philip J. King and Lawrence E. Stager, *Life in Biblical Israel* (Louisville: Westminster John Knox, 2001) 171.

75. K. William Whitney Jr., trans., in Gunkel, *Creation and Chaos*, 324 n. 90.

Sea/Red Sea flowing from the four corners of the *terra cogna* toward the center of the biblical world.[76] Noort, who did not appear to have been aware of the Kuwait River, nonetheless linked the Pishon to the Haulān, a tribal federation in southwest Arabia. But Noort was unable to decide whether the Pishon was the Red Sea or the Persian Gulf or an unknown river in Arabia, while Radday thought Havila and Kush were intentionally ambiguous.[77] But while mainstream scholars have yet to digest this river, its discovery has been of interest to evangelicals.[78] The recognition that all four rivers were real and known to the original audience buttresses the interpretation that the author was dealing with the real world.

This dried-up river apparently flowed northeast across the Arabian Peninsula, with its mouth near the mouth of the Tigris and Euphrates at the head of the Persian/Arabian Gulf. The Kuwait River originated adjacent to Mahd edh-Dhahab, "the Cradle of Gold," an area in the Arabian Peninsula known for its gold. Thus it fits the biblical description of the Pishon. The biblical references to the products of the Havilah were not, as Gunkel suggested, "a rather immature method of geographical description" expressed concerning the products of the land, but a savvy means of identifying a land through the products that his audience knew firsthand, even if they did not know the land firsthand.[79] It was comparable to adding "in the east" to Eden: some additional information to help guide the audience into understanding the proper noun with possible allusions to the king and temple. The Kuwait River disappeared between 3500 and 2000 B.C.E. in a time of increased aridity.[80] The land it had watered did not disappear, and Saba/Sheba was part of the world view of the author's audience. The Kuwait River with its fabled riches left its legacy in oral tradition, just as the Bronze Age destruction of Sodom was remembered long after it had occurred. This memory may be considered part of Gunkel's "precompositional stage."

The existence of a fourth river in the third millennium B.C.E. changes the world view potentially possessed by the biblical writer. It provides a new element to the schematic four-corner universe regarded as standard. Gunkel was right to interpret the passage as referring to all the major rivers of the ancient Near East but wrong to exclude the Nile from consideration. Instead, the bib-

---

76. Stordalen, "Heaven on Earth," 43; idem, *Echoes of Eden*, 279.

77. Noort, "Gan-Eden," 30–31; Radday, "Four Rivers," 31.

78. See Carol A. Hill, "The Garden of Eden: A Modern Landscape," *Perspectives on Science and Christian Faith* 52 (2000) 32–38; Edwin M. Yamauchi, *Africa and the Bible* (Grand Rapids, MI: Baker Academic, 2005) 38–39.

79. Gunkel, *Genesis*, 9. The Sheba story (1 Kgs 10:2, 10–11) without the wisdom insert seems rooted in real-world geography and products that are consistent with the Gen 2:10–14 addition.

80. Sauer, "A New Climate," 64.

lical writer has gone beyond Breasted's Fertile Crescent to create a Circle of Life. This Circle is a metaphorical and iconographic statement, not an Edward Robinson field map. In the eighth and seventh centuries B.C.E., the Babylonians created a world map where the firmament was surrounded by water, and the Tigris was excluded.[81] Albright noted in the Langdon-Jastrow-Albright exchange that both the Egyptians and the Babylonians "evolved the theory of four great rivers, flowing from a common source to water the four quarters."[82] The fact that the Nile flows the wrong way in this scenario was irrelevant (although it can be said to flow south of the rapids at the First Cataract). No one knew where it originated anyway. Kramer's insight into the Sumerian geographical perception, expressed in a footnote and meant for the Tigris and the Euphrates, illuminates the perception that the biblical author brought to his four-river, world-encompassing addition to J:

> For it is important to bear in mind that for the Sumerian poets and priests, the *real* sources of the Tigris and Euphrates in the mountains of Armenia were of little significance. . . . Indeed, their view was just the opposite [of ours]; it was the Persian Gulf which was responsible for the waters of the Tigris and the Euphrates and for their all-important overflow. . . . In short, as the Sumerians saw it, it was not the rivers that "fed" the sea, it was not the Tigris and Euphrates that "fed" the Persian Gulf, but rather the sea that "fed' the rivers. Thus the Sumerian "mouth" of the rivers, while it coincides geographically with the actual mouth of the rivers as we understand it today, is nevertheless not to be understood in terms of our modern usage, as the place where the rivers "empty" their waters (*into* the Persian Gulf) but rather as the place where they "drink" the waters (*from* the Persian Gulf).[83]

Thanks to this bird's-eye view, modern Etana can now recognize that the Tigris, Euphrates, Nile, and Kuwait rivers all could be imagined in ancient times as having flowed from the Garden of Eden at fresh-water Dilmun. This revised view reveals the biblical author to have been a sophisticated, erudite writer of consummate skill and knowledge. It contradicts Gunkel's perception of him as geographically "immature." He was painting a picture story of the world through images and metaphors that the audience knew and recognized,

---

81. Wayne Horowitz, "The Babylonian Map of the World," *Iraq* 50 (1988) 147–65.

82. Albright, "The Mouth of the Rivers," 188. Contra Stordalen, who envisions the flow from the four corners to the cosmic center (*Echoes of Eden*, 270–85).

83. Kramer, "Dilmun, the Land of the Living," 28 n. 41; cited by Speiser, "The Rivers of Paradise," in *Festschrift Johannes Friedrich zum 65. Geburtstag am 27 August 1958 gewidmet* (ed. R. von Kienle et al.; Heidelberg: Carl Winter, 1959) 478; reprinted in *Oriental and Biblical Studies: Collected Writings of E. A. Speiser* (ed. J. J. Finkelstein and M. Greenberg; Philadelphia: University of Pennsylvania Press, 1967) 28; and in *I Studied Inscriptions from before the Flood: Ancient Near Eastern, Literary, and Linguistic Approaches to Genesis 1–11* (ed. Richard S. Hess and David Toshio Tsumura; Winona Lake, IN: Eisenbrauns, 1994) 179.

and he was doing so with only a few words. There is a real king and a real temple within the garden story. The author's vision was not restricted to the immediate physical world with which Israel was in proximity and as it had been related in the original J; his vision consisted of the entire known and frequently distant world. This conscious addition to the written text set the stage for the additions to follow as this biblical writer crafted a new narrative through the judicious use of proper nouns that transformed a local narrative into a global one.

Excavating Tell Genesis 2:4b–25

Gunkel, himself, recognized that primeval J was not a unity:

> We distinguish three sources in the primal history of J, two of which offer originally independent, sometimes parallel threads.[84]

He identified the sources as J^{j}, who always used *Yahweh*; J^{e}, who began by using *elohim* and then switched to *Yahweh*; and J^{r} for the compiler. Indeed, he commented on the then-current debate among German scholars over the number of sources in primal J.[85] Recent scholars similarly advocate multiple authors or versions within J.

> I do not of course deny that this apparently well composed story may have gone through a literary process with several 'sources' or redactions. . . . Indeed, the *story* Genesis 2–3 seems to connect several plots—possibly one reason why this relatively short text is rather more complex than most other narratives in the Hebrew Bible.[86]

Thompson states that "the original version of Genesis 2:4b–25 has been subjected to extensive editing before it was used by P," including the creation of the woman and the addition of the trees in this anti-Baʿal story.[87] Vermeylen posits three levels to the story:

1. an oral or written mythical version that could itself be the result of multiple expressions;
2. the written J version in Solomonic times that established the legitimacy and sacred character of royal power, which used the preexisting myth in the service of its own propaganda;
3. a series of Deuteronomic, moral, historical additions.

84. Gunkel, *Genesis*, lxxii–lxxiii. For a historical recap, see Stordalen, *Echoes of Eden*, 190–98.

85. Gunkel, *Genesis*, 2–4, 25–26.

86. Terje Stordalen, "Man, Soil, Garden: Basic Plot in Genesis 2–3 Reconsidered," *JSOT* 53 (1992) 5, 7.

87. P. E. S. Thompson, "The Yahwist Creation Story," *VT* 21 (1971) 197–208.

He sees the serpent as a symbol for the great danger of Canaanite synchretism that was menacing the fidelity of Israel.[88] For the purposes of this essay, the tiered approach seems reasonable, with the Mesopotamian motifs (those included here and the remaining ones in Genesis 2 and primeval J) suggesting an ongoing dialogue that extended into the patriarchal narrative and beyond.[89]

There are useful diagnostics differentiating writers within J as well as in contrast to P and D. Examples include the familiar tensions that have been identified: the two trees, the double departure from the garden, using the name of Yahweh before Moses did, dual city builders, dual spreading out over the earth, and the confused curses of a son or grandson of Noah. These expressions were not the result of diverse oral traditions' being collected by a redactor. Quite the contrary: I argue that they represented conscious assaults on opposition political parties, even though they were called priests and prophets. Gunkel's mythic approach misses the political battles for power in the texts. Consider the following two contrasting comments on him:

> His legacy: It has been customary since Hermann Gunkel to refer to Genesis 2–3 as myth or mythic on account of . . . its affinity to mythical literature of the ancient Near East. This affinity . . . is now undeniable[90]
>
> The picture drawn by Hermann Gunkel in his monograph *Legends of Genesis* proposing a family and tribal context [now] gives way to a more *real politick* description.[91]

Indeed, for people schooled in seminaries and departments of religion, embracing the dark side of religious history, the real-world power politics in the Beltway may be anathema. The Mesopotamian motifs analyzed here were the creation of a zealous writer, a powerful advocate for the king, the cosmic center, and building a temple in the garden Eden.[92] These stories were not mythical; nor were they about the human condition. They were expressions of real-world power politics, using a story form for which no one needed footnotes to recognize who the players were.

88. Vermeylen, "Le Récit du Paradis," 230–50.

89. This approach is consistent with the view that primeval J is not an independent narrative. See Ronald Hendel, "Is the 'J' Primeval Narrative an Independent Composition? A Critique of Crüsemann's 'Die Eigenständigkeit der Urgeschichte,'" in *The Pentateuch: International Perspectives on Current Research* (ed. Thomas B. Dozeman and Konrad Schmid, with Baruch Schwartz; Tübingen: Mohr Siebeck, 2011) 181–205.

90. Stordalen, *Echoes of Eden*, 205.

91. Stephen Breck Reid, "Review of Robert B. Coote, *The Bible's First History: From Eden to the Court of David with the Yahwist*," *JAAR* 63 (1995) 379.

92. Stordalen concurs but with Ezek 47:1–12 accomplishing the same (*Echoes of Eden*, 367).

Babel-Bible-Baal

Aaron Tugendhaft

Ludwig Maximilian University, Munich

I. *"Babel-Baal Streit"*

On January 13, 1902, Friedrich Delitzsch delivered his first *Babel und Bibel* lecture before the Deutsche Orient-Gesellschaft and the Kaiser of the German Reich. As part of Delitzsch's general argument that much in the Hebrew Bible depended on Babylonian culture, the Assyriologist provided his audience with a lengthy paraphrase of *Enūma eliš*. "At the very beginning of all things," Delitzsch informed the Kaiser, "a dark, chaotic, primeval water, called Tiâmat, existed in a state of agitation and tumult," but the god Marduk later cleaved it "clean asunder like a fish."[1] Delitzsch proceeded to explain the relevance of the ancient Babylonian poem to his theme: "As Marduk was the tutelary deity of the city of Babylon, we can readily believe that this narrative in particular became very widely diffused in Canaan. Indeed, the Old Testament poets and prophets even went so far as to transfer Marduk's heroic act directly to Yahwè."[2] Delitzsch was only popularizing an opinion that many scholars of his day were already taking for granted—that the origin of Israelite ideas about creation was to be found in Babylonia.[3] This groundbreaking thesis had been presented seven years earlier, when, in *Schöpfung und Chaos in Urzeit und Endzeit*, Hermann Gunkel argued that the Babylonian narrative of Marduk's defeat of Tiʾāmat had influenced the Bible's conception of creation, as well as its depiction of the eschatological end of days.[4]

---

1. Friedrich Delitzsch, *Babel and Bible: Two Lectures* (trans. C. H. W. Johns; Eugene, OR: Wipf & Stock, 2007; original: New York: Putnam, 1903) 47, 49. On Delitzsch's ideological commitments, including his nationalism and anti-Semitism, see Bill T. Arnold and David B. Weisberg, "A Centennial Review of Friedrich Delitzsch's 'Babel und Bibel' Lectures," *JBL* 121 (2002) 441–57, with bibliographical references. For a discussion of Delitzsch's lecture in its larger cultural context, see Suzanne L. Marchand, *German Orientalism in the Age of Empire: Religion, Race, and Scholarship* (Cambridge: Cambridge University Press, 2009) 212–51.

2. Delitzsch, *Babel and Bible*, 49.

3. The principal biblical passages that have come under discussion in this regard are Genesis 1; Isa 17:12–14; 27:1; 51:9–10; Pss 104:5ff.; 46:3–4; 74:12ff.; 89:10ff.; Job 26:12; 9:13; Daniel 7; Revelation 12, 13, 17.

4. H. Gunkel, *Creation and Chaos in the Primeval Era and the Eschaton: A Religio-Historical Study of Genesis* 1 and Revelation 12 (trans. K. William Whitney, Jr.; Grand Rapids,

Uncertainty emerged about Babylon as the source of the divine combat imagery in the Bible when the Ugaritic mythological texts were discovered in 1931. As early as 1936, just one year after the initial publication of the *Baʿal Cycle* passage presenting the storm god's combat with Yamm, W. F. Albright raised the issue of influence between Mesopotamian and Ugaritic mythology.[5] Albright observed that "Yammu plays essentially the same role in Canaanite cosmogony that Tiâmat and Labbu, etc., do in Mesopotamian"[6] but remained agnostic regarding the direction of influence. In a note, he remarked: "It is too early to reach any definite conclusion with regard to the original provenience of these monsters, whether from the East or the West."[7]

Thirty years later, Thorkild Jacobsen believed he could resolve the question of the combat motif's geographical origin. In a short article devoted to the combat between Marduk and Tiʾāmat, Jacobsen reflected on the relationship between the Babylonian creation epic and the myth of Baʿal from Ugarit:

> To find the same mythological motif: a battle between the god of thunderstorms and the sea from which the god of the thunderstorm emerges victorious, both in *Enuma elish*—composed in Babylonia around the middle of the Second Millennium B.C.—and in an Ugaritic poem written down on the coast of the Mediterranean at roughly the same date naturally raises the question whether we are dealing with a case of independent invention, or with a motif that has wandered from East to West or from West to East.[8]

Earlier in his essay, Jacobsen had concluded that "the battle between Marduk and Tiʾāmat described in *Enūma eliš* is a battle of the elements, of forces in nature, a battle between the thunderstorm and the sea."[9] This meteorological interpretation constitutes the basis for Jacobsen's answer to the question of origins. Considering which geographical location—coastal Syria or southern Mesopotamia—is the more likely original environment to have produced this myth, he concludes that the meteorology of coastal Ugarit makes for the more likely candidate. The environment surrounding Babylon, Jacobsen argued,

---

MI: Eerdmans, 2006); cf. idem, *Israel and Babylon: The Babylonian Influence on Israelite Religion* (trans. E. S. B. and K. C. Hanson; Eugene, OR: Wipf & Stock, 2009 = Göttingen: Vandenhoeck und Ruprecht, 1903) 42–43.

5. Willam Foxwell Albright, "Zabûl Yam and Thâpiṭ Nahar in the Combat between Baal and the Sea," *Journal of the Palestine Oriental Society* 16 (1936) 17–20. See Dennis Pardee, "La mythologie ougaritique dans son cadre historique," *Res Antiquae* 7 (2010) 168–69.

6. Albright, "Zabûl Yam," 18.

7. Ibid., 18 n. 1.

8. Thorkild Jacobsen, "The Battle between Marduk and Tiamat," *JAOS* 88 (1968) 104–8; quotation from p. 107.

9. Ibid., 106.

would have supplied no incentive for such a mythopoeic rendering of the storm and sea, and so the idea that the Babylonians "should independently have thought up a myth about a battle between the thunderstorm and the sea and should then have made the myth central in [their] cosmogony is exceedingly difficult to imagine, and common sense must exclude it as a probable possibility."[10] Jacobsen ends his article by considering when this migration may have taken place. Basing his opinion on the time when the uncontracted form *tiʾamtum* would most likely have arrived in the east, he states that his "personal preference is for assuming that the motif was brought to Babylon late, with the Amorites."[11]

Jacobsen's "common sense" seemed to be proved right when, in 1993, Jean-Marie Durand published a letter from Mari containing a prophecy of the storm god of Aleppo.[12] The prophecy contains a reference to the combat between the storm god and the sea and thus provides an attestation of the motif several hundred years older than both the Ugaritic and the Babylonian poems. This early appearance of the combat motif in the west lent support to the contention that the Mesopotamian use was derivative of an earlier Amorite tradition. Exorcism rituals from Ebla, published four years later by Pelio Fronzaroli, further localized the tradition in Syria at an early date.[13] Scholarly opinion has accordingly shifted toward identifying an Amorite origin for the mythic motif of divine combat against the sea.

The discovery of these western sources has necessitated a reconsideration of the question of influence on the Bible that produced the *Babel-Bibel-Streit*. With numerous attestations of the mythic motif now available from locations more proximate to ancient Israel, one must wonder whether the biblical authors took from Babylon at all or instead acquired their mythical material closer to home. Though proponents of Babylonian influence on the Bible have not disappeared—especially with respect to biblical texts considered to be later productions—the discovery of the Ugaritic mythological texts have dramatically shifted scholarly attention to Israel's "Canaanite" background. According to Mark S. Smith, for example, "the Baal Cycle expresses the heart of the West Semitic religion from which Israelite religion largely developed."[14]

10. Ibid., 107.

11. Ibid., 108.

12. A. 1968. Published in Jean-Marie Durand, "Le mythologème du combat entre le dieu de l'orage et la mer en Mésopotamie," *MARI* 7 (1993) 41–61.

13. Pelio Fronzaroli, "Les combats de Hadda dans les textes d'Ébla," *MARI* 8 (1997) 283–90.

14. Mark S. Smith, *The Ugaritic Baal Cycle*, vol. 1: *Introduction with Text, Translation and Commentary of KTU 1.1–1.2* (VTSup 55; Leiden: Brill, 1994) xxvi.

Israel's use of the combat motif has come to be seen mainly as an inheritance of local Syro-Palestinian traditions, not an importation from Mesopotamia. This revision of Gunkel and Delitzsch's position has resulted, above all, from the displacement of Mesopotamian by Ugaritic mythology as the principal source for reconstructing the background to Israelite religion.

In contrast to the furor that broke out in the wake of Delitzsch's famous lecture, the replacement of *Enūma eliš* with the *Baʿal Cycle* as the key text for understanding the Bible's mythological background has been a tame academic affair. There has been no "Babel-Baal Streit" akin to the *Babel-Bibel Streit* of a century ago. This is understandable. The idea that the biblical texts reflect prebiblical traditions has, of course, become more palatable over the years. Besides, compared with the problem of whether to admit the existence of outside influences on the Bible at all, the question whether these influences come from near or far can hardly cause blood to boil; particularly so because—as Albright's early comment about Yamm's resembling Tiʾāmat attests—little effort has been placed on distinguishing the meaning of mythological material in Mesopotamia and Ugarit. Instead, Jean-Marie Durand has referred to the *Baʿal Cycle* and *Enūma eliš* as attesting "la même histoire,"[15] while Albright's student Frank Moore Cross has contended that both poems are cosmogonies that share the same basic structure.[16] If there is little fundamental difference between the mythical attestations of the combat motif in Ugarit and Babylon, then the question of which provides the more direct source for the Bible is at best a secondary concern.

Consensus has begun to break down, however, regarding the similarity of the Ugaritic and Babylonian poems.[17] Already in the first volume of his *Baʿal Cycle* commentary, Smith provided an extensive list of points at which the characterization of Baʿal differs from that of Marduk.[18] In his contribution to this volume, Wayne Pitard continues to distinguish the two poems by arguing against claims that the *Baʿal Cycle* is a cosmogony. It is an opportune time, therefore, to reconsider the relevance of the discovery of the Ugaritic myth to our understanding of the motif of divine combat against the sea as it occurs in the literature of the ancient Near East.

15. Durand, "Le mythologème du combat," 42.

16. Frank Moore Cross, *From Epic to Canon: History and Literature in Ancient Israel* (Baltimore: Johns Hopkins University Press, 1998) 73–83.

17. To be sure, there have always been those who objected to the tendency of reading the *Baʿal Cycle* in light of *Enūma eliš*; see, for example, Jonas C. Greenfield, "The Hebrew Bible and Canaanite Literature," in *The Literary Guide to the Bible* (ed. Robert Alter and Frank Kermode; Cambridge: Harvard University Press, 1987) 557.

18. Smith, *Ugaritic Baal Cycle*, xxv–xxvi.

II. Motifs and Meanings

The corpus of texts that attest the mythic motif of a storm god who fights the sea has grown since the days of Gunkel and Delitzsch. Nevertheless, the predilection has been to approach these new finds with the same basic questions that motivated those German scholars a century ago. Focus has remained on tracking influence and transmission. This has often had the effect of diverting attention away from the particularities of each specific occurrence. This procedure makes sense if the goal is to plot a motif's historical trajectory but often stands in the way of understanding the meaning of the material in our possession. Because meaning is not present intrinsically in a mythological motif but, rather, results from the way that a motif is employed within a specific context, concern with origins can prove to be an obstacle to understanding. Knowing where something comes from is not the same as understanding what it is doing once it is there.[19] The tendency to focus on influence and transmission and thus to abstract from what particularizes each attestation must be balanced by investigation into the ways that a common motif can produce a variety of meanings, sometimes quite at odds with one another.

Jacobsen, for instance, failed to consider this latter issue when he wrote about the relationship between *Enūma eliš* and the *Baʿal Cycle*. For him, the meaning of the myth derived from "which realities may be thought to underlie it."[20] He determined that the two combatants stood for meteorological phenomena and that these phenomena corresponded to the climate of Ugarit, not Babylonia. As a result, the Ugaritic poem was designated original, and the Babylonian poem was treated as derivative. Jacobsen never explained what good a meteorological myth that did not correspond to the Babylonian climate would have done for the people of Babylon. Employed as a means to convey ideas about political order and authority, however, the motif achieves a function at Babylon despite its meteorologically foreign origins. The combat motif, even if foreign in origin, was integrated into an elaborate Babylonian account of Marduk's reign, how that reign overturned an earlier chaotic era, and how it manifested itself on earth in the institution of Babylonian kingship. The motif's meaning in *Enūma eliš* derives from the way this poem uses it to imagine the conquest of chaos by the current lord of the universe.[21]

19. See Marc Bloch, *The Historian's Craft* (trans. Peter Putnam; New York: Knopf, 1953) 29–35.

20. Jacobsen, "Battle between Marduk and Tiamat," 105.

21. Elsewhere, Jacobsen does address the political meaning of Marduk's combat with Tiʾāmat; see Thorkild Jacobsen, *The Treasures of Darkness: A History of Mesopotamian Religion* (New Haven, CT: Yale University Press, 1976) 183–91.

By contrast, the *Baʿal Cycle* does not employ the combat with Yamm to depict the overcoming of a primordial past. That is—to employ a generic definition proposed by Cross—the *Baʿal Cycle* is not a cosmogony. According to that definition, a cosmogony tells the story of how the "olden gods" were overcome by the "younger gods."[22] Though Cross offered this definition as part of an argument aimed at identifying both *Enūma eliš* and the *Baʿal Cycle* as cosmogonies, his criteria only hold good for the Babylonian poem. The two criteria he offered for identifying a god as "olden" are that such a god would not have received cultic sacrifices and would not have been taken as a theophoric element in personal names.[23] This test works for Marduk's antagonist in *Enūma eliš*, since Tiʾāmat did not receive offerings in Mesopotamia, nor was she taken as a namesake. At Ugarit, however, the picture for Yamm is rather different. The sea god is found listed as a recipient of cult—along with El, Baʿal, and Athirat—in local ritual texts.[24] Likewise, the Ugaritic onomasticon attests Yamm as a theophoric element in such personal names as *yammuʾilu* ("Yamm is god"), *iluyammu* ("A god is Yamm"), *milkuyammu* ("A king is Yamm"), and *ʿabduyammi* ("Servant of Yamm").[25] Unlike Tiʾāmat, therefore, Yamm fails both tests for being an "olden god." Not a deity of the distant past, Yamm belongs to the coterie of gods that make up the present world. Battle with him, therefore, is not about transitioning from a chaotic past to an ordered present; rather, in the *Baʿal Cycle* the combat motif belongs to a depiction of struggle as present within the current world order.

Though both the poets of Ugarit and of Babylon employed the motif of combat between the storm god and the sea, they characterized the sea in different ways—with the result that the combat takes on a different meaning in each case. At Babylon, the motif was used to mark a transition from one eon to another, with the concomitant political implication that the current order has replaced a previous disorder; at Ugarit, one finds no reference to a displaced primordial chaos but, rather, a suggestion that the current world itself is constituted by ongoing struggle. The ramifications of this distinction for the respective myths' messages regarding earthly political life are profound. Any attempt to elucidate the meaning of the *Baʿal Cycle* in relation to *Enūma eliš* must take into account how each applies the combat motif differently.

22. Cross, *From Epic to Canon*, 78.

23. Ibid.

24. See *KTU* 1.39 13; 1.46 6; 1.148 9, 41; and 1.162 11.

25. *Ymʾil*: *KTU* 4.75 V 14; *ʾilym*: *KTU* 4.116 13; *mlkym*: *KTU* 4.126 19; *ʿbdym*: *KTU* 4.7 7; 4.103 18 and 47; 3.3 10; 4.341 3 (restored).

III. Myth and Politics

Nicolas Wyatt has asserted that, following Durand's publication of the Adad letter, "it became clear that the whole narrative tradition of the *Chaoskampf* had an intimate relationship with rituals of kingship, new kings receiving from the gods a charter guaranteeing divine sanction in their military campaigns." According to Wyatt, "[E]very petty local king present[ed] himself to his people in the same guise. It really had become a cliché for legitimacy."[26] Wyatt's conclusion flattens out the differences between the various attestations of the combat motif. His use of the term *Chaoskampf* obfuscates how the *Baʿal Cycle* is able to make use of a narrative tradition without telling a story about the conquest of chaos. Wyatt may well be right that there was an affinity between the combat motif and political thinking in the ancient world, but this affinity should not be mistaken for a fixed political message. Rather, the politics of myth are malleable in conformity with the ways a motif can be variously applied.

A typological approach furnishes a powerful corrective to the emphasis on origin and influence that has dominated discussion of the combat motif since Gunkel's pioneering work. Attention to typological distinctions provides for a richer account of the political implications of myth because it puts focus on variation and adaptation and therefore necessitates political explication consonant with that variety. I will therefore conclude by proposing two typological distinctions that are helpful for understanding the combat motif in its various manifestations. The following comments should be taken as a preliminary sketch, the purpose of which is to orient inquiry, not supply a definitive account.

The first typological distinction is between narratives that use divine combat to depict a transgenerational conflict and narratives in which combat occurs within a single generation. Call this the distinction between "diachronic" and "synchronic" applications of the combat motif. Only the former would be an appropriate mythopoeic means for describing the transition from one temporal epoch to another. Other purposes should be sought when explicating a synchronic application. The contrasting temporal horizons of *Enūma eliš* and the *Baʿal Cycle* put the Babylonian poem in the diachronic category and the Ugaritic myth in the synchronic.

Notably, the Bible's attestations of the combat motif tend to resemble the usage at Babylon more closely than at Ugarit—a point that holds true regardless of how one maps out the trajectories of influence and transmission. When, in Psalm 89, David's kingship is associated with Yahweh's primordial subduing

26. Nicolas Wyatt, "The Religious Role of the King in Ugarit," *UF* 37 (2005) 698–99.

of the sea, explicit reference is being made to an earlier time. Politically, Psalm 89 is also closer to *Enūma eliš* than to the *Baʿal Cycle*. Yahweh's relationship to the House of David resembles Marduk's position vis-à-vis Babylon. Despite Ugarit's greater proximity to Israel, the *Baʿal Cycle*—which neither associates the combat motif with the overcoming of a primordial past nor identifies divine rule with kingship on earth—provides less of a parallel to Israel's use of the motif than does the Babylonian poem.

However, the Bible also attests its own complex renderings of the mythic trope. As Gunkel recognized, the combat motif was not only used in the Bible to express ideas about creation (as in *Enūma eliš*) but also to describe the future end of days (an idea that is absent from the Babylonian poem). For instance, Isaiah predicts that "on that day" Yahweh will visit his sword on Leviathan; "He will slay the dragon of the sea" (Isa 27:1). As in the beginning, so too in the end. This prophetic eschatology is intertwined politically with the messianic hope that the future will bring an end to Israel's suffering. The eschatological adaptation of the combat motif belongs to Israel's particular rethinking of politics' relationship to the divine—one that emerged in part as a reaction to imperial subjugation.

This leads to my second typological distinction: between victory at work in the present and victory projected into the future. According to *Enūma eliš*, Marduk achieved his victory in the past and thus is ruling now, in the present. Biblical eschatology, on the other hand, recalls Yahweh's past triumph as a way to anticipate his reign in the future. Isaiah announces that Yahweh's combat at the end of days will reproduce his victory at the dawn of creation. The period between these two endpoints of history, however, the time in which we ourselves live, does not manifest the reign of a victorious god—the prophet implies—as does the world according to *Enūma eliš*. By applying the combat motif to the future as well as the past, biblical authors produced a distinct picture of the present. This picture of the present was unlike either Babylon's optimistic portrayal of Marduk's current reign or Ugarit's representation of a present characterized by continuous conflict.

There is something appropriately imperial about the Babylonian account that coordinates present Babylonian domination with Marduk's rule over the entire universe. It similarly stands to reason that Israel developed its own eschatological use of the combat motif in response to its political circumstances as a small state oppressed by imperial power. Like Israel, Ugarit also developed its political understanding in the shadow of imperial power. However, unlike the Israelite prophets who saw hope in the future, whoever composed the *Baʿal Cycle* did not apply the combat motif eschatologically. Rather, the Ugaritic poem embraces a picture in which there is neither beginning nor end but only the ongoing struggles of today. These three cases attest three entirely different approaches to understanding the relationship among politics, history, and the divine—all three making use of the combat motif. A typological approach makes these distinctions apparent in a way that concern with transmission and influence cannot.

The *Babel-Bibel Streit* was explicitly theological. At stake were the authority of the Old Testament, the nature of revelation, and the character of God's working through history. Of the many permutations of theological thinking that came to expression in those early years of the twentieth century, I will conclude with a comment that C. H. W. Johns makes in the introduction to his 1903 English translation of Delitzsch's two lectures. The Cambridge Assyriologist and Church of England clergyman defended his German colleague by situating Babylonian culture within the history of salvation. The discoveries announced by Delitzsch are not a challenge to faith, Johns argued, but rather, an occasion for celebrating God's grace:

> The men of deep religious faith, who alone count for the progress of the race, will rejoice and take courage at a fresh proof that the Father has never left Himself without witness among men, and that even the most unlikely elements have gone to prepare the world for Him who was, and still is, to come.[27]

From Johns's perspective, the discovery of religious expression that anticipates the writings of ancient Israel only goes to prove that recognition of God has been richer and more extensive than previously appreciated. The tracking of transmission takes on a particular value when one is tracking the manifestations of grace.

We inherit the research questions of our predecessors. If the motivations that defined those questions have faded from view, it is incumbent on us to reacquaint ourselves with the concerns of former scholars. Do we share the concerns that motivated their research? If not, why continue to pursue the same questions? By turning away from questions of transmission and continuity, I have tried to refocus inquiry on the different ways that the same inherited materials could be used to fashion three vastly different visions of the world. This may not speak to the unity of divine care, but it does attest the range and significance of human creativity.

---

27. C. H. W. Johns, "Introduction," in Delitzsch, *Babel and Bible: Two Lectures*, xxix. There is reason to believe that Delitzsch would not have shared his apologist's position, but that is another matter.

Part 4

Power and Politics

The Combat Myth as a Succession Story at Ugarit

Wayne T. Pitard

University of Illinois at Urbana-Champaign

With the discovery in the early 1930s of the Ugaritic literary tablets in the House of the High Priest, we came into possession of narrative texts that both geographically and culturally stand between Mesopotamia and ancient Israel. The appearance of a mythological text in which the young storm-god Baʿal fights with the god of the sea, Yamm, provided a key parallel in pre-Israelite northwest Semitic literature for the *Chaoskampf* motif that had played such an important role in the study of biblical creation stories since Gunkel's great *Schöpfung und Chaos* appeared in 1895. But the *Baʿal Cycle* was different from the Mesopotamian and biblical exemplars in that it did not appear to have a creation account within the story. The other two primary elements, the battle with the sea and the construction of the palace/temple, were clear, but what to make of the absence of the creation?

During our years of work on a commentary on the second episode of the *Baʿal Cycle* on tablets 3 and 4,[1] Mark Smith and I came to the realization that the best way to understand the narrative arc of the cycle is to recognize that creation essentially has little to do with the story. Rather, we have here an account of royal succession set onto the mythological plane. This succession

1. Mark S. Smith and Wayne T. Pitard, *The Ugaritic Baal Cycle*, vol. 2: *Introduction with Text, Translation and Commentary of KTU/CAT 1.3–1.4* (Vetus Testamentum Supplement 114; Leiden: Brill, 2009).

narrative is the focus of the first two episodes of the cycle—that is, the conflict between Baʿal and Yamm (tablets 1 and 2) and the building of Baʿal's palace (3 and 4).

It also became clear to us as we worked through these two tablets that the narrative of how Baʿal gained permission from El to build his grand palace is best understood as the central story of the *Baʿal Cycle*, not just physically (where, after all, it is flanked on each side by the narratives about the conflicts between Baʿal and Yamm [tablets 1 and 2] and Baʿal and Mot [tablets 5 and 6]), but also theologically. The climactic image of the episode in 1.4 VII—in which Baʿal, now in his new palace, sits enthroned, lord of heaven and earth, the mighty warrior whose voice is the thunder and who sends forth the rains to water the earth—is certainly the fundamental image of the god for his worshipers at Ugarit. Although he must surmount several difficulties in achieving his kingship, he does arrive at this epiphany with full power and no rivals. The previous episode concerning Yamm shows his ability to overcome great challenges. The following episode depicting his challenge of Mot points out something that everyone knew: even the god of life must share the universe with death. But on earth, life remains the more powerful and more durable. At the end of each of the three episodes of the cycle, Baʿal's rulership is proclaimed (*CAT* 1.2 IV 32–37; 1.4 VI 38–VII 42; 1.6 VI 33–35). The truly defining image of his kingship, however, is the image in 1.4 VII.[2]

In the commentary, Mark and I proposed a number of new interpretations of elements of the *Baʿal Cycle*. Some of these grew out of the recognition that too much emphasis has been placed on interpreting the *Baʿal Cycle* through the lens of the Mesopotamian creation epic, the *Enūma Eliš*, with scholars often reading aspects of the latter's narrative into the former. It is indeed the case that the two narratives have a number of common elements, in that both tell stories of the rise of a young god to power through combat with the sea. However, the contrast between the larger contexts within which these narrative elements appear in the two stories has often been downplayed. The broader contexts of the *Enūma Eliš* and the *Baʿal Cycle* are in fact quite different from one another.

First, one may note the substantial contrasts between the two sea deities who play the important role of antagonist in each epic, Tiʾāmat of the *Enūma Eliš*, and Yamm of the *Baʿal Cycle*. The former is the mother of all the gods and, until the rise of Marduk, the most powerful force in the universe. While she is related to all the gods as progenetrix, she is consistently marked off in the epic as separated from the primary deities of the Sumero-Akkadian pantheon who

2. Ibid., 2:1–3. On Baʿal's relationship to Mot, see p. 19.

play the leading roles in the religion of Mesopotamia and who are several generations removed from her. She has no personal relationships with them; they do not belong to the same social sphere. She is, from the point of view of the storyteller, an outsider, representing chaos, the periphery and danger, while Marduk, the poem's hero, represents order, the center of the universe, and the great pantheon of gods.[3] The relationship between Baʿal and Yamm, however, is strikingly different from this. Unlike Mesopotamian mythology, where the gods are seen as an extended family of numerous generations, the genealogy of the Ugaritic gods is very short and constricted.[4] There are essentially only two primary generations of deities: Generation One being El and Athirat as the divine parents; followed by Generation Two, their children, often called the 70 children of Athirat. Baʿal and Anat seem to be somewhat outside this setup, since neither is the offspring of Athirat, but both are probably children of El by a different mother (Baʿal is sometimes identified as a son of El and sometimes as a son of Dagan—but El and Dagan may have been merged at Ugarit).[5] Whatever their exact situation, they are portrayed as contemporaries with the generation of the children of El and Athirat. Yamm is also a member of that generation, a son of El and probably one of Athirat's offspring. He thus is not a primeval deity like Tiʾāmat, nor does he represent chaos or the periphery in the story. Rather than being an outsider like Tiʾāmat, he is very much an insider, a member of the divine council in good standing, and El proclaims him ruler of the council in the first episode (*CAT* 1.1 IV). Although Baʿal objects to the appointment, there appear to be few who are discontented with this choice among the members of the council. So Yamm is not an outside force that threatens the very existence of the younger generation of the gods, as Tiʾāmat is, but is part of the young generation, an ambitious member of the council who rises to power through the support he receives from the older king of the gods. This presentation of Yamm is quite foreign to the depiction of Tiʾāmat and provides a completely different context for his struggle with Baʿal, since the conflict between Baʿal and Yamm is a power struggle within the divine council and not a cosmological conflict that will lead to creation of the world. In the *Baʿal Cycle*, the world already exists, and it is already peopled by humans (see *CAT* 1.3 II 3–35; 1.4 VII 5–13). It may be that at some other point in Ugarit's religious history the Combat Myth was related to creation,

3. On the discussion of "periphery" and "center," see Mark S. Smith, *The Origins of Biblical Monotheism: Israel's Polytheistic Background and the Ugaritic Texts* (Oxford: Oxford University Press, 2001) 27–35; and Smith and Pitard, *Ugaritic Baal Cycle*, 2:52–55.

4. See ibid., 2:46–52.

5. Cf. Lluis Feliu, *The God Dagan in Bronze Age Syria* (trans. Wilfred G. E. Watson; CHANE 19; Leiden: Brill, 2003) 264–66.

but in the *Baʿal Cycle* it is not such a narrative, and there is nothing in the preserved text to suggest that it should be so understood.

In addition to these substantial differences between the two narratives, another contrast must be noted as well. While both Marduk and Baʿal rise to kingship during the course of the story, the type of office and the circumstances under which they assume power are significantly different. In the *Enūma Eliš*, Marduk rises to uncontested kingship in circumstances that can be described as a power vacuum—all the gods, including Marduk's father and grandfather have proven to be ineffective in facing the threat of Tiʾāmat's attack (*Ee* II 49–126). Marduk steps into a dire situation and saves the younger gods from certain doom. He has no rivals for the position. Tiʾāmat, the enemy he fights, is intentionally portrayed as an external threat to all the young gods, not a personal rival. The account of Baʿal's rise to power, however, is placed in a completely different context. Here, we have a story of royal succession rather than an existential crisis for the gods. El is portrayed as the old king looking for a young successor among his children who will act as co-regent and take on the active responsibilities within the divine council. He first appoints Yamm to the position, but Baʿal refuses to accept this arrangement, believing himself to be the more appropriate choice. The story here is much closer, thematically, to the account of the succession to David's throne in 1 Kings 1 than to the *Enūma Eliš*. There too we have an elderly king who is called upon to designate his heir while still alive, an heir who will take over the day-to-day business of kingship, while sharing the title of king with the old ruler. There also we have two sons in conflict over who should take the position. In this story, appropriate protocol plays an important role, in both its usage and in its breach. In 1 Kings 1, Adonijah ignores protocol by proclaiming himself successor without bothering to consult David (1 Kgs 1:5–10: "Now Adonijah son of Haggith exalted himself, saying, "I will be king"). This bit of arrogance is used against him when Bathsheba goes to David to ask him to appoint Solomon as king (1 Kgs 1:18: "But now suddenly Adonijah has become king, though you, my lord the king, do not know it"). Adonijah's breach of protocol is emphasized in the passage to indicate his lack of faithfulness to David (the author describes Adonijah's actions in terms reminiscent of those he uses to describe the beginning of Absalom's rebellion) and thus his lack of suitability for the position. Bathsheba then carefully follows the proper protocol of consulting with the old king to gain his support for Solomon.

The importance of appropriate court etiquette that we see in the David story is also a major factor in the Baʿal-Yamm episode of tablets 1.1 and 1.2. A key scene in the narrative, found in 1.2 I, appears to be used in much the same way within the Baʿal story as the description of Adonijah's seizure of power is used in 1 Kings 1. In 1.2 I, it appears that Yamm's new position goes to his head, and in an action that breaks with royal protocol and etiquette in a shocking and highly political way, Yamm arrogantly sends his messengers to El and the council with specific instructions to refuse to bow before either and to demand Baʿal as his slave. This is a direct attack on El's position as the primary king and ultimate authority, and a usurpation of power by the younger ruler. Although El gives in to the request, the shameful behavior of Yamm here was almost certainly intended by the storyteller to impress upon the audience the unsuitability of Yamm to rule over the council, thus justifying both Baʿal's refusal to accept Yamm's authority and his eventual overthrow of the god. This breach of protocol will be punished by his removal from office.

An obvious but significant difference between the David story and the *Baʿal Cycle* is, of course that, while the former occurs in the human sphere of activity, the latter takes place in the mythological sphere. The person whom David appoints as co-regent will succeed to the throne as the single ruler when David dies. But in the *Baʿal Cycle*, we are among the gods, and while El is on one level appointing a successor, he is not mortal—the gods are essentially frozen in time. El will not die and leave the kingdom to his successor. The relationship between El and Baʿal here, the elderly ruler and the young co-regent, is mythologically permanent, just as the relationships between Baʿal and Yamm and Baʿal and Mot are permanent. Thus, within the episode concerning Baʿal's palace, the subordinate position of Baʿal vis-à-vis El is crucial to understanding the events described.

When we turn to the parallel stories in the *Enūma Eliš* and the *Baʿal Cycle* about the building of the god's palace/temple, we see a number of important similarities. In both narratives, the temple itself is seen as a physical confirmation of the new position of the god. The attendance of all the gods at a banquet in the new palace (*Ee* VI 69–120 and *CAT* 1.4 VI 38–VII 6) is the clear indicator that the gods fully accept the new ruler and his authority. But again, there are major differences between the contexts of these scenes in the two stories. The most important thing to note in the *Enūma Eliš* is that the defeat of Tiʾāmat is the conclusion and climax of Marduk's rise to kingship. From that moment on, he acts as ruler, creating the world and giving the gods their new functions within it. The building of Esagila for Marduk (*Ee* VI 39–68) is an action of the gods themselves as a gift of appreciation for his benevolent deeds. The situation in the *Baʿal Cycle* is dramatically different. First of all, the Baʿal/Yamm story has been about two gods fighting, not for independent kingship, but for co-regency with the old king. At the end of the story of the battle between Baʿal and Yamm (*CAT* 1.2 IV), Baʿal's quest of the position as co-regent has not yet been completed. A few gods (his allies) have proclaimed his kingship but, for Baʿal to take his position, it is imperative that he have the approval of El, the king, who has not yet so proclaimed. The second episode of the *Baʿal Cycle*, in tablets 3 and 4, is the story of how Baʿal gains El's support as co-regent, although it is told through the metaphor of Baʿal's obtaining El's permission to build a new palace. By approving Baʿal's request for the construction of a palace appropriate to his status, El also indicates his approval of Baʿal as co-regent. The importance of El's approval is evident in the narrative itself. An astonishing 8 of the 11 columns of the second episode deal with Baʿal's complicated struggle to gain this permission, indicating the central importance of this specific story element for understanding the overarching theme of the epic. The story of the construction of the palace (1.4 V 35–VI 38) takes a relative back seat in the episode to the process of gaining El's consent to build it.

As in the Baʿal and Yamm episode in tablets 1.1 and 1.2, appropriate royal protocol plays a key role here.[6] The two scenes in which first Anat, then Athirat approach El on Baʿal's behalf provide narrative examples of the futility of a breach of protocol (Anat) and the successful outcome based on using the appropriate protocol (Athirat). In the first scene (1.3 V 4–44), Anat's attempt at persuasion is poorly handled on her part, as she breaks divine protocol with her belligerent attitude, and El does not give his permission. Baʿal and Anat then visit El's wife Athirat and convince her to talk to her husband on Baʿal's behalf. The meeting between Athirat and El is successful, because Athirat follows every aspect of proper court etiquette, and El grants his permission (1.3 VI–1.4 V).

But the key focus in all of this is the relationship between Baʿal and El, between the elder king and the young successor, the importance of recognizing the authority of the elder king in establishing the legitimacy of the younger co-regent and the proper protocol necessary in this circumstance. This issue and its resolution overwhelm everything else in the episode and must be the overriding concern of the storyteller. It fits well into the larger theme of the first four tablets of the cycle, which deals with disputed succession to the throne, with what the qualities of a successor should be, and the fact that, in the case of a dispute, proper protocol and etiquette must be observed.

If we are correct in understanding the primary theme of the cycle, then we would argue that the palace itself, unlike the situation in the *Enūma Eliš*, is

6. The importance of recognizing the key role of protocol within the narrative of 1.3 and 1.4 is discussed in general in Smith and Pitard, *Ugaritic Baal Cycle*, 2:36–39, and in more detail in the detailed commentary.

somewhat peripheral to the main theme of the episode.[7] It is only significant in that El's granting of permission to Baʿal for building the palace symbolizes his acceptance of Baʿal as co-regent. Likewise, the inaugural celebration in which the children of Athirat join the banquet at the palace indicates their acceptance of Baʿal as the legitimate ruler of the divine council. Thus all of the focus of the episode is on legitimation of a process of royal succession, rather than on legitimation and glorification of the Temple of Baʿal or of the city and/or king of Ugarit as such. In the *Enūma Eliš*, the palace/temple constructed is the physical temple Esagila in Babylon, and the story legitimates Babylon's status as the political/religious center of the universe. In the *Baʿal Cycle*, the same motif is used as a symbol for the legitimation of Baʿal as El's co-regent (and thus, the process by which legitimation occurs) and acts as a subordinate motif to the much more significant motif of royal succession.

Thus, the *Baʿal Cycle* provides an excellent example of the fluidity with which complex motifs could be used in narrative constructions across the Near East. It issues a warning to interpreters, reminding them that the appearance of a similar motif in more than one story does not mean an identical function of the motif within the stories.

---

7. See the more detailed discussion of the relation between the poem's palace and the Temple of Baʿal at Ugarit in ibid., 2:42–44.

What Are the Nations Doing in the Chaoskampf?

Robert D. Miller II

The Catholic University of America / The University of Pretoria

In the book of Psalms, images associated with the *Chaoskampf* or with whatever we decide Israel to have used that was *Chaoskampf*-like occur in clusters. That is, motifs and terms borrowed from the Baʿal stories are found in combination: the defeat of chaos, Mount Zaphon, and rivers of paradise, for example. The foreign nations also form an essential element of these psalms, both as enemies defeated and as peacefully coming in pilgrimage to Zion. There seems to be no counterpart for these motifs in the ancient Near Eastern *Chaoskampf*. In this essay, I examine the inclusion of the nations and find it to be an element of Judean royal propaganda in the context of Neo-Assyrian expansion.

First, let me present the image cluster as it is found in the Psalms. I think it is fair to call this a "constellation," as Jan Assmann defines this term, as a set of reference points or motifs that recur together both in and out of narrative myth.[1] One element of this constellation is the identification of Mt. Zion with the mythical highest mountain in the utmost North, Mt. Zaphon of Canaanite mythology. This is evident in Ps 48:2: "Mount Zion, the heights of Zaphon, the city of the great king." Zaphon hardly means simply "north" in this psalm.[2] In some cases, this first theme includes the related idea of God's dwelling on Zion, as in Psalm 48, but this is not uniform.

1. Jan Assmann, *The Search for God in Ancient Egypt* (trans. David Lorton; Ithaca, NY: Cornell University Press, 2001 (= *Ägypten: Theologie und Frömmigkeit einer frühen Hochkultur* [Kohlhammer Urban-Taschenbücher 366; Stuttgart: Kohlhammer, 1984]) 107; idem, "Die Zeugung des Sohnes: Bild, Spiel, Erzählung und das Problem des ägyptischen Mythos," in *Funktionen and Leistungen des Mythos: Drei altorientalische Beispiele* (OBO 48; Freiburg: Universitätsverlag / Göttingen: Vandenhoeck & Ruprecht, 1982) 13–61.

2. As per Corinna Körting, *Zion in den Psalmen* (FAT 48; Tübingen: Mohr Siebeck, 2006) 169.

Second, streams—perhaps of paradise—flow from this mountain, as seen in Pss 87:7and 46:4: "There is a river whose streams make glad the city of God, the holy habitation of the Most High."[3]

Third, this is the location of Yahweh's primordial victory over the sea of chaos. This motif appears in Ps 46:3–4, "the sea, though its waters roar and foam"; 65:6–7, where defeating the sea is linked to creation; and 67:3.[4] Psalm 46 plays on this dual image of water: rivers of paradise and sea of chaos.[5] The victory over chaos may also lie in Psalm 68. In v. 22, Bashan is parallel with Yamm. Bashan can be equated with the Ugaritic *bṯn* (cf. Akk. *bašmu*, Aram. *ptn*, Arab. *bathan*; KB³ 1.165), which is identified as Leviathan in *KTU* 1.5 i 1–2.[6] The "Beast of the Reeds" in v. 31, then, could be not Egypt but is the Chaos Dragon.[7]

These elements derive from Canaanite mythology. The mythical Mt. Zaphon, the highest mountain of the utmost North, is 1700 meters-high Cassius Mons (Gk. Kasion), modern Jebel el-Aqra (Keldağ in Turkish), a bit north of Ugarit—sacred even in pre-Canaanite Hittite documents.[8] The word *zaphon* never means simply "north" in Ugaritic.[9]

In Canaanite mythology, Zaphon is the home of Baʿal (*KTU* 1.3 i 21–22). Thus, in the *Baʿal Epic*, we hear repeatedly of "Baʿal on the peaks of Zaphon" (1.3 i 22; 1.5 i 11).

---

3. For discussion and support of this reading, see Christl M. Maier, "Psalm 87 as a Reappraisal of the Zion Tradition and Its Reception in Galatians 4:26," *CBQ* 69 (2007) 475 n.12.

4. John Day, *God's Conflict with the Dragon and the Sea: Echoes of a Canaanite Myth in the Old Testament* (Cambridge: Cambridge University Press, 1985) 35.

5. Jacques Vermeylen, *Jérusalem centre du monde: Développements et contestations d'une tradition biblique* (Lectio Divina 217; Paris: Cerf, 2007) 66.

6. James H. Charlesworth, "Bashan, Symbolism, Haplography, and Theology in Psalm 68," in *David and Zion: Biblical Studies in Honor of J. J. M Roberts* (ed. Bernard Batto and Kathryn L. Roberts; Winona Lake, IN: Eisenbrauns, 2004) 355–56, 358.

7. Ibid., 362; John Herbert Eaton, *The Psalms* (New York: T. & T. Clark, 2003) 249. On the other hand, *bṯn* already enters Hebrew as *peten* (Day, *God's Conflict*, 115). There are other mythical overtones associated with Bashan, particularly with its king, Og (Numbers 1, 3, 21, etc.). Deut 3:11 makes Og the "last of the Rephaim." Some Ugaritic Rephaim (*Rpu*) lived in Ashteroth and Edrei, just as Josh 13:31 says Og did (*Aqhat* 1 108; Scott B. Noegel, "The Aegean Ogygos of Boeotia and the Biblical Og of Bashan," *ZAW* 110 [1998] 416). Deut 3:8–9 associates Og with Mount Hermon, abode of Baʿal in 1 Chr 5:23 and of Leviathan according to two Aramaic Incantation Bowls cited by Noegel (p. 418).

8. John Healey, "From Ṣapānu/Ṣapunu to Kasion: The Sacred History of a Mountain," in *"He Unfurrowed His Brow and Laughed": Essays in Honour of Professor Nicolas Wyatt* (ed. Wilfred G. E. Watson; AOAT 299; Münster: Ugarit-Verlag, 2007) 141.

9. Richard J. Clifford, *Cosmic Mountain in Canaan and the Old Testament* (HSM 4; Cambridge: Harvard University Press, 1972) 57.

The rivers of paradise signify the residence of the high god El, "at the springs of the rivers" in both the *Baʿal Epic* (*KTU* 1.4 iv 21; 1.6 i 33) and in *Aqhat* (*KTU* 1.17 vi 47). El has his own mountain ("Mount LL" of *KTU* 1.2 ii 19–20), which is not the same as Baʿal's mountain, Zaphon.

Baʿal receives his temple on Zaphon after his defeat of the sea (*KTU* 1.3–4, esp. 1.3 iii 28–31).[10] Therefore, *Aqhat* says, "In the hands of Zaphon are victory and triumph" (*KTU* 1.19 ii 34–36).[11]

Another element, found only in Ps 48:8, is Yahweh as the destroyer of ships, a title of Baʿal Zaphon in Esarhaddon's treaty with the king of Tyre (*ANET* 534 = Borger, *Ash.* 112).[12]

Two additional elements are not as easy to tie to Canaanite mythology, however. God also defeats the nations of the earth here, in a great battle at dawn. This is reflected in Ps 46:6, 48:5–8, and 68:13–15. Psalm 46 places the "roaring" of the chaos waters (v 4) in parallelism with the "roaring" of the nations (v 7).[13] By means of his victories, God destroys war forever, as in Pss 46:9 and 76:2.[14] Psalm 76 highlights this peace-bringing by playing on the folk etymology of "Jerusalem" from *shalom*.[15]

A separate element is the so-called *Völkerwallfahrt*—the nations make pilgrimage to Zion to worship Yahweh, as in Ps 86:9, "All the nations you have made shall come and worship before you, O Lord, and shall glorify your name"; and 87:1–7. Psalm 48 may also belong, if the kings in v. 5 are "streaming" (*nāhărû*) to Jerusalem and not attacking it.[16] In Psalm 68, the *Völkerwallfahrt* comes at the end of the psalm. Verse 31 can either be translated "Ethiopia will hurry its hands," implying the bringing of tribute, or, following Akkadian parallels, "Ethiopia will stretch out its hands," implying an act of worship.[17] Since this immediately follows the coming of Israelites to the temple in vv. 25–28,

10. Nicolas Wyatt, *The Mythic Mind* (London: Equinox, 2005) 133.

11. Idem, "Le Centre du monde dans les littératures d'Ougarit et d'Israël," *JNSL* 21 (1996) 133.

12. Day, *God's Conflict*, 128.

13. Sidney Kelly, "Psalm 46: A Study in Imagery," *JBL* 89 (1970) 306.

14. Luis Alonso Schökel, *Treinta Salmos: Poesía y oración* (Valencia: Institución San Jerónimo, 1986) 360; Norbert Lohfink, "Psalm 46: Ein Beispiel alttestamentlicher Friedenslyrik," *Bibel und Kirche* 44 (1989) 152.

15. Beat Weber, "'In Salem wurde sein Versteck . . .': Psalm 76 im Lichte literarischer und historischer Kontexte neu gelesen," *BN* 97(1999) 89.

16. James Chukwuma Okoye, *Israel and the Nations* (American Society of Missiology Series 39; Maryknoll, NY: Orbis, 2006) 112.

17. Robert G. Bratcher and William David Reyburn, *A Handbook on Psalms* (New York: United Bible Societies, 1993) 591.

it should be seen as parallel.[18] Finally, the kingdoms of the earth are called to sing to and ascribe power and glory to God in vv. 32–35.[19]

Psalm 87 is a unique case. Since antiquity, many have emended and rearranged it in hopes of clarifying its meaning.[20] But Booij and Emerton have argued quite convincingly that the text should be left as it is.[21] Emerton has argued that the *šām* in v. 4 refers not to Jerusalem but to each of the places mentioned and that the sense of the verse is that "each one severally" (*ʾîš wĕʾîš*, translated following Isa 6:2 and Esth 1:8) was born in the places mentioned earlier in the verse.[22] The meaning, then, is that being born in Zion "is incomparably more distinguished than having been born anywhere else."[23]

However, Emerton's primary reason for rejecting a more universalistic interpretation of the verses is "the implausibility of supposing that people (whether Jews or Gentiles) would be said to have been born in Zion, when in fact they had been born elsewhere."[24] He maintains that even Isaiah 49 does not go that far and that "[t]he theory that Ps. lxxxvii makes such a statement is implausible, and it is difficult to suppose that such a legal fiction was intended, let alone that in v. 6 Yahweh falsifies his records."[25] Crenshaw[26] and a few other scholars share Emerton's view.[27] But in view of the Korahite psalms' propensity to summon the nations to pay homage (Psalms 46, 48) and the use of *ʿelyôn* in 87:5 with its universalistic overtones (cf. Ps 47:3; 97:9; Deut 32:8), Booij is probably correct that the text means that "it is shown in these nations who was born in Zion, namely the non-Israelite nation, or the non-Israelite of any nation."[28] As long as Elyôn establishes Zion, they are included in the circle of the covenant community.[29] *Šām* is clearly Zion, and the plain grammatical

18. Lucien Legrand, *Unity and Plurality: Mission in the Bible* (Maryknoll, NY: Orbis, 1990) 17.

19. W. Creighton Marlowe, "Music of Missions: Themes of Cross-Cultural Outreach in the Psalms," *Missiology* 26 (1998) 448.

20. Norbert Lohfink and Erich Zenger, *The God of Israel and the Nations* (Collegeville, MN: Liturgical Press, 2000) 124; Christl M. Maier, "'Zion wird man Mutter nennen': Die Ziontradition in Psalm 87 und ihre Rezeption in der Septuaginta," *ZAW* 118 (2006) 583.

21. T. Booij, "Some Observations on Psalm lxxxvii," *VT* 37 (1987) 18; John A. Emerton, "The Problem of Psalm lxxxvii," *VT* 50 (2000) 187. The psalm is, admittedly, incomplete because the opening *yswdtw*'s third-person masculine-singular pronoun has no antecedent (John William Wevers, "Psalm 97 and Its Sitz im Leben," *Teologinen Aikakauskirja* 82 [1977] 274)!

22. Emerton, "Problem," 194–96.

23. Ibid., 197.

24. Ibid., 188.

25. Ibid., 189.

26. James Crenshaw, *The Psalms* (Grand Rapids, MI: Eerdmans, 2001) 30.

27. Cited in Lohfink and Zenger, *God of Israel,* 129–31.

28. Booij, "Some Observations," 20.

29. Ibid., 21; Johanna W. H. Bos, "Psalm 87," *Int* 47 (2001) 282.

sense is that the various nations mentioned (and not Jews from those lands) are counted as belonging to the people of God.[30] The list of nations, moreover, moves from large "evil empires" (Rahab and Babel) to smaller neighboring enemies (Philistia and Tyre) and ends with the alien and distant Cush.[31] They mark the four compass points, with Zion in the center.[32] Smith has shown that the *šām* and *b-* particles' structure places "the nations' existence in the context of Zion's destiny."[33]

Furthermore, the Gentiles are not tangential to the issue of the *Chaoskampf*. In Psalm 87, for example, Zion's central importance in the world and to God is its destiny for the nations.[34] As Lucian Legrand wrote, in these songs, "the 'Zionism' of the Psalms of the Temple opens wide to the nations."[35]

A few scholars argue that the victory over the nations is unknown in the Canaanite literature and cannot be derived directly from the victory over chaos, and thus it must have been derived from Israelite historical experience.[36] Other scholars argue that the war with the nations is simply a historicization of the war with the waters,[37] a view that goes back to Gunkel and Mowinckel. Nevertheless, Ugaritic texts attest Baʿal's victory over "many enemies (*KTU* 1.4 vii 35) who would drive Baal from the heights of Zaphon."[38] Even if Yamm, Tannin, and Leviathan are the same, *KTU* 1.3 iii 43–47 also lists defeat of "Desire, the Beloved of El; Rebel, the Calf of El; Fire, the Dog of El; and Flame, the Daughter of El." Baʿal's victory, according to *KTU*1.3 iii 13–16, will "pour peace upon the earth."[39]

A number of explanations have been offered for the origin and placement of the *Völkerwallfahrt*. Each of these can be considered in turn, and each explanation fails in one or more of three ways: it takes for granted unexamined postulates, accepted blindly as dogmas without being able to put forward the

30. Bratcher and Reyburn, *Handbook*, 759; Maier, "Zion," 585–86; idem, "Psalm 87," 478.

31. Bos, "Psalm 87," 283.

32. Lohfink and Zenger, *God*,134.

33. Mark S. Smith, "The Structure of Psalm LXXXVII," *VT* 38 (1988) 358, italics mine.

34. Smith, "Structure," 358; Marlowe "Music," 449.

35. Legrand, *Unity*, 17.

36. Gunter Wanke, *Die Zionstheologie der Korachiten* (BZAW 97; Berlin: Alfred Töpelmann, 1966) 77; Annemarie Ohler, *Mythologische Elemente im Alten Testament* (Dusseldorf: Patmos, 1969) 165–66; J. J. M. Roberts, "The Davidic Origin of the Zion Tradition," *JBL* 92 (1973) 337.

37. Werner H. Schmidt, *Alttestamentlicher Glaube in Seiner Geschichte* (Neukirchener Studienbücher 6; 7th ed.; Neukirchen-Vluyn: Neukirchener Verlag, 1990) 257.

38. Clifford, *Cosmic Mountain*, 59.

39. Leopold Sabourin, *The Psalms* (Staten Island, NY: Alba, 1969), 232. Peace through the destruction of the weapons of war is a common image in the ancient Near East, as seen in *Sefire* IA.38–39.

rational basis of acceptance; or it does not perceive the implications of what it affirms to be true; or it does not appreciate the extent of the field of discussion.

Some recent scholars have seen the *Völkerwallfahrt* as simply a reversal of the victory over the nations.[40] Just as water has two qualities, the sea to be conquered and the rivers of paradise that flow from the mountain, so also the nations show a poetic inversion. As I have shown, however, both the sea and the streams are integral to the constellation that the Israelites received, while the pilgrimage of the nations is not.

John Day (personal communication) sees the *Völkerwallfahrt* as being derived from the gathering of the various gods to Baʿal's home on Zaphon for a feast following his victory. This *is* an integral part of the story, found also in the Hittite *Illuyanka* myth (§4). But it is difficult to see how the gods who are Baʿal's peers and allies can be transformed into nations that any Israelite would have seen as unmistakably "other."

More commonly, the *Völkerwallfahrt* is a labeled postexilic addition, reflecting the theology of Isaiah 2 and 18; Micah 4; and Zechariah 14.[41] Ezekiel 38 and Zech 14:10–11, 20–21 seem to be good sources for the victory over the nations. Psalm 86 seems to be modeled on David's thanksgiving uttered after the prophecy of Nathan.[42] Jürgen Vorndran argues that it also draws on the complete canonical book of Isaiah, with language taken from Isaiah 2, 7, 25, 51, and 66.[43] Corinna Körting argues that Psalm 87 is a postexilic twist on Psalm 49;[44] Christl Maier, that it presupposes Jeremiah 4 and Psalms 46 and 48;[45] and much of 48 she assigns to a postexilic redaction.[46]

But several problems obtain with this explanation. What is unexamined is the difference between the *Völkerwallfahrt* of Isaiah/Micah and that of the Psalms. These should not be conflated: in Micah and Zechariah, the *Völkerwallfahrt* has a tenor *against* the nations, and certainly this is true of Isa 61:5–6 and 62:8.[47] In Isaiah 2 and Micah 4, there are no gifts or sacrifice being

40. Joachim Schaper, "Psalm 47 und sein Sitz im Leben," *ZAW* 106 (1994) 267; Thilo Alexander von Rudnig, "'Ist den Jahwe nicht auf dem Zion?' (Jer 8,19): Gottes Gegenwart im Heiligtum," *ZTK* 104 (2007) 285; Matthew J. Lynch, "Zion's Warrior and the Nations: Isaiah 59:15b–63:6 in Isaiah's Zion Traditions," *CBQ* 70 (2008) 249.

41. Ben C. Ollenburger, *Zion the City of the Great* King (JSOTSup 41; Sheffield: JSOT Press, 1987) 15; Rudnig, "Ist den Jahwe!" 285.

42. Enzo Cortese, *Preghiera del Re: Formazione, redazione e teologia dei Salmi di Davide* (Rivista Biblica Supplementi 43; Bologna: Dehoniane, 2004) 167.

43. Jürgen Vorndran, *Alle Völker werden kommen: Studien zu Psalm 86* (BBB 133; Berlin: Philo, 2002) 145, 150, 157–59, 168, 178–79.

44. Körting, *Zion*, 177.

45. Maier, "Psalm 87," 476–77, 479.

46. Christl M. Maier, *Daughter Zion, Mother Zion: Gender, Space, and the Sacred in Ancient Israel* (Minneapolis: Fortress, 2008) 41.

47. Christopher T. Begg, "Foreigners in Third Isaiah," *The Bible Today* 23 (1985) 99–100.

brought by the nations (although there is in Isa 18:7 and chap. 60). There is no "Torah" in the *Völkerwallfahrt* of the Psalms, an essential element of Isaiah 2's *Völkerwallfahrt*, as it is in that of Psalms 99 and 138, where there is no *Chaoskampf*.[48] Watson considers Psalms 99 and 138 to be developments to the motif in these psalms.[49] The universal peace of Isa 11:1–9 seems far more political than what is presented in Pss 46:9–12; and 87,[50] and the equation of Zion with the community, found in Deutero-Isaiah, is absent in these psalms.[51] Furthermore, insisting that the *Völkerwallfahrt* is postexilic is to "deny any connection between this motif and the very similar motif which occurs in the royal Psalms."[52]

One implication of a postexilic origin for the *Völkerwallfahrt* is postexilic dating of these psalms. Psalm 68, however, has a great deal of archaic vocabulary (note vv. 7, 11, 17, 19, 23, 37).[53] The title, "Rider of the Clouds" in v. 7 and again in 33, is identical with *rkb ʿrpt*, a standard Ugaritic title of Baʿal (*KTU* 1.2 iv 8). Archaisms abound in Psalm 48, as well.[54] God as "Great King" in Psalm 48 could easily reflect Assyrian royal propaganda.[55] Lam 2:15 clearly offers a reinterpretation of something like Psalm 48. The use of the passive *yullad* in Ps 87:4–5, which must be a periphrasis of God's action (on the basis of Isa 9:5), may serve as evidence of an early date for this psalm,[56] and Watson highlights a number of other archaisms in this psalm.[57]

We must also extend the field of discussion. There are other psalms that are undoubtedly postexilic, and these have their own distinct view of the Gentiles that is not what obtains in Psalms 48, 68, 86, and 87. Psalm 102 presents a theophanic revelation of God to the whole earth.[58] In vv. 17–23, Israel and

48. Norbert Lohfink, "The People of God of the Old Covenant Never Revoked by God," *Service international de documentation Judéo-Chrétienne periodical* 24 (1991) 4; Michael Tilly, *Jerusalem—Nabel der Welt: Überlieferung und Funktionen von Heiligtumstraditionen in antiken Judentum* (Stuttgart: Kohlhammer, 2002) 161, 165.

49. Rebecca S. Watson, *Chaos Uncreated* (BZAW 341; Berlin: de Gruyter, 2005) 125; although she believes Isaiah 2 is "First Isaiah" (p. 126). Maier identifies it with Third Isaiah (*Daughter Zion*, 199–200).

50. Otto Eissfeldt, "Psalm 46," in *Kleine Schriften* (ed. Rudolf Sellheim and Fritz Maass; 6 vols.; Tübingen: Mohr, 1968) 4:11.

51. A. Robinson, "Zion and Ṣāphôn in Psalm XLVIII 3," *VT* 24 (1974) 123.

52. Roberts, "Davidic Origin," 338.

53. Cortese, *Preghiera*, 102.

54. Mitchell Dahood, "The Language and Date of Psalm 48 (47)," *CBQ* 16 (1954) 15, 19.

55. Michael L. Barré, "Seven Epithets of Zion in Ps 48, 2–3," *Bib* 69 (1988) 559.

56. Fr. Luke, "The Songs of Zion as a Literary Category of the Psalter," *Indian Journal of Theology* 14 (1965) 89 n. 69.

57. Watson, *Chaos*, 175–76.

58. Raymond Jacques Tournay, *Voir et Entendre Dieu avec les Psaumes ou la liturgie prophétique du second Temple a Jérusalem* (CahRB 24; Paris: Gabalda, 1988) 88.

the Gentiles together, as a new people of God, will recognize and praise him in a spirit of mutual confidence.[59] All of this is eschatological, because v. 27 implies an entirely new creation.[60] The image is clearly of a Jerusalem in ruins, presumably in the exilic period, sharing the renewal vision of Deutero-Isaiah and approaching that of Trito-Isaiah.[61]

I propose to consider this problem anew. Zion is a multivalent symbol. It denotes Yahweh's kingship;[62] note Ps 48:3: "Within her citadels God has made himself known as a fortress." Yahweh's kingship is the guarantee of order versus the chaos vanquished. Zion is Yahweh's royal residence, and therefore, Zion is a symbol of this security against chaos,[63] as seen in Ps 87:5b: "for the Most High himself will establish her." By analogy, as Zion is the site of Yahweh's victory over chaos, it is also the site of his victory over the nations (Ps 48:8–9). Yahweh's presence equals security, and the safety of Zion is proof of this (Psalm 48). Both Yahweh and Zion are a refuge, and Zion is thus a symbol of refuge (Ps 48:12–15).

But why Zion? The actual hill called Zion in the Psalms is Mt. Moriah on which the temple stood. This hill rises only 743 m, lower than the surrounding Mount of Olives, Mt. Scopus, and the hill now called "Mt. Zion," to the southwest. The actual Mt. Zaphon is a huge mountain.[64] Perhaps Zion is sanctified as such a mountain by its temple (Ps 48:2).[65] This is the case in Mesopotamia, where the temple is the *axis mundi* both vertically and horizontally, as Zion is in Psalm 48.[66]

But Zion is also a political capital. These psalms present "systemically distorted communication."[67] This distortion is accomplished to legitimate domination and power.[68] Representations are a means whereby rulers establish what is "common sense" and convince the public that life is in *order*, which

59. Gunild Brunert, *Psalm* 102 im Kontext des Vierten Psalmenbuches (Stuttgarter Biblische Beiträge 30; Stuttgart: Katholisches Bibelwerk, 1996) 296–97, 306.

60. Ibid., 297.

61. Ibid., 234

62. Ollenburger, *Zion*, 19 and passim.

63. Lohfink, "Psalm 46," 151; Ollenburger, *Zion*, 66–67, 147; Rudnig, "Ist den Jahwe?" 267.

64. Although the fact that Zion is a hill is also ideologically important; Körting, *Zion*, 221.

65. Rudnig, "Ist den Jahwe?" 269.

66. Piotr Michalowski, "Space and Place in Sumerian 'Epic,'" Paper read at 202nd annual meeting of the American Oriental Society (Cambridge, MA, 1992); Körting, *Zion*, 217.

67. Ian Hodder, *Reading the Past: Current Approaches to Interpretation in Archaeology* (Cambridge: Cambridge University Press, 1986) 165.

68. Louis Althusser, *Essays on Ideology* (London: Verso, 1984) 17, 20.

is so key to these psalms (Psalm 48).[69] I have argued elsewhere that the so-called Zion Hymns can be read as propaganda, designed to make one see the Jerusalem government as society's assurance of security, refuge, and order.[70]

Turning to the Gentiles in these psalms—Psalm 72 should also be considered, where the Gentiles' bringing of tribute to the king in vv. 11–12 is an "incarnation" of the *Völkerwallfahrt*: "May the kings of Tarshish and of the isles render him tribute, may the kings of Sheba and Seba bring gifts. May all kings fall down before him, all nations give him service." Now, Eckart Otto and Martin Arneth have shown that this psalm is based on Assurbanipal's Enthronement Hymn.[71] Recall my earlier suggestion, following Michael Barré, that "Great King" in Psalm 48 derives from Neo-Assyrian usage. There are ready impulses for sentiments such as the *Völkerwallfahrt* earlier than Second and Third Isaiah in the context of Assyrian imperialism.[72] Scholars have regularly seen in the description of Yahweh's global rule echoes of Assyrian royal ideology.[73] Christl Maier sees this as the context for Psalm 87.[74]

There is abundant evidence to show that Judah's intelligentsia during the Neo-Assyrian period was regularly employing Assyrian royal propaganda—in Psalm 2, Isaiah, the Deuteronomistic History, and Deuteronomy.[75] And in

69. Ibid., 45; Marlies Heinz and Marian H. Feldman, "Introduction: Representation—Tradition—Religion," in *Representations of Political Power: Case Histories from Times of Change and Dissolving Order in the Ancient Near East* (ed. Marlies Heinz and Marian H. Feldman; Winona Lake, IN: Eisenbrauns, 2007) 1; Rudnig, "Ist den Jahwe?" 271.

70. Robert D. Miller, "The Zion Hymns as Instruments of Power," *Ancient Near Eastern Studies* 47 (2010) 217–39.

71. Eckart Otto, "Political Theology in Judah and Assyria: The Beginning of the Hebrew Bible as Literature," *SEÅ* 65 (T. N. D. Mettinger FS; 2000) 66–71; Martin Arneth, "Psalm 72 in seinen altorientalischen Kontexten," in *"Mein Sohn bist du" (Ps 2:7): Studien zu den Königspsalmen* (ed. Eckart Otto and Erich Zenger; Stuttgarter Bibelstudien 192; Stuttgart: Katholische Bibelwerk, 2002) 155–64.

72. Okoye, *Israel,* 12–13. Roy Rosenburg argued that Second Isaiah itself drew this from Assyrian influence: "Yahweh Becomes King," *JBL* 85 (1966) 297–99.

73. James A. Wharton, "Psalm 47," *Int* 47 (1993) 163.

74. Maier, "Zion," 589.

75. *Psalm 2*: Eckart Otto, "Politische Theologie in den Königspsalmen zwischen Ägypten und Assyrien," in *"Mein Sohn bist du" (Ps 2:7): Studien zu den Königspsalmen* (ed. Eckart Otto and Erich Zenger; Stuttgarter Bibelstudien 192; Stuttgart: Katholisches Bibelwerk, 2002) 33–65; idem, "Psalm 2 in neuassyrischer Zeit: Assyrische Motive in der judäischen Königsideologie," in *Textarbeit: Studien zu Texten und ihrer Rezeption aus dem Alten Testament und der Umwelt Israels. Festschrift für Peter Weimar* (ed. Klaus Kiesow and Thomas Meurer; AOAT 294; Münster: Ugarit-Verlag, 2003) 335–49.

Isaiah: Peter B. Machinist, "Assyria and Its Image in First Isaiah," *Journal of the American Oriental Society* 103 (1983) 719–37; Pinhas Artzi, "All the Nations and Many Peoples," in *Treasures on Camels' Humps: Historical and Literary Studies from the Ancient Near East Presented to Israel Ephʿal* (ed. Mordechai Cogan and Dan'el Kahn; Jerusalem: Magnes, 2008) 41–53.

many cases, while God is the Great King who replaces the Assyrian emperor, some places show that a clear echo of Assyrian propaganda about the Assyrian Great King, representative of Aššur, was to be found in statements about Israel's own king in Jerusalem and his relationship to Yahweh (e.g., Psalm 2; 2 Kgs 19:21–28).[76]

I am not arguing that the *Völkerwallfahrt* was directly borrowed from Assyrian propaganda, although this is possible. On Prism A, Esarhaddon mentions that he summoned the kings of Ḫatti-land and those beyond the river, including Manasseh, to Nineveh in 676 (Leichty, RINAP 4, Esarhaddon 1 v 54–vi 1).[77] Vassal ambassadors were required to deliver tribute to Assyria annually.[78] Still less am I arguing that the intention is anti-Assyrian resistance literature. There was no "imposition of Assyrian ideology" against which to revolt.[79]

But the image of the pilgrimage of the nations is not so obscure as to require copying or parroting. The motif was added to the Canaanite *Chaoskampf* in the face of Assyrian rhetoric; like the king of Ugarit, the Jerusalem king epitomizes the divine victor.

Deuteronomistic History: Nadav Na'aman, "Solomon's District List (1 Kings 4:7–19) and the Assyrian Province System in Palestine," *UF* 33 (2001) 419–36.

Deuteronomy: Hans Ulrich Steymans, *Deuteronomium 28 und die Adê zur Thronfolgeregelung Asarhaddons: Segen und Fluch im alten Orient und in Israel* (OBO 145; Freiburg: Universitätsverlag / Göttingen: Vandenhoeck & Ruprecht, 1995); Otto, "Political Theology," 59–76; Jan Christian Gertz, *Die Gerichtsorganisation Israels im deuteronomischen Gesetz* (FRLANT 165; Göttingen: Vandenhoeck & Ruprecht, 1994); Ernest Nicholson, "Do Not Dare to Set a Foreigner over You," *ZAW* 118 (2006) 46–49; Nili Wazana, "Are Trees of the Field Human?" in *Treasures on Camels' Humps: Historical and Literary Studies from the Ancient Near East Presented to Israel Ephʿal* (ed. Mordechai Cogan and Dan'el Kahn; Jerusalem: Magnes, 2008) 274–95.

76. Mark W. Hamilton, *Body Royal: The Social Poetics of Kingship in Ancient Israel* (Biblical Interpretation 78; Leiden: Brill, 2005) 256, 260.

77. Eduard Nielsen, "Political Conditions and Cultural Development in Israel and Judah during the Reign of Manasseh," in *Law, History, and Tradition* (Copenhagen: Gads, 1983) 130.

78. Shigeo Yamada, *The Construction of the Assyrian Empire* (CHANE 3; Leiden: Brill, 2000), 307, with evidence especially from Shalmaneser.

79. See, inter alia, Mordechai Cogan, "Judah under Assyrian Hegemony: A Reexamination of Imperialism and Religion," *JBL* 112 (1993) 404, 409, 412; Carla M. Sinopoli, "Archaeology of Empires," *Annual Review of Anthropology* 23 (1994) 168–70; J. Nicholas Postgate, "The Land of Assur and the Yoke of Assur," *World Archaeology* 23 (1992) 252, 255; Walter Mayer, *Politik und Kriegskunst der Assyrer* (Abhandlungen zur literatur Altsyrien-Palästinas und Mesopotamiens 9; Münster: Ugarit-Verlag, 1995) 481.

Part 5

KAMPF AND CHAOS

The Combat Myth in Israelite Tradition Revisited

BERNARD F. BATTO

DePauw University, Emeritus

Introduction

The theory of the Combat Myth is almost as old as Assyriology. A quarter of a century after George Smith published his revolutionary (for biblical studies) work *The Chaldean Account of Genesis*[1] (an account of the flood story from the *Gilgameš Epic*), Hermann Gunkel in 1895 published his own groundbreaking *Schöpfung und Chaos*.[2] With the aid of Assyriologist Heinrich Zimmern, Gunkel became aware of the newly discovered Babylonian text *Enūma eliš*. Using insights from the new discipline of history of religions with its form-critical approach, Gunkel recognized commonalities between this new Babylonian myth and various biblical texts. This led him to postulate his thesis of *Chaoskampf*, that a common ancient Near Eastern form undergirds both *Enūma eliš* and various biblical passages, including the Priestly creation account in Genesis 1.

1. George Smith, *The Chaldean Account of Genesis* (London: Sampson, Low, Marston, Searle, & Rivington, 1875), revising and expanding earlier work dating back to 1872.

2. Hermann Gunkel, *Schöpfung und Chaos in Urzeit und Endzeit: Eine religionsgeschichtlich Untersuchung über Gen. 1 und Ap. Jon 12* (Göttingen: Vandenhoeck & Ruprecht, 1895); ET: Herman Gunkel, with contributions by Heinrich Zimmern, *Creation and Chaos in the Primeval Era and the Eschaton: A Religio-Historical Study of Genesis* 1 and Revelation 12 (trans. K. William Whitney Jr.; Grand Rapids, MI: Eerdmans, 2006).

Although Gunkel's thesis has not been without its critics, it did persuade many, especially biblical scholars. The subsequent discovery of additional texts from Mesopotamia and other areas—notably Egypt and Ugarit—have led to numerous refinements and modifications of Gunkel's original thesis. One of the chief criticisms was that the term *Chaoskampf* interjects Greek concepts of *chaos* and *cosmos* that are not appropriate for ancient Near Eastern cultures.[3] Accordingly, the term *Combat Myth* has now become the preferred term to refer to the phenomenon that Gunkel identified. More than just a simple substitution of one name for another, the term Combat Myth carries with it a set of characteristics that are somewhat different from those of the *Chaoskampf*, as I will address below.

The transition from *Chaoskampf* to Combat Myth has not been consistent, however. One finds both terms used in the literature, sometimes interchangeably and without discrimination. For my part, I will use the term Combat Myth, except when I wish to refer explicitly to Gunkel's own thesis (or to the ideas of scholars who rely explicitly on Gunkel's thesis).

The history of scholarship regarding the Combat Myth has been controversial, to say the least.[4] On the one side, supporters have at times claimed too much, purporting to find evidence of this form in far too many biblical texts. I confess that I may be guilty of this in some of my earlier publications. On the other side, critics have been too reluctant to admit allusions to the Combat Myth in various biblical passages. In particular there has been much controversy concerning whether or not Genesis 1 is dependent on *Enūma eliš* and, even more specifically, whether Combat Myth motifs are even present in Genesis 1. Reversing an opinion common among critical biblical scholars of the last century, recent biblical scholars increasingly find that Genesis 1 is not literarily dependent on its Babylonian counterpart. I think it may be granted that the so-called Priestly creation account is not *literarily* dependent on *Enūma eliš*, but I am not ready to concede that the Priestly creation account is devoid of Combat Myth motifs or even that the Babylonian creation story formed no part of the mental background of the Priestly Writer. I will return to this point.

---

3. John H. Walton, *Ancient Near Eastern Thought and the Old Testament: Introducing the Conceptual World of the Hebrew Bible* (Grand Rapids, MI: Baker Academic, 2006) 184–88.

4. For an annotated bibliography, see my "Myth in the Hebrew Bible," in *Oxford Bibliographies in Biblical Studies* (ed. Christopher Matthews; New York: Oxford University Press, 2013), particularly the section on "the Combat Myth in the Hebrew Bible."

An Evaluation of Rebecca S. Watson's Thesis

The most recent as well as the most substantial attempt to discredit the whole *Chaoskampf* idea in the Hebrew Bible is by Rebecca S. Watson in her 2005 monograph, *Chaos Uncreated: A Reassessment of the Theme of "Chaos" in the Hebrew Bible*. For that reason alone, it behooves me to address her thesis and the evidence on which it is based. Watson's overall judgment is negative:

> the so-called "chaos imagery" is expressed in such variable terminology, in so many different types of context and genre, and is juxtaposed with such a vast array of motifs drawn from so many areas of life, that the validity of clustering together such material under a single unifying theme must be called into question.[5]

More specifically, Watson argues that Israel proper was unacquainted with a "chaos" motif. In her analysis, this motif is not found in biblical literature from the preexilic period; it appears first in very late texts, she claims, where it was probably introduced under the influence of the Babylonian Exile.

I, for my part, find both Watson's methodology and her assessment of individual passages to be so prejudicial in numerous instances that I in turn must call her conclusions into question. But first, it must be acknowledged that Watson is correct that advocates have been much too quick to posit chaos motifs in passages where the evidence may be ambiguous (e.g., Psalm 29) or where an alternate explanation seems more suited (e.g., the Red Sea event or the crossing of the Jordan: Psalms 77,[6] 114, 136; Isa 51:9–16;[7] or a theophany with its typical concomitant terrestrial tumult: Psalm 68; Nah 1:2–8).

Nevertheless, Watson herself is doggedly singular in her reading of individual passages; methodologically, she looks for a single referent within each passage. She does not allow that a passage may contain multiple levels of reference—for example, that *yām*, "sea," may refer *not only* to the exodus event

5. Rebecca S. Watson, *Chaos Uncreated: A Reassessment of the Theme of "Chaos" in the Hebrew Bible* (BZAW 341; Berlin: de Gruyter, 2005) 1. David T. Tsumura (*Creation and Destruction: A Reappraisal of the* Chaoskampf *Theory in the Old Testament* [Winona Lake, IN: Eisenbrauns, 2005]) similarly rejects Gunkel's hypothesis that the *Chaoskampf* motif of *Enūma eliš* lies behind the biblical idea of creation in Genesis on the grounds that in the Babylonian myth all things, including the gods, emanate from two preexistent primordial waters, divine Apsu and Tiʾāmat, whereas in Genesis the waters and earth are created by Yahweh. Tsumura maintains that Combat Myth motifs are absent in the rest of the Hebrew Bible as well; biblical poetic texts that supposedly have been influenced by the Combat Myth in fact use the language of storms and floods metaphorically and have nothing to do with primordial combat.

6. Watson, *Chaos Uncreated*, 78.

7. For Watson's conclusion on Isa 51:9–11 as referring to the Red Sea only, see ibid., 298.

but also to the cosmic sea, or that "Rahab" can reference simultaneously *both* Egypt *and* a primeval cosmic enemy of Yahweh. She claims to entertain both possibilities in her discussion but invariably opts for a historical or naturalistic explanation, usually without serious consideration of the alternative. There is neither time nor space here for a thorough review of each biblical passage examined by Watson, but a few examples may suffice.

Psalm 18

Watson's examination of the "chaos" theme in Psalm 18 provides a good example of her methodology. She pays particular attention to this psalm because, in her opinion, "Ps. 18 arguably exhibits the earliest and fullest example" of a common motif, "that of the waters of the underworld, and the related idea of the waters as the embodiment of the psalmist's enemies."[8] She considers Psalm 18, though not archaic, to have been composed fairly early in the preexilic period but also showing signs of having been adapted over time. Watson finds in this psalm a "comfortable synthesis" of the various elements of a divine epiphany:

> Yahweh is in heaven/his temple (v. 7), from whence he thunders and sends forth lightnings (vv. 14–15), but he also bows the heavens and comes down (v. 10), riding on a cherub (v. 11). The statement that he reached from on high to deliver his servant (v. 17) is slightly ambiguous, insofar as the petitioner is being drawn out of "many waters," the depths beneath. . . . [T]he terminology also indicates Yahweh's transcendence, his distance from the shadowy realms below. . . . The storm phenomena, thunder, wind and rain, now incorporate hailstones and coals of fire (vv. 13–14), thus functioning more directly as ammunition (v. 15).[9]

Nothing in all of this, Watson insists, has anything to do with chaos imagery. Rather it is a standard description of a divine appearing and the concomitant tumult in nature at the deity's appearance, albeit in elevated, poetic language. Moreover, this being a royal thanksgiving psalm, the deity has come to deliver the supplicant king from certain death at the hands of some historical enemy, here described metaphorically as being drawn out of the watery depths of Sheol.

Of particular significance is Watson's assessment of the "waters" imagery of Psalm 18. In contrast to scholars who see an association with "chaos" and "non-existence" or "uncreation" in Sheol here, with its "torrents [*or* rivers] of

8. Ibid., 74. In this category Watson groups also Psalms 32, 42–43, 69, 88, 124, and 144.

9. Ibid., 79.

perdition" (נחלי בליעל, v. 5) and its "mighty waters" (מים רבים, v. 17), Watson sees only a metaphorical reference to the king's close encounter with death. She warns against seeing here any "*Chaoskampf* allusions." "In particular, the fact that the waters represent death (Mot) and not the cosmic sea (Yam) distinguishes the content of this psalm from Canaanite epic, both in substance and in essence."[10]

It is incredible to me that Watson finds no reference here to "the cosmic sea (Yam)." Indeed, she boldly states that the vocable *yam*, "sea," does not occur in this psalm. This is most surprising in light of v. 16, which in the NRSV is translated:

> Then the channels of the sea were seen,
>   and the foundations of the world were laid bare
> at your rebuke, O Lord,
>   at the blast of your nostrils.

In Watson's defense, she reads v. 16 in accordance with the MT, which in the first colon of the verse has אפיקי מים (*ʾăpīqê mayîm*), "the channels of (the) water(s)." The parallel text in 2 Samuel 22, however, has אפקי ים (*ʾăpīqê yām*), "the channels of (the) sea." In a footnote, Watson acknowledges the reading of 2 Sam 22:16 but quickly dismisses it in preference to the reading of Psalm 18 "as the *lexio difficilior* and because it is intrinsically more probable that the initial *mem* of מים should drop out than that the same letter should be inserted from nowhere before ים."[11] In my opinion, however, it is more likely that 2 Samuel 22 retains the original reading. Given both the cosmic allusions in the surrounding verses and the evidence of an analogous phrase in the Ugaritic *Baʿal Myth*,[12] it is appropriate for this psalm to refer to the channels of "the sea" explicitly.

Moreover, it seems impossible not to see this as a reference to "the cosmic Sea (Yam)." The mention in this same verse of Yahweh's "rebuke" (גערה), at which the "foundations of the world were laid bare," bolsters the argument that, in the parallel colon, the correct reading is that "the channels *of (the) sea*" were revealed (and not "the channels of waters"). It is true that

10. Ibid., 80.

11. Ibid., 80 n. 26. Watson also dismisses the proposal of Frank Moore Cross and David Noel Freedman (*Studies in Ancient Yahwistic Poetry* [Biblical Resource Series; Grand Rapids, MI: Eerdmans, 1997] 100 n. 41) that an enclitic *mem* was transferred to ים from the preceding word—which in my opinion seems quite possible. The simplest explanation, however, is that, since the phrase *ʾăpīqê yām* does not appear elsewhere in the Hebrew Bible, a copyist of Psalm 18 either inadvertently or advertently changed the text to *ʾăpīqê mayîm* as in Joel 1:20 (cf. 4:18) and Song 5:12.

12. Ugaritic *ʾpq . thmtm . tgly*, "the channels of the deep(s) were revealed," *KTU* 1.6 i 34; and restored in *KTU* 1.3 v 6–7.

מים, "waters," is the object of God's *rebuke* in Ps 104:7; but there, "waters" is parallel to "the deep." Moreover, the context of celestial commotion as well as terrestrial commotion at the arrival of Yahweh makes a cosmic interpretation of "waters" likely in that psalm as well. Watson's claims that, in the Hebrew Scriptures, when some watery entity that is the object of Yahweh's rebuke is identifiable, it is either the Red Sea (e.g., Ps 106:9) or other terrestrial waters, such as desert streams (e.g., Nah 1:4). She ignores the possibility that the biblical writer may have a cosmic or mythical allusion in mind as well. This is almost certainly the case for Isa 50:2–3:

Is my hand withered,[13] that it cannot redeem?
  Or have I no power to deliver?
By my rebuke I dry up the sea,
  I make the rivers a desert;
their fish stink for lack of water,
  and die of thirst.
I clothe the heavens with blackness,
  and make sackcloth their covering. (Isa 50:2–3)

Returning to Psalm 18, because Watson has ruled out any reference to "sea" in this composition, it is easier for her to ignore other potential allusions to Combat Myth motifs. For her, one of the principal criteria for the presence of "chaos" in a composition is that there must be mention of creation in the immediate context. Since there are no explicit references to creation in Psalm 18, she takes this as confirmation that Psalm 18 contains no allusions to "chaos." She ignores all too easily, however, the presence of motifs ancillary to the Combat Myth: Yahweh's appearance as divine warrior to do battle, ostensibly against the supplicant's enemies, which include Death (Mot) and Sheol (vv. 5–6), in addition to "sea"—all part of the "mighty waters" (מים רבים, v. 17) from which God drew out the supplicant. Other mythic images in the preceding vv. 7–15 seem to confirm that the divine warrior's battle is not just with historical enemies: from his heavenly temple, he hears the supplicant's cry for help; his arousal causes great terrestrial tumult as he bows the heavens and descends in his cherub chariot; the weapons he brandishes are those familiar to us from various ancient Near Eastern myths: storm clouds, arrows of lightning, thunder, and wind. Moreover, creation per se is not an essential component in a Combat Myth, as the Ugaritic *Baʿal Myth* shows. (But

13. For קצר with the meaning "to be powerless," hence "withered," see Michael Barré, "The Crux of Psalm 22:17c: Solved at Long Last?" in *David and Zion: Biblical Studies in Honor of J. J. M. Roberts* (ed. Bernard F. Batto and Kathryn L. Roberts; Winona Lake, IN: Eisenbrauns, 2004) 287–306, esp. pp. 290–91 n. 18.

more on this later.) In my judgment, there is no way to avoid the attribution of motifs in Psalm 18 to the Combat Myth.

Isaiah 27:1

Turning to Isa 27:1, "On that day the LORD with his cruel and great sword will punish Leviathan the fleeing serpent, Leviathan the twisting serpent, and he will kill the dragon that is in the sea"—Watson readily concedes that this passage derives from a draconic mythic tradition about killing the sea serpent Leviathan and is related to the similar passage found in *KTU* 1.5 i 1–3. Nevertheless, she argues that the Isaianic passage is not to be associated with *Chaoskampf* because (1) context suggests that the passage probably contains an echo of the Exodus tradition (comparing the preceding verse [26:21] with Exod 12:23) and is directed against Egypt, a historical enemy, not primordial chaos; (2) there is no reason to associate Leviathan with the primeval chaos myth in which the deity vanquishes Tiʾāmat/the Sea; and (3) Isaiah 27 is in any case probably postexilic in date and thereby disqualified as a barometer of authentic Israelite thought.[14]

Watson's contention that Leviathan is to be equated with Egypt here is difficult to sustain, however, since (1) it is not clear that structurally Isa 26:21 and 27:1 belong to the same oracle, and (2) Egypt is not mentioned until 27:12—which patently belongs to a separate oracle—wherein Egypt is paired with Assyria as common enemies.

Moreover, when discussing Job 26:12–13, Watson equates the Sea, Rahab, and the fleeing serpent—together with Leviathan—as different appellations of the same figure. By contrast, here she wishes to dissociate Leviathan and the other figures from the sea/Sea. She cannot have it both ways.

Job 7:12

> Am I Sea/the Sea or Dragon/a dragon, that you place a guard on me?
> הים־אני אם־תנין כי־תשים עלי משמר

Job 7:12 is not an allusion to the chaos myth, Watson argues, because the evidence is not incontrovertible.[15] Each of the four points of her argument fail to convince, however, as shown by my italicized counterarguments:

1. Because Watson has not found convincing (to her) evidence for the chaos myth elsewhere in the Hebrew Bible, a priori, one may not assume it here. *This constitutes a clear case of circular reasoning and deserves to be dismissed.*

---

14. Watson, *Chaos Uncreated*, 327–32.
15. Ibid., 281–88.

2. Watson says that the terms ים and תנין rarely appear in proximity in the Hebrew Bible, and where they do, there appears to be no intrinsic connection between them. *The fact that the two terms do appear close together elsewhere in the Hebrew Bible—Ps 74:13* being a prime example, where the two terms are intrinsically connected—shows that Watson's point here carries little weight in making a decision about Job 7:12.
3. The vocable משמר commonly refers to a watch or guard, not a prison. Moreover, there seems to be no allusion to a Babylonian or Canaanite chaos myth, since there is no taking captive, imprisonment, or binding as with the forces of Tiʾāmat in *Enūma eliš* (IV 111–120), nor any taking captive as with Yam (*KTU* 1.2 iv 29–30), and no killing afterwards. The "guarding of the sea is not an idea which is attested elsewhere in the Old Testament," Watson insists. *To the contrary, the idea of Sea's being restrained or placed under guard is given expression not only elsewhere in Job* (38:8–11), but also in Prov 8:29. (Jer 5:22 and Ps 104:6–9 may also be mentioned as allusions to a raging cosmic sea, though these last two passages could also be interpreted as referring to the seashore's serving as barrier to a [naturally occurring] stormy sea.)
4. Finally, because the construction ה . . . אם normally expresses disjunctive interrogation in the Hebrew Bible, ים and תנין may not be understood as "virtually synonymous manifestations of cosmic 'chaos'," as is commonly done by the proponents of a chaos myth. *In point of fact, the construction . . . ה אם does link synonymous concepts in Jer 31:20*, as Watson herself acknowledges.[16] *Moreover, even though Hab 3:8 may be "staircase parallelism,"*[17] *this does not disqualify this verse as an additional example of the construction* ה . . . אם *used to link synonymous concepts. Thus, against Watson, these examples demonstrate that* ים *and* תנין *could be linked, synonymous concepts in Job 7:12.*

Job 26:12–13

By his power he stilled the Sea;
  by his understanding he struck down Rahab.
By his wind the heavens were made fair;
  his hand pierced the fleeing serpent. (NRSV)

Watson says that this passage is the *locus classicus* for those who posit a *Chaoskampf* in the Hebrew Bible. Accordingly, she expends great effort to disprove the presence of chaos motifs in this passage.[18]

Admittedly, this passage is difficult, most notably because of problems involved in determining the correct reading of v. 13a. As it stands in the MT, v. 13a (ברוחו שמים שפרה) yields little sense, and various attempts to emend the text have met with resistance from other scholars. The NRSV translation "By his wind the heavens were made fair" is an attempt to retain the MT

16. Ibid., 285 n. 70.
17. Ibid.
18. Ibid., 301–12.

text; however, שפרה (*šiprâ*), "beauty," "brightness," is an abstract noun—not a masculine-plural adjective or a verbal, as would be required for the NRSV translation. A literal translation of the MT would be "By his wind/breath the heavens are brightness" or the like. An attempt has been made to relate the MT's *šiprâ*, "brightness," to the "boundary between light and darkness" mentioned in v. 10, on the assumption that there is here a reference to God's illuminating "the heavens" when he overcame precreation darkness. That solution hardly fits within the context of the other three cola in vv. 12–13, however. Tur Sinai noted that *šiprâ* bears similarities to Akkadian *saparu*, "net," one of the instruments that Marduk used, along with "wind," to subdue Tiʾāmat in *Enūma eliš;* by dividing consonantal שמים (*šmym*) into two words, *śm ym*, he posited that the original text read "By his wind he put Sea (in) a net."[19] This certainly fits the context of vv. 12–13 better. Pope accepted this proposal but translates "By his wind he put Sea (in) a bag."[20] The comparison with Akkadian *saparu* is very attractive both because of the cognate literature and because it yields two nicely balanced bi-cola (the stilling of Sea // striking down Rahab; capturing Sea // piercing the fleeing serpent). The problem is that no Hebrew cognate of Akkadian *saparu* is attested. The LXX ("The bars of heaven feared him"), although it confirms the consonantal reading שמים, is of little help for determining the Hebrew original.

Watson's contention that Job 26:12–13 is devoid of Combat Myth motifs is completely unacceptable, however. Three of the four cola explicitly reference the principal act of the Combat Myth, the subjugation and slaying of the "chaos monster" under three of its common designations: (the) Sea, Rahab, and the "fleeing serpent." ("Fleeing serpent" is, one recalls from Isa 27:1, another designation for Leviathan.) Moreover, the fourth colon plausibly also references the same motif.

Watson would discount the presence of authentic myth, however, by positing that the Joban author is merely using poetic license via heightened language to describe God's creative acts in the beginning. The logical contortions that Watson must employ to accomplish this thesis is illustrated by her attempt to place Rahab in waters above the firmament, despite Rahab's patent association elsewhere with the underworld or the depths of the sea, the Great Deep (תהום רבה). She argues that "the heavens both provide the focus of the

19. N. H. Tur-Sinai, *The Book of Job: A New Commentary* (rev. ed.; Jerusalem: Kiryath Sepher, 1967) 382–84.

20. M. H. Pope, *Job: A New Translation with Introduction and Commentary* (3rd ed.; AB 15; New York: Doubleday, 1973) 185–86; similarly N. Wyatt, *Myths of Power: A Study of Royal Myth and Ideology in Ugaritic and Biblical Tradition* (UBL 13; Münster: Ugarit-Verlag, 1996) 95.

preceding verses (vv. 8–11) and seem to register an effect of the slaying of the dragon (v. 13a)."[21] By a series of admittedly conjectural proposals, she places Rahab within the celestial ocean, where this "fleeing serpent," comparable to Apophis in Egyptian myth and to Mot in the Ugaritic *Baʿal Myth*, darkens the sky by obliterating the divinely created light. Apparently, this action is to be associated with the process of creation itself. The deity then "struck down Rahab," "pierced the fleeing serpent," thereby making the heavens bright once more.

An alternative interpretation, Watson suggests, is to see in all this a poetic depiction of a naturally occurring storm—that is, the deity is depicted as "stilling a storm in the heavens and blowing away the remnants of cloud."[22] Either explanation, Watson insists, is preferable to invoking a *Chaoskampf* reading.

It is unclear how the first alternative avoids invoking the Combat Myth, however. The striking down of the fleeing serpent Rahab and associated mythemes are the basic elements of the Combat Myth, as least in my understanding. The second alternative is more consistent with Watson's overall thesis but fails to convince, as even Watson seems to concede.

Essential Features of Chaos according to Watson

My dissatisfaction with Watson stems in part from her definition of "chaos" myth. She seems to be doing battle still with Herman Gunkel and his thesis as enunciated in *Schöpfung und Chaos*. To judge from Watson's own conclusions, any finding for "chaos" in the Bible must include at minimum the following six features:

1. *A struggle between opponents of relative parity.*[23] In this regard, she constantly references the Babylonian narrative *Enūma eliš*, confirming that her perspective is focused principally on Gunkel and his thesis. Since such a Combat Myth narrative is nowhere to be found in the Hebrew Bible, Watson easily concludes that "chaos" is not a feature of Israelite literature.
2. *The deity's archenemy is "the Sea," the watery entity that is known in Mesopotamia as Tiʾāmat and in Ugarit as Yamm.* Watson finds no certain evidence in the Hebrew Bible that "(the) sea" or "(the) deep" is ever depicted as a genuinely personal power or deity. Everywhere there is only a metaphorical personification of the sea and the deep; that is, references to these are but figures of speech and not authentic myth.[24]

21. Watson, *Chaos Uncreated*, 303.
22. Ibid., 312; cf. p. 372.
23. Ibid., 369.
24. Ibid., 369–70.

3. *An indication that Yahweh slew "the sea," whether by hacking it to pieces, piercing, entrapping, or the like*. Even mention of Yahweh's sword, which is said to slay Leviathan in Isa 27:1, is lacking with reference to the sea.[25]
4. *"The sea" cannot be a true opponent to God if God created the sea and the deep(s)*. That God created the sea is stated in Ps 95:5, 146:6, 148:4–6; cf. Prov 3:20 [where it may be implied]; and is probably implied also in Gen 1:1–2.[26] The sea(s) is (are) everywhere presented as a natural phenomenon controlled by God, not as "a counter-cosmic power."[27]
5. *"Chaos" is defined as "the chaotic mass of power(s) preceding creation" and as such is "preexistent"; accordingly, the idea of chaos applies to the "event" of creation in the beginning only*.[28] No extensions of combat or chaos into historical time or to historical agents are recognized. A passage cannot reference *both* original creation *and* the exodus sea event, or the chaos monster *and* Egypt (or Babylon or Assyria). To state this differently, "chaos" applies to "an originating act of creation," not to *creatio continua* (God's control of the natural world).[29] And, finally,
6. *A narrative or story of God's conflict with Sea/Chaos*. "Chaos" is not applicable to the Old Testament, Watson claims, because it contains no "clear expression of the idea that Yahweh engaged in combat with the sea or a sea monster in primordial times," nor is there a narrative about "the control or confinement of the sea" or "the overcoming of a dragon."[30]

Essential Characteristics of a Combat Myth

It may be readily conceded that the Hebrew Bible contains no actual narrative of Yahweh engaged in combat with a chaos monster. Nevertheless, biblical writers were familiar with one or more versions of the ancient Near Eastern Combat Myth, and they used motifs and mythemes from the Combat Myth to further their own theological agenda of Yahwism. Indeed, given their location within the greater cultural setting of the ancient Near East, it would have been well nigh impossible for them to be impervious to its influence, in much the same way that they were not impervious to the polytheism of the ancient Near East. In order to make my own thesis clear, I need to provide a definition

25. Ibid., 370.
26. Ibid., 370–71.
27. Ibid., 382. Even if Watson's argument can be sustained that everywhere in the Hebrew Bible the sea was created by God, this argument does not apply to other chaos figures; Leviathan is everywhere assumed to be primordial, except in Ps 104:26, as emphasized by Jon D. Levenson, *Creation and the Persistence of Evil: The Jewish Drama of Divine Omnipotence* (San Francisco: Harper & Row, 1988) 49, 53–54.
28. Watson, *Chaos Uncreated*, 379.
29. Ibid., 382. Though no narrative per se, Job's words "Let those curse it who curse the Sea, those who are skilled to rouse up Leviathan" (Job 3:8) bemoaning the day of his birth surely indicate a contemporary belief that these primordial monsters continue into the present.
30. Ibid., 397.

of the Combat Myth as I understand it, together with its constituent components or characteristics.

1. The primary function, or purpose, of the Combat Myth was to account for the existence of the universe—the heavens and the earth (and the underworld)—as a "place" where gods, humans, animals, and plants might thrive in safe, well-ordered existence. In the idiom of the ancient Near East, this is what was meant by "creation." Sometimes the divinities had to emerge or evolve from some earlier form (condition), sometimes not; but invariably they had to arrive at a final, definitive state, and a proper place for them to reside had to be prepared. Humans and their realm by definition had to be formed through the agency of their divine creator(s). Not all creation stories were Combat Myths. Neither did all Combat Myths narrate a story of original creation, but they did narrate a story about how the continuing existence of that creation is secured.[31]
2. The opposite of creation in the Combat Myth is non-creation. Countering the divine will to bring about a well-ordered universe was a force (or forces) of anti-creation. This negative force was personalized as some kind of being that would prevent and extinguish good order, if possible. The identity of this being, often referred to as the "chaos monster," varied from culture to culture, and from one period to another; indeed, this monster might exist in more than one form at the same time. This monster may also be depicted in various forms: aquatic, bird-like, serpentine, draconic, seven-headed, or fully anthropomorphic; moreover, the monster may even exhibit multiformism, appearing in more than one shape within the same composition.[32] Among its most common designations were Nun and Apophis in Egypt; Anzu and Tiʾāmat in Mesopotamia; Yamm, Mot, and Litan in Canaan and Ugarit; and in Israel, certainly Leviathan, Rahab, and very likely also Behemoth and Yam ("Sea").[33]
3. The protagonist in the Combat Myth is the divine sovereign, whose benevolence is manifest in that he guarantees the continued existence of the divinely conceived right order. The divine sovereign is usually—though not always—credited also as being the divine creator. At Ugarit, for example, Baʿal appears to have succeeded his father, El, in his capacity as the divine sovereign, even though El and Athirat continued to be acknowledged as the

31. Wayne T. Pitard in this volume argues that the Ugaritic *Baʿal Myth* belongs to the genre of "succession story" rather than, as commonly posited, a variant of the common Semitic Combat Myth. Even so, this Ugaritic text patently employs motifs derived from the Combat Myth.

32. On the multiformism of the chaos monster, see Wayne T. Pitard, "Just How Many Monsters Did Anat Fight (*KTU* 1.3 III 38–47)?" in *Ugarit at Seventy-Five* (ed. K. Lawson Younger, Jr.; Winona Lake, IN: Eisenbrauns, 2007) 75–88, esp. pp. 82–83. For examples of iconographic multiforms on cylinder seals, see F. A. M. Wiggermann, "Transtigridian Snake Gods," in *Sumerian Gods and Their Representations* (ed. Irving L. Finkel and Markham J. Geller; Cuneiform Monographs 7; Groningen: Styx, 1997) 33–55, esp. pp. 37–39.

33. The Hittite Illuyanka myth, sometimes included here, seems best left aside as belonging to a different genre.

divine creators.[34] In *Enūma eliš*, Marduk was elevated by the gods to the role of divine sovereign and also was credited as the primary creator, though the creation of humankind was carried out by Enki/Ea, a traditional role of this deity retained from the *Atrahasis* myth and elsewhere.

4. The enmity between the divine sovereign and the chaos monster is invariably depicted as a conflict, normally some form of primordial battle. In literary texts, however, such battle(s) may only be alluded to as a past event. In the *Baʿal Cycle*, an alarmed Anat queried the messengers sent to her, "Surely I fought Yamm, the Beloved of El, / Surely I finished off River, the Great God, / Surely I bound Tunnan and destroyed (?) him. / I fought the Twisty Serpent, / the Potentate with Seven Heads" (*KTU* 1.3 iii 38–42); and Mot mocked a weakened Baʿal with the taunt, "When you killed Litan, the Fleeing Serpent, / Annihilated the Twisty Serpent, / The Potentate with Seven Heads" (*KTU* 1.5 i 1–3).[35] In the Hebrew Bible, Yahweh is said to have battled some of these same opponents in Isa 27:1 and Ps 74:13–14.
5. Although the chaos monster may have been vanquished in primordial time, the divine sovereign must remain perpetually vigilant. At any time, the force(s) of anti-creation may rise up again to threaten the good order established by the divine sovereign. For this reason, it was common to depict this recrudescent monster as having seven heads.[36] Three or four heads may already have been disposed of, but the monster always seems able to raise up another of its ugly, threatening heads. In *Enūma eliš*, tucked away among the 50 glorious names of Marduk is this prayer that implies that Marduk's battle against Tiʾāmat is neverending:

   May he vanquish Tiʾāmat, constrict and shorten her life.
   Until the last days of humankind, when even days have grown old,
   May she depart, not be detained, and ever stay away
   (*Ee* VII 132–34)

   The additional heads of the monster may arise in the form of historical enemies. For example, in Israel, both Egypt and Babylon were cast in the role of Rahab or Leviathan. The scope of the Combat Myth, therefore, is not restricted to original creation in primordial time, as Watson supposes, but was thought to extend into historical time as well.[37]
6. It is unclear whether an eventual, complete defeat (or killing) of the forces(s) of anti-creation is implicit in the original ancient Near Eastern Combat Myth,

34. For the *Baʿal Cycle* as a succession narrative, see n. 31. Others assume that Baʿal was only proclaimed ruler of the divine council, with El retaining his authority as king of the gods, so Wayne T. Pitard, "How Many Monsters?," 75–76; Nicolas Wyatt, "The Religious Role of the King in Ugarit," in *Ugarit at Seventy-Five* (ed. K. Lawson Younger, Jr.; Winona Lake, IN: Eisenbrauns, 2007), 41–74, esp. p. 46.

35. Trans. Mark S. Smith, "The Baal Cycle," in *Ugaritic Narrative Poetry* (ed. Simon B. Parker; SBLWAW 9; Scholars Press, 1997) 111, 141.

36. James B. Pritchard, *ANEP* no. 671; Dominique Collon, *First Impressions: Cylinder Seals in the Ancient Near East* (Chicago: University of Chicago Press, 1987) 179.

37. Levenson addresses well the duality of evil in the Hebrew Bible as both primordial and historical (*Creation and the Persistence of Evil*, 14–25).

but certainly this motif did develop in postexilic versions of the Combat Myth, as is evident from texts such as *1 Enoch* (especially chaps. 10, 21, and 53–56) and in Revelation 12–22, especially chap. 20.

7. It would be more accurate to speak of ancient Near Eastern Combat *Myths*, since each culture or region developed its own version of cosmogonic conflict, adapted to its particular theological assumptions about its god(s) and their involvement with the world. Nevertheless, there were shared motifs, derived from common larger culture, and thus, it is not inappropriate to refer to this phenomenon as if it were a phenomenon.
8. The narrative of a particular version may have originated in oral tradition, though of course, only written versions have been preserved. Moreover, a particular version may not have survived as a complete narrative but only in myth fragments or in literary allusions. Egyptian myths seem not to have been written down but were passed from generation to generation of priests, who wrote down only mythic fragments as necessary for their esoteric needs. Also at Mari, no narrative of the Combat Myth has survived, though an allusion to the storm god's combat with the Sea survived.[38]
9. In the Hebrew Bible, we are dealing with written materials, obviously. But patently, for many biblical passages there is an underlying oral or written tradition that is no longer available to us. For most biblical passages, the closest analogies are from Canaan-Ugarit. For the primeval stories in Genesis, however, the closest analogies are from Mesopotamia.
10. With regard to literary versions of the Combat Myth, specifically, it is apparent that at times we must reckon with conscious adaptations of older traditions designed to further the theological and political agenda of a given society, as in the case of *Enūma eliš*'s having been composed originally to undergird Babylonian hegemony but later rewritten in support of Assyrian hegemony. The Ugaritic *Baʿal Cycle* may have been composed by the writer Ilimilku himself, using *Chaoskampf* motifs to undergird Ugaritian royal ideology in order to lend legitimacy to the current dynastic fiction.[39] Myths of necessity change and adapt as the societies that formulate them change. Again, *Enūma eliš* provides an obvious example of the way that a new version of the Combat Myth was composed by borrowing elements from traditional stories, particularly from the Akkadian myth of *Anzu*, to promote Marduk to the position of divine sovereign and also, implicitly, to acknowledge Babylon's accession to political dominance. We may posit an analogous situation for Israel; any use of Combat Myth motifs was done consciously to promote Israel's own national deity, Yahweh.

38. See J.-M. Durand, "Le mythologeme du combat entre le dieu de l'orage et la mer en Mésopotamie," *MARI* 7 (1993) 41–61.

39. See Wyatt, "Religious Role of the King in Ugarit," 48–51.

Examples of Biblical Passages with Patent Combat Myth Motifs

In my estimation, there are a number of biblical passages in which combat motifs are present. Moreover, at least four of them meet Watson's criterion that not only must a passage contain a conflict but also this conflict must be within the context of creation: Ps 74:13–17, 89:9–13; Job 9:5–10, 26:7–13.[40]

Psalm 74 is perhaps the most explicit in terms of actual combat terminology:[41]

You divided the sea by your might;
  you broke the heads of the dragons in the waters.
You crushed the heads of Leviathan;
  you gave him as food for the creatures of the wilderness.
  (74:13–14)

The reference to the "heads (plural) of Leviathan" make it clear that God's conflict here is with the primordial, seven-headed "twisty serpent" known at Ugarit as Litan (Lotan; *KTU* 1.5 i 1–3; cf. 1.3 iii 40–42), who also makes its appearance in Isa 27:1. God's drying up "ever-flowing springs" in Ps 74:15 is probably another reference to the deity's conflict with primordial aquatic foes. This is followed in the next verses by patent creation statements:

To you belongs the day, to you also the night;
  you established the luminaries and the sun.
You fixed all the boundaries of the earth;
  you fashioned summer and winter. (Ps 74:16–17)

Ps 89:10–14, in particular, manifests a similar confluence of creation motifs and God's primordial conflict with aquatic foe(s)—Rahab and sea are paralleled here:

You rule the ragings of the sea,
  When its waves surge, you quiet them.
You crushed Rahab, he was like a corpse;
  With your mighty arm you scattered your enemies.

---

40. J. Richard Middleton (*The Liberating Image: The IMAGO DEI in Genesis 1* [Grand Rapids, MI: Brazos, 2005] 244–50) likewise finds that Combat Myth themes are bound together with creation themes in Job 26:7–14 and in Ps 74:12–17, 89:5–14.

41. It should be noted that Watson disqualifies this psalm from invalidating her thesis because it is clearly late—exilic or later; note that the Jerusalem temple lies in ruins (vv. 3–10). I fail to see what difference it makes whether a composition is (post)exilic or not. But even granting this point, Watson acknowledges that Psalm 89, which also has Combat Myth motifs, dates to no later than 587 B.C.E., too early for exilic influences to have shaped this psalm substantially. Patently, knowledge of the Combat Myth in Israel predated the exile.

To you belongs the heavens, to you also the earth;
The world and its fullness—you established them.
The north and the south—you created them;
Tabor and Hermon—they celebrate your name.
Yours is a mighty arm;
powerful is your hand,
exalted is your right hand.

This psalm is strongly reminiscent of Isa 51:9–10, where also Yahweh's mighty arm is celebrated for having cut Rahab into pieces, pierced the dragon, and dried up the sea. But I leave it out of consideration here because there are no clear creation motifs in this passage (though creation motifs are ubiquitous in Second Isaiah). Isa 51:9–10 is important also because, contrary to Watson's claim, it shows that a passage may simultaneously reference both original creation and a historical event, in this case the exodus and the [Red] Sea crossing.[42] The strong arm of the deity is also recalled in Ps 74:11–12.

Job 9:5–10 also combines creation and combat motifs. Note in particular the reference to God in v. 8: "who alone spread out the heavens, and trod on the back of the Sea."

Especially intriguing is Job 26:12–13, treated above, where once again combat motif(s) occur(s) within a context of creation. Even with the textual variants of v. 13, which make an allusion to the sea here less certain than one would like, Job 26:12–13 seems to be out of the same cloth as the passages just considered and thus is best seen as yet another example of Combat motifs' being appropriated by a biblical writer.[43]

There are other biblical texts that could be included here, but I trust I have made my case that biblical writers were acquainted with the Combat Myth and appropriated motifs from it—mostly by allusion—to enhance their own theological and literary agendas.

Genesis 1 and the Combat Myth

Finally, I turn to the question of whether there are Combat Myth motifs present in the Priestly (P) account of creation in Gen 1:1–2:3. It is fair to concede that this P account is not itself a Combat Myth narrative; patently, there is no battle narrated here. Moreover, contrary to some opinions of a previous generation of scholars, it is also not immediately obvious that the P account is

42. Levenson, *Creation and the Persistence of Evil*, 7–9, 18–20.

43. Watson (*Chaos Uncreated*, 312) faults "the *Chaoskampf* interpretation" for not providing a unitary reading of this text; but her own solution, to read v. 12a as a naturalistic event by which God calms a stormy sea and parallel it to v. 13a, read appropriately as in the NRSV translation, fails to address the grammatical difficulties in v. 13a.

literarily derived from the Babylonian creation story *Enūma eliš*. Despite similarities noted by Heidel and others,[44] there are major differences both in form and in content. The real question is whether the P creation account contains Combat Myth *motifs*, and if so, can their source be identified as one specific version of the Combat Myth, namely, the Babylonian version, *Enūma eliš*.

It is well established that ancient Near Eastern writers were not mere scribes recording traditional tales; in many cases, they acted as true authors, creatively adapting existing materials for their own purposes and even composing new literary works. Like all authors, however, they were children of their time, and their ideas were shaped in large measure by their cultures. No author can completely divorce herself or himself from cultural winds swirling about, and certainly not ancient Near Eastern authors, who were even more tradition bound than are moderns. One should expect to encounter traditional motifs in biblical writings, even when they are placed in the service of new ideas.

The Priestly author of the opening chapters of Genesis was no exception. Elsewhere I have argued that this author was a highly original theologian who, living in the shadow of the Babylonian Exile, recomposed Israel's "traditional" story for the purpose of bolstering the sagging faith of fellow Judahites. To this end, he reused many existing materials, including the Yahwistic primeval story, and freely adapted them to fit in a new setting.[45] Is there evidence that P adopted motifs from the Combat Myth as well? I contend that he did; and more specifically, that the model of the Combat Myth that P had in mind was the Babylonian creation story—though I concede that the case for actual *literary* dependence is perhaps less patent than I argued in 1992 in *Slaying the Dragon*.[46] The Priestly author referenced this Babylonian myth more by allusions, however, than by outright borrowings:

1. The cosmology that P presupposes is congruent with that of *Enūma eliš*: primeval waters that have to be divided to allow for dry land and a suitable living space;[47] some sort of solid barrier to form this separation of primeval

44. Alexander Heidel pointed to similarities but cautioned that evidence for literary dependence was inconclusive (*The Babylonian Genesis* [2nd ed.; Chicago: University of Chicago Press, 1951] 82–140, with a diagram on p. 129). Ephraim Speiser argued for clear literary dependency (*Genesis* [AB 1; Garden City, NY: Doubleday, 1964] 9–13).

45. Batto, "The Priestly Revision of the Creation Myth," chap. 3 in *Slaying the Dragon: Mythmaking in the Biblical Tradition* (Louisville: Westminster John Knox, 1992) 73–101.

46. Middleton (*Liberating Image*, 240–63) was critical of my thesis stated in *Slaying the Dragon*. Nevertheless, Middleton's own conclusions are very similar to my current, more nuanced views, as articulated in my essay "The Divine Sovereign: The Image of God in the Priestly Creation Account," *In the Beginning: Essays on Creation Motifs in the Ancient Near East and the Bible* (Siphrut 9; Winona Lake, IN: Eisenbrauns, 2013) 96–138.

47. In Egypt, the primordial waters of Nun are kept apart by barriers formed by the god Geb stretched out as the earth and the goddess Nut arched above as the sky and supported

waters; an illumination of primordial darkness; specific stations for the heavenly luminaries. Of course, these features were common in cosmological conceptions of the ancient Near East—but not invariably present—so that, alone, they cannot be taken as definitive evidence of close association.

2. The creation of humankind is the apex of the divine sovereign's creative activity in both texts.
3. Both texts also culminate in the establishment of a "resting place" or sanctuary from which the divine sovereign rules and guarantees the continuance of the newly established divine order.[48] In other words, "temple building is represented as the climax or purpose of a creation story."[49] This is explicit in *Enūma eliš* (V 92–155; VI 45–81); it is implicit in P (Gen 2:1–3), as has been argued by many scholars.[50]
4. In addition to the internal evidence from the Priestly creation account itself, there is evidence from other biblical passages that, taken together, confirm the presence of Combat Myth motifs in Genesis 1.
5. Psalm 8, which clearly is dependent on Genesis 1 because of its specific listing of creation motifs, explicitly notes that Yahweh as the (divine) sovereign "founded a fortress (עֹז) because of your foes, to silence the enemy and the avenger" (Ps 8:2). Who are these unnamed foes against whom the divine sovereign is guarding? They could be the historical enemies of Israel. But given the context of creation motifs that permeate this psalm, it is not unreasonable to assume that these unnamed opponents are none other than the cosmic

from beneath by the air-god Shu; no text exists that recounts any battle involved in the separation of the chaotic waters of Nun, though there are pictorial representations of the god Horus presiding over and maintaining this division that provides a bubble or living space in which (human) existence is possible. In Mesopotamian cosmology, by contrast, a division of primordial chaotic waters is atypical, because it is related only in *Enūma eliš*; see Wilfred G. Lambert, "A New Look at the Babylonian Background of Genesis," *JTS* n.s. 16 (1965) 287–300, esp. p. 293. Thorkild Jacobsen has proposed that the Combat Myth may have been imported into Mesopotamia from the west via the Amorites ("The Battle between Marduk and Tiamat," *JAOS* 88 [1968] 104–8), a view once shared by Lambert, in the just-cited article. Lambert has since modified his view, allowing for a more distant ancestor common to both traditions; see his two postscripts to the 1965, reprinted article in "*I Studied Inscriptions from before the Flood*": *Ancient Near Eastern, Literary, and Linguistic Approaches to Genesis 1–11* (ed. Richard Hess and David Toshio Tsumura; Winona Lake, IN: Eisenbrauns, 1994) 96–113, esp. pp. 110–13.

48. For a full exploration of this motif, see my article "The Sleeping God: An Ancient Near Eastern Motif of Divine Sovereignty," *Bib* 68 (1987) 153–77 (repr. in my *In the Beginning*, 139–57); an updated bibliography is provided by Victor (Avigdor) Hurowitz, *I Have Built You an Exalted House* (JSOT/ASOR Monograph 5; JSOTSup 115; Sheffield: Sheffield Academic Press, 1992) 330–31.

49. Ibid., 94. See also Mark S. Smith, "Recent Study of Israelite Religion in Light of the Ugaritic Texts," in *Ugarit at Seventy-Five* (ed. K. Lawson Younger Jr.; Winona Lake, IN: Eisenbrauns, 2007) 1–25, esp. p. 6.

50. In addition to Hurowitz (*I Have Built You an Exalted House*), see Levenson, *Creation and the Persistence of Evil*, 66–127; Walton, *Ancient Near Eastern Thought and the Old Testament*, 197–99; idem, *The Lost World of Genesis One: Ancient Cosmology and the Origins Debate* (Downers Grove, IL: IVP Academic, 2009) 72–92.

force(s) of anti-creation—in short, the monsters well known from the Combat Myth.

6. Various biblical passages, we have seen, mention Rahab, Leviathan, and dragons—in additions to "sea"—as opponents of God. Some of these occur in contexts that contain creation motifs, making it virtually impossible not to conclude that these inimical figures were derived from the Combat Myth. Every biblical occurrence of "dragons" seems to refer to these mythical figures. Accordingly, it seems impossible also to avoid the conclusion that in Gen 1:21 the mention of "the great dragons" (התנינם הגדלים) as the very first of the aquatic creatures made by God was a deliberate and strategic move by the Priestly Writer to reduce these feared figures to mere creatures completely under divine control, much like Leviathan tamed by God and led about by hooks in its mouth (Job 41:1–2).[51] An analogous situation may have been posited at Babylon for Marduk who, following his defeat of Tiʾāmat and her allies, also captured the 11 fearsome demonic creatures specially created by Tiʾāmat; these creatures Marduk put on lead ropes before trampling them under foot (*Ee* IV 115–118; V 73–76). Among these creatures was the *mušḫuššu* snake dragon (*Ee* I 141; II 27). The occasional portrayal of Marduk standing on the snake-dragon *mušḫuššu* may in part be an allusion to this primordial battle.[52]
7. If one accepts the conclusion of critical scholars that Gen 9:1–17 is from the same writer as Genesis 1 and that it serves as a conclusion of the Priestly primeval story, then it is legitimate to mine this passage for evidence of Combat Myth motifs in the creation story. In Gen 9:1–17, the author has God make adjustments to his original creation by allowing the eating of meat under specified conditions, apparently in recognition of the "violence" to which both animals and humankind seem all too prone. More importantly for our investigation, the author has God showing remorse for having brought about the flood, promising never again to allow such a catastrophic event. Elsewhere I have argued that in P the flood is partially the result of chaotic waters of תהום escaping their divinely imposed confines by rupturing the barriers placed by God both from below and from above (see Gen 7:11). This interpretation cannot be confirmed from the passage itself. But when one reads in Gen 9:11–17 that God placed his bow in the heavens as a reminder to himself never again to bring about a flood, one finds more than a hint of the Combat Myth.[53] The bow (קשת) is literally a war bow, even though it appears

51. Note also that in Ps 104:26 Leviathan has been "downgraded" to a kind of divine plaything created by God for his own amusement.

52. The snake-dragon *mušḫuššu* was originally tamed by Ninazu and then inherited by Tishpak when the latter replaced Ninazu as the city god of Eshnunna. This dragon was transferred to Marduk following Hammurapi's conquest of Eshnunna. In other contexts, the snake-dragon is also associated with other supreme gods such as Enlil, Nabu, and Aššur. On the snake-dragon, see Jeremy Black and Anthony Green, *Gods, Demons and Symbols of Ancient Mesopotamia: An Illustrated Dictionary* (London: British Museum Press, 1992) 166.

53. On the (rain) bow as one of many cosmic signs employed by ancient Near Eastern writers to proclaim the end of combat, see my article "The Covenant of Peace: A Neglected Ancient Near Eastern Motif," *CBQ* 49 (1987) 187–211, esp. pp. 190–92.

in the sky as a rainbow. God is depicted as literarily "hanging up" his weapons of war. What war? The only war known from primeval time is the war that the divine sovereign waged against the forces of anti-creation—which brings us once again to the Babylonian version of the Combat Myth. In *Enūma eliš* (VI 82–92), Marduk, following his rout of Tiʾāmat and her allies and after his completion of creation, also placed his war bow in the sky. This appears to be shorthand for saying that the divine sovereign is firmly in control, and no power can ever threaten the divinely imposed order. Since the motif of "hanging up the war bow" is known only from these two texts, it is likely that the Priestly Writer was at least partially aware of the Babylonian version of the Combat Myth and that he used it as rhetorical foil to suggest that Yahweh was the true divine sovereign, and not Babylon's god Marduk.

8. Although critical scholars do not attribute the Babel story (Gen 11:1–9) to P, the Priestly Writer was certainly cognizant of the polemical character of this story and likely retained it as reinforcement of his anti-Babylonian campaign.
9. After the flood, in Gen 8:1 we read that God sent "a wind" (רוח) across the earth to dry up the waters. This appears to be the same as the רוח אלהים, "wind of God" in Gen 1:2 that was stirring over "the face of the waters" at the beginning of creation. Given the hints already noted that P probably intended a polemic against Babylon, it is not inconceivable that P may have intended an allusion to the winds that Marduk used to subdue his foe in *Enūma eliš*. If so, this would be confirmation that P also thought of "the waters" and "the deep" (תהום) as some type of anti-creation power and that the divine sovereign used his "wind" to subdue it.

None of these points taken individually proves that the Priestly Writer was conscious of the Combat Myth as he penned his creation account. But given the ubiquity of the Combat Myth as one paradigm for creation in the ancient Near East, the aggregate of these motifs in a single text does strongly suggest that the Priestly Writer used the Combat Myth as a backdrop or a foil against which he composed his own original version of creation, in order better to portray Israel's god Yahweh as the true divine sovereign.[54]

54. See further my article "The Divine Sovereign: The Image of God in the Priestly Creation Account" (see n. 46 above).

The Three "Daughters" of Baʿal and Transformations of Chaoskampf *in the Early Chapters of Genesis*

Richard E. Averbeck

Trinity Evangelical Divinity School

Some years ago, while I was reworking a certain passage in the Ugaritic Baʿal myth with students, it occurred to me that there may be an important and as-yet unrecognized correspondence between a certain set of passages in the myth, Genesis 1, and Psalm 104, one of the creation psalms. The extant Baʿal myth dates to the Late Bronze Age, although the mythic story was probably around long before that. Whatever the case may be with the dating, if I understand the data correctly about Baʿal's ***three*** daughters as reviewed briefly below, it seems that the same ***three***fold sequence of light followed by the sky and the waters above and then earth and vegetation below as seen in Genesis 1 and Psalm 104 is also found there. It seems that this is an instance where both the Bible and the Baʿal myth reflect the same underlying cosmological pattern, suggesting that it was common to the world in which both of them were written.

In general, the Baʿal myth falls into three major episodes. First, there is a battle for supremacy between Baʿal, the fertility god, and Yamm, the god of the sea. The first two tablets of the myth are devoted to this part of the story. Second, since Baʿal is victorious over Yamm, he earns a place of supremacy among the gods. So he petitions El, the head of the pantheon, to commission the building of a suitable palace from which to exercise his dominion.[1] Eventually, El grants the petition, and the celestial palace of Baʿal is built. Tablets three and four tell this second part of the story. Third, and finally, in tablets five and six, Baʿal and Mot, the god of death, do battle over the issue of who is more powerful. Baʿal loses this battle and ends up captive in the netherworld

1. It seems that El, the chief god of the pantheon, had previously granted supremacy over the other gods to Yamm and commissioned the building of a temple for him. Baʿal objected and rebelled, which led to the battle between Baʿal and Yamm. See Mark S. Smith, *The Ugaritic Baal Cycle* (2 vols.; VTSup 55; Leiden: Brill, 1994) 1:218–19 and 224–38.

but then comes to life again through the urgent intervention of certain other deities.

There are several different interpretations of the Baʿal myth and all sorts of difficulties in understanding many of the specific elements within it.[2] The fact is, however, that in spite of this diversity in scholarly opinion, there are points on which there is general agreement. In particular, most scholars would agree that the myth has some relationship to vegetative growth and fertility.[3] The text is, therefore, cosmologically related, although it is most certainly not a cosmogony. Perhaps we should think of it as an ecological myth. Moreover, this mythical cycle is somehow related to kingship among the gods and most likely corresponds in some way to royal concerns on the human level as well. It is of special significance that Baʿal's kingship in the myth is a rather precarious affair on several counts.[4] This brings us to the elements of the myth that are most important for the purposes of this essay.

The Daughters of Baʿal and the Window in the Palace

One of the most important, intriguing, and difficult features of the palace building account in the second section of the Ugaritic Baʿal myth is the concern over having a window in the palace (CAT 1.4 vi 1–15; vii 14–37) and the relationship that this has to Baʿal's three daughters. For the time being, I refer to them as Pidray, daughter of light, Ṭallay, daughter of showers, and ʾArṣay, daughter of the wide world (CAT 1.3 i 22–27; iii 6–8; iv 49–51). There was some sort of threat to the daughters that caused Baʿal great consternation when considering whether or not a window would be installed in his palace (CAT 1.4 vi 10–11). What this threat might have been is an ongoing subject of debate among scholars. This is not the place to deal with all the technical details,[5] so I will review only the most relevant points.

First, after defeating Yamm, in due course Baʿal calls for the craftsman-god, Kothar-wa-Ḫasis, who would naturally be responsible for designing and constructing Baʿal's palace. Baʿal issues his command to build the house and, in anticipation of the construction, Kothar-wa-Ḫasis proposes at the end of the fifth column of tablet 4 that he should install a window (CAT 1.4 v 49–65). Baʿal rejects his proposal twice. In spite of this, Kothar-wa-Ḫasis is convinced

2. See the review of the history of scholarly interpretation in ibid., 1:58–114.

3. Dennis Pardee, "The Baʿlu Myth," COS 1:242.

4. Smith, *The Ugaritic Baal Cycle*, 1:104–10.

5. For the technical details and full discussion, see my forthcoming publication "Pidray, Tallay, ʾArsay, and the Window in Baal's Palace" (paper delivered at the Society of Biblical Literature Ugaritic Studies and Northwest Semitic Epigraphy Section, November 20, 2010).

that Baʿal will eventually agree to allow him to install a window in the palace. He says as much, but Baʿal vehemently refuses to allow it for reasons that have something to do with two of his three daughters and Yamm, the enemy he had defeated to earn kingship among the gods in the first place. Unfortunately, the first negative response appears at a place on the tablet that is completely broken. The text is also partially broken at the point of Baʿal's second negative response to the window plan, but we can determine a good number of the cuneiform ***signs*** and, from these, the basic rendering of the passage is relatively clear and certain (CAT 1.4 vi 7–13):[6]

7. *wʿn . ʾalʾi [ ]bʿl*	And Almighty Baal answered:
8. *ʾal . tšt . ʾů[ ]t . bbhtm*	"Do not put a wi[ndo]w in the house,
9. *ḥln . bq[ ]k̊lm*	a window opening in the mi[dst of the pa]lace.
10. *ʾal . tx[ ]ẙ . bt ʾar*	Let not [Pidr]ay, daughter of light . . .
11. *[ ]xx[ ]ẙ . bt . rb*	. . . [Ṭall]ay, daughter of showers . . .
12. *[ ]dd . ʾil ym*	[The be]loved of El, Yamm . . .
13. *[ ]q̊lṣn . wpṯm*	. . . abase me and spit . . .[7]

It is of interest that only the first two of Baʿal's daughters appear here. The last of the three in their regular order of appearance, Arṣay, daughter of the wide world, is left out.

Between Baʿal's initial refusal and his later agreement to the installation of the window, there are three units: (1) the actual construction and furnishing of Baʿal's palace (CAT 1.4 vi 16–40); (2) the inaugural banquet (CAT 1.4 vi 40–vii 12); and (3) his tour of the realm, taking possession of his cities (CAT 1.4 vii 7–12). After this, returning to his palace, Baʿal calls for the installation

6. I have followed Smith, *The Ugaritic Baal Cycle*, vol. 1; and Mark S. Smith and Wayne T. Pitard, *The Ugaritic Baal Cycle*, vol. 2 (VTSup 114; Leiden: Brill, 2009) in the transliterations here. CAT sometimes reads or restores somewhat differently, so it seemed wise to provide a simple base transliteration from which to work. Smith and Pitard also provide a transliteration with restorations supplied, which I have generally followed in my translations.

Fortunately, Smith and Pitard, *The Ugaritic Baal Cycle*, vol. 2 comes with a CD of the cuneiform for tablets 3 and 4 attached to the back cover of the book. Although the text is quite broken, especially down the middle of the lines, there are clearly visible wedges for almost all the signs given in the transliteration. Where the signs are not clear at the edges of the break, the restoration is quite sure because of the combination of signs, words, and expressions with which the damaged signs are associated.

7. For line 13, compare CAT 1.4 iii 13–14a, *yqm . ydd , w yqlṣn yqm . wywpṯn*, "He (Yamm) rose up, stood, and abased me; He stood up and spat on me." See Smith and Pitard, *The Ugaritic Baal Cycle*, 2.462, 472 for the translation and interpretation of the lines as presented here.

of the window, just as Kothar-wa-Ḫasis thought he would eventually do (CAT 1.4 vii 13–20):

13. . . .[ ]*b* . *bʿl* . *bqrb̊*	Baal [ent]ered(?) into the midst of the
14. *bt* . *wyʿn* . *ʾalʾiyn*	house, and Almighty
15. *bʿl*[ ]*ʾaštm* . *kṯr bn*	Baal answered: "I will install, O Kothar, son
16. *ym* . *kṯr* . *bnm* . *ʿdt*	of the sea, O Kothar, son of the confluence,
17. *ypth̩* . *h̩ln* . *bbhtm*	let a window opening be opened in the house,
18. *ʾůrb̊t* . *bqrb* . *hkl*	a window in the midst of the palace.
19. *m̩* . *w*[ ]*th̩* . *bdqt* . *ʿrpt*	So let a break be [op]ened in the clouds,
20. *ʿlh̊*[ ]. *kṯr* . *wḫss*	according to the wo[rd of] Kothar-wa-Ḫasis."

Soon after, this the text reports (CAT 1.4 vii 25–29):

25. . . . *ypth̩* . *h̩*	He (Kothar-wa-Ḫasis) opened a window
26. *ln* . *bbhtm* . *ʾurbt*	opening in the house, a window
27. *bqrb* . *hkl̊*[ ]*ẙp̊th̩*	in the midst of the palace. Baal opened
28. *bʿl* . *bdqtʿr̊p̊t*	a rift in the clouds,
29. *qlh* . *qdš*[ ]*bʿ*[ ]*ytn*	gave his voice (thunder) in the clouds.

Although not all scholars agree,[8] it appears to me that Kothar-wa-Ḫasis is the agent performing the action in lines 25–27a, where the window is actually installed in the palace, since he is the builder of the house and the one speaking in the immediately previous lines. Baʿal, however, is introduced by name as the agent performing the action in lines 27b–29, which are about his opening a rift in the clouds. The juxtaposition of these two units distinguishes between the installation of the window and the opening of the rift in the clouds but does so in a way that clearly shows they are parallel acts. For Kothar-wa-Ḫasis (or Baʿal) to open the window in the celestial palace was for Baʿal to open a rift in the clouds.

Mark Smith and Wayne Pitard conclude:

> [T]he window is equated with a break in the clouds through which Baʿal issues his voice, the thunder, the sign of approaching rains. There can be little doubt then that the key function of the window involves Baʿal's primary characteristic as fertility deity . . . the opening of the window is the climax of the entire story of the construction of the palace.[9]

8. See the summary discussion in Smith and Pitard, *The Ugaritic Baal Cycle*, 2:672, where, in the end, Baʿal is taken to be performing both actions; in contrast to Pardee's opinion in COS 1:262 n. 184.

9. Smith and Pitard, *The Ugaritic Baal Cycle*, 2:608. See this point also in Wayne T. Pitard, "Temple Building in Northwest Semitic Literature of the Late Bronze and Iron Ages," in *From the Foundations to the Crenellation: Essays on Temple Building in the Ancient Near East and Hebrew Bible* (ed. Mark J. Boda and Jamie Novotny; AOAT 366; Münster:

The window, therefore, is crucial to Baʿal's central functions from his palace. Without the window, there would be none of the rains that were so essential to fertility. At this point, Dennis Pardee makes special note of the fact that "the Ugaritians were well aware of the metaphors with which they were dealing."[10]

The names of the three daughters of Baʿal are especially important to us in the present discussion. At the least, if the derivations proposed here are anywhere near correct, the first daughter has something to do with light, the second with water from the sky, and the third with either the ground water or the ground itself, or both. Although some of the elements are unclear, for each of the daughters there is at least one part of each of the combined names and epithets that is relatively transparent in meaning. The first daughter, Pidray, has the epithet "daughter of light": the term *ʾar* is cognate with Hebrew *ʾôr*, which is used, for example, in Gen 1:3, when God said, "Let there be light." At least, this is one of the major views regarding the meaning of *ʾar* in this epithet. Others are convinced that it should be a term for "dew," perhaps "honey-dew," the sweet liquid that exudes from the leaves of certain plants in hot weather.[11] However, further analysis has convinced me that this is not the case. The reason for proposing the latter derivation is the *supposition* that this name must correspond somehow to the name of the second daughter, *ṭly . bt . rb*, "Ṭallay, daughter of rain," where the meaning is clear. This supposition is misleading and should be reconsidered.

The name Pidray itself is a difficult matter. The Hebrew term *peder* appears three times in the Bible, referring to the fat of animals being sacrificed (Lev 1:8, 12; 8:20). Some, therefore, have suggested that the name would have the meaning "Fatty," or "Chubby," or something similar.[12] Of course, fat did not have the negative connotations then that it does today. Instead, it indicated abundance and prosperity and was thus a function of fertility.

The name of the middle daughter, Ṭallay, "daughter of showers," is relatively easy to analyze, and its significance is clear. The basic root itself means "dew" or "light rain." Compare Hebrew *ṭal* and cognates in Arabic and other

Ugarit-Verlag, 2010) 98 and see also pp. 101–3 for another text from Ugarit about putting a window in a temple.

10. COS 1:262 nn. 183–84.

11. Johannes C. de Moor (*The Seasonal Pattern in the Ugaritic Myth of Baʿlu* [AOAT 16; Kevelaer: Butzon & Bercker, 1971] 82–83) argues that, if it were related to Hebrew *ʾôr*, "light," it would be written *ʾur*, but there are other uses of *ʾar* in Ugaritic that unquestionably mean "light" in the context. Moreover, *ʾur* in Ugaritic has more of a connotation of "warmth, heat," or "fire"; see Gregorio del Olmo Lete and Joaquín Sanmartín, *A Dictionary of the Ugaritic Language in the Alphabetic Tradition* (trans. Wilfred G. E. Watson; HO 1/67; Leiden: Brill, 2003) 1:94–95.

12. Dennis Pardee, *Ritual and Cult at Ugarit* (SBLWAW 10; Atlanta: Society of Biblical Literature, 2002) 215, text 58, line 7; and p. 219 n. 4; see also the glossary entry on p. 282.

Semitic languages. Some translate the name "Dewy." In her epithet "daughter of showers," Ugaritic *rb(b)* is cognate with Hebrew *rĕbîbîm*, which appears only a few times in the Hebrew Bible, most often for the sort of rain showers that are good for crops. The linkage to Baʿal as a fertility god is straightforward.

The third daughter of Baʿal is Arṣay, "daughter of the wide world" (Ug. *ʾarṣy btyʿbdr*; at least, this is how it is sometimes translated). The linguistic analysis of the epithet is obscure, but her name is not. She is Arṣay, which most certainly has something to do with earth or the ground. Arṣay corresponds to Hebrew *ʾereṣ* and thus apparently means something like "Earthy." She appears sporadically with the other two in the Baʿal myth. As is well known, Hebrew *ʾereṣ* can also refer to the grave or netherworld, as can the same word in Ugaritic and other cognate languages, such as Akkadian *erṣetu.*[13] My own inclination is to look at Arṣay in terms of the larger picture of the earth as both the land surface and the underworld—including the ground as well as the underground and underground waters. This is the territory in dispute between Baʿal and Yamm. I cannot go into a full discussion of this here, but the text suggests that a battle victory by one of them over the other does not eliminate the defeated one because *ʾarṣ*, "earth," is the primary realm for neither of them. This is because Baʿal is celestial, and Yamm is the god of the sea. The situation in the Mot part of the cycle is different. Here, Baʿal intends to invade and take over Mot's primary realm, which is death and the underworld. His bravado over having defeating Yamm and having a palace shows that his dominion has gone too far.

Baʿal is sometimes referred to as *zbl . bʿl ʾarṣ*, "Prince, Lord/Baʿal of the Earth." It is of particular importance here that this title first appears in the Baʿal myth right after he defeats Yamm. Apparently, using this title corresponds to Baʿal's gaining dominion over the earth (*ʾarṣ*) through defeating Yamm. Baʿal is a celestial deity, but his dominion is terrestrial as well, because his rain is a source of water for the ground and, therefore, abundant produce. As noted above, the building of the palace and installing of the window in the fourth tablet clearly corresponds to Baʿal's opening a rift in the clouds in association with sending rain. The main point of building Baʿal's celestial palace is to enable Baʿal to function well as this provider of rain and the fertility that comes with rain.

Regarding the problem of the window in the palace, as noted above, it is clear that it corresponds to Baʿal's function as the celestial fertility god who sends forth the rains on the earth and, along with them, thunder and lightning to assert his overwhelming power and dominion. But how do the daughters

13. See Pardee, COS 1:251 n. 84; and Smith and Pitard, *The Ugaritic Baal Cycle*, 2:221.

fit into this? More specifically, what was Baʿal's reason for initially refusing to have a window installed in the palace, and what was the nature of the problem with the daughters as it related to the installation of a window?[14]

First, with regard to Yamm, the reason that Baʿal initially did not want a window in his palace was that his archenemy could still be a threat to Baʿal's dominion. Even though he had defeated Yamm, Baʿal was not yet assured and secure in his kingship among the gods and, as noted above, Yamm still had his own primary realm. Baʿal feared that Yamm would rise up again to attack him and reassert his rule among the gods, who would then turn back to Yamm in loyalty. After all, Yamm was indeed "the beloved of El." This fear was apparent in Baʿal's second refusal of Kothar-wa-Ḫasis's proposal of a window. It had something to do with his first two daughters and, this, in turn, was somehow related to Yamm. Although the text is broken, what remains of the part about Yamm suggests that, if there was a window in the palace, Yamm might once again gain some sort of advantage and "abase and spit" upon Baʿal: (12) [ ] *dd . ʾil ym* (13) [ ]*q̊lṣn . wpṯm*, "(The be)loved of El, Yamm, . . . abase me and spit . . ." (CAT 1.4 vi 12–13).

Yamm also appears later in a broken passage (CAT 1.4 vii 3–4), where we read *mdd ʾil y*[*m*], "the beloved of El, Yamm" (cf. line 12 of the earlier broken passage cited just above). This comes after the construction and furnishing of the palace and Baʿal's subsequent celebration banquet with the other gods (CAT 1.4 vi 16–vii 6). This is before Baʿal took possession of numerous towns and cities (CAT 1.4 vii 7–12), and only after that did he order Kothar-wa-Ḫasis to include a window in the palace after all (CAT 1.4 vii 13–25). It is fairly certain, therefore, that fear of Yamm's resurgence was behind Baʿal's initial refusal to have a window installed in his palace.

Second, with regard to his first two daughters, Pidray daughter of light and Ṭallay daughter of showers, it was Baʿal's concern for them that caused him initially to reject the proposal of installing a window in his palace, for they might somehow be harmed or taken over by Yamm upon his resurgence. Again, the text is broken, so in the story we do not know exactly what sort of harm Yamm would do to Baʿal's daughters or how he might gain control of them: (8) *ʾal . tšt . ʾů*[ ]*t . bbhtm* (9) *ḥln . bq*[ ]*k̊lm* (10) *ʾal . tx*[ ]*ẙ . bt ʾar* (11) [ ]*xx*[ ]*ẙ . bt . rb*, "Do not put a wi[ndo]w in the house, a window opening in the mi[dst of the pa]lace. Let not [Pidr]ay, daughter of light . . . [Ṭall]ay, daughter of showers . . ." (CAT 1.4 vi 8–11). The point seems to be that, if Yamm could somehow stop Baʿal and his daughters from performing effectively, he would again take control. What is relatively clear in analogical

14. See the full review and analysis of these questions in ibid., 2:602–10.

ecological terms, therefore, is that Baʿal has authority over these two daughters, who represent his celestial power to promote fertility on the earth from above. As noted previously, there is a direct correspondence between Kothar-wa-Ḫasis's inserting the window into the palace and Baʿal's actually opening an aperture in the clouds (see CAT 1.4 vii 25–29, cited and discussed above).

The third and final point brings us to the third daughter, Arṣay, daughter of the wide world. The three daughters of Baʿal, two of whom are threatened by the installation of the window in Baʿal's palace, correspond to the three essential ecological features of the landed earth. As with most scholars, I do not see the Baʿal myth as a cosmogony, but it does reflect on the cosmology of Ugarit as it relates to kingship in heaven among the gods and this, in turn, affects kingship on earth among humans.[15] The myth draws and speculates on the larger ecological framework of the world, which is based on three elements or spheres; namely, light, rain, and earth or ground, respectively. The first two are celestial by nature, while the third is terrestrial. The first two, therefore, correspond to Baʿal's natural celestial realm, where his palace is located, while the third does not. Thus Arṣay, "Earthy," was not under threat in the matter of the window in Baʿal's palace and, therefore, is not mentioned in the context of the threat.

As noted above, the window was essential for Baʿal to function appropriately as the bringer of rain; apparently, however, Baʿal had developed a fortress mentality from his confrontation with Yamm, so he wanted to allow him no possible access into his palace—no window. This would have been self-defeating of course, but this is often the case with fortress mentalities, which may be part of the reason that so much attention is paid to the window in the myth. This element of the myth has puzzled scholars so much that they sometimes resort to the notion that it is largely a literary elaboration intended to raise the tension and suspense in the story to a higher level.[16] The interpretation offered here, however, suggests that it was much more than that, having to do with Baʿal's essential functions, the retention of his dominion, and the risks involved.

In sum, with regard to the interpretation of the Baʿal myth overall, I am suggesting that the three daughters of Baʿal correspond to the overall framework of the natural world that is necessary for fertility and abundance of vegetation, animals, and people. In order for Baʿal to function effectively, all three features of the ecological framework with which the daughters are analogous must work together in concert. This is what the meanings of the three names

15. See the helpful discussion of the probable connection to human kingship at Ugarit in Pitard, "Temple Building in Northwest Semitic Literature," 96–101.

16. Smith and Pitard, *The Ugaritic Baal Cycle*, 609–10.

and their epithets are all about. Thus, all the consternation over having a window in Baʿal's palace relates to the maintenance and stability of the basic underlying ecological system, without which there would be catastrophe. It would threaten the entire ecological system of the cosmos.

The Three Daughters, Genesis 1, and Psalm 104

The descriptions of creation in Genesis 1 and Psalm 104 are built on this same fundamental structure. This is especially true of Genesis 1 with its first set of three days corresponding exactly to the names of Baʿal's three daughters, which correspond to the three fundamental structures or elements of the cosmos: light, sky/rain, and earth/dry ground. The second set of three days in Genesis 1 (days 4 through 6) elaborate on the first three days, taking the creation story beyond this basic underlying ecological framework.

The following chart displays and summarizes the overall sequential pattern common between Genesis 1 and Psalm 104:

DAYS 1–3

Gen 1:3–5 *Day 1*—Ps 104:1b–2a, light
Gen 1:6–8 *Day 2*—Ps 104:2b–4, sky with its clouds, winds, and lightning
Gen 1:9–13 *Day 3*—Ps 104:5–18, dry land and vegetation, expands to:

1. The recession of the waters so dry land appears, Ps 104:5–9 (cf. the first "God said" in Gen 1:9–10)
2. The flowing springs and streams that water the *animals*, Ps 104:10–13
3. The growth of vegetation as food and habitat for the *animals*, and as crops for *humans* to cultivate their own food, Ps 104:14–18 (cf. the second "God said" in Gen 1:11–13)

DAYS 4–6

Gen 1:14–19 *Day 4*—Ps 104:19–23, sun and moon, explained in terms of:

1. The night for *animals* to prowl, Ps 104:20–21
2. The day for *humans* to do their work, Ps 104:22–23

Gen 1:20–23 *Day 5*—Ps 104:24–26, sea and sea animals, including Leviathan
Gen 1:24–31 *Day 6*—Ps 104:27–30, land animals and humankind[17]

There is not enough space to explain all the details of either Genesis 1 or Psalm 104 here, much less both of them. In general, Psalm 104 follows the pattern of the six days in Genesis 1 but in a more extended and overlapping manner that highlights the relationships among various elements of the six-day pattern. Genesis 1 strictly separates the various elements of the natural

17. For additional analysis and discussion, see my "Psalms 103 and 104: Hymns of Redemption and Creation," in *Interpreting the Psalms for Teaching and Preaching* (ed. Herbert W. Bateman IV and D. Brent Sandy; St. Louis, MO: Chalice, 2010) 132–48 and 274–76, esp. pp. 141–46 and the additional bibliography cited there.

order by means of the six-day units as delimited by the regular evening and morning formula. Moreover, it does so as a cosmogony—that is, a description of God as the Creator of the cosmos.

Rhetorically, Psalm 104 sometimes does, in fact, present God as the Creator, such as in the description of the waters in vv. 5–9.

5. He established the earth (Heb. *ʾereṣ*) on its foundations; it shall never totter.
6. You made the deep cover it like a garment; the waters stood above the mountains.
7. They fled at your rebuke, rushed away at the sound of your thunder,
8. mountains rose, valleys sank down, to the place you established for them.
9. You set a boundary—they will not pass over (it)—they will not return to cover the earth (Heb. *ʾereṣ*).[18]

But at other times, and for most of the psalm, it describes and lauds God's ongoing care for creation by virtue of the way he designed it in the first place. There is reference to the way he created it, but the attention is given to the way it currently works—to these wonders. Moreover, Psalm 104 does not use the six-day pattern in any explicit way but orders its poetic description of the natural order in a sequence that corresponds largely to the six-day sequence in Genesis 1. Both Genesis 1 and Psalm 104 describe the structure of the world and the way it works, but Psalm 104 does not always treat it in terms of God's acts of original creation. Psalm 104 is as much about how the ecosystem works as it is about the origin of it, although some would argue that Genesis 1 is also more about how the cosmos works than it is about its material creation.[19]

It is especially important to note that light and sun or sunlight are not treated as the same thing or coequal in Ugaritic, Genesis 1, or Psalm 104. The sun and other luminaries visible in the sky are not treated as the only sources of all light. Clearly, Shapash is the sun goddess at Ugarit, not Pidray, the daughter of light, and Shapash does not appear in the Baʿal myth scenes where Pidray is involved.[20] Similarly, Genesis 1 has "light" on Day 1 and the greater and lesser "lights" on Day 4, created mainly for delimiting seasons, days, and years (v. 14). Although it is also true that "God set them in the

18. English translations of Hebrew Scripture here and elsewhere are my own.

19. See esp. John H. Walton, *Genesis 1 as Ancient Cosmology* (Winona Lake, IN: Eisenbrauns, 2011).

20. In fact, Shapshu is especially relevant to the overall interpretation of the myth as distinct from Pidray (see, e.g., the resurrection of Baʿal in CAT 1.6 I 7–15; VI 22–29, 41–48), but this is not the place to develop that point.

expanse of the sky to give light (Heb. *ʾôr*) on the earth" according to v. 17, one must keep in mind that this did not happen until Day 4 in the account. Thus, it seems that the sun is not thought to be the same "light" as the light of Day 1. The same separation between "light" and the sun(light) appears in Psalm 104, where light is referred to in v. 2, but the sun does not enter the picture until vv. 19–22:

19. The moon marks off the seasons (Heb. *môʿᵃdîm*), and the sun knows when to go down.
20. You bring darkness, it becomes night, and all the beasts of the forest prowl.
21. The lions roar for their prey and seek their food from God.
22. The sun rises, and they steal away; they return and lie down in their dens.
23. Then man goes out to his work, to his labor until evening.

The word for the sun and moon marking "seasons" in Gen 1:14 (Heb. *môʿădîm*) is also used in Ps 104:19 for the function of the moon. Night is the time for the predatory animals to prowl for prey (vv. 20–21), while day is the time for people to go out to work (vv. 22–23). Perhaps this explains why the light and the lights are separated in Genesis 1 (i.e., v. 3, Day 1 versus v. 14, Day 4). There has been no end of discussion about the idea that this separation shows that the chapter is not in chronological order: how can there be light without the sun, moon, and stars? If the threefold foundation of the natural order proposed here is correct, then it would have seemed natural to the ancient readers, not problematic, to talk about light first without the sun, moon, and stars. Yes, the lights on Day 4 provide light, but they come into the telling of the story as natural indicators of seasons, days, and years. As strange as it may sound to us, for the ancient audience there had to be light before there were lights. Thus, the Genesis 1 account simply begins here, but it follows the first three days with another three, thus making a total of six days. Likewise, as noted above, Psalm 104 begins with light (vv. 1–2), not the lights (vv. 19–23).

Transformation of Chaoskampf *in the Early Chapters of Genesis*

This brings us to the beginning of the story in Gen 1:1–2 and the issue of *Chaoskampf*. In a groundbreaking work written over 30 years before the Ugaritic texts were recovered, Hermann Gunkel argued for the incorporation of the ANE cosmic battle myth into the Bible from the story about Marduk versus Ti'āmat in the Babylonian creation epic (*Enūma eliš*). Since then, much scholarly debate has revolved around a supposed cosmic battle in Genesis 1.[21] Gunkel argued that, even though "Deutero-Isaiah" does not allow for the idea of chaos in creation, "a cosmogonic-mythological fragment is added to Genesis 1," that "Genesis 1 is not the composition of an author, but rather the written deposit of a tradition," and that "this tradition stems from a period of high antiquity."[22] He concluded that, in light of the background of all the other allusions to the cosmic battle in Scripture (e.g., Rahab, Leviathan, Behemoth, the Dragon in the Sea, and Tannin), ultimately, "the Babylonian . . . myth was taken up by Israel and there became a myth of YHWH."[23] There are scholars who still follow this basic line of argument.

Bernard Batto, for example, is fully committed to it, with refinements and expansions from *Atrahasis*, the Baʿal myth, and other ANE texts discovered since Gunkel. He argues that Genesis 1 retains reminiscences of the belief that God created us and our world through defeating the great sea monster known elsewhere in the Bible and the ancient Near East as Leviathan, Yamm, Tannun, Ti'āmat (cf. *tĕhôm* in Gen 1:2), and so on.[24]

Others hold to alternate forms of this view—for example, that Gen 1:2 refers to a chaotic state that is unformed and unfilled because of the ravages of precreation evil chaos. According to this view, Gen 1:3 begins an account of God's **re**creation of the world.[25] Still others reject the cosmic battle interpretation of Genesis 1 altogether, including the notion that there are traditions of this sort lying behind the current text. Claus Westermann, for example, reviews Gunkel's hypothesis and more recent elaborations of it in some detail. He concludes that, "[F]or the most part it is quite clear that the victory over the monster of Chaos has nothing to do with creation" in Genesis 1.[26] Even in regard to the parade example of *tĕhôm* (cf. "Ti'āmat" in *Enūma eliš*) and other terms in Gen 1:2, he argues that:

21. See Hermann Gunkel, *Schöpfung und Chaos in Urzeit und Enzeit: Eine religionsgeschichtliche Untersuchung über Gen 1 und Ap. Jon 12* (Göttingen: Vandenhoeck & Ruprecht, 1895). The citations in this essay are taken from Hermann Gunkel, *Creation and Chaos in the Primeval Era and the Eschaton: A Religio-Historical Study of Genesis 1 and Revelation 12* (with contributions by Heinrich Zimmern; trans. K. William Whitney Jr.; Grand Rapids, MI: Eerdmans, 2006).

22. Gunkel, *Creation and Chaos*, 7 and 11.

23. Ibid., 77.

24. Bernard F. Batto, *Slaying the Dragon: Mythmaking in the Biblical Tradition* (Louisville: Westminster/John Knox, 1992) 73–84.

25. See, e.g., Allen P. Ross, *Creation and Blessing: A Guide to the Study and Exposition of the Book of Genesis* (Grand Rapids, MI: Baker, 1988) 106–7.

26. Claus Westermann, *Genesis 1–11: A Commentary* (trans. John J. Scullion; Minneapolis: Augsburg, 1984) 33.

> We can be certain then that Gen 1:2 belongs to a history of creation narratives in which the motif of the primeval deep, with or without darkness, very often represents the situation before creation, but that the link between creation and the struggle of the gods is ***not part of its pre-history.***[27]

In this matter, I agree with David Tsumura that there is no serpentine sea monster in Genesis 1 and no hint of cosmic battle either.[28] The great sea creatures known as *tnnynym* (see Ug. *tunnan* in some of the texts cited above) are created on Day 5 along with all the other water animals (v. 21). They raise no challenge to God. The term *tĕhôm*, "deep," in v. 2 is cognate with the goddess Tiʾāmat, who did battle with Marduk in the Babylonian creation epic, but this *tĕhôm* is not personal, neither is it a demythologized borrowing from Mesopotamia, and it expresses no resistance to God's creative activity. Even if there is a shrouded allusion to Tiʾāmat or a reflection on ANE traditions that lie behind the Tiʾāmat motif in *Enūma eliš*,[29] it has the same effect as the reference to the *tnnynym* in Gen 1:21. *Tĕhôm*/Tiʾāmat raises no challenge to God or his creative work.

It is indeed true that, according to Genesis 1, God progressively through the six creation days eliminated the totally dark and watery unformed and unfilled conditions of v. 2. Moreover, darkness, as opposed to light, is often used as a metaphor for evil or catastrophe in Scripture. However, in Genesis 1 God progressively pronounces that what he has made is "good," and then finally "very good" (v. 3). This includes even the fact that light and darkness alternate to create the cycle of day and night. To argue that the darkness in v. 2 stands for a state of destruction caused by evil is, in my opinion, an instance of "illegitimate totality transfer."[30] Westermann is correct. The point of v. 2 is to provide a starting point for God's creative activity that the ancient Israelites

27. Westermann, *Genesis 1–11*, 106. He argues that it is not just a matter of the current text not holding to or reacting against the ANE cosmic battle motif, but that this does not even lie behind the text in its prehistory. This flies directly in the face of Gunkel's argument that the prehistory of the text of Genesis 1 is found primarily in the Babylonian myth. See also the very helpful review of the history of scholarship and helpful discussion in Gordon J. Wenham, *Genesis 1–15* (WBC; Waco, TX: Word, 1987) 8–17 and secondary references cited there.

28. David Tsumura, *Creation and Destruction: A Reappraisal of the* Chaoskampf *Theory in the Old Testament* (Winona Lake, IN: Eisenbrauns, 2005) 1–140.

29. Gunkel was right; there is no article on *tĕhôm* in Gen 1:2, suggesting that perhaps this is more than simply a term for the deep (Gunkel, *Creation and Chaos*, 7). But see the careful analysis of *tĕhôm* in the OT in Westermann, *Genesis 1–11*, 104–5, where he argues that there is no personification of *tĕhôm* in the Hebrew Bible even though it has no article in all but two of its 35 occurrences.

30. "Illegitimate totality transfer" occurs when meanings and/or implications of terms and expressions from various other contexts are illegitimately piled together and forced on a context where the argument does not call for it. See James Barr, *The Semantics of Biblical*

could understand. In their ancient Near Eastern world, numerous creation accounts from Mesopotamia and Egypt began with a deep dark watery abyss. In these texts, this condition is seen as uncreated but ***not*** evil.

Even at the beginning of *Enūma eliš* (= "when on high," a temporal beginning similar to *bĕrēʾšît*, "In the beginning" or "When God began," Gen 1:1), this point of departure carries no evil meaning or implication, even though Tiʾāmat is on the scene. Instead, the watery abyss conditions provide the starting matrix for creation:

> When on high no name was given to heaven,
> Nor below was the netherworld called by name,
> Primeval Apsu was their progenitor,
> And matrix-Tiʾāmat was she who bore them all,
> They were mingling their waters together.[31]

A theogony follows. The battle between the forces of evil and good associated with creation does not come into play until later in *Enūma eliš*, when Marduk defeats the enraged Tiʾāmat and creates heaven and earth out of her corpse (tablets IV–V).[32] The original conditions are treated neither as inherently evil nor as reflective of cosmic battle imagery. Moreover, even in the Ugaritic Baʿal myth, one would be hard-pressed to show that Baʿal's battle with Leviathan had anything at all to do with the creation of the world.

I am not trying to argue here, as some have recently attempted to do, that there is no place in the Bible where the *Chaoskamf* or cosmic battle motif comes into play. Some of the Leviathan passages clearly turn in this direction, although others do not, for example, Ps 104:25–26: "Yonder is the sea, great and wide, creeping things innumerable are there, living things both small and great. There go the ships, and Leviathan that you formed to sport in it" (NRSV). On the other hand, consider, for example, Isa 27:1. I have treated

---

Language (Oxford: Oxford University Press, 1961) 218, and virtually all the books written since then on theological hermeneutics and esp. biblical word usage and definition.

31. As in Gen 1:1–2, this is the very beginning of the composition. Translated by Benjamin R. Foster, "The Epic of Creation (Enūma Elish)," COS 1:391:1–5.

32. Actually, earlier in the myth (*Enūma eliš* I 21–84), after the begetting of the gods by the divine progenitors, Tiʾāmat and Apsû (*Enūma eliš* I 1–20), Ea vanquished Apsû, who planned to destroy the lower gods, the divine brothers and sisters, because their clamor was interrupting his rest during the day and his sleep during the night. By defeating Apsû, Ea took over the cosmic territory known as the *apsû* and made it his home territory. This became part of the ongoing world order that would underlie the creation of the larger cosmos by Marduk later in the myth. So in this sense, Ea and his son Marduk together were responsible for the creation of what we know as the cosmos: heaven and earth and all that is in them.

this in a publication elsewhere and will only summarize the main points here.[33] Isaiah 27 belongs to the so-called "little apocalypse" of Isaiah 24–27, which looks forward to the day when the Lord will set all things right.[34] It is the corresponding opposite of Psalm 74, which looks into the distant past and perhaps even to creation according to some scholars, rather than forward into the distant future. Accordingly, in the coming day, it will be the Lord, *not* Baʿal, who will defeat the great enemy of God and his people. One can hear the polemic against Baʿal in favor of the Lord resounding, even as Isaiah baldly alludes to the "twisted serpent" Leviathan. In fact, as is well known, the allusion directly to the Baʿal myth seems undeniable in this case. As Isa 27:1 puts it:

> In that day the LORD will punish Leviathan (Heb. *lwytn* = Ug. *ltn*),
> the fleeing (Heb. *brḥ* = Ug. *brḥ*) serpent with his harsh and great and mighty sword,
> even Leviathan, the twisted (Heb. *ʿqltwn* = Ug. *ʿqltn*) serpent;
> and he will kill the dragon (Heb. *tnnyn*) who is in the sea (Heb. *ym*; cf. the Ug. god Yamm).

Here is a passage as it appears in the Baʿal myth at the beginning of tablet 5 (CAT 1.5 i 1–3). Mot speaks:

ktmhṣ.ltn.bṯn.brḥ	When you smote *Litan* (=Leviathan) the *fleeing* serpent,
tkly. bṯn.ʿqltn.[ ]	made an end of *the twisted serpent*,
šlyt.d.šbʿt.rʾašm	the tyrant with seven heads.[35]

33. Richard E. Averbeck, "Ancient Near Eastern Mythography as It Relates to Historiography in the Hebrew Bible: Genesis 3 and the Cosmic Battle," in *The Future of Biblical Archaeology: Reassessing Methodologies and Assumptions* (ed. James K. Hoffmeier and Alan R. Millard; Grand Rapids, MI: Eerdmans, 2004) 328–56, especially pp. 338–40. See also Tryggve N. D. Mettinger, *The Eden Narrative: A Literary and Religio-Historical Study of Genesis 2–3* (Winona Lake, IN: Eisenbrauns, 2007) 80–83, where he has independently come to essentially the same view of Genesis 3 as in my earlier article cited above, and which I am reviewing in this essay. His references back to Paul Ricoeur's work in this regard are especially interesting. I thank Robert B. Chisholm Jr., Professor of Hebrew and Old Testament Studies at Dallas Theological Seminary, for calling my attention to this reference.

34. See the helpful discussion in Bernhard W. Anderson, "The Slaying of the Fleeing, Twisted Serpent: Isaiah 27:1 in Context," in *Uncovering Ancient Stones: Essays in Memory of H. Neil Richardson* (ed. Lewis M. Hopfe; Winona Lake, IN: Eisenbrauns, 1994) 3–15; and, more recently, see the dissertation on the little apocalypse by William Dale Barker, *Isaiah 24–27: Studies in a Cosmic Polemic* (Ph.D. diss., Cambridge University, 2006).

35. For the iconography of the seven-headed serpent, see, e.g., Othmar Keel, *The Symbolism of the Biblical World: Ancient Near Eastern Iconography and the Book of Psalms* (trans. Timothy J. Hallet; New York: Seabury, 1978; repr., Winona Lake, IN: Eisenbrauns, 1997) 54; and John W. Hilber, "Psalms," in *Zondervan Illustrated Bible Backgrounds Commentary* (ed. John H. Walton; Grand Rapids, MI: Zondervan, 2009) 5:382.

The close parallels are highlighted in the citations as given here. "Leviathan" is obvious even in the English translations, but consider also the adjectives "fleeing" and "twisted." The adjective *brḥ*, rendered "fleeing," appears only two or perhaps three other times in the Hebrew Bible. Other possible meanings are "flashing" as in "fast," or "hairless, slippery," as serpents are. Whatever the correct meaning might be, it is obviously the same in Ugaritic and in Hebrew. The term *ʿqltwn*, "twisted," appears only here in the Hebrew Scripture, which makes it difficult to avoid the conclusion that this is some kind of free quotation or perhaps close allusion to the Baʿal myth, depending on how you want to put it. The term for "serpent" here is Hebrew *nāḥāš*, not the same as Ugaritic *bṯn* in the parallel passage, but it is the same word used in Gen 3:15, for example. The significance of *tnnyn* in this verse is apparent from its use in Ps 74:13–14:

13. You divided the sea by your might; you broke the heads of the dragons (Heb. *tnnynym*; cf. sing. *tnnyn* in Isa 27:1) in the waters.
14. You crushed the heads (Heb. *raʾšîm*) of Leviathan (*lwytn*); you gave him as food for the creatures of the wilderness.

A comparison of a combination of passages in the Ugaritic Baʿal myth and other mythic texts reveals that Leviathan, Yamm "sea," Tunnan (Heb. *tannîn*) "sea monster," and other such terms all refer to one and the same enemy of Baʿal in the Ugaritic material, as Wayne Pitard has shown.[36] The association of Leviathan with "the dragon" (Heb. *tnnyn*) who is in the "sea" (Heb. *ym*; cf. the Ug. god Yamm) in Isa 27:1 makes perfectly good sense against the backdrop of the world of the Ugaritic Baʿal myth. The point of all this is that, in the biblical text, we have clear allusions to an ancient Near Eastern myth about an evil serpent with whom Yahweh does battle, whether in the distant past, the distant future, or sometime between.

Chaoskampf *in Genesis 3*

Genesis 1, of course, does not include a theogony, and this is part of the underlying polemic against the ancient Near Eastern environment of the Israelites. This polemic, it seems to me, also includes a reaction to the notion that God created the world by defeating the evil forces of chaos, although even *Enūma eliš* does not begin with *Chaoskampf*, so "polemic" might not be the right word here. In any case, the lack of *Chaoskampf* in Genesis 1 is not

36. Wayne T. Pitard, "The Binding of Yamm: A New Edition of the Ugaritic Text *KTU* 1.83," *JNES* 57 (1998) 261–80.

the end of the story. The fact of the matter is that there is a cosmic battle in the early chapters of Genesis, but it has been transformed in accordance with the nature and concerns of Yahweh. The battle really begins in Genesis 3, and it is here where the correspondences to *Chaoskampf* in the early chapters of Genesis appear, but in a thoroughly transformed way.

Some of the most important works either completely exclude this chapter or underplay the relationship between Genesis 3 and the complex of cosmic battle references in the ancient Near East and the Hebrew Bible.[37] Others follow and continue to develop the groundbreaking work of Gunkel. In this scholarly tradition, on one level, the serpent story in Genesis 3 is largely an etiological fable that explains the snake's mode of transport and the natural enmity between people and snakes.[38] Or the serpent is a magical source of life and wisdom as, for example, in the cult of the serpent in Numbers 21 and 2 Kgs 18:4. In this case, the Genesis 3 curses have the heathen practice

37. See Mary K. Wakeman (*God's Battle with the Monster* [Leiden: Brill, 1973] 84–86, 136–38), according to whom the myth is obscured in Genesis 3; cf. also Tremper Longman III and Daniel G. Reid, *God as Warrior* (Grand Rapids, MI: Zondervan, 1995) 72–74.

Susan Niditch (*Chaos to Cosmos: Studies in Biblical Patterns of Creation* [Chico, CA: Scholars Press, 1985] 35–36) sees the serpent as "a betwixt and between creature, one appropriate for linking paradise and reality," a wise creature who introduces humankind to wisdom, the ability to distinguish between good and evil; cf. also eadem, *Oral World and Written World: Ancient Israelite Literature* (Louisville, KY: Westminster John Knox, 1996) 28–38. Batto (*Slaying the Dragon*, 59–62, 96) argues, on the one hand, that the serpent was an enemy of God but not of people, since he enabled the latter to obtain a divine level of knowledge and, on the other hand, that "the serpent embodied the illegitimate human aspiration to divine wisdom" (p. 60). So, by enticing two people to overstep the boundary of knowledge that distinguished humankind from God, the serpent brought a curse upon all animals and humankind as well. For a treatment of the two different sides of serpent imagery in Egypt—wise and protective versus evil and destructive—see the essay by Joanna Töyräänvuori in the present volume. The Genesis 3 story, in my view, conceives of the serpent as the enemy of both God and those who were created in his image and likeness. The serpent simply used the created to attack the Creator.

Jon D. Levenson (*Creation and the Persistence of Evil: The Jewish Drama of Divine Omnipotence* [Princeton: Princeton University Press, 1994]); John Day (*God's Conflict with the Dragon and the Sea* [Cambridge: Cambridge Univ. Press, 1985]); Hugh Rowland (*The Myth of Cosmic Rebellion: A Study of Its Reflexes in Ugaritic and Biblical Literature* [VTSup 65; Leiden: Brill, 1996]); Rebecca S. Watson (*Chaos Uncreated: A Reassessment of the Theme of 'Chaos' in the Hebrew Bible* [BZAW 341; Berlin: de Gruyter, 2005]); and K. William Whitney (*Two Strange Beasts: Leviathan and Behemoth in Second Temple and Early Rabbinic Judaism* [HSM 63; Winona Lake, IN: Eisenbrauns, 2006]), for example, do not bring the serpent in Genesis 3 into their discussion at all.

38. Hermann Gunkel, *Genesis* (trans. Mark E. Biddle; Macon, GA: Mercer University Press, 1997) 21; Westermann, *Genesis 1–11*, 260–61. Gerhard von Rad (*Genesis: A Commentary* [OTL; rev. ed.; Philadelphia: Westminster, 1972] 92–93) argues that the narrative is not just etiological but also sets forth the basic struggles that humankind has with evil.

of deriving higher knowledge through magic and divination as their object of concern.[39]

On another level, however, Gunkel also argued that behind the etiological fable in Genesis 3 lurks another tradition. There was an original mythological serpent that had demonic characteristics, but this one in Genesis 3 derives from an ANE tradition different from that of Tiʾāmat in the Babylonian tradition reflected in Genesis 1. The two are "separate figures" altogether.[40] Moreover, the mythical foundation of the more ancient story in Genesis 3 has receded further into the background, so here we have an actual serpent rather than a serpent-demon.[41] With help from the Ugaritic texts not available in Gunkel's day, other scholars have carried this interpretation forward. Brevard Childs, for example, argues that

> the Yahwist employs the language of the myth, carefully altered and held in a delicate balance. Demonic elements of a Canaanite myth were associated with the serpent who epitomized that which is sinister and strange among the animals. The Yahwist retained the demonic character of the snake arising out of the myth, but affirmed that it was a mere creature under God's power.[42]

In my opinion, Gunkel's proposed shift in the ANE mythological analog away from *Chaoskampf* in Genesis 3 to another analog was a mistake from the beginning. The serpent in Genesis 3 would naturally have called the image of Leviathan and the *Chaoskampf* cosmic battle to mind for the ancient author(s) and readers. It is true that one of the most basic methodological rules for comparing extrabiblical ancient Near Eastern texts with the Bible is that careful analysis of the biblical passages and their innerbiblical parallels should always take precedence over comparisons with external texts. Having said that, however, the fact is that in the biblical text we do indeed have clear allusions to an ancient Near Eastern myth about an evil serpent with whom Yahweh does battle. We have discussed a few of the most important instances above.

In plain terms, then, Genesis 3 is where conflict first appears in the Bible. Gen 3:1 is the first appearance of a serpent in the Bible. This serpent issues a direct and carefully crafted sinister challenge to Yahweh's rule by attacking what in Genesis 1 is referred to as his image and likeness—people. As Gen 1:26–28 puts it, we are his statue, his "image and likeness," so to speak, created

39. See the summary of this view and the bibliographical references cited in Westermann, *Genesis 1–11*, 237–38.

40. Gunkel, *Genesis*, 16.

41. Ibid., 15 and 39.

42. Brevard S. Childs, *Myth and Reality in the Old Testament* (SBT 27; 2nd ed.; London: SCM, 1962) 49.

and placed within creation to represent him, his authority, and his character.[43] If we stay within the Genesis 2–3 account, something similar is reflected here in a different way. Thus, the serpent's actions are an attack on the Lord himself and his creative design. Yahweh responds with curses on the serpent (Gen 3:14–15; and the ground, v. 17) that involve, among other things, the woman's seed crushing, striking at, or bruising (or whatever[44]) the "head" of the serpent's seed in Gen 3:15. There is a battle engaged here—a theomachy between God and the serpent—and we stand right in the middle of it all.

Conclusion

The chaos of the *Chaoskampf* in Genesis 3 is the corruption of the world, beginning with human beings. The battle is a battle of redemption—re-creation, not creation—but it began during the time of creation. The writer of Genesis 3 and the ancient Israelites overall would have seen this in the account and viewed it as the core of the cosmic battle, although in a way that transforms it into the form in which we have it here from the cosmic battle imagery readily available to them in that day. The ancient Israelites were living in an ancient Near Eastern world and were, in fact, ancient Near Easterners themselves. And, like the ancient Ugaritians, they were fully aware of the figures and metaphors from their world that underlay their particular account of the *Chaoskampf*.

The main point of all this is that, according to Genesis 3 and certain other biblical passages, the battlefield in the *Chaoskampf* cosmic battle is us: people. We are the "territory" under dispute. And an attack upon us is by its very nature an attack on Yahweh himself. According to the Bible, we were the crowning act of God's ***creative activity*** when he made us in his image and likeness and put us in charge in Genesis 1–2. We are also the focal point of his ***redemptive activity***. Thus, for the time being, we stand right in the middle of a great, vicious cosmic fray that is the only cosmic battle there has ever really been or will be. This concept and its imagery continues to be transformed to one degree or another, in one way or another, through the remainder of the

43. This is not the place to delve into the details of the interpretation of "image and likeness" in Gen 1:26–28; 5:1–3; etc. Briefly, like the statue of a king, we are the "statue" of a king too, the divine king. And we have been set up in the midst of God's creation to represent him and his interests. It is not that we look like God physically, but that we are physical beings who stand within physical creation as God's stewards. We stand before God to serve as his authoritative representatives on this earth "in his image as his likeness." We have been put in charge and made responsible for the way things go here. For now, see the helpful discussion in J. Richard Middleton, *The Liberated Image: The IMAGO DEI in Genesis 1* (Grand Rapids, MI: Baker, 2005).

44. For the lexical difficulty here, see *HALOT* 1146–47.

Old Testament and on into the New, but that discussion will need to wait for another time. All I want to add here is that Revelation 12 transforms it back into an actual battle again, with battlefield imagery. This chapter in John's Apocalypse is virtually a Christian midrash on Genesis 3. Here again is the *Chaoskampf* of the ages, beginning to end, and all through history. Gunkel was right on this count: there really is an *Urzeit* and an *Endzeit* in all this.

Part 6

Chaos and (Re)Creation

Chaoskampf *Lost*—Chaoskampf *Regained*

The Gunkel Hypothesis Revisited

JoAnn Scurlock

Elmhurst College (retired)

It has often been argued that there is a close relationship between the Genesis creation account (Gen 1:1–2:4a) and the Babylonian creation epic *Enūma eliš* that extends even to the order in which the various elements of the universe were created.[1] Most of those who accept that there is a relationship between the two prefer to see it as a (mediated) cultural borrowing. The closeness of the comparison, however, suggests an alternative interpretation—namely, that the first creation account in Genesis was intentionally patterned after the *Enūma eliš* and intended to dispute with it,[2] although what exactly the point of the disputation would have been is less clear. Kenton L. Sparks, taking the conventional interpretation of the Genesis passage as an assertion of monotheism, argues that the main difference is that Yahweh

1. Hermann Gunkel, *Creation and Chaos in the Primeval Era and the Eschaton: A Religio-Historical Study of Genesis* 1 and Revelation 12 (trans. K. William Whitney Jr.; Grand Rapids, MI: Eerdmans, 2006 [Göttingen: Vandenhoeck & Ruprecht, 1895]) 78–111; cf. E. A. Speiser, *Genesis* (AB 1; Garden City, NY: Doubleday, 1964) 8–13. For the contrary extreme, see Victor P. Hamilton, *The Book of Genesis, Chapters 1–17* (NICOT; Grand Rapids, MI: Eerdmans, 1990) 110–11. For a more neutral approach, which neither accepts nor quite refuses a connection, see Alexander Heidel, *The Babylonian Genesis* (Chicago: University of Chicago Press, 1942) 82–140.

2. See, for example, Kenton L. Sparks, "Enūma Eliš and Priestly Mimesis: Elite Emulation in Nascent Judaism," *JBL* 126 (2007) 629–32.

has an exclusive kingship: "By imitating the Mesopotamian myth of divine sovereignty with a monotheistic setting, the Priestly Writer has clearly articulated the belief that his God is the king, not only because he is the Creator but because he has no rivals at all."[3]

However, in the *Enūma eliš*, Marduk is also given an exclusive kingship: *Marduk-ma šar*, "Marduk alone is king."[4] There are, of course, other gods, but *Enūma eliš* goes out of its way to emphasize that they are completely at his mercy and exist only because of his sufferance.[5] Indeed, it has long been remarked that Marduk's rise to the head of the pantheon resembles the rise of a monarch to absolute power.[6] Moreover, the creation of the visible world is carried out by Marduk and Marduk alone, without any helpers.[7] Ea turns up as assistant only in the creation of humankind (VI 31–38), just as the rest of the elohim make an appearance in Genesis at this point in the narrative (Gen 1:26).

What **is** a noticeable contrast is the omission in Gen 1:1–2:4a of any mention of the *Chaoskampf* in connection with creation.[8] Mark Smith follows Sparks's general line of argument but interprets the omission of a *Chaoskampf* as an assertion of a Priestly vision of God rather than an anti-Marduk polemic per se: "The aim would appear to be to substitute divine speech for divine conflict and thus read conflict out of creation. In this way, God can be viewed as a power beyond conflict, indeed the unchallenged and unchallengeable power beyond any powers." He also argues that this Priestly vision is a "paradigm shift" away from the "traditional" understanding of God as a sort of Marduk figure who destroyed monsters in order to create the world.[9] A similar formulation is given in M. Fishbane, *Biblical Myth and Rabbinic Mythmaking*, where the "logos" model is contrasted with the "agon" model as competing views of the nature of creation, with the "agon" model representing the older view.[10]

Actually, I see no evidence of this allegedly prior belief in an agonistic creation at any point in the biblical narrative. To be sure, Yahweh is given credit

3. Ibid., 632.

4. *Ee* IV 28.

5. *Ee* II 159–63; III 60–64, 118–22; IV 5–18; VI 17–25, 95–100; VII 151–54.

6. Henri Frankfort, *Kingship and the Gods: A Study of Ancient Near Eastern Religion as the Integration of Society and Nature* (Chicago: University of Chicago Press, 1948) 218, 220.

7. *Ee* IV 132–V 62.

8. W. G. Lambert ("A New Look at the Babylonian Background of Genesis," *JTS* n.s. 16 [1965] 287–300) accepts a connection between biblical and Mesopotamian accounts of creation but argues that divine combat between Marduk and Tiʾāmat which precedes creation in the *Enūma eliš* should not be included among the common elements.

9. Mark S. Smith, *The Priestly Vision of Genesis 1* (Minneapolis: Fortress, 2010) 69.

10. Michael Fishbane, *Biblical Myth and Rabbinic Mythmaking* (Oxford: Oxford University Press, 2003) 63–69.

for defeating a whole host of monsters, many of whom also feature in victories attributed in Ugaritic epics to Baʿal and in Hurro-Hittite songs to Teššub: Nahar (River), Leviathan (Coiled One), Tannin (Dragon), Rahab (Arrogant One) and Yam (Sea).[11] Nonetheless, in no case, as we shall have more occasion to discuss later, is the defeat of such a monster in any way foundational to the original creation of the world as opposed to the creation of Israel after the crossing of the Red Sea and the sojourn in the desert or the re-creation of the temple after its destruction by Nebuchadnezzar.[12]

The same may, of course, be said of the *Baʿal Epic* itself, which foregrounds the defeat of Yam but does not refer to anything, apart from Baʿal's palace, as having been created.[13] This fact has been used to argue for an early date of composition for Gen 1:1–2:4a, since Sumerian accounts of creation and the battles against monsters also treat *Chaoskampf* and creation as two separate topoi, carried out at different times and by different types of gods.[14]

Given the closeness of the parallels between Genesis 1 and *Enūma eliš*, a preexilic dating for the former is rather questionable. And Westermann's early dating would need to be early indeed, since it is a generally accepted consensus that the *Enūma eliš* is to be dated to the second millennium. But even assuming for the moment that Westermann is correct, the presentation of Genesis 1 would still involve a conscious choice between two competing images of God.

In the ancient Mesopotamian religious universe, as at Ugarit, the separation of creation from monster bashing springs from a contrast between fatherly, if sometimes elderly and ineffectual, leaderly El-type gods[15] and young competitive-warrior Baʿal-type gods,[16] a contrast that is only partly obscured

11. Isa 27:1; 51:9–10; Job 26:12–13; Ps 9:9–12, 74:12–17, 104:9; Prov 8:27; Job 9:13–14; 26:10, 12–13; 38:8–11.

12. See also David Toshio Tsumura, *Creation and Destruction* (Winona Lake, IN: Eisenbrauns, 2005); and Rebecca S. Watson, *Chaos Uncreated: A Reassessment of the Theme of "Chaos" in the Hebrew Bible* (BZAW 341; Berlin: de Gruyter, 2005); cf. Heidel, *Babylonian Genesis*, 102–14; H. W. F. Saggs, *The Encounter of the Divine in Mesopotamia and Israel* (London: Athlone, 1978) 54–63; Yehezkel Kaufmann, *The Religion of Israel from Its Beginnings to the Babylonian Exile* (trans. Moshe Greenberg; Chicago: University of Chicago Press, 1960).

13. On this point, see, inter alia, Arvid S. Kapelrud, "Baʿal, Schöpfung und Chaos," *UF* 11 (1979) 407–12.

14. Claus Westermann, *Genesis 1–11* (trans. John J. Scullion; Minneapolis: Augsburg, 1984) 28–33.

15. For El as the Creator god at Ugarit, see Smith, *Priestly Vision*, 200–202 nn. 20–21; and Mark S. Smith, *The Ugaritic Baal Cycle*, vol. 1: *Introduction with Text, Translation and Commentary of KTU 1.1–1.2* (VTSup 55; Leiden: Brill, 1994) 83–84. For a creation myth at Ugarit featuring El as Creator, see my "Death and the Maidens: A New Interpretive Framework for KTU 1.23," *UF* 43 (2011) 411–34.

16. See Smith, *Ugaritic Baal Cycle*, 1:102–5.

by the presence of two levels of Creator gods in Mesopotamia and a host of other gods with a myriad of different functions to perform.

Sumerian creation accounts are mostly about the evolution of the world we know from primordial elements such as earth, water, time and sky (air).[17] Insofar as active creation is contemplated, it is the work of the divine assembly (the Mesopotamian equivalent of the biblical Elohim),[18] with the Creator Anu (= Ugaritic El) forming the heavens[19] and initiating a chain of creation in the midst of which Enki/Ea[20] or a usurping Enlil[21] appears to produce humankind.[22] Battles against monsters existed for Sumerians but took place at some point after the creation of the world—as, for example, during solar and lunar eclipses[23]—and were handled by gods such as Tišpak[24] and, most spectacularly, Ninurta.[25] Both were young warrior gods (= Ugaritic Baʿaluma) who acted on behalf of their superiors, not on their own account.

One of the more striking features of the reassessment of the Ugaritic *Baʿal Epic* by Wayne Pitard and Mark Smith[26] is the realization that El plays no minor or insignificant role in the story and, being immortal, may be imagined as leaving Baʿal forever[27] trapped in the position of crown prince to his father-

---

17. W. G. Lambert, "Kosmogonie," *RlA* 6:218–22.

18. CT 13.34, apud Georgio Castellino, "The Origins of Civilization according to Biblical and Cuneiform Texts," in *"I Studied Inscriptions from before the Flood": Ancient Near Eastern, Literary, and Linguistic Approaches to Genesis 1–11* (ed. Richard S. Hess and David Toshio Tsumura; Winona Lake, IN: Eisenbrauns, 1994) 89; cf. Thorkild Jacobsen, "The Eridu Genesis (1.158)," *COS* 1:513–15. References to the divine assembly appear in 1 Kgs 22:19–22; Isaiah 6; Dan 7:10; Job 1; *1 En.* 14:22–23; Revelation 4.

19. *Rit. Acc.* 46:24–38, apud Castellino, "Origins," 89; cf. Heidel, *Babylonian Genesis*, 64–75.

20. Jacob Klein, "Enki and Ninmah (1.159)," *COS* 1:515–18.

21. See Gertrude Farber, "The Song of the Hoe (1.157)," *COS* 1:511–13. Enlil uses the hoe to separate heaven and earth and to create mankind by molding him like a brick. In other words, we are talking about creation by deed.

22. As Tsumura (*Creation and Destruction*, 132) points out, only Ea is referred to as "creator of living creatures," and in only one or two texts is anyone but Ea involved whenever living things need to be produced.

23. See ibid., 153–54 for the moon's being represented as containing a warrior god armed with a sickle sword and holding a lion serpent by the tail. Tsumura completely misses the fact that this and the references in "late expository texts" are in the specific context of eclipses, as he should have gathered from pp. 155–56, where a statue of the moon-god Sîn in eclipse has at its base a flood monster (Leviathan) and a wild beast (Behemoth).

24. Heidel, *Babylonian Genesis*, 141–43.

25. See Amar Annus, *The God Ninurta* (SAAS 14; Helsinki: The Neo-Assyrian Text Corpus Project, 2002) for full details.

26. Smith, *Ugaritic Baal Cycle*, vol. 1; and Mark S. Smith and Wayne T. Pitard, *The Ugaritic Baal Cycle*, vol. 2: *Introduction with Text, Translation and Commentary of KTU/CAT 1.3–1.4* (VTSup 114; Leiden: Brill, 2009).

27. Even as late as Philo of Byblos, Baʿal ("Zeus"), although king of the gods and ruling over the land, must still do so "with the consent of Kronos" (PE 1.10.31; see Harold W.

in-law's position of king and having literally to beg for his palace through the intercession of his wife and mother-in-law.[28] Pitard and Smith rightly point out the numerous differences between this epic and the *Enūma eliš*.[29]

Nonetheless, the contrast between El-like sky gods and Baʿal-like warrior gods is very much a part of Mesopotamian religion, and that from Sumerian times. Ninurta receives kingship as his reward for the defeat of monsters and the rescuing of the Tablet of Destinies (just as Ugaritic Baʿal receives a palace) and is similarly in an awkward position vis-à-vis the head of the Sumerian pantheon, Enlil. Ninurta is actually an illegitimate child, which is why the god Sîn, Enlil's oldest son, gets first crack at the position of king and must be replaced by Ninurta due to Sîn's inadequacies.[30] Similarly, Ugaritic Athar is dwarfed by Baʿal's throne in the *Baʿal Epic* and must give up trying to exercise the kingship.

The issue of legitimacy is center stage in the Ugaritic *Baʿal Epic*, with Yam, El's first choice for sovereignty, being narrowly defeated by Baʿal, who subsequently fails in his attempt to take over the netherworld from Mot.[31] Indeed, it appears that, not only do warrior gods typically occupy subordinate positions,[32] but they are only legitimate insofar as they recognize their subordination and do not overstep the boundaries of their authority or abuse the powers delegated to them.

Moreover, in Mesopotamia, neither Tišpak nor Ninurta is portrayed as creating anything. So, for example, in the Song of the Hoe, it is Enlil who uses the hoe to create mankind, not Ninurta, who instead uses it as an offensive weapon against enemy lands.[33] Thus, like Ugaritic Baʿal, it is not actually clear that Sumerian warrior gods are anything more than monster bashers, playing the role occupied by human kings vis-à-vis the city god, inspiring the

Attridge and Robert A. Oden Jr., *Philo of Byblos: The Phoenician History: Introduction, Critical Text, Translation, Notes* [CBQMS 9; Washington, DC: Catholic Biblical Association, 1981] 55).

28. Smith, *Ugaritic Baal Cycle*, 1:xxv–xxvi, 95–96. Compare also Daniel Schwemer, "Storm-Gods of the Ancient Near East: Summary, Synthesis, Recent Studies, Part 2," *JANER* 8 (2008) 10–12.

29. See especially Smith, *Ugaritic Baal Cycle*, 1:104–5, 296, 314–16, 361; and Smith and Pitard, *Baal Cycle*, 2:16–20, 35–41, 43–46, 53–55, 57.

30. As pointed out by Maria Grazia Masetti-Rouault, "Fathers and Sons in Syro-Mesopotamian Pantheons: Problems of Identity and Succession in Cuneiform Traditions," paper read at the 55th Rencontre Assyriologique Internationale; Paris, 2009.

31. For a discussion of these issues, see Pierre Bordreuil and Dennis Pardee, "Le combat de Baʿlu avec Yammu d'après les textes Ougaritiques," *MARI* 7 (1993) 66–67.

32. At Ugarit, Baʿal is at the head of the younger generation of gods but still listed after Ilu-ibi, El, and Dagan (Schwemer, "Storm-Gods 2," 10).

33. Gertrud Farber, "The Song of the Hoe."

monarch's manly deeds as a combater of human enemies of the community,[34] and reminding him that he is working for his superiors and not on his own account.[35]

Neither the drunk and disorderly Ugaritic El nor the dead Sumero-Akkadian Anu seems a very promising choice as an image of the God of Israel,[36] but then nobody said that a Creator God **had** to be either retired or dead. Ugaritic Baʿal looked grand as the storm cloud, thundering in his wrath or sending the gentle rain of his mercy[37]—attributes that were clearly appropriated for Yahweh.[38] Baʿal was, nonetheless, a muscle-bound behemoth with personality problems of his own, who was only good for bashing monsters and did not have the power to create.[39] What is worse, the warrior god was only legitimate when there was someone above him—which is the most basic violation of "Thou shalt have no other gods before me"! And did I mention that he died periodically and needed to be rescued from the netherworld by his wife, who was a better monster basher than even he was?[40] It was a foregone conclusion, then, that if a choice had to be made, Creator El was going to be the choice, and warrior Baʿal, if he was unwilling to behave himself and disappear into anonymity among the elohim, leaving God to take over his victories, was going to have to be anathematized.

And this is what appears to have happened, regardless of how we wish to date Genesis 1. In some of the earliest references in the Hebrew Bible to the god of Abraham (Gen 14:19, 22), he appears as *El elyon*, *qoneh*, literally, "purchaser" of heaven and earth, a very unusual way of expressing creation, at-

34. See Annus, *The God Ninurta*, on this score, and note that, in later periods, Nabû essentially takes on all of the attributes of Ninurta, including the patronage of kingship. For the patronage of West Semitic kingship by Baʿalim, see Smith, *Priestly Vision*, 19–21 with nn. 58–67; cf. Schwemer, "Storm-Gods 2," 10; and Dominique Charpin, "'Le roi est mort, vive le roi!' Les funérailles des souveraines amorrites et l'avènement de leur successeur," in *Studies in Ancient Near Eastern World View and Society Presented to Marten Stol on the Occasion of His 65th Birthday* (ed. R. J. van der Spek; Bethesda, MD: CDL, 2008) 89.

35. Perhaps the most striking expression of this is the "slap in the face" to which Babylonian kings were annually subjected in the Babylonian New Years' Festival (*Rit. Acc.* 145:449–52).

36. So, for example, Smith (*Priestly Vision*, 17–23, 32–33, 200 n. 14) assumes that Israelites imaged their god as Baʿal.

37. See Schwemer, "Storm-Gods 2," 23; cf. idem, "Storm-Gods of the Ancient Near East: Summary, Sythesis, Recent Studies, Part 1," *JNER* 7 (2007) 134–35 (Iškur). Baʿal as the gentle rain is attested in KTU 1.19 i 41–46 and 1.3 ii 38–41.

38. The references are numerous; to cite only the most spectacular examples: Ps 68:5, 8–11; 104:3–4; Sir 43:13–27.

39. On this point, see also Tsumura, *Creation and Destruction*, 55–56; Smith, *Ugaritic Baal Cycle*, 1:83–84; and Smith and Pitard, *Baal Cycle*, 2:244–45.

40. See Schwemer, "Storm-Gods 2," 7–8, 12–13, 24; cf. idem, "Storm-Gods 1," 134 (Iškur).

tested otherwise only of Ugaritic El.[41] Equally striking for the equation of God with El is Proverbs 8's presentation of Wisdom (the Asherah)[42] as the daughter of God (Prov 8:22) and a "craftsman" (8:30) assisting in some unspecified way in the creation of the universe (8:27–31).

We may unpack this by comparing the relationship of Ugaritic El and Kothar[43] to their Mesopotamian equivalents, Anu and Ea.[44] Ea was somewhat of a super craft god who formed human beings from clay in the way one might make a pot (*Atrahasis* 189–305) or by coagulating blood (*Enūma eliš*). His specialty, in other words, was creation by deed. The creation of heavens and earth, by contrast, went to gods like Anu (in cosmologies) and Anšar (in the *Enūma eliš*), who were themselves spontaneously generated. When power is delegated to Marduk in the *Enūma eliš*, it is explicit that creative power at this level is by word (*Ee* IV 19–26).[45] Unlike Mesopotamian Anu, Ugaritic El was not above creation by deed, but he confined his creation to "creatures"[46] and invariably entrusted the manufacture of objects—such as, for example, Baᶜal's palace—to Kothar, so there is a consistent pattern of more- and less-important creative acts, reflecting a division of labor between the Creator and his assistants.

Thus, when God in Genesis 1 employed a speech act—such as, for example, "Let there be light" in Gen 1:3—it would have been God qua Ugaritic El who was speaking; whereas, when an object was being manufactured—such as, for example, the "making" of the two great lights in Gen 1:16—it would have been Wisdom qua Ugaritic Kothar who was acting as "craftsman."[47] The manly deeds of Ugaritic Baᶜal were, of course, claimed for God in the same way

41. The references are collected in Daniel O. McClellan, "El Elyon, Begetter of Heaven and Earth," a paper read at the Society of Biblical Literature annual meeting in Atlanta, 2010 (now at http://danielomcclellan.wordpress.com/tag/el-elyon/). The view that "purchase" is literally meant is **not** his interpretation. The reference is to the need to purchase clay used in manufacture

42. For references for this equation, see Smith, *Priestly Vision*, 261 n. 88. Note also that Wisdom appears as the World Tree in Ben Sirah 24.

43. For numerous parallels between the characterization of El in his dealings with Kothar in the *Baᶜal Epic* and biblical texts, see Smith, *Ugaritic Baal Cycle*, 1:173–80, 184–86, 188–89. Note also ibid., 207–8.

44. El's vizier at Ugarit is identical with the vizier of Anu in Mesopotamia.

45. Compare "Let all the earth fear the Lord; let all who dwell in the world revere him. For he spoke, and it was made, he commanded and it stood forth" (Ps 33:8–9).

46. See now also my "Death and the Maidens," 411–34, esp. 426–29.

47. Compare Ovid, *Metamorphoses*, which has God himself separating heaven from earth, but when it is humankind's turn to be created: "The son of Iapetus (Prometheus) fashioned that earth, mingled with the waters of rain, into the image of the gods that guide the world" (Publius Ovidius Naso, *Metamorphoses* [trans. Z. Phillip Ambrose; Newburyport: Focus, 2004] 1:76–83), where Gen 1:26 has "Then God said: Let us make man in our image, after our likeness."

that a human king may claim victories won by his generals, whether or not he himself actively participates in warfare. Nevertheless, God was never, and could not be Baʿal. What is more, if Baʿal began to act independently in the land and to be approached by himself in his own temple and by his own ritual, as in the episode of Elijah and the priests of Baʿal, then Baʿal was essentially in rebellion against God.

This tension would have problematized the close relationship between human kings and Baʿaluma, so clearly attested outside Israel.[48] It nonetheless survived, if in attenuated form, in the idea of the king as an agent or weapon of God and of God as the king's special protector. Thus, in Ps 18:5–20, we find God mounted on a cherub (Ps 18:11) defeating the sea in the style of Ugaritic Baʿal's taking on Yam in order to rescue his faithful king from danger. The reference to the *Baʿal Epic* is no doubt intentional, and conspicuous by its absence in this retelling is any mention that Yam was, in fact, a legitimate authority that God was having to displace or that, after the battle, God was going to need to send his wife and mother-in-law to beg the real boss for a palace. Also conspicuous by its absence is any mention of creation in connection with this incident.

Southern Mesopotamian views on the subject of creation had taken a radical turn by the end of the second millennium B.C. with the emergence of Babylonian theology, the composition of the *Enūma eliš*, and the rise of Marduk to the head of the pantheon. For Marduk was not just a warrior god but a Creator as well. Simultaneously, Aššur morphed from the *numen loci* of Mt. Ebiḫ and the city of Aššur to an imperial god. In the process, an El-type Creator god (literally, "The God" or "The Lone God") became a very alive, effectual warrior in his own right.

So, if Genesis 1 is late enough to be contemporary with the Neo-Assyrian and Neo-Babylonian empires, the choice presented to Israel and Judah by apparently unstoppable and victorious enemies was between Aššur and Marduk as images of God. The new choice presented by the contrast between the national gods of these two Mesopotamian empires with whom first Israel and then Judah found itself in intimate contact was between a Creator god who, by the by, was also a warrior; and a warrior god who, by the by, was also a Creator. The contrast was, then, a matter of emphasis rather than function. What is God's primary purpose—not just what can he do?

In this light, it is essential to understand the significance of the apparent omission of the *Chaoskampf* from Genesis 1's account of creation. With Gun-

48. For a discussion, see Jean-Marie Durand, "Le mythologème du combat entre le dieu de l'orage et la mer en Mésopotamie," *MARI* 7 (1993) 41–61. See also Smith, *Ugaritic Baal Cycle*, 1:105–10; Smith and Pitard, *Baal Cycle*, 2:21.

kel, did the Priestly author just sort of forget to mention it or, with Sparks and Mark Smith,[49] was the omission deliberate? And if the latter is the case, why? When we understand that the question is whether the primary activity of God on earth is creation or combating the forces of evil, it is painfully obvious why Gunkel made the choice that he did.

For Christians, the primary purpose of Christ, and it is Christ whom Gunkel (following Zimmern, from whom he got his Assyriological material) is seeing in Marduk's image, is to bring salvation to mankind. The creation of the world, while of course impressive, is secondary to the cosmic conflict with the forces of evil that leads to the Last Judgment or, in other words, Christ is a warrior God who, by the by, creates. Of course, Gunkel never imagined primitive minds as having grasped the concept of salvation, which is why he relegated the Mesopotamian version to the "traditional" analogue of *Chaoskampf*.[50] The struggle between Marduk and Qingu is not, however (as Karen Sonik has shown),[51] about Chaos[52] but about the legitimate exercise of power, which ironically makes the so-called *Chaoskampf* a better analogue to salvation as specifically a Cosmic Battle in which a Fallen Angel is brought to book by a Warrior Christ as representative of legitimate divine authority than Gunkel could have dreamed.

Gunkel was not, then, entirely mistaken in seeing, at the urgings of his Assyriologist colleague Zimmern, a Christ figure in Marduk. And it followed, again a sine qua non of Christian belief, that the God of Genesis must be equated with the Jesus of Revelation. It also appealed that reading the defeat of evil into the account of original creation made human existence into a full circle, echoing the repetitive defeats and releases of Leviathan in Revelation.[53]

Unfortunately, Genesis 1 was not written with a salvation religion in mind. And from a pre-salvation point of view, I argue that the choice was still a "no-brainer," but in the opposite direction and for a number of reasons. Of course,

49. Smith, *Priestly Vision*, 69. Following the conventional assignment of Genesis 1 to the P source, Smith regards this as a Priestly vision—one, that is, that was primarily confined to a handful of intellectuals. Indeed, it remains, in his estimation, the most difficult to grasp, even today (pp. 36–37).

50. Mytho-poetics is what those who think they can think, think those whom they think cannot think, do in place of thought.

51. Karen Sonik, "Bad King, False King, True King: Apsû and His Heirs," *JAOS* 128 (2008) 737–43.

52. For Mesopotamians, foreigners and other monsters were never disordered (chaotic); they were simply wrongly ordered. See Karen Sonik in this volume. This being the case, the obvious thing to do was to domesticate them (as with Tiʾāmat's demonic ally, the *mušḫuššu*-dragon, who ends up as Marduk's pet) and, failing that, to take them apart and put them back together again the right way (as with Tiʾāmat herself).

53. See Smith, *Priestly Vision*, 245 n. 235.

the choice between El-gods and Baʿal-gods had already been made, so it would have required a momentous about-face to change this. On the other hand, the destruction of Judah and Jerusalem and the temple and the breach of the covenant, which these events represented, almost demanded a reassessment of the understanding of God and his purpose in history. In this head-on confrontation between Aššur and Marduk as images of God, was not Marduk the winning choice?

Actually, no, or at least not for the prophets. Marduk—so much the equivalent of Ugaritic Baʿal that Isa 14:13 assigns him Mt. Zaphon as preferred throne emplacement—remains always and ever just a warrior god. In *Enūma eliš*, Marduk takes on the role of Ninurta fighting the Anzû-bird, an episode that consumes the bulk of the narrative. Of the three heavens and the three corresponding earths that represented, for ancient Mesopotamians, the created world, Marduk never claims to have created any but the third and innermost set. The outermost set still belongs to Anu, who creates it without a battle and by procreation in the *Enūma eliš*. Elsewhere, Anu creates it by word and ex nihilo, again without a battle. It is Anu, the Mesopotamian equivalent of Ugaritic El and, in his creative aspects, of the Assyrian god Aššur (= Anšar), who is the model for Genesis 1 as the Creator of the single heaven and single earth of Jewish tradition.

And there is more. Not only were Marduk's powers given to him by the other gods, but they are not the powers one might expect. Marduk does not, properly speaking, create but simply re-creates, one might even say reassembles, what he has first destroyed.

> They set up a constellation among them and said to Marduk their first-born. . . . Let the constellation be destroyed (by) what comes from your mouth. Speak to it again and let the constellation be whole (again). He spoke from his mouth and the constellation was destroyed. He spoke again to it and the constellation was created. (*Ee* IV 19–26)

Put another way, Marduk had the warrior god's power to "destroy and create," whereas Creator gods such as Anšar (= Aššur) had the power to "create and destroy" (*Ee* II 61–64). Creation by Marduk thus came at the end of the creative process rather than at its beginning. [54] Or, to put it another way, the Creator cum warrior creates, then pauses for a rest; the warrior cum Creator defeats monsters, then pauses for rest and re-creation.

54. See Frankfort, *Kingship and the Gods*, 232–35.

Not only this, but Marduk's creation is exclusively of inanimate objects.[55] Unlike Ea, Marduk is not a "creator of living creatures."[56] When living beings such as humans (plants and animals) need to be produced, then, Ea still must be involved—even if like a marionette on strings. This is the force of Isa 45:18's indirect critique of Marduk: "The creator of heavens, who is God, the designer and maker of the earth who established it, not creating it to be desert waste (*tōhû*), but designing it to be lived in." That is, Marduk was only capable of creating an empty structure, completely devoid of living things, whereas God created the world as a place that could support life.

The combination of the *Chaoskampf* and creation was, then, presumably designed to allow the young warrior god (Baʿal) to take on a role more properly suited to the heavenly father (El). And the *Chaoskampf* cannot be omitted from the narrative without making it impossible for our warrior god to have been the true creator of the universe.

And this is by no means all. One might suppose that Marduk was at least free of the chains that trapped Ugaritic Baʿal and Sumerian Ninur̃ta in subordinate positions in the pantheon. Not so! A careful reading of the *Enūma eliš* reveals the same relationship between Anšar and Anu on the one hand and Marduk on the other as between El and Baʿal in the Ugaritic *Baʿal Epic*. And as with the *Baʿal Epic*, legitimacy for Marduk as king is intimately tied up with his recognition of that subordination. So, when Marduk defeats Tiʾāmat, he does not put up his own triumphal cry, but that of Anšar (*Ee* IV 125), and he does not keep the rescued Tablets of Destinies for himself but gives them to his grandfather Anu (*Ee* V 69–70). Mesopotamian Qingu is another Ugaritic Yam, a warrior god who ceases to be legitimate and must be taken out by a rival claimant (Marduk/Baʿal) due to his abuse of power.[57]

The only saving of Gunkel's hypothesis is to latch onto the fact that the primordial waters that form the substance of creation in Genesis 1 are referred to as *tĕhôm*, which has long been related to Tiʾāmat. Tiʾāmat is, in turn, related to monsters such as Leviathan and Rahab, whose defeat is claimed

55. On this point, see also Andrea Seri, "The Role of Creation in Enūma eliš," *JANER* 12 (2012) 11–12.

56. As Tsumura (*Creation and Destruction*, 132–34) points out, only Ea is referred to as "creator of living creatures," and it is only he who actively creates them. Even the mighty Enlil can only provide a model and wait for mankind to sprout like some odd plant (see Castellino, "Origins," 90–91). On the other hand, one can go too far in elevating Ea. He creates always by deed and casts/molds (*patāqu*) the heavens and the earth or whatever else he makes. Creation by word is well beyond his powers.

57. Compare Ḫadad of Aleppo who, speaking through a medium, commands King Zimri-Lim of Mari to be a just judge and offers him the weapon with which Ḫadad defeated the sea. See Durand, "Combat entre le dieu de l'orage et la mer," 41–61.

for Yahweh. However, although sea creatures abound in the Bible, they are second-generation progeny of the sea, and their bodies are never disarticulated and used as raw material for creation; instead, they are fed to sea animals, which apparently already existed at the time that they were slaughtered.[58]

Leviathan's Mesopotamian equivalent is the *mušḫuššu*-dragon, who was one of Ti'āmat's monstrous children—again, second-generation progeny of the sea. He was slain by Marduk but was not used as raw material for creation. Instead, the beast was resurrected and became a sort of pet, as also Leviathan did in Ps 104:26 and Job 40:26–32.

In Psalms 74 and 89, an account of creation follows the defeat of Leviathan and Rahab, respectively. The context of both psalms is, however, the fall of Assyria, which ultimately included the fall of Jerusalem to the Babylonians, which is graphically described in Psalm 74. What is contemplated is, therefore, not an original creation but a literal re-creation of Jerusalem, which may only take place after Judah's monstrous enemies have been defeated by God.

Nor is it Baʿal's defeat of Yam that is the model for this mythic monster bashing.[59] Instead, inspiration for these narratives is the separate topos of divine defeat of eclipse cum sea monsters, which is found not only in Jewish tradition but also in Egypt, Ugarit, and Mesopotamia, and which is incorporated secondarily into *Enūma eliš* by way of allowing Marduk to rise to the head of the pantheon. In short, these passages describing monster bashing may profitably be compared with the book of Revelation's defeat of the forces of evil and the creation of the heavenly Jerusalem but have nothing to do with the creation of the world in Genesis.

Genesis 1 was written with *Enūma eliš* in mind and with a view to disputation with it. The image of God presented in Genesis 1 is of an El-type Creator God with secondary, warrior-like characteristics. This is in sharp contrast to Marduk as presented in *Enūma eliš*, who is a Baʿal-type warrior god with secondary, Creator-like characteristics. Finally, the omission of the combat motif was deliberate and was designed to prove that it was God, not Marduk, who created the universe.

58. Ps 74:14.

59. Smith (*Ugaritic Baal Cycle*, 1:xxvi–xxviii) insists otherwise. His defense of Ugaritic mythology against blatantly anti-Semitic criticism is fully warranted, and there is indeed more congruence between the Hebrew Bible and Ugarit than is often acknowledged. However, the book of Revelation and the *Baʿal Epic* have essentially nothing in common.

Making All Things New (Again)

Zephaniah's Eschatological Vision of a Return to Primeval Time

David Melvin

McKendree University

Introduction

The origins of apocalypticism remain a matter of debate, as do the defining characteristics that mark apocalyptic literature. As early as 1895, Hermann Gunkel sought the roots of apocalyptic eschatology in the ancient Near Eastern chaos myth.[1] Gunkel posited that the creation account of Genesis 1 along with several other biblical references to creation derived from the Babylonian chaos myth *Enūma eliš*. This myth served as the basis for the development of an eschatology which envisioned a future destruction of the world which would entail the return of primeval chaos, its defeat, and the renewal of creation.[2]

It is not necessary for our purposes to determine the precise origin of the phenomenon of apocalyptic literature as a clearly defined genre, but merely to note that (1) the reappearance and transformation of mythic material is a common motif in apocalyptic literature, and (2) already in the book of Zephaniah one observes this eschatological transformation of primeval myth.[3]

---

1. H. Gunkel, *Creation and Chaos in the Primeval Era and the Eschaton: A Religio-Historical Study of Genesis 1 and Revelation 12* (trans. K. William Whitney Jr.; Grand Rapids, MI: Eerdmans, 2006); translation of *Schöpfung und Chaos in Urzeit und Endzeit* (Göttingen: Vandenhoeck & Ruprecht, 1895).

2. Ibid., *Creation and Chaos*, 58–59. It is, of course, now widely recognized that any connection between Genesis 1 and *Enūma eliš* probably came by way of intermediaries. The discovery of the Ugaritic texts now indicates that a much closer West Semitic Chaos myth existed and provides a more likely source for the biblical creation/Chaos myth that underlies apocalyptic (see Frank Moore Cross, *Canaanite Myth and Hebrew Epic: Essays in the History of the Religion of Israel* [Cambridge: Harvard University Press, 1973] 346).

3. On the eschatological transformation of myth in apocalyptic, see Stephen L. Cook ("Mythological Discourse in Ezekiel and Daniel and the Rise of Apocalypticism in Israel," in *Knowing the End from the Beginning: The Prophetic, the Apocalyptic and Their Relationships*

Well-known examples of this eschatological reuse of creation myth include Jer 4:23–28[4] and Isaiah 24–27, the so-called Isaiah Apocalypse.[5] The motif of eschatological reversal of creation also appears in Zeph 1:2–3, as pointed out most notably by Michael De Roche and further developed by Adele Berlin.[6] However, in Zephaniah, the eschatological transformation of primeval myth is carried further than in either Jer 4:23–28 or Isaiah 24–27, because allusions to Genesis 1–11 run throughout the entirety of the book and follow the canonical sequencing of Genesis 1–11.[7] This fact suggests a conscious employment of the *Urzeit-Endzeit* pattern, which does not appear again until the emergence of apocalyptic literature. I propose that Zephaniah's recasting of materials from Genesis 1–11 constitutes a more fully-developed example of the apocalyptic motif of the eschatological transformation of primeval myth than either Jer 4:23–28 or Isaiah 24–27 and that it marks an important step in the transition from prophetic literature to apocalyptic literature.

[ed. Lester L. Grabbe and Robert D. Haak; JSPSup 46; London: T. & T. Clark, 2003] 85–106) and Frank Moore Cross (*Canaanite Myth and Hebrew Epic*, 343–46).

4. The text of Jer 4:23–28 is loaded with creation language that echoes Genesis 1–2, including the only appearance of the phrase תהו ובהו outside Gen 1:2. The passage takes the form of a vision beheld by the prophet of a world that has receded into a chaotic, uncreated state. In a fourfold pattern, the prophet describes what he "saw" (ראיתי), and in each instance the sight corresponds to the undoing of a particular element of creation. Thus, in Jer 4:23 the earth (הארץ) returns to a chaotic, unformed state, the lights of the heavens are extinguished. In v. 24, the mountains quake, and in v. 25, humans and birds have fled from the land. Finally, in v. 26, the fruitful land is transformed into a desolate wasteland, and all of its cities lie in ruins. The frequent use of the word ראיתי, "I saw," may also allude to Genesis 1, in which the verb ראה appears frequently as God looks upon his creation.

5. Mark S. Smith notes especially that in Isa 27:1 "pre-Israelite polytheistic narrative set in the future appears in monotheistic form as Israelite apocalyptic set in the future" (*The Memoirs of God: History, Memory, and the Experience of the Divine in Ancient Israel* [Minneapolis: Fortress, 2004] 94). Here, the defeat of Leviathan is set, not in the primordial past, but in the eschatological future. Most scholars have tended to view Isaiah 24–27 as a late addition (see Brevard S. Childs, *Isaiah* [OTL; Louisville: Westminster John Knox, 2001] 171–74). Wildberger regards these chapters as postexilic, and considers the case against Isaianic authorship as "more sure than virtually any other conclusion established by the modern analysis of the written material of the OT" (Hans Wildberger, *Isaiah 13–27* [trans. Thomas H. Trapp; Minneapolis: Fortress, 1997] 445; see also Otto Kaiser, *Isaiah 13–39: A Commentary* [trans. R. A. Wilson; OTL; Philadelphia: Fortress, 1974] 173–79).

6. Michael De Roche, "Zephaniah I 2–3: The 'Sweeping' of Creation," *VT* 30 (1980) 104–9; Adele Berlin, *Zephaniah: A New Translation with Introduction and Commentary* (AB 25A; New York: Doubleday, 1994) 13, 81–83.

7. Berlin comments on the relationship between Zephaniah and Genesis 1–11 at length, noting that "[t]hemes from the early chapters of Genesis appear in all three chapters of Zephaniah" (ibid., 13).

Zephaniah in Recent Scholarship

Since the groundbreaking work of James Nogalski on the Book of the Twelve,[8] redactional analysis has become increasingly important for the study of the Minor Prophets, and Zephaniah is no exception. Nogalski argues for the formation during the exilic period of a "Book of the Four" consisting of the core materials in Hosea, Amos, Micah, and Zephaniah.[9] This proposal has been taken up and further developed by Aaron Schart, who questions whether Zeph 3:11–13 ought also to be included in the Book of the Four.[10] More recently, Rainer Albertz has examined the theme of exile as "purification" in this hypothetical four-book collection. With regard to Zephaniah, particularly Zeph 3:8, Albertz argues, contra Nogalski, that

> such a prophetic composition [the Book of the Four] cannot end in total destruction and hopelessness, particularly since it started with a much more hopeful perspective in the book of Hosea (2:16–17; 3:5; 11:8–11; 14:2–9). Thus, it is very unlikely that Zeph 3:8a formed the end of the Book of the Four, as Nogalski proposed.[11]

Albertz finds evidence in the redaction of the Book of the Four for reflection on the experience of exile as Yahweh's act of punishment and purification, as well as the expectation of renewal following Israel's purification by exile. This renewal, however, would not consist of the restoration of the preexilic monarchy, as anticipated by Haggai and Zechariah, but a completely new beginning in which Yahweh is king (Zeph 3:15).[12]

Paul Redditt takes up and refines Albertz's main thesis by positing a late exilic setting for the Book of the Four, including Zeph 3:1–13, with vv. 14–20 being added slightly later. These final verses presuppose the fall of Jerusalem while at the same time looking forward to a restoration, thus serving as a bridge to Haggai and Zechariah 1–8.[13]

8. James Nogalski, *Literary Precursors to the Book of the Twelve* (BZAW 217; Berlin: de Gruyter, 1993); idem, *Redactional Processes in the Book of the Twelve* (BZAW 218; Berlin: de Gruyter, 1993).

9. Nogalski includes within this initial collection Hosea 1–14; Amos 1:1–9:6; Micah 1–3, 6; Zeph 1:1–3:8 (Nogalski, *Literary Precursors*, 278–80).

10. Aaron Schart, *Die Entstehung des Zwölfprophetenbuchs* (BZAW 260; Berlin: de Gruyter, 1998).

11. Rainer Albertz, "Exile as Purification: Reconstructing the 'Book of the Four,'" in *Thematic Threads in the Book of the Twelve* (ed. Paul L. Redditt and Aaron Schart; BZAW 325; Berlin: de Gruyter, 2003) 236.

12. Ibid., 250.

13. Paul L. Redditt, *Introduction to the Prophets* (Grand Rapids, MI: Eerdmans, 2008) 304–7. With Albertz, Redditt understands the restoration anticipated in Zeph 3:14–20 as

Finally, in two recent studies Jakob Wöhrle concludes that the first stage in the formation of the Book of the Twelve was the collection during the exilic period of Hosea, Amos, Micah, and Zephaniah into a corpus (*Das exilischen Vierprophetenbuch*) heavily colored by Deuteronomistic thought.[14] Haggai and Zechariah combined to form an independent, two-book corpus in the early fifth century.[15] Later still, a "Joel corpus" (*Das Joel-Korpus*) consisting of Joel, Amos, Micah, and Zephaniah emerged, as Joel temporarily displaced Hosea in the Book of the Four.[16] His second study examines the continued formation of the corpus through the insertion of common thematic material into the books (compare with Nogalski's "catch-words"), thus binding the collection together. In the first stage, which Wöhrle dates to the early fourth century, Joel, Amos, Micah, Nahum, Zephaniah, Haggai, Zechariah, and Deutero-Zechariah and, slightly later, Obadiah and Malachi as well are united by the theme of universal divine judgment (*Das Fremdvölker-Korpus I* and *Das Fremdvölker-Korpus II*).[17] Passages announcing salvation, first for Yehud, then later for the nations as well were added in the mid-fourth and third centuries, respectively (*Die Davidsverheissungen*, *Das Heil-für-die-Völker-Korpus*, and *Das Gnaden-Korpus*).[18]

The significance of the above redactional analyses for the present study is twofold. First, given the complex redactional history of Zephaniah, arguments of this sort bear tremendous importance for the dating of the emergence of the apocalyptic motif in question. Second, if, as I will argue, the macrostructure of Zephaniah indicates a recasting of motifs from Genesis 1–11, this could suggest that all of these allusions belong to a single redactional layer of the book, which sought to cast Zephaniah's message as a vision of the reversal and reprise of creation. On the other hand, the present essay has implications for the redactional history of Zephaniah, since, as I demonstrate below, Zephaniah contains allusions to both P and non-P (traditionally J) material from Genesis 1–11, suggesting that the major redactional work of the book took place in the postexilic period, after Genesis 1–11 had achieved its basic shape.

fundamentally different from the conditions that existed under the monarchy. Yahweh, rather than a Davidic heir, will rule as Jerusalem's king.

14. Jakob Wöhrle, *Die frühen Sammlungen des Zwölfprophetenbuches: Entstehung und Komposition* (BZAW 360; Berlin: de Gruyter, 2006) 51–284.

15. Ibid., 285–385.

16. Ibid., 387–435.

17. Jakob Wöhrle, *Der Abschluss des Zwölfprophetenbuches: Buchübergreifende Redaktionsprozesse in den späten Sammlungen* (BZAW 389; Berlin: de Gruyter, 2008) 23–171, 191–288.

18. Ibid., 173–90, 335–419.

Genesis 1–11 and Eschatology in Zephaniah

The book of Zephaniah begins with a superscription attributing the prophecy to Zephaniah, son of Cushi, son of Gedaliah, son of Amariah, son of Hezekiah, and dating his activity to the reign of Josiah (1:1).[19] Following the superscription a vivid description appears of divine judgment against humanity, animal life, and the earth itself. Verses 2–3 are of special note due to their use of creation language and their description of a world that has, in essence, been "uncreated" and has returned to a state of primordial Chaos:

אסף אסף כל מעל פני האדמה נאם־יהוה
אסף אדם ובהמה אסף עוף־השמים ודגי הים והמכשלות את־הרשעים
והכרתי את־האדם מעל פני האדמה נאם־יהוה

"I will completely sweep away[20] everything from upon the face of the ground," utterance of YHWH.

"I will sweep away human and beast. I will sweep away the birds of the sky and the fish of the sea, and the stumbling blocks with the wicked.[21]

19. The extension of Zephaniah's genealogy back four generations is unique among the biblical prophets, and the reason for this intense interest in the prophet's ancestry is not entirely clear. Redditt suggests that the name of Zephaniah's father, "Cushi," could have prompted a defense of Zephaniah's Israelite/Yahwistic pedigree, since Cushi could be understood as a gentilic (Cushite; Redditt, *Introduction*, 308).

20. The phrase אָסֹף אָסֵף is problematic. The word אָסֹף is the Qal infinitive absolute of אסף, "to sweep," while אָסֵף appears to be a Hiphil form of סוף, "to bring to an end." Since it would be unusual for an infinitive absolute to be paired with a finite verb from a different root, a number of scholars have proposed emending the word to אֹסֵף (Qal active participle; *BHS*). Others suggest that the second verb is also a form of אסף and that an original imperfect prefix א has been lost (Julius Wellhausen, *Die kleinen Propheten* [4th ed.; Berlin: de Gruyter, 1963] 150). The latter proposal has the advantage of a comparable construction in Mic 2:12 (אסף אאסף יעקב כלך). On the other hand, Berlin decries all such attempts to emend the text and suggests instead that there are indeed two different roots being used here. She argues that their usage here is an intentional literary device designed to produce heightened assonance and notes, along with Széles, that אסף and סוף overlap semantically and that two roots together suggest complete destruction (Berlin, *Zephaniah*, 72; Mária Eszenyei Széles, *Wrath and Mercy: A Commentary on the Books of Habakkuk and Zephaniah* [trans. George A. F. Knight; International Theological Commentary; Grand Rapids, MI: Eerdmans, 1987] 75).

21. The phrase והמכשלות את־שרשעים has sometimes been regarded as a late addition to the text, designed to mitigate the sweeping judgment of vv. 2–3 by directing them specifically at the wicked (J. M. P. Smith et al., A *Critical and Exegetical Commentary on Micah, Zephaniah, Nahum, Habakkuk, Obadiah and Joel* [ICC; Edinburgh: T. & T. Clark, 1911] 186; cf. De Roche, "The 'Sweeping' of Creation," 105). Redditt does not go so far, although he does view the verses that follow (vv. 4–6), which he attributes to the redactor of the Book of the Four, as limiting judgment to idolaters from Judah and Jerusalem (*Introduction*, 310, 312).

A second problem relates to the referent of המכשלות. The feminine form disagrees with the masculine הרשעים, making it unlikely that the two stand in apposition. Some have

I will cut off humanity from upon the face of the ground," utterance of YHWH.

Michael De Roche sees in the vocabulary and syntax of these verses allusions to the creation accounts of both Genesis 1 and Genesis 2, although his case for connections with Genesis 2 is much less convincing than for Genesis 1.[22] Others have drawn connections primarily with the Genesis flood account, particularly the appearance of the phrase מעל פני האדמה ("from upon the face of the ground") in Gen 6:7, 7:4, 8:8 (cf. Zeph 1:2, 3).[23] In the case of Zephaniah, the divine decree may be viewed as Yahweh's retraction of his promise in Genesis 8 not to "curse the ground (האדמה) again because of humanity" or to "strike again every living thing as I have done" (Gen 8:21). The appearance of the phonetically similar and orthographically identical אֹסִף in Gen 8:21 (cf. אָסֹף/אָסֵף in Zeph 1:2, 3) appears to support this conjecture, however disconcerting the idea of divine reneging on a covenant promise may be. As Stulman and Kim note, "Once destroyed by a flood because of human wickedness (Genesis 6–9), the earth can again be swept away by divine decree."[24] The theme of cosmic judgment against not only humanity but creation as well is common in apocalyptic literature (Isa 24:1ff.; 2 Pet 3:7, 12–13; Rev 21:1; *4 Ezra* 7:30–44; *2 En.* 33:11; 70:8–10), as is interest in the flood as a prototype of the final judgment (Matt 24:36–44; 2 Pet 3:3–6; *1 Enoch* 1–36; *2 Enoch* 33–35; 70; *2 Baruch* 56).

Although he does not necessarily deny that the flood account lies in the background of Zeph 1:2–3, De Roche argues that closer associations exist with the creation accounts of Genesis 1–2. Zeph 1:3 begins, אסף אדם ובהמה אסף עוף־השמים ודגי הים ("I will sweep away human and beast. I will sweep away

---

suggested emending to read a Hiphil verb הכשלתי, "I will cause [the wicked] to stumble" (*BHS*; Smith et al., *Zephaniah*, 186; De Roche, "The 'Sweeping' of Creation," 104–5). While the confusion of a י with a ו and metathesis with ת are both plausible, the insertion of a מ is less easily explained. It is best to follow Berlin and Széles in reading את as a preposition and translating "and the stumbling blocks with the wicked" as an attack both on idolaters and on their idols, which lead to their destruction (Berlin, *Zephaniah*, 73–74; Széles, *Wrath and Mercy*, 76).

22. "The 'Sweeping' of Creation," 106–8. De Roche argues that the use of אדם and אדמה echo Genesis 2, but Genesis 1 also uses אדם, and the phrase מעל פני האדמה is better understood as an allusion to the flood story (cf. Gen 6:7; 7:23) than to Genesis 2.

23. Berlin notes that the phrase is reminiscent, if not completely identical, to several passages throughout Genesis 1–11 (2:6; 4:14; 6:1, 7; 7:4, 23; 8:8) (*Zephaniah*, 13, 81–82). See also Ralph L. Smith, *Micah–Malachi* (Word Biblical Commentary 32; Waco: Word, 1984) 127; John Goldingay and Pamela J. Scalise, *Minor Prophets II* (New International Biblical Commentary; Peabody: Hendrickson, 2009) 100.

24. Louis Stulman and Hyun Chul Paul Kim, *You Are My People: An Introduction to Prophetic Literature* (Nashville: Abingdon, 2010) 223.

the birds of the sky and the fish of the sea"), which is similar to Gen 6:7; 7:23, מאדם עד־בהמה עד־רמש ועד־עוף השמים ("from human to beast to creeping thing and to the birds of the sky"). Zeph 1:3, however, lacks any mention of רמש ("creeping things") and adds דגי הים ("the fish of the sea"). For De Roche, the inclusion of fish in Zeph 1:3 distances this judgment from that of the flood, which did not affect fish. Instead, he points to the parallel with the sequence of creation in Genesis 1 and notes that, while the vocabulary is identical, the order is reversed.[25] In Genesis 1, sea life (שרץ נפש חיה) is created first on Day 5 (v. 20a), followed by the birds of the sky (v. 20b); and land animals (including בהמה, vv. 24–25), followed by humans (vv. 26–27) are created on Day 6. Zephaniah maintains this same basic sequence but reverses it, thus implying "man's loss of dominion over the earth, and more importantly, *the reversal of creation*" (emphasis original).[26]

De Roche's observations have been widely accepted.[27] The parallel in the sequencing as well as the frequent invocation of themes of creation (and its undoing into primeval chaos) in eschatological and especially apocalyptic contexts are indeed persuasive.[28] His argument is, however, not without difficulties. Several items present in Gen 1:24–25, such as נפש חיה, רמש, and חיתו־ארץ are not mentioned in Zeph 1:3. There does not seem to be a good explanation for the fact that only בהמה is mentioned from among the land animals, except that this term often refers to cattle and other beasts of burden that were domesticated by humans. This fact suggests that Zephaniah's vision of judgment is closely tied to humanity and the elements of creation that live closely with humans. Additionally, even though De Roche builds his case for the linking of Zeph 1:2–3 with Genesis 1 rather than the flood account, the term for fish used in Zephaniah (דגי הים) is not the same as in Gen 1:20a. In Genesis, fish are subsumed under the broader category of sea life, שרץ נפש חיה. The phrase "over the fish of the sea" (בדגת הים) does, however, appear in Gen 1:28, alongside "humanity" (אדם), "birds of the sky" (עוף השמים), and "beast" (בהמה)—all elements of creation that are also mentioned in Zeph 1:2–3.

25. De Roche, "The 'Sweeping' of Creation," 106. See also J. Alec Motyer, "Zephaniah," in *The Minor Prophets: An Exegetical and Expository Commentary* (ed. Thomas Edward McComiskey; 3 vols.; Grand Rapids, MI: Baker, 1992–98) 3:911–12.

26. De Roche, "The 'Sweeping' of Creation," 106.

27. Széles, *Wrath and Mercy*, 75; Berlin, *Zephaniah*, 81–83; Goldingay and Scalise, *Minor Prophets II*, 100; Stulman and Kim, *You Are My People*, 223; Motyer, "Zephaniah," 3:911–12. See also René Vuilleumier and Carl-A. Keller, *Michée, Nahoum, Habacuc, Sophonie* (Commentaire de l'Ancien Testament 11b; Neuchâtel: Delachaux et Niestlé, 1971) 188.

28. Note especially the references to chaos dragons in Isa 27:1; Daniel 7; Revelation 12–13; *1 En.* 60:7–10, 24–25; *4 Ezra* 6:49–52; *2 Bar.* 29:4–7; Add Esth 1:4–9; cf. Gunkel, *Creation and Chaos*, 200–238.

It is not necessary to isolate either Genesis 1 or the flood account as the pattern that Zeph 1:2–3 replicates, because the flood account itself is cast as an undoing of creation.[29] Broadly speaking, creation is also reversed in Gen 6:7:

> אמחה את־האדם אשר־בראתי מעל פני האדמה מאדם עד־בהמה עד־רמש ועד־עוף השמים כי נחמתי כי עשיתם
>
> I will wipe out humanity which I created from upon the face of the ground, from human to beast to creeping thing to the birds of the sky, for I regret that I made them.

Gen 6:7 explicitly refers to creation (בראתי; cf. ברא in Gen 1:1) and states that Yahweh regretted having made his creations. Furthermore, the sequence here is roughly the reverse of that in Genesis 1. Humanity (האדם) is mentioned first, then repeated (as also in Zeph 1:3), followed by land animals (בהמה and רמש), and finally birds (עוף השמים). In the flood, the world returns to the uncreated, chaotic, watery state mentioned in Gen 1:2, and the motif of Chaos as the sea or a sea monster is widespread throughout the ancient Near East, so that echoes of *Chaoskampf* may be heard in the story of the deluge.[30]

Following the sweeping declaration of global destruction proclaimed in Zeph 1:2–3, vv. 4–13 are direct condemnations of Judah and Jerusalem, and the royal house in particular (see vv. 8–9). An announcement of the Day of Yahweh follows in 1:14–18, in language similar to Amos 5:18–20 and Joel 2:1b–2. The final portion of this announcement (vv. 17–18) may once again envision a global judgment, as Yahweh declares, ובאש קנאתו תאכל כל־הארץ כי־כלה אך־נבהלה יעשה את כל־ישבי הארץ ("With the fire of his jealousy all the earth shall be consumed, for a full, indeed, a sudden end shall he make of all the inhabitants of the earth," Zeph 1:18b). As Berlin notes, "Chapter 1 ends as it began, with the destruction of the whole earth."[31] The universality of this judgment recalls the flood, while the description of a fiery end to the world anticipates apocalyptic visions of the destruction of the earth and its

29. Berlin, *Zephaniah*, 82; Goldingay and Scalise, *Minor Prophets II*, 100.

30. See Mark S. Smith, *The Ugaritic Baal Cycle*, vol. 1: *Introduction with Text, Translation and Commentary of KTU 1.1–1.2* (VTSup 55; Leiden: Brill, 1994) 84–87. It is surely significant to both biblical and extrabiblical flood stories that the agent of the world's destruction—water—is so closely associated with Chaos in myths of creation. Note especially the chaos and disorder brought even to the divine realm during the deluge in *Atrahasis*, Old Babylonian Version III iii 11–iv 25 (Benjamin R. Foster, *Before the Muses: An Anthology of Akkadian Literature* [3rd ed.; Bethesda, MD: CDL, 2006] 249–51).

31. Berlin, *Zephaniah*, 92.

inhabitants (cf. 2 Pet 3:7, 10, 12; Rev 8:7; 20:9b–10, 14–15; *L.A.E.* 49:3; *Sib. Or.* 3:53–54, 689–90).[32]

Although the portrayal of universal judgment and allusions to Genesis 1–11 in Zephaniah 1 have received the most attention, there are other points of contact with Genesis 1–11 in Zephaniah 2–3. Following what some have interpreted as a call to repentance in Zeph 2:1–3 (or perhaps just v. 3),[33] Zephaniah includes a number of oracles against foreign nations. These include Philistia (2:4–7), Moab (2:8–11), Ammon (2:8–11), "Cushites" (2:12),[34] and Assyria/Nineveh (2:13–15). Berlin sees in these oracles another allusion to the primeval history, specifically to the Table of Nations in Genesis 10. She points to the use of unusual terms and unexpected associations that point toward Genesis 10, such as the identification of the land of the Philistines with Canaan (Zeph 2:5b; cf. Gen 10:19), the mentioning of Sodom and Gomorrah (Zeph 2:9b; cf. Gen 10:19b), and the "islands of the nations" (איי הגוים; Zeph 2:11b; cf. Gen 10:5).[35] While Moab and Ammon do not appear in the Table of Nations, they may here be identified with the Canaanites, especially via the comparison of Moab and Ammon with Sodom and Gomorrah (Zeph 2:9). Perhaps the strongest connection with Genesis 10 is the mentioning of the

32. On the motif of cosmic destruction by fire in apocalyptic literature, see especially D. S. Russell, *The Method and Message of Jewish Apocalyptic* (OTL; Philadelphia: Westminster, 1964) 281.

33. Stulman and Kim, *You Are My People*, 224; Julia M. O'Brien, *Nahum, Habakkuk, Zephaniah, Haggai, Zechariah, Malachi* (Abingdon Old Testament Commentaries; Nashville: Abingdon, 2004) 90–91; Smith, *Micah–Malachi*, 132; Széles, *Wrath and Mercy*, 89–93; Berlin, *Zephaniah*, 100–102; Charles L. Taylor and Howard Thurman, "Zephaniah," *IB* 6:1021–22. There is certainly an imperative thrust to these verses, as the people are called upon to "gather together" (התקושׁשו), "assemble" (קושו), and "seek" (בקשו) Yahweh. It should be noted, however, that the coming of the Day of Yahweh is spoken of as inevitable. The people are urged to repent "before" (בטרם) the coming of the day of Yahweh's wrath, and the possibility that the humble of the land who heed the call may be "hidden" (תסתרו) on that day is mentioned, but there is no indication that disaster may be averted through repentance (Goldingay and Scalise, *Minor Prophets II*, 110). Much like the Genesis flood and the final judgment, the righteous may be preserved through the disaster, but the disaster will come.

34. Berlin identifies five possible referents for כושים: (1) Egypt, (2) Ethiopia, (3) Midian, (4) Arabia, and (5) Assyria. She dismisses Egypt, arguing that, while Cush (Ethiopia) is often associated with Egypt, it is not identical with it. Ethiopia is the region most commonly designated by Cush, and this interpretation creates a geographical symmetry for the Oracles against the Nations (cf. Goldingay and Scalise, *Minor Prophets II*, 112; Smith, *Micah–Malachi*, 135–36; Széles, *Wrath and Mercy*, 93–94). Midian seems unlikely, because it is not typically listed among Judah's enemies at this time. Berlin prefers the identification with Assyria, largely on the basis of a perceived allusion to Gen 10:5–11, in which Cush is the father of Nimrod, who founds Ashur (Assyria) and Nineveh (Berlin, *Zephaniah*, 111–13).

35. Ibid., 120–24.

"islands of the nations" (איי הגוים) in Zeph 2:11b, since the only other place in which this exact phrase appears is Gen 10:5.

Of special note is the reference to the "Cushites" (כושים) in Zeph 2:12. Berlin reads this not as a reference to the Ethiopians or Nubians, who are usually identified as Cush, but to the father of Nimrod in Gen 10:8. She notes that the sequence Cush→Assyria→Nineveh appears both in Zeph 2:12–13 and in Gen 10:8–11, in which Cush begets Nimrod, who settles in Assyria and builds the city of Nineveh. Thus, Berlin offers a reading of Zephaniah's Oracles against the Nations in which judgment is proclaimed against Assyria and its loyal vassal states, and the reason that Egypt (and, in her reading, Ethiopia) is not included is explained.[36]

If this reading of Zeph 2:4–15 is correct, the book of Zephaniah couches its polemic against Assyria and its vassals in the mythological language of Genesis 10. The foreign nations here condemned are all identified with descendants of Ham, whom Genesis 9–10 portrays negatively (cf. Gen 9:20–27) and who is associated with most of the traditional enemies of ancient Israel. Judah represents Shem, and Japheth is represented by the "islands of the nations" in Zeph 2:11b (cf. Gen 10:5, in which the איי הגוים are among the descendants of Japheth). Thus, in Zeph 2:4–15, we find a prophetic (and perhaps eschatological?) reprisal of Gen 9:25–27:

ארור כנען עבד עבדים יהיה לאחיו
ויאמר ברוך יהוה אלהי שם ויהי כנען עבד למו
יפת אלהים ליפת וישכן באהלי־שם ויהי כנען עבד למו

> "Cursed be Canaan! May he be a slave of slaves to his brothers!"
> And he said, "Blessed be YHWH, the God of Shem. May Canaan be his slave.
> May God enlarge Japheth. May he reside in the tents of Shem, and may Canaan be his slave."

A final allusion to Genesis 1–11 appears in Zeph 3:9–10, which may draw on the motif of the confusion of human languages at the Tower of Babel in Gen 11:1–9. Zephaniah 3 returns the focus of judgment, which had shifted from Judah to foreign nations in 2:4–15, back to the city of Jerusalem. Following a reprisal of the theme of global destruction in 3:8, Yahweh declares: כי־אז אהפך אל־עמים שפה ברורה לקרא כלם בשם יהוה לעבדו שכם אחד ("For then I will turn over to the peoples purified language, for all of them to invoke the name of YHWH, to serve him together as one," Zeph 3:9). Berlin suggests that, in the mention of "purified speech" (שפה ברורה) and the uniting of all peoples, "[i]t is as if the story of Babel were being reversed and all peoples reunited in the

36. Ibid., 120.

worship of the Lord."[37] The phrase שפה ברורה immediately calls to mind the confusion of languages at Babel in Gen 11:7–9. The Babel story, moreover, served as a polemic against the city of Babylon by offering an alternative myth of the city's foundation through a play on the verb בלל ("to mix up"; cf. בבל "Babel/Babylon").[38] The similarity between the verbs ברר ("to purify") and בלל ("to mix up") invites association. Formulated one way, in Zeph 3:9 the שפה בלולה ("mixed up language") of Gen 11:7 becomes שפה ברורה ("purified language").

Zeph 3:10 continues, מעבר לנהרי־כוש עתרי בת־פוצי יובלון מנחתי ("From beyond the rivers of Cush my supplicants, my scattered ones, shall bring my gifts"). If the "Cushites" mentioned in Zeph 2:12 are indeed a reference to Assyria, rather than Ethiopia, then it is likely that the "Cush" referred to here is likewise in Mesopotamia.[39] The idea of scattered peoples' returning from Mesopotamia makes better sense than their returning from Ethiopia, especially if these verses date to the late exilic period, as suggested by some.[40] On the other hand, if the "scattered ones" referred to here are foreign peoples, rather than exiled Jews, then Cush could refer to Ethiopia as a representative of very distant lands.[41] These "scattered ones" (בת־פוצי) may also constitute an allusion to Gen 11:1–9, as the same verb פוץ describes the scattering of the peoples in Gen 11:4, 8–9.[42] Further reinforcing the link between Zeph 3:9–10 and Gen 11:1–9 is the fact that in the three-year cycle of Torah reading, the Haftarah reading corresponding to Gen 11:1 is Zeph 3:9–17, 20, which suggests that early interpreters detected a common theme in the two passages.[43]

37. Ibid., 14. See also Smith, *Micah–Malachi*, 141–42; Motyer, "Zephaniah," 951–52; Goldingay and Scalise, *Minor Prophets II*, 125; O'Brien, *Nahum, Habakkuk, Zephaniah, Haggai, Zechariah, Malachi*, 123.

38. Speiser, *Genesis*, 75–76. Compare the foundation of Babylon in *Enūma eliš* V 117–56 (Foster, *Before the Muses*, 467–68).

39. This is the interpretation offered by Berlin here as well, in which she sees "rivers of Cush" as possibly echoing the rivers associated with Eden in Genesis 2, as well as perhaps the mythological motif of rivers at the ends of the earth (see *Epic of Gilgamesh*, SBV XI 204–5: Andrew George, *The Epic of Gilgamesh: A New Translation* [London: Penguin, 2000] 95); Berlin, *Zephaniah*, 134.

40. Albertz, "Exile as Purification," 236; Redditt, *Introduction*, 304–7.

41. See Taylor, "Zephaniah," 1031–32; Goldingay and Scalise, *Minor Prophets II*, 126; Motyer, "Zephaniah," 952; Széles, *Wrath and Mercy*, 108. But see also O'Brien, who argues that the reference to Cush indicates a particular concern with Ethiopia itself, rather than a representation of faraway lands in general (*Nahum, Habakkuk, Zephaniah, Haggai, Zechariah, Malachi*, 123).

42. Ibid.

43. Ehud Ben Zvi, *A Historical-Critical Study of the Book of Zephaniah* (BZAW 198; Berlin: de Gruyter, 1991) 24.

The Book of Zephaniah: A Precursor to Apocalyptic Eschatology

As the above analysis has shown, the book of Zephaniah in a number of instances draws on Genesis 1–11 as a pattern for the prophet's visions of judgment and restoration. The reuse of earlier traditions and motifs is not unusual for biblical prophets (e.g., Jer 4:23–27; Hos 12:2–6, 12–14). Zephaniah's use of Genesis 1–11, however, goes well beyond mere allusions. Zephaniah's sequencing of these allusions follows the canonical ordering of Genesis 1–11. Zeph 1:2–3 uses the language of creation (Genesis 1) and the flood (Genesis 6–8) to describe universal divine judgment as the reversal of creation and a return to primordial Chaos. The Oracles against the Nations in Zeph 2:4–15 parallel the Table of Nations (Genesis 10) in a number of details and may be read as a reprisal of Noah's curse on Ham/Canaan in Gen 9:25–27. Finally, Zeph 3:9–10 describes restoration as a reversal of the Tower of Babel (Gen 11:1–9), with the granting of "purified speech" (שפה ברורה) to the peoples and the gathering of Yahweh's "scattered ones" (בת־פוצי). The book of Zephaniah begins with the "un-creation" of the world and ends with the re-creation of the unity of primeval humanity. This sequencing suggests that Zephaniah's vision of the future of Israel and of humanity is cast in terms of an eschatological replaying and transformation of the primeval history.

There is much in Zephaniah's reuse of motifs from Genesis 1–11 that anticipates the development of later apocalyptic eschatology. The primeval history seems to have held a special place of significance in the minds of Jewish apocalypticists, because much of apocalyptic literature features characters and events from Genesis 1–11. John Collins notes that "primordial events" occupy an important place in a large number of the earliest apocalyptic texts, such as The Book of Watchers (*1 Enoch 1–36*), *4 Ezra*, *2–3 Baruch*, and *The Apocalypse of Abraham*.[44] Several apocalyptic books (e.g., *1 Enoch*, *Jubilees*, *The Apocalypse of Adam*, *The Life of Adam and Eve*) largely consist of expansions and elaborations of pentateuchal traditions, especially the primeval history. The apocalyptic fascination with creation, the flood, and other elements of the primeval history has been described by Russell as a principal belief that "the End should in some way correspond to the Beginning."[45] This tendency is exemplified perhaps nowhere better than in *4 Ezra* 7:30–31:

44. See Collins's reproduction of a chart from the apocalyptic genre project in *Semeia* 14 (J. J. Collins, *The Apocalyptic Imagination: An Introduction to Jewish Apocalyptic Literature* [2nd ed.; Grand Rapids, MI: Eerdmans, 1998] 7).

45. Russell, *The Method*, 282. See also Cook, "Mythological Discourse," 85–104.

> And the world shall be turned back to primeval silence for seven days, as it was at the first beginning; so that no one shall be left. And after seven days the world, which is not yet awake, shall be roused, and that which is corruptible shall perish.[46]

This is the *Urzeit-Endzeit* pattern, pointed out long ago by Gunkel, and it appears prominently in the book of Zephaniah.

Conclusion

Gunkel's identification of the important place of the ancient Near Eastern *Chaoskampf* myth in apocalyptic eschatology, although not without its difficulties and mistaken assumptions,[47] continues to influence discussions of the relationship between ancient Near Eastern mythology and apocalyptic literature.[48] Although not personified as a dragon, a similar portrayal of an eschatological reversion of creation into chaos is found in the book of Zephaniah, as the world is "uncreated" in a manner reminiscent of the flood (Zeph 1:2–3; cf. Gen 1:20–28; 6:7; 7:23). This cosmic destruction is also described as the consumption of the earth by fire (Zeph 1:18b), as is also the case in several later apocalyptic texts (2 Pet 3:7, 10, 12; Rev 8:7; 20:9b–10, 14–15; *L.A.E.* 49:3; *Sib.Or.* 3:54, 690). Additional allusions to Genesis 1–11 in Zephaniah's Oracles against the Nations (Zeph 2:4–15; cf. Gen 9:25–27; 10:5–14) and Oracles of Restoration (Zeph 3:9–10; cf. Gen 11:1–9) indicate that Zephaniah's eschatology is shaped by the primeval history in a manner that anticipates later apocalyptic eschatology and its recasting of themes of creation/re-creation and the antediluvian epoch as foreshadows of the end of time.

46. Trans. B. M. Metzger, "The Fourth Book of Ezra," in *The Old Testament Pseudepigrapha*, vol. 1: *Apocalyptic Literature and Testaments* (ed. James H. Charlesworth; Garden City, NY: Doubleday, 1983) 537–38.

47. Chief among these is his unawareness of the West Semitic *Chaoskampf* myths now known from Ugaritic texts. The Canaanite/Ugaritic myths, rather than *Enūma eliš*, are more likely sources for the form of the *Chaoskampf* myth that stands behind many Old Testament passages (e.g., Isa 27:1; Daniel 7).

48. See, for example, Cook, "Mythological Discourse," 85; Andrew R. Angel, *Chaos and the Son of Man: The Hebrew* Chaoskampf *Tradition in the Period 515* BCE *to 200* CE (Library of Second Temple Studies 60; London: T. & T. Clark, 2006).

Index of Authors

Index of Scripture

New Testament

Apocrypha

Pseudepigrapha

Index of Subjects

Index of Ancient Texts and Objects

Index of Ancient Texts

Index of Objects

Index of Words

Akkadian
alimbû 85
apsû 46
āribu 75, 91
ašrātu 77–78 n. 49
banû 50–51 w/n. 9, 59 n. 53
barû 59 w/n. 53
bašmu 207
ditānu 84–85, 88–90
/dnn/ 66
dunānu 66
edinu 177
enūma eliš 250
epēšu 131
erṣetu 242
ḫabaṣirānu 90
ḫiāṭu 56–60
izbu 17 n. 51
karšānu 84–85
kispu 168, 170
kūbu 16–17 w/n. 51
kusarikku 76, 84–85 w/n. 60, 88–90 w/n. 71
labbu 99
laḫmu 90
/lḫm/ 15 n. 42
-ma 131 w/ n. 13
māliku 87
mušḫuššu 70, 136–37, 235 w/n. 52, 265 n. 52, 268
ra'ābu 52–53
saparu 225
šamādu 129
tiāmtu 3 n. 8, 46, 99, 192

Arabic
/br'/ 45
baṣara 59
bathan 207
raḥafa 52–53
tihāmah 3 n. 8

Arabic (cont.)
tubalû 93

Aramaic
ptn 207

Eblaite
tihām(a)tum 3 n. 8

Egyptian
ʿ3pp 113–14
ḥq3 120–21 n. 52
isfet 125
k3 116
ma'at 125
matet 114 n. 15
nṯr 115
semket 114 n. 15
snk n mw 116
tnt-amw 122
tz pn n ʿ3pp 114
w3ḏ-wr 117

Greek
ankulometis 26
argeion hudrion 91–92
bie 26, 43
epipotheō 52
epipherō 53
ēris 26
ēros 26
korax 91–92
korē 92
kourotrophos 27
kosmos 4 n. 11
kratos 4 n. 11
metis 26 w/n. 1, 43
paradeisos 173
pheromenoi theoi 53
pneuma 54
hudrokhoos 92
chainō/chaskō 5 n. 13
chaos 5–6 w/n. 13, 7 n. 20
ōon 55 n. 30

Hebrew
'ādām 273–76
'adāmâ 273–74, 276
'ôr 241 w/n. 11, 247
'îyê haggôyim 277–78
'El elyōn qoneh 262–63 w. n. 41
'sp 273–74
'apīqê 221
'ereṣ 242, 246, 270, 275–76
bābel 279
behēma 273–76
bll 250, 279
beliʿal 220–21
bṣr 59
berē'šît 45, 250
berûrâ 278–80
brḥ 251–52
br' 45, 50–52 w/n. 9, 59 n. 53, 276
geʿarah 221
dāg 273–75
dīšōn 86
zemām 78–79, 81
ṭal 241–242
yām 220–25, 251–52, 273–74
kûš 277–79
krt 273
lwytn 251–52
môʿadîm 247
mayîm 221–22
mišmar 223–24
nāharû 208
naḥal 220–21
nāḥaš 252
sm ym 225
sāpâ 278–80
ʿôp 273–76
ʿqltwn 251–52
ʿz 234
peder 241
pwṣ 279
qdm 174, 177 n. 30